SPECIFIC LEARNING DIFFICULTIES (DYSLEXIA) PERSPECTIVES ON PRACTICE

Edited by Gavin Reid

SCOTTISH DYSLEXIA TRUST

This publication has been funded by the Scottish Dyslexia Trust. The Trust was set up in 1988 to encourage the development of teacher training, so that all teachers will eventually have a grounding in recognition and teaching of dyslexic children.

Open Learning Courses in Specific Learning Difficulties

General Editors – Gavid Reid and Fernando Almeida Diniz

Course Reader
PERSPECTIVES ON PRACTICE
Edited by Gavin Reid

Moray House Publications
Holyrood Road, Edinburgh,
EH8 8AQ.

Current and forthcoming titles:

Course Reader – Perspectives on Practice
Edited by Gavin Reid

**Course Handbook – Specific Learning Difficulties
A Handbook for Study and Practice**
Gavin Reid

**Module Workbooks and Study Guide
for the Open Learning Courses in Specific Learning Difficulties**
Gavin Reid and Fernando Almeida Diniz

All rights reserved. No part of this publication may be reproduced, stored in a retrieval system, or transmitted in any form or by any means, electronic, mechanical, photocopying, recording or otherwwise, without prior permission of the Co-ordinator, Specific Learning Difficulties Project, Moray House Institute of Education, Edinburgh.

First published 1993
ISBN 0 901580 50 3
© Moray House Institute of Education

Printed and bound by Bell & Bain Ltd., Glasgow

CONTENTS

		Page
Foreword:	Jackie Stewart	7
Acknowledgments:		9

Section 1. **Introduction**
Chapter 1:	Perspectives on Practice	Gavin Reid and Fernando Diniz	2

Section 2: **Assessment**
Chapter 2:	Difficulties, Discrepancies and Differences	Gavin Reid	14
Chapter 3:	Principles of Assessment	Gordon Booth	26
Chapter 4:	Formal Assessment	Rosemary McGhee	34
Chapter 5:	Psychological Dimensions and the Role of the Educational Psychologist in Assessment	Sionah Lannen and Gavin Reid	45
Chapter 6:	A Doctor's Perspective	Anne O'Hare	65

Section 3: **Teaching and the Curriculum**
Chapter 7:	The Role of the Teacher	Margaret Crombie	80
Chapter 8:	Access to the Curriculum	Sylvia Russell	93
Chapter 9:	Curriculum Differentiation in the Secondary School	David Dodds	114
Chapter 10:	A Phonic Attack Structured Skills Programme (PASS)	Helen Calcluth	128
Chapter 11	Spelling – Diagnosis and Strategies	Catriona Collins and Jean C Miller.	135

				Page
Chapter 12:	Perceptual Motor and Neurodevelopmental Dimensions in Identifying and Remediating Developmental Delay in Children with Specific Learning Difficulties	Sheila Dobie		143
Chapter 13:	Information Technology and Specific Learning Difficulties	Marie Dougan and George Turner		154
Chapter 14:	Integrated Support: Working on the System in the System.	Ros Hunter		173
Chapter 15:	Supporting Learning Through A Whole School Approach	Morven Brown		183

Section 4: **Reading, Writing and Mathematics**

Chapter 16:	Perspectives on Reading	Gavin Reid	200
Chapter 17:	Reading Disorders -Do Poor Readers have Phonological Problems?	Rhona Johnston	225
Chapter 18:	Parents and Peers as Tutors for Dyslexic Children	Keith Topping	232
Chapter 19:	The Skilled Reading Experience	Janet Hunter	246
Chapter 20:	Handwriting-Skills, Strategies and Success	Mary Kiely	257
Chapter 21:	Specific Difficulties and Mathematics	Charles Weedon	273

Section 5: **Metacognition**

Chapter 22:	The Learner – Metacognition in Reading	Patricia Brown	291
Chapter 23:	Strategies for Effective Learning	Vicky Hunter	307

Section 6: **Speech and Language**

Chapter 24:	Specific Language Impairment: Explanations and Implications.	Jennifer Reid and Morag Donaldson	318
Chapter 25:	Language and Literacy – Connections and Implications.	Marysia Nash	338

Chapter				Page
Chapter 26:	Role of the Speech Therapist	Nicola Robinson		354
Chapter 27:	Language in Context	Eileen Francis		381

Section 7: **Emotional Considerations**

Chapter 28:	The Emotional World of Specific Learning Difficulties	Stewart Biggar and Jennifer Barr		394

Section 8: **Practice, Provision and Resources**

Chapter 29:	Specific Learning Difficulties, Learning Support Teachers and the Impact of Changing Policy	Sheila Riddell, Sally Brown and Jill Duffield		409
Chapter 30:	A Framework for Practice	Linda Cumming		430
Chapter 31:	The Use of Resources to Access Learning Skills.	Anne F. Philip		438

Notes on Contributors — 460

Subject Index — 469

Author Index — 485

FOREWARD

JACKIE STEWART

Three-Time World Driving Champion

Dyslexia, or any of the derivative learning disabilities, can be one of the most mentally damaging and painful issues that the young can face. A large percentage of sufferers are abused and ridiculed by their peers, their elders, and even their teachers, in the traditional education system. The anguish and frustration and resulting lack of self-esteem can linger long in a person's life if the correct help and assistance is not forthcoming.

Dyslexia often causes the young to take the easy route – since they are often laughed at and humiliated in the circles in which they would traditionally mix at school and after school – and frequently they are dragged into the 'wrong crowd'. It can lead from truancy and crime, to alcohol and drugs. A life can be ruined or even lost. In an enormous percentage of cases, a young person with a fantastic mind can never reach true potential because they are convinced, due to the insensitivities of others and the inadequacy of the system, that they could never be achievers or successful in anything.

All of this can be avoided by understanding teachers and educators who are prepared to change the system and accommodate a group of people that require a different kind of education which, in some cases, would only mean 'decimal points of change'. With good communication the victims of learning disabilities, their friends and peers, could be made to understand that the ability to consume information, by either the written word, the spoken word, or even visual diagrams, cannot be done in the 'traditional manner'. It could also be emphasised that in some cases, those same individuals have skills, talents, and minds, much more expansive than the traditional 'bright' children have. If such a thing were done, humiliation could be avoided, self-esteem could be established, potential developed, a better social life created and pain and suffering avoided.

To a very large extent this difference can be created only by educators and by teachers who are prepared to be shown and understand that, by doing things a little differently, those young minds can be taught and trained, in a large percentage of cases, to handle most of the challenges of life that otherwise might be immovable obstacles.

In the United Kingdom it has taken a remarkable amount of time for the traditional education system to recognise that there are special needs within its domain which have to be provided for. The obstinacy of the system to fully appreciate this is extremely frustrating for a sufferer, such as myself, to accept.

What has been achieved at Moray House and what can be achieved in the future with a properly funded programme, will help innumerable people, not only of this generation, but more importantly future generations, to contribute and benefit our country and society in general, not to mention the possibility for dyslexia sufferers, to be proud achievers.

ACKNOWLEDGMENTS

This publication is part of the open learning materials being developed by the Specific Learning Difficulties Project at Moray House. As coordinator of the project I am well placed to acknowledge the efforts and expertise of the wide range of professionals and representatives of parents' groups who have given support and advice throughout the project. Guidance and support have also been readily offered from representatives of Regional Education Authorities who formed consultative task groups; colleagues from the Department of Professional and Curriculum Support Studies at Moray House and the Advisory Committee of the Scottish Dyslexia Trust. The efforts of the Trust, and those who helped to provide funding and support to the Trust highlights the determination to address the clearly obvious gap in teacher training in relation to dyslexia which is the principal aim of the project and this publication. The Specific Learning Difficulties Project at Moray House is steering a path towards the fulfilment of this objective.

In relation to this publication particular thanks should be extended to all contributors who despite heavy commitments were still able to provide a quality product. Special acknowledgment should also be given to Stephen Iliffe for helping with proofreading and providing insightful suggestions, Janet Hunter for assisting with the indexing, Pat Hill the Project Secretary and the Central Text Production Unit for typesetting and graphics, Tanja Lannen for the cover design and Fernando Diniz for his guidance and support.

Gavin Reid

SECTION 1

INTRODUCTION

Chapter 1

PERSPECTIVES ON PRACTICE

GAVIN REID and FERNANDO DINIZ

Perspectives on Practice in Specific Learning Difficulties (Dyslexia) is the Reader prepared to accompany the Moray House modular programme of courses leading to advanced postgraduate awards in the field of Specific Learning Difficulties (Dyslexia). It forms part of a package of open-learning materials designed to provide staff development which is capable of being delivered throughout Scotland. When completed (August 1994), the package will include:

- the Reader
- the Course Handbook
- Module Workbooks
- the Study Guide which includes details of programme planning, tutorial arrangements and assessment regulations leading to various awards (certificate, diploma, Masters degree) validated by Moray House Institute of Education, Heriot-Watt University, Edinburgh.

The package is the outcome of the Specific Learning Difficulties Project, funded for a four-year period by The Scottish Dyslexia Trust.

WHY FOCUS ON PRACTICE?

Moray House was commissioned by The Scottish Dyslexia Trust to provide a coherent and professionally relevant package to support teachers, psychologists and allied practitioners to respond to the particular needs of pupils who may experience barriers to learning associated with specific learning difficulties (dyslexia). Emphasis was to be given to disseminating *good practice* whilst also capitalising on current research evidence. The Reader offers a blend of theory and practice with contributions from professionals involved in the day-to-day challenge of teaching, as well as researchers in the field.

Secondly, this is a positive attempt to facilitate cooperation between all interested parties in the practice of specific learning difficulties (dyslexia), including teachers, parents, voluntary organisations and statutory services. Relations between them have for too long been bedevilled by acrimonious disputes over the validity of the *'syndrome'* of dyslexia, what is (or is not) a specific learning difficulty or dyslexia, about the essentially middle-class basis of the claim and whether dyslexic pupils have a higher priority in the distribution of resources than other pupils with special needs.

For example, in a report on the most comprehensive inquiry yet carried out, Pumfrey and Reason (1991) present their analyses of pertinent theoretical, policy and practice issues and offer recommendations which they regard as reflecting current trends of good practice. A selection is offered below:

- *All professionals [should] encourage cooperation between statutory and voluntary organisations concerned with any pupil currently identified as experiencing specific learning difficulties (1.3).*

- *Efforts should be made by educationalists to reach provisional agreement on the presenting characteristics of pupils experiencing specific learning difficulties, using theoretically based empirical definitions (1.5).*

- *Given the present state of knowledge, dogmatic assertions concerning either the conceptual basis or the incidence of specific learning difficulties be treated with caution (6.1).*

- *Local educational authorities [should] have an explicit policy on pupils with specific learning difficulties to be either particular to these difficulties or set in the context of a policy for learning difficulties in general (13.1).*

- *Local education authorities [should] ensure that a range of in-service training opportunities exists whereby teachers and educational psychologists are enabled to identify, assess and alleviate special educational needs stemming from specific learning difficulties (13.8).*

- *The term 'specific learning difficulties' [should] be used and seen as part of a continuum of special educational needs whilst acknowledging that the term dyslexia has considerable currency (15.1).*

(Pumfrey and Reason, 1991).

In Scotland, the results of recent research conducted by Riddell, et al (1992) accord with many of the recommendations cited above. The need for clear policies by education authorities, partnership between parents and teachers, whole-school approaches and both pre-service and in-service training opportunities are all highlighted.

Chapter 1

This modular programme for staff development is an example of cooperation between the voluntary and higher education sectors, resulting in the first university validated course leading to postgraduate awards in specific learning difficulties (dyslexia) in Scotland. Given the complex scientific, pedagogic, administrative and financial issues involved, it is perhaps unrealistic to always achieve a consensus of opinion. However, enough is known to provide a basis for positive action to provide equal opportunities for pupils with specific learning difficulties (dyslexia).

A final reason for focusing on the practice of specific learning difficulties (dyslexia) is to emphasise its location within an overall policy framework for special educational needs. There can be little doubt that, over the last two decades, special education has undergone major change in policy and practice; some would argue that it has been brought from the periphery to centre stage in the debate about *Education for All*. The Warnock (1978) and Progress (1978) reports, followed by the Education Act 1981 and now the reforms in curriculum and assessment in the UK have all signalled a significant shift from the philosophy of *Is the child good enough for the school?* to one in which schools are expected to cater for a diversity of learners, through developing whole-school policies, curriculum differentiation, in-school support systems, partnership with parents and staff development (Allan et al, 1991: Bell and Best, 1986: Brennan, 1987: Blythman, 1989: Wolfendale, 1992). There has also been an increase in the number of local authority advisers and support teachers. What is now the concern is how the delivery of special needs services will develop in the future. Recent government policy concerning *Choice and Diversity* (DfE 1992a), the consultation document *Access to the System* (DfE 1992b), the Education (Schools) Act 1992, the restructuring of local government, the effects of local management of schools (about to come to Scotland) and school development planning will have far-reaching implications for children, parents, schools, services and local education authorities (Audit Commission and HMI 1992; Evans and Lunt 1992: Moore 1991: SOED 1992a and b).

It is against this uncertain backdrop that changes recommended by Pumfrey and Reason (1991) and Riddell, et al (1992) will have to be addressed. This in turn, emphasises the neccessity for locating policy and practice of specific learning difficulties (dyslexia) firmly within an overall framework for education in general and special educational needs in particular.

OVERVIEW OF THE READER

No single teaching programme, strategy or perspective can effectively overcome or explain the learning difficulties presented by dyslexic children. It is important therefore to examine a range of practices and perspectives in dealing with dyslexia in order that a successful outcome can be achieved for both the teacher and the learner. The range of perspectives and practices which will be discussed in 'The Reader' reflects the interest and the energy extended by professionals in this field. 'The Reader' aims to illustrate, examine and reflect on these practices to provoke thought and help conceptualise ideas to assist professionals undergoing initial training, or further specialist studies in dyslexia; and indeed all practitioners engaged in this field. It is hoped therefore that the chapters which follow will influence practice and promote early and insightful assessment, provide clear guidelines for teaching and help identify the individual needs of the learner.

- **Section 2: Identification and Assessment.**

Identification and assessment is without doubt an area of crucial importance. A high profile should be accorded to the task of early identification in order to minimise the adverse effects which result from the 'cycle of failure' which many dyslexic children experience through failure to respond to the literacy demands of the curriculum. The section on assessment is intended to provide readers with a framework and strategies which can be utilised to help in the identification and assessment process.

Gavin Reid presents an introduction to assessment by examining some difficulties, discrepancies and differences. He provides some guidelines on the nature of the difficulty and the need to preserve and respect the individualism of children with dyslexia by acknowledging variations in learning styles.

Gordon Booth sets out a number of principles and some assessment issues which relate to them. The purpose of assessment is addressed, in addition to criteria for the selection of tests and pre and post assessment consultancy. This is followed by Rosemary McGhee's analysis of formal assessment. She illustrates how such assessment can be used both as a diagnosis and a guide to developing an appropriate teaching programme.

Neurological and cognitive aspects of assessment are considered by Anne O'Hare, Sionah Lannen and Gavin Reid. In looking at the role of the paediatrician Dr O'Hare considers the links with other health professionals and other agencies in the education and voluntary sector. A number of neuro-developmental issues are also discussed which provides fascinating and helpful aetiological insights into the relationship between 'dyslexia' and neuro-psychology, genetics, sensory aspects, perinatal factors and the visual perceptual area.

Sionah Lannen and Gavin Reid, in looking at the role and function of the educational psychologist in assessment, address some key cognitive aspects of formal and informal assessment which they relate to both teaching and student's learning styles.

- **Section 3: Teaching Programmes and the Curriculum**

Teaching programmes and the Curriculum should be considered together. Teaching programmes require a context, and that context is the classroom and the curriculum. The class teacher has therefore a key role and Margaret Crombie addresses this by commenting on early intervention, preparation and planning of programmes and the importance of the classroom context and parental involvement.

Curriculum issues are addressed in more detail in the chapters on Differentiation by Sylvia Russell and David Dodds. By examining the holistic needs of the child Sylvia Russell draws attention to teaching, curriculum and resource approaches and the detailed case study highlights how these approaches may be implemented. David Dodds focuses on the importance of the learner's language skills through discussion tasks and the learner's existing knowledge. Using a Modern Studies unit as an example, he shows how skilled development of materials, and flexibility in the mode of learning and teaching, can assist in the organising of information and in responding to that information in an imaginative and evaluative manner.

Some examples of particular teaching approaches feature in the chapters by Helen Calcluth, Catriona Collins and Jean Miller. Helen Calcluth provides a sample of the Phonic Attack Structured Skills programme (PASS) which she has developed, implemented and evaluated. It was the recognition of the inflexibility of some other similar programmes to accommodate to different classroom and teaching situations which inspired her to develop the programme. PASS recognises many key aspects in teaching children with dyslexia; it can also be adapted to meet whole class requirements which can be extremely beneficial in the quest for early recognition and preventative teaching approaches to minimise the difficulties associated with dyslexia.

Catriona Collins and Jean Miller provide a useful overview of spelling difficulties. With reference to some aids and strategies they highlight the need to help children develop a positive attitude towards spelling to help overcome the stigma and failure which often accompanies children's perception of their spelling abilities.

Chapter 1

Sheila Dobie examines factors in relation to poor motor performance which impinge upon early development. Through highlighting research in perceptual motor and neuro developmental dimensions she proposes that problems rooted in developmental delay are both identifiable and remediable.

The important contribution of information technology is highlighted by George Turner and Marie Dougan. They illustrate the importance of developments in micro-technology and provide evaluative comment on particular programmes to show how technology can assist in the development of literacy skills in a manner which promotes enjoyment and motivation.

Ros Hunter provides an illuminative account of supporting pupils with specific learning difficulties through the transition period from primary to secondary school. She provides a clear framework, highlighted by case studies and, following on from the previous chapter, she displays how micro-technology can provide useful support at this stage. She also acknowledges the importance of the teacher's perceptions and particularly the classic dilemma experienced constantly by teachers of the need to provide 'equal allegiance to all the pupils'.

Morven Brown's chapter on supporting learning through a whole-school approach develops some of the themes of the previous one. She highlights how a learning resource centre can be used to coordinate whole-school issues to help meet the needs of children with specific learning difficulties – one such issue being staff in-service training programmes. Identification, teaching, resources and consultancy are also discussed in relation to the whole school. Her contribution is particularly useful because she offers, due to her particular school context, a summary of whole-school issues from **Nursery** to **6th Year Secondary**. Her conclusion, in which she uses the phrase 'whole-school community' provides an ideal of an educational setting which would be a commendable aspiration for all.

- **Section 4: The teaching of Reading, Writing and Mathematics**

The teaching of reading, writing and mathematics are areas where debate on methodology and practices are rife. It is therefore important that teachers of dyslexic children have some understanding of the theoretical models underlying the practices which are recommended, acknowledge the key principles and appreciate the range of strategies which dyslexic children can utilise to help in the acquisition of literacy. Gavin Reid therefore presents a chapter examining various perspectives on reading, looking at some of the underlying competencies such as phonological skills, word recognition and comprehension and strategies such as analogous reading, the utilisation of visual skills and imagery.

The research and the debate on the role of phonological skills in reading is addressed by Rhona Johnston. She critically examines studies on phonological awareness and the performance of poor readers on reading tasks and then attempts to resolve some of the controversies by explaining children's reading difficulties from both visual and phonological perspectives. She argues that the interaction between visual and phonological segmentation can help to explain how poor readers approach reading tasks and she discusses the implications of this for the teaching of reading.

Keith Topping's work on paired reading is widely acclaimed. He provides an outline and an evaluation of paired reading and shows how parents and peers can perform an important function in assisting dyslexic children, particularly in the area of motivation and self-esteem.

Some practical aspects relating to the experience of reading are addressed by Janet Hunter. She provides a number of useful points to consider in affecting successful reading and readers. Her chapter closely identifies with the needs and experiences of the child and should provide an excellent framework for the teacher.

The area of handwriting is skilfully dealt with by Mary Kiely. She provides an insight into a recipe for success by considering not only the craft of handwriting but considerations relating to the organisation and implementation of a writing programme. Her chapter, abundantly illustrated with examples, highlights the importance of motivation and self-esteem in effecting change and improvement in the pupil's attainments.

Specific learning difficulties in mathematics is discussed in Charles Weedon's chapter. He examines this area from a holistic perspective by looking at the sources of difficulties experienced by students in mathematics. He addresses 'institutional features' relating to the school curriculum and teaching as well as student focused aspects relating to personality factors and learning styles. He also discusses a 'network model' to explain the link between language difficulties and mathematical difficulties. This explains the co-existence and overlay between the areas of language and calculation. An interesting interpretation of the pupil-deficit model is also presented by Dr. Weedon. He argues that the starting point of the pupil and his difficulty may be preferable to over-zealous attempts to abolish 'institutional labelling and segregation'. He pin-points the challenge facing all educators to 'build upon the hard won strengths and advantages of our current provision, whilst developing at the same time an organisational and curricular flexibility where it is needed.'

- **Section 5: Metacognition**

The recent interest shown in the area of *Metacognition* reflects the long overdue acceptance and importance of an understanding of the process of learning. Pat Brown examines the metacognitive process of learning focusing particularly on reading strategies. Her assertion that 'some pupils with Specific Learning Difficulties may also be at risk from poor metacognitive knowledge and strategy use' is one that should not be lost to teachers. Vicky Hunter in answering the question 'what makes learning effective for children?' provides a useful framework of strategies to assist with reading, writing, spelling and comprehension.

- **Section 6: Speech and Language**

Speech and Language is without doubt an area of extreme importance in the assessment and teaching of dyslexic children.

Jennifer Reid and Morag Donaldson argue that research into specific language impairment has so far failed to identify an underlying cause of the disorder, and that the linguistic problems which characterise children with specific language impairment are heterogeneous. In their chapter they discuss the implications for instruction and advocate an individualised, eclectic but principled approach. The aim of this approach is to target those specific aspects of language which are posing problems for an individual child, while at the same time retaining an emphasis on the communicative and cognitive functions of language.

Following on from this Marysia Nash examines the connections and implications between language and literacy. She offers some insight into language disorders by reference to the research evidence and examines the implications of this in the acquisition of literacy.

Nicola Robinson discusses the role of the speech therapist, examines early language development and offers pointers for early recognition and assessment. She touches on some key issues when she uses the phrases 'a description rather than a label should be provided' and 'if dyslexia reflects a difference in learning then it requires a difference in teaching'. These two points are indeed central to the whole area of assessment and teaching of dyslexic children.

Eileen Francis provides an insight into the use of language in the educational context. She addresses communication issues in school, describes different communication styles and highlights the centrality of language in the learning process; the importance of discussion, differentiation and the curriculum context are stressed.

Chapter 1

- **Section 7: Emotional Considerations**

Self-esteem is an important consideration in the teaching of all children. Dyslexic children, faced with the difficulties of acquiring literacy skills are a particularly vulnerable group and many of the chapters in 'The Reader' consider this aspect.

Emotional aspects are considered in more detail however by Dr Stewart Biggar and Dr Jenni Barr. They describe some recent research and examine the feelings which children with specific learning difficulties can experience. A major theme is the way in which a child deals with difficulties and attempts to understand or come to terms with them. The feelings and behaviour of parents and teachers can clearly influence these attempts and this is given considerable focus in this chapter.

- **Section 8: Practice, Provision and Resources**

Provision for children with specific learning difficulties is a matter of some debate. Sheila Riddell, Sally Brown and Jill Duffield referring to the results of a research project to investigate policy, practice and provision for children with specific learning difficulties (Riddell, *et al* 1992) highlight the impact of the redefinition of the role of learning support teachers. This chapter encapsulates the classic dilemma of implementing whole-school approaches and also engaging in individual help and offering a 'detailed and specialised approach to learning'. They also discuss learning support teacher's conceptualisation of specific learning difficulties and dyslexia, appropriate forms of identification and assessment and the crucial issue of education provision for specific learning difficulties.

In the following chapter Linda Cumming presents a framework for such provision by highlighting some aspects which may be considered quite crucial. She achieves this by addressing issues relating to staff development, intervention procedures and specialist provision and exemplifies these factors through the use of case studies.

The accumulating availability of resources for specific learning difficulties can be both confusing and helpful for the teacher. Anne Philip attempts to unravel the confusion by presenting a guide to some of the useful resources available and how they can most effectively be used. She also displays how the generation of creative and imaginative ideas can help in the development of 'custom made' resources which can help dyslexic children cope more effectively with curriculum demands, including the 5-14 programme, study skills and preparation for examinations.

Chapter 1

In *conclusion* this Reader, by presenting *Perspectives on Practice,* from a wide range of practitioners, highlights the holistic needs of learners. The 'Reader' examines neurological, cognitive, curriculum and teaching perspectives and recognises the value of the interchange of ideas among professionals.

During the last twenty years the field of dyslexia has been associated with controversy and anxiety. During that time, however, considerable efforts have been made to highlight the needs of dyslexic children using positive and constructive methods, by commissioning and referring to research, through the development of teaching programmes and packages and through consultancy and communication. Central to all these aspects is the crucial issue of teacher training – such training would aim to instil confidence, acquire skills and to disseminate knowledge. It is hoped that this *Reader*, and the *Specific Learning Difficulties Project,* will help to achieve these aims.

REFERENCES

ALLAN J. BROWN S. and MUNN P. (1991) *Off the Record: mainstream provision for pupils with non-recorded learning difficulties in primary and secondary schools* . SCRE, Edinburgh.

Audit Commission/HM Inspectorate (1992). *Getting in on the Act. Provision for Pupils with Special Educational Needs*. HMSO, London.

BELL P. and BEST R. (1986). *Supportive Education*. Blackwell, London.

BLYTHMAN M. (1989). 'From The Other Side of the Wall'. L. Barton (ed). *The Politics of Special Educational Needs*. Falmer Press

BRENNAN W. (1987) *Changing Special Educational Needs*. Open University Press. Milton Keynes.

DEPARTMENT OF EDUCATION AND SCIENCE (1978). *Special Educational Needs*. (Warnock Report). HMSO London.

DEPARTMENT FOR EDUCATION (1992a). *Choice and Diversity: A New Framework for Schools*. HMSO. London.

DEPARTMENT FOR EDUCATION (1992b). *Access to the System*. DFE. London.

EVANS and LUNT I. (1992). *Developments in Special Education under LMS*. Institute of Education, University of London. London.

HER MAJESTY'S GOVERNMENT UK (1981). *Education Act 1981*. HMSO.

HER MAJESTY'S GOVERNMENT UK (1992). *Education (Schools) Act, 1992*. HMSO.

MOORE J. (1991) Local education authority restructuring under ERA: Meeting or creating special educational needs? *Support for Learning*. Vol. 6, No. 1, 16-21.

PUMFREY P. D. and REASON R. (1991) *Specific Learning Difficulties (Dyslexia)* NFER Routledge.

RIDDELL S., BROWN S., DUFFIELD J. and OGILVY C. (1992) *Specific Learning Difficulties: Policy, Practice and Provision*. Report to SOED. University of Stirling.

SCOTTISH EDUCATION DEPARTMENT (1978) *The Education of Pupils with Learning Difficulties in Primary and Secondary Schools in Scotland* (Progress Report). HMSO Edinburgh.

SCOTTISH OFFICE EDUCATION DEPARTMENT (1992a). *Using Performance Indicators in Primary School Self-Evaluation*. SOED Edinburgh.

SCOTTISH OFFICE EDUCATION DEPARTMENT (1992b). *Using Performance Indicators in Secondary School Self-Evaluation*. SOED Edinburgh.

WOLFENDALE S. (1992) *Empowering Parents and Teachers: Working for Children*. Cassell.

SECTION 2

ASSESSMENT

Chapter 2

DIFFICULTIES, DISCREPANCIES AND DIFFERENCES

GAVIN REID

INTRODUCTION

Assessment for specific learning difficulties is a process which considers a variety of different forms of evidence; it should not be portrayed as a rigid formula. A single test or assessment strategy is insufficient since one needs to look for a pattern of evidence which would indicate a specific learning difficulty. It is necessary therefore to focus on at least three principal elements: difficulties; discrepancies and differences. Potential 'difficulties' such as phonological processing, word recognition, use of context, visual and auditory aspects should be considered. Attention should also be given to the 'discrepancies' which may be evident such as that between decoding and reading comprehension, oral and written work and between different subject areas in the school curriculum. At the same time one must also attempt to incorporate a holistic perspective and identify the child's learning style and reading style preferences. Ideally, the learning task should be presented in a manner which matches the child's learning style. These factors can provide an indication of the likelihood of the presence of a specific learning difficulty and provide some information to direct the teacher to appropriate methods and programmes.

The Assessment also needs to consider the curriculum and classroom teaching approaches to obtain a full and clear picture of the child's difficulties, the discrepancies in performance and the individual preferences in learning style.

DIFFICULTIES

- **Decoding.**

A decoding difficulty is the common factor among the difficulties displayed in relation to specific learning difficulties. It is the problem of decoding the symbols which make up letters of the alphabet, identifying the letter sounds and recognising the word patterns which account for the specific learning difficulty. Poor mastery of letter-sound correspondences is present because of a difficulty in learning the phonetic code. The decoding difficulty may also be due to segmenting and blending problems. The child would have some difficulty in breaking words down into their component parts and in blending these component parts. One may also observe sound sequencing errors and indeed other sequencing errors at the letter and word level.

- **Phonological Processing**

There is considerable evidence to suggest that phonological processing difficulties are at the root of these decoding difficulties. Stanovich (1991) suggests there is a lack of phonological awareness, and that the child does not have the ability or awareness to recognise the constituent sound segments which make up words. This is supported by Bradley (1988, 1991) who has identified such difficulties among nursery school children and has shown, in a longitudinal study, that the children so identified have difficulty reading after entry to school. Mann (1986) sees the phonological problem as one of phonetic coding, implying that the child has difficulty in processing verbal information into the working memory. Mann believes that these memory differences between dyslexic and other readers do not pertain to non-verbal information but to information which needs to be linguistically coded.

There is also some evidence to suggest that auditory perception problems may determine the extent of the phonological processing difficulty (Brady and Fowler, 1985). Interestingly, there is evidence which may rule out the possibility of a generalised auditory perception impairment since Mann also found no difference between dyslexic children and other readers in their perception of non-verbal environmental sounds.

Brady and Fowler (1988) provide evidence for a phonological decoding problem which restricts access to words and names. This type of problem, name retrieval difficulty, does appear to be a significant factor among children with dyslexic difficulties. Stanovich (1985) found that children with dyslexia were slower at naming familiar words from pictures than a control group.

- **Early Identification**

The issue of early identification is one of crucial importance. Early recognition can help to minimise the degree of potential failure by identifying appropriate preventative intervention strategies.

Experimental research in early diagnosis has included areas and skills not necessarily related to reading (Singleton, 1993; Nicolson and Fawcett, 1993). It is necessary therefore to recognise the broader perspective of dyslexia and appreciate that dyslexic children may have difficulty in developing skills and carrying out tasks in activities not directly related to the reading task. Such areas can include manual dexterity, reaction times, memory span, non-word repetition, motor skills and balance, awareness of rhyme, visual deficits, automatisation deficits, and picture, colour and number naming. These factors have been the focus of ongoing research on the development of diagnostic early screening procedures involving the use of microtechnology (Singleton, 1993; Nicolson and Fawcett, 1993).

Nicolson and Fawcett, (1993) contend that early screening, together with appropriate pre-reading support could help dyslexic children overcome difficulties in literacy acquisition. They argue that microcomputers offer an historic opportunity for the development of diagnostic pre-reading tests. Their present work focuses on the development of an objective and valid 'Dyslexia Early Screening Test' which can be easily and cheaply administered. These tests principally examine performances in a range of activities not dependent on taught skills such as reading.

The Humberside Early Identification Project (Singleton, 1990, 1992, 1993) is another example of a development programme to devise effective early recognition of dyslexia using microcomputer technology. The purpose of the tests devised by this project which includes analysis of children's performances in memory, phonological processing and visual-perceptual skills, is to identify those children who will possibly experience some difficulty in the acquisition of literacy due to some fundamental difficulty in cognition.

Such developments clearly offer some promise in the area of early recognition and can complement some other procedures in early recognition such as observational assessment (Lannen and Reid, 1993) and formal and informal testing (McGhee, 1993; Evans, 1989). Some attempts at early recognition have centred on the association between phonological awareness and literacy acquisitions (Lundberg et al, 1988; Bradley, 1989; Bradley, 1992). These studies identify a lack of phonological awareness, such as the inability or difficulty to categorise sounds and recognise and repeat rhyme and alliteration, as being of some significance in early recognition of potential reading difficulties. This part is reinforced by the success of the intervention studies (Bryant et al, 1989; Bradley, 1990, 1992) which introduces training in phonological awareness at an early stage to prevent subsequent reading failure. Bradley's longitudinal study suggests that training children to appreciate the connection between rhyming and letter patterns is effective in helping children develop an understanding of the relationship between phonological awareness and the letters of the alphabet (Bradley, 1988).

VISUAL FACTORS

- **Binocular Control**

Stein and Fowler (1982, 1985, 1993) suggest that a considerable number of children with dyslexic difficulties have an unfixed reference eye, which results in binocular instability thus impairing progress in reading.

This viewpoint has met with some criticism (Bishop, 1989) who argued that stable binocular control is acquired as a result of learning to read, rather than as a prerequisite for reading.

Stein and Fowler (1993), however, disputed this and claimed that dyslexic children have in fact less binocular control than a group of younger children matched for IQ and reading age with the dyslexic group. Furthermore these researchers demonstrated that an improvement in dyslexic readers' binocular control was often followed by reading improvement without any additional tutoring in reading skills. Stein and Fowler therefore argue that unstable binocular control is a feature of dyslexia and a factor which does impede reading.

The responses from the Stein and Fowler research have been obtained through the use of the Dunlop Test (Dunlop, 1972). This test is said to "indicate the lateral preference of the ocular motor system" and it is argued that it can determine the 'dominant' eye in a binocular situation – that is by studying the movements of both eyes simultaneously (Stein and Fowler, 1993).

Some criticism, however, has been voiced in the use of this test. The test does have a high level of subjectivity – children have to indicate the movement of a visual stimulus, which they do not directly focus on – which makes it not entirely reliable, especially in inexperienced hands (Stein et al, 1985; Bigelow and McKenzie, 1985). Stein and Fowler (1993), however, did attempt to overcome this in their research design by adaptations to the test providing for more objective responses.

The intervention which they argued was followed by improved reading was based on the practice of monocular occlusion. This, they argue, helped to establish a fixed reference eye of binocular control. While they argue that unstable binocular control is a common cause of reading difficulties, they do acknowledge that it is seldom the sole cause. This is an important point to consider since although it has been shown that, for example, visual segmentation skills can be an important aspect in reading difficulties (Johnston, Anderson & Duncan, 1991), phonological aspects need also to be highlighted both in assessment and in teaching (Stanovich, 1988; Goswami and Bryant, 1990).

- **Visual Tracking**

A number of studies have shown a high incidence of right to left tracking of information among dyslexic children. The implication of this is that confusion may occur when the child is trained to read from left to right if this conflicts with his/her natural instincts to read from right to left. This may well account for reversals and misreading of print. It is important therefore that a teaching programme emphasises the directional aspect of left to right.

Extensive research (Pavlidis, 1990) suggests that children with dyslexia make more eye fixations and fixate for longer than other children. He suggested they have less efficient control over eye movements.

- **Eye Sensitivity**

Irlen (1983, 89) claims that some dyslexic children may have a sensitivity syndrome (scotopic sensitivity syndrome) which results in excessive glare and an inability to see print without distortions. According to Irlen the treatment for this involves the use of coloured Perspex overlays or tinted lenses. The research on this, however, is far from clear cut. Stone and Harris (1991) claim that it is difficult for the dyslexic child to cope with the full range of spect... light, but they argue that the present form of assessment, which takes the form of screening procedures, such as that used by the Irlen Institute, is too subjective. Wilkins (1990) provided evidence for significant improvements in visual acuity in those children who were identified by the screening procedures and subsequently used overlays or lenses.

A study involving 75 children with specific learning difficulties (Kyd, Sutherland and McGettrick, 1992) presented evidence for visual perceptual dysfunction. Almost half the sample tested positive using the Irlen Screening Test. Subsequent intervention involved the use of appropriate, self-selected, coloured overlays. This was accompanied by significant improvements in reading rate. The researchers are currently engaged in follow-up studies to examine the long-term effects of the Irlen overlays in comprehension and accuracy as well as reading rate. Similarly the preliminary results from an evaluation project of the Irlen overlays and lenses (Wright, 1993) has provided some impressive data on reading rate progress.

Pumfrey and Reason (1992), however, suggest that improvements using overlays can often be due to a 'placebo effect'. They argue that the evidence that dyslexia is primarily due to visual difficulties is not convincing, since much of the literature focuses on language, information processing, and other cognitive aspects such as attention, concentration and memory.

DISCREPANCIES

The identification of discrepancies in ability and performances is an important factor in the assessment of children who may have a specific learning difficulty.

- **Decoding/Reading Comprehension Discrepancy**

Aaron (1989) presents a case for focusing on the discrepancy between decoding and listening/reading comprehension. Thus one would expect a child with dyslexia to be poor at decoding and good or relatively better at listening/reading comprehension. Features of other types of readers can be described using the same decoding/comprehension discrepancy measure. For example Aaron describes a group, the 'non-specific reading disabled', as being poor at both decoding and comprehension. He also describes a 'hyperlexic' group as displaying a reverse trend from the dyslexic group, being good at decoding but poor in comprehension.

How, therefore, should one attempt to identify a decoding/reading comprehension discrepancy? To test for decoding, words in isolation may be presented, but this is also testing memory for letter and word patterns which may produce some criteria contamination which would mean that other factors in addition to decoding are being assessed. To eradicate these criteria contamination factors, decoding can be assessed through the use of non-words. By using pronounceable non-words based on grapheme-phoneme relational rules one can obtain some measure of the child's actual decoding ability.

Clearly, it is difficult to obtain a reading comprehension measure if the child has a decoding difficulty. This though can be overcome by testing for listening comprehension. Aaron (1989) in a study of school children from six different years found an impressive correlation (0.78) between reading comprehension and listening comprehension. Indeed, among the nine year old group the correlation was even higher (0.87). Often it is around the nine year age group that concern is quite high in relation to reading progress because by that stage other factors, such as developmental lag, have usually levelled out and are therefore less influential as a possible cause of the reading difficulty.

- **Oral/Written Discrepancies**

One may also identify a discrepancy between a child's oral performance and written work or reading fluency. It is, therefore, important to assess the child's oral skills and oral contributions in class in relation to his performance through other modalities. One must, however, bear in mind that some children's oral performance can be affected by other factors such as low confidence and self-esteem, and phonological processing difficulties. Children with a specific learning difficulty may therefore also have a difficulty with oral communication.

• Subject Discrepancies

Most children display some level of variance in their performances in school between different subject areas. Children with specific learning difficulties, however, may display extreme discrepancies. A discrepancy may be seen for example, between science subjects and English, or subjects which demand significant amounts of reading. Such children may have abilities at non-verbal problem solving which can readily be developed in some curricular subjects, although their performance may still be restricted by reading difficulties, since some reading is usually necessary in all curricular areas. To help deal with this some schools now provide extensive learning support including readers, scribes and tapes of notes and texts.

DIFFERENCES

Extensive research on learning styles (Dunn and Dunn, 1992) raises the issue of assessing not just the product of learning, but also the process by which learning takes place. It is important, therefore, to appreciate that dyslexic children are all individuals and each will have a specific preference in their learning style. Reid (1992) has tackled the identification of learning styles through an observational schedule which can provide data on the range of learning and contextual factors which can influence children's learning outcomes. Dunn and Dunn (1992) have produced a learning styles inventory, a self-report questionnaire, which has been extensively validated in many countries. Dunn and Dunn's factors include: the environment including sound, light, temperature and design; emotional aspects which relate to the need for structure and responsibility; sociological aspects, such as student preferences in learning alone or in pairs, physical factors such as mobility and time of day; psychological aspects identifying styles such as analytic (preference to piece details together before attempting to understand the whole) and global (preference for obtaining the overall comprehension of the whole first and then attend to details). Dunn and Dunn found significant differences between the global and analytic groups, and that each group learnt best under different conditions. An example is that global learners tend to be less bothered by sound in learning than analytics.

Carbo, Dunn and Dunn (1987) looked at the implications of the Dunn and Dunn model and postulated that no single reading method is best for every child, and that lack of mastery of a reading sub-skill doesn't necessarily indicate a need for that sub-skill. She also found that most primary aged children are global, tactual and kinaesthetic learners and prefer to read in pairs.

The research in learning styles does, therefore, warrant some attention from those involved in the assessment process. Observational assessment or self-report questionnaires can provide useful information on children's learning which can be complimented by other aspects of the assessment.

CONCLUSION

An assessment should be an all embracing activity and should be viewed as a process not a product. All forms of assessment, norm-referenced; criterion-referenced; curriculum based and metacognitive assessment (where one looks at the process of learning) are of value and all can provide information which can help to identify children with specific learning difficulties and help to provide information which can be useful in the development of support programmes. There are some key questions one must ask when embarking on an assessment for specific learning difficulties. These include:

- What is being assessed? Is one looking at children's skills, abilities or strategies?
- Why is the assessment taking place – is it to be diagnostic, prescriptive, predictive or normative?
- How is it to be done? What assessment strategies will be used – norm-referenced, criterion-referenced, observational , metacognitive?
- What will be the effect of the assessment? To what extent will it link with teaching and in what way will it have an affect on the student's self concept?

Clearly, there are many questions relating to assessment and these are encapsulated in four of the recommendations made following extensive research on assessment (Pumfrey and Reason, 1992). These are that:

- identification procedures should consider the child's previous learning history;
- both normative and criterion referenced assessment should be supplemented by the observations of pupils, parents, teachers and psychologist;
- attention should be given to strategies, strengths and weaknesses that children bring to their attempts to read and write;
- the symbolic relationship between assessment and teaching should be appreciated by all practitioners involved with pupils identified as having specific learning difficulties.

These recommendations provide a clear framework with which to embark on the process of assessment. In implementing an assessment for specific learning difficulties it is important therefore to:

- obtain a clear rationale of why the assessment is being carried out;
- appreciate the importance of consultancy with parents and other professionals;
- recognise the value of observation and learning styles;
- embrace a range of strategies to identify strengths and difficulties displayed by the child in addition to any discrepancies in performance which may be present.

Consideration of these factors helps to ensure that assessment is constructive, productive and positive and will be recognised as an integrated element of both teaching and the curriculum.

REFERENCES

AARON, R G (1989). *Dyslexia and Hyperlexia*. Kluwer Academic Publications.

BIGELOW, E R and McKENZIE, B E (1985). 'Unstable occular dominance and reading ability.' *Perception*, 14, 329-335.

BISHOP, D V M (1989). 'Unfixed reference, monocular occlusion and developmental dyslexia - a critique'. *British Journal of Opthalmology*, 73, 8-5.

BRADLEY, L (1988). 'Rhyme recognitions and reading and spelling in young children' in Masland, R L and Masland, M U (eds.), *Pre-school presentation of reading failure*. Parkton, Maryland. York Press.

BRADLEY, L (1989). 'Predicting learning disabilities' in Dumont, J and Nakken, J (eds.), *Learning Disabilities: Cognitive, Social and Remedial Aspects*. Amsterdam. Swets and Zeitlinger.

BRADLEY, L (1991). 'Rhyming connections in learning to read and spell' in Pumfrey, D D and Elliott, C D (eds.), *Children's Reading, Spelling and Writing Difficulties: Challenges and Responses*. Neumes. Falmer Press.

BRADLEY, L (1992). *Early Identification of Specific Learning Difficulties*. Paper presented at Conference held by Specific Learning Difficulties Project, Inverness, June 1992.

BRADY, S, and FOWLER, A E (1988). 'Phonological precursors to reading acquisition' in Masland, R L and Masland, M U (eds.), *Preschool Prevention of Reading Failure*. 204-215. Parkton, Maryland. York Press.

CARBO, M, DUNN, R, and DUNN, K (1987). *Teaching students to read through their individual learning styles*. Prentice Hall.

DUNLOP, P (1972). 'Dylexia: the orthoptic approach.' *Australian Orthoptic Journal*, 12, 16-20.

DUNN, R and DUNN, K (1992). *Teaching Elementary Students through Their Individual Learning Styles*. Allym and Bacon, Mass.

EVANS, A (1990).

GOSWAMI, U and BRYANT, P (1990). *Phonological Skills and Learning to Read*. Hove, Sussex. Erlbaum.

IRLEN, H (1983). *Successful treatment of learning disabilities*. Presented at 91st annual convention of American Psychological Association, Anaheim, California.

IRLEN, H (1989). *Scotopic Sensitivity Syndrome*. Screening manual, 3rd Ed. Perceptual Development Corporation.

JOHNSTON, R, ANDERSON, M and DUNCAN, L (1991). 'Phonological and visual segmentation problems in poor readers', in Snowling, M and Thomson, M, *Dyslexia, Integrating Theory and Practice*. Whurr Publishers.

KYD, L, SUTHERLAND, G and McGETTRICK, P (1992). 'A preliminary appraisal of the Irlen screening process for scotopic sensitivity syndrome and the effect of Irlen overlays on reading.' *British Opthalmic Journal* 1992: 49: 25-30.

LANNEN, S and REID, G (1993). 'Psychological dimensions and the role of the educational psychologist in assessment', in Reid, G (ed.), *Specific Learning Difficulties (Dyslexia) - Perspectives on Practice*. Edinburgh. Moray House Publications.

LUNDBERG, I, FROST, J and PETERSON, O (1988). 'Effects of an exercise program for stimulating phonological awareness in pre-school children.' *Reading Research Quarterly*, 12,3 pp.263-284.

MANN, V A (1986). 'Why some children encounter reading problems: The contribution of difficulties with language processing and phonological sophistication to early reading disability', in Torgeson, J K and Wong, B Y L (eds.), *Psychological and Educational Perspectives on Learning Disabilities*, 133-59. New York. Academia Press.

McGHEE, R (1993). 'Formal assessment', in Reid, G (ed.), *Specific Learning Difficulties (Dyslexia)—Perspectives on Practice*. Edinburgh. Moray House Publications.

NICOLSON, R and FAWCETT, A J (1993). *Early Diagnosis of Dyslexia: An Historic Opportunity?* Keynote address presented at BDA 'Early Diagnosis' Conference, London, June 1993.

PAVLIDIS, G T (1990). Perspectives on dyslexia. *Neurology, Neuropsychology and Genetics*. Vol. 1. Chichester. Wiley.

PUMFREY, P D and REASON, R (1992). *Specific Learning Difficulties (Dyslexia) Challenges and Responses*. NFER Routledge.

REID, G (1992). *Learning Difficulties and Learning Styles – Observational Criteria*. Paper presented at S.E. Learning Styles Center, 5th Annual Conference. November 1992. George Mason University, Virginia, USA.

SINGLETON, C H (1990). *Software Developments in Cognitive Assessment and Remediation*. Paper delivered to the British Dyslexia Association Conference 'Advances in Computer Applications for Dyslexics', University of Hull.

SINGLETON, C H (1992). *The Use of Computers in the Early Identification of Dyslexia* Paper presented at Fourth Cambridge Conference, Helel Arkell Dyslexia Centre, April 1992.

SINGLETON, C H (1993). *Early identification of Specific Learning Difficulties*. Paper presented at Specific Learning Difficulties Conference, Moray House, Edinburgh, June 1993.

STANOVICH, K E (1985). 'Explaining the variance in reading ability in terms of psychological processes: What have we learned?' *Annals of Dyslexia* 35:67-95.

STANOVICH, K E (1988). 'Explaining the differences between the dyslexic and the garden-variety poor reader: the phonological-core variable-differentiation model.' *Journal of Learning Disabilities* 21, 590-612.

STANOVICH, K (1991). 'Discrepancy definitions of reading disability: has intelligence led us astray?' *Reading Research Quarterly*, XXVI, 1, 7-29.

STEIN, J F (1991). 'Vision of language', in Snowling, M and Thomson, M (eds.), *Dyslexia: Integrating Theory and Practice*. London. Whurr Publishers.

STEIN, J F and FOWLER, S. (1982). 'Diagnosis of dyslexia by means of a new indication of eye dominance'. *British Journal of Opthalmology*, 66, 332-236.

STEIN, J F and FOWLER, S (1985). 'Effect of monocular occlusion on visuomotor perception and reading in dyslexic children.' *Lancet*, 13/7/85.

STEIN, J F and FOWLER, M S (1993). 'Unstable binocular control in dyslexic children.' *Journal of Research in Reading*, 16 (1), 30-45.

STONE, J and HARRIS, K (1991). 'These coloured spectacles: what are they for?' *Support to Learning*, vol. 6, no. 3 (1991).

WILKINS, A (1990). *Visual Discomfort and Reading*. MRC, APU Cambridge.

WRIGHT, A (1993). *IRLEN - The Never Ending Story*. Paper presented at the 5th European Conference of Neuro-Developmental Delay in Children with Specific Learning Difficulties, London.

Chapter 3

PRINCIPLES OF ASSESSMENT

GORDON BOOTH

THE PURPOSE OF ASSESSMENT

The importance of skilled assessment of any pupil's progress is fully acknowledged today, although in the past practice in the classroom has often failed to live up to precept. If careful assessment is judged essential for the average school pupil, it is even more crucial in the case of a pupil with specific learning difficulties, whose problems are still frequently misunderstood and are all too often attributed to 'laziness' or 'lack of ability'.

Teachers taking part in a diploma course for the education of pupils with specific learning difficulties volunteered the following reasons for carrying out assessment:

- to diagnose learning difficulties;
- to check on progress;
- to provide feedback to the student(s) themselves;
- to assist with record keeping;
- to explore the pupil's thinking and learning strategies;
- to discover the student's strengths and weaknesses;
- to establish baselines for an intervention programme;
- to monitor the success of a particular programme;
- to enable a report to be written.

These are all valid and important reasons for carrying out assessment and others might well be added. Nevertheless it is not uncommon for extensive testing to be carried out without the teacher having any very clear purpose in mind – perhaps in the hope that by using a barrage of tests something of value will emerge to throw light on the nature of the problem and the scale of the task ahead. All assessment should be founded upon a systematic and thoughtful approach, bearing in mind that:

- each element in a battery of tests should be presented with a specific purpose in mind;

- over-testing is wasteful of time;
- testing should be economical and efficient, providing the maximum of information in the minimum of time;
- testing should be a positive, enlightening experience for the student and teacher alike;
- the qualitative information elicited may ultimately prove more significant than the quantitative data (the test scores);
- successful assessment depends on an effective relationship between teacher and student;
- assessment should always be used to generate hypotheses

Assessment is an ongoing process and forms an integral part of an educational cycle that will be familiar to most teachers but which is worth re-emphasising schematically.

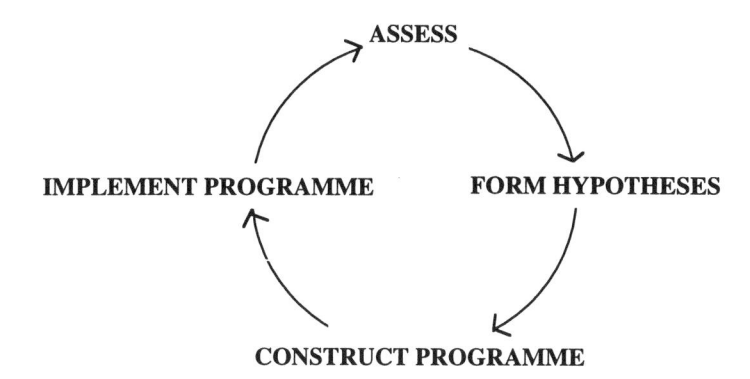

```
          ASSESS
    ↗            ↘
IMPLEMENT PROGRAMME    FORM HYPOTHESES
    ↖            ↙
      CONSTRUCT PROGRAMME
```

THE RELATIONSHIP

Where ongoing assessment forms part of the familiar routine between teacher and pupil, it will be incorporated naturally within the framework of the lesson; and the pupil, just as much as the teacher, should find it a rewarding and illuminating experience. The older student should be helped to understand what the numerical scores mean and be enabled to gauge the degree of progress made, but even the younger child will understand progress made in terms of 'number right this time' by comparison with a previous occasion.

When assessment is being carried out for the first time, possibly in unfamiliar surroundings, care must be taken to establish a friendly, easy relationship. Whatever the age of the pupil or student, he or she should have some understanding

Chapter 3

of the reason for the testing and should have an opportunity to chat beforehand. Talking about home, family, personal preferences and interests not only helps to place a child at ease but may provide important information.

Take brief notes unobtrusively, but not covertly, and with a first-time assessment always double-check basic information such as name, age and address. It is very worthwhile offering a child or young person scope for free drawing in the course of an assessment but, unless time is unlimited, it is generally advisable to tackle much of the more difficult testing first. Obviously it is important to be aware of fatigue setting in and this forms part of the task of monitoring the child's reaction generally: is there a pattern, for example, of 'high energy, low efficiency' or is the student's output well-paced and methodical?

Indeed, the 'first five minutes' are a vital stage of any new assessment, shedding light on the student's characteristic personality attributes, social attitudes and individual style of approach: whether he is, for example, predominantly outgoing or withdrawing, attentive or distractable, good-humoured or irritable, interested or apathetic, systematic or disorganised in his general approach. At the same time this information may only be fully obtained once the pupil has settled and established a relationship with the tester.

ATTAINMENT TESTING

Testing is a standardised procedure and every effort should be made to adopt a uniform approach, following the instructions provided in the test manual and, so far as possible, knowing these sufficiently thoroughly to avoid having to refer to them during the test administration. It is obvious that one should ensure the best possible conditions, with a minimum of noise or distraction, and it is important not to feel under pressure of time. On the other hand, there is a tendency for inexperienced teachers to adopt an unduly slow style of testing and this does not encourage interest or high-level attention on the child's part. Despite the need to follow test instructions carefully, it is vital that teachers should be able to exercise their own judgement as to how far to prolong testing or when to intervene and offer a change of activity.

Regardless of the type of test form provided for a specific test, a teacher should establish a systematic personal style of approach to note-taking during testing, remembering that scores form only a small part of the data provided by the child in making his sequence of responses. Pay close attention to – and make a record of – such potentially important details as:

- varying levels of confidence;
- changes in pace or fluency;
- fluctuations in persistence and motivation;
- indications of altering emotional attitude;
- flexibility of approach and capacity to adopt alternative strategies.

CHOOSING THE RIGHT TESTS

Use tests that are reasonably up-to-date, are well standardised and have proven reliability, (implying that the same pattern of results would emerge if the test was repeated) and validity, which indicates that the test contents are appropriate and consistent with the aims of the test. Test manuals should always give clear information about the date of standardisation, the population sample used and technical data concerning reliability and standard error of measurement. Where test norms are provided in the form of reading ages alone, teachers should be aware of the limitations of these and should have some familiarity with alternatives such as standard scores or centiles.

The range of tests given should in part be determined by the stated reasons for referral: i.e. the child's difficulties as perceived by class teacher or parent. However, a child may well have problems in areas of work not mentioned in the referral. For example, because the specific learning difficulties pupil essentially has weaknesses in processing of auditory or visual data, computation skills are almost certain to be affected, although this may be obscured by good understanding of number concepts.

Reading should be assessed on more than one dimension: it is important to look at a child's capacity to deal with continuous text and a test such as the **Revised Neale Analysis of Reading** is invaluable in providing separate scores for accuracy, comprehension and speed – but, like any test, it has its limitations and is not particularly suited to the needs of very young or secondary age pupils. A word recognition test (e.g. the Revised Burt) could complement a test of continuous reading and observations made whilst the child reads the passages in the test. Either type of test will afford a great deal more information than simply a set of right and wrong scores: not only will you want to establish generally whether a child:

- uses a whole word or phonic approach;
- has ability to segment words into syllables;
- shows evidence of useful predictive strategies;

Chapter 3

- has a grasp of vowel and consonant digraphs;
- has eye movement problems;

but close analysis of each individual response (especially the incorrect ones) will build up a picture of how the child understands the reading task, what particular tactics are available and not available to him, and which faulty procedures are characteristic of his approach. It is through this analytic technique that one begins to form hypotheses about a child's way of working.

From now on the tasks for the teacher are to establish where to begin afresh the learning process for the individual pupil and what the key elements of the teaching approach are to be. Neither should ever be a matter of guess-work or random choice but should always emerge from the observed data elicited from the child or student in the course of the assessment and subsequently organised by the teacher into a meaningful pattern. Scores provide one kind of baseline but qualitative analysis of how the pupil is actually operating or thinking provides the key to the development of a logical and effective teaching programme which aims to build on the child's demonstrated strengths and works to mitigate his weaker abilities.

Both spelling and basic number tests should be given the same detailed error analysis: indeed the identification of simple operational errors in arithmetic affords the best starting point for a teacher to discover the power of this approach to elucidating what a child knows and does not know, how he thinks, and how he utilises the skills he possesses. With older pupils (or adults) this detective work becomes a real partnership – a mutual voyage of discovery for teacher and student – and should form part of the continuous assessment process which is integral to the interaction of teacher and pupil in any learning situation. Children with specific learning difficulties have an especial contribution to make here and need to be encouraged to talk about how they perceive each learning task: how, for instance, they decipher words in the course of reading, which particular components of a word constitute spelling obstacles for them, or which elements of an arithmetical operation pose especial difficulty.

Written work needs to be a constant feature of the diagnostic interaction between teacher and pupil, always bearing in mind that handwriting output is certain to be slow, effortful and fatiguing for the pupil with specific learning difficulties. Assessment here begins with taking account of basic factors such as body posture, hand preference, pencil grasp and muscle tone; it moves on to scrutiny of letter and digit formation, the spacing between words and the general 'flow' of a child's handwriting. It hardly needs to be stressed that a sample of the student's free writing, no matter how elementary, is essential evidence for a first assessment. It needs the same care in analysis as the responses to formal testing and should always be preserved for future reference.

For younger and older pupils alike opportunities for free drawing are important, both for relaxation and as a means of comparing executive skills in this area with the youngster's level of conceptual awareness. Detecting a 'mismatch' in this way between technical skill and intellectual grasp is fundamental to all diagnostic assessment of specific learning difficulties: it is often dramatically articulated by the pupil himself in a characteristic expression of frustration, 'I should be able to do this but I can't!'

RECORDING

Spoken words are ephemeral and therefore systematic record-keeping is vital, not just at the initial assessment stage but in the course of all interactive teaching which incorporates continuous assessment. Tape-recording has a certain value for later analysis, and also for preserving evidence of a pupil's speed and fluency in reading, but it can be intrusive and should be used with economy and discretion. Effective, economical note-taking throughout a lesson or assessment is more generally useful and has the major advantage of capturing a record, not only of how the pupil has responded, but of one's own moment-to-moment insights, impressions and ideas. These can prove to be of immense usefulness later. You are, after all, aiming to discover which aspects of a child's performance are characteristic features – not just chance occurrences – and it is the recurring elements in the pattern of a child's response which are significant.

After the assessment take time to review your notes and to sift out the relevant pieces of information. Write these up in a more coherent form, fleshing out your initial thoughts and making preliminary inferences. These will lead on either to the formulation of a programme or to the compilation of a complete report for parent or teacher colleague. In many instances both will be necessary and to rely mainly on memory is guaranteed to ensure that major gaps in your overall picture will occur.

WRITING UP THE ASSESSMENT

This is an art in itself, to be successfully mastered only through practice. There are certain fundamentals of good report-writing which are self-evident, such as the need to set out test results clearly, adjacent always to the child's chronological age. State accurately the names of the tests and where appropriate, the particular version used. Interpretation of what the test scores imply should follow on logically from this setting out of the basic data and, ideally, your eventual conclusions should be seen to emerge quite inescapably from your interpretation of the evidence. Jargon should be avoided since reports should be understandable by the intended audience and further explanation from the writer should be unnecessary.

PRE AND POST ASSESSMENT CONSULTANCY

Effective, accurate diagnosis depends on objective assessment carried out under the best possible conditions. This does not mean that assessment should be carried out in a vacuum without reference to the information available from teachers and parents, nor that the child's behaviour in the classroom is irrelevant.

Pre-assessment discussion with the class teacher (and possibly head teacher and parent also) will help clarify or amplify those concerns which should already have been stated in writing. The only caveat is that one should take care to avoid being unduly influenced by strongly-held views that may be quite forcibly expressed in the context of informal conversation. For the same reason classroom observation is generally best deferred until after the formal assessment is completed: at that point it helps illuminate facets of behaviour that cannot easily be judged in the individual setting, such as the child's social and educational interaction with other children, his ability to cope with classroom distraction or the degree to which he is capable of becoming truly 'engaged' in the range of different learning activities. In addition there is, of course, the opportunity to form a general impression of the classroom's atmosphere and dynamics.

Consultation with teachers and parents following an assessment is essential, possibly at more than one stage. The written report is of fundamental importance, not only as a record of your findings and recommendations but as a point of reference now and in the future for all concerned. By itself, however, it is insufficient as a means of communication. Discussion is a two-way process and you will need to know whether teacher and parent 'recognise' the picture of the child that you have given in your report. If they don't then you have almost certainly not succeeded in your task. Equally, you may wish to have further information on certain points, just as those to whom you are speaking will want you to elaborate on some of your findings and recommendations. 'Listening' on both sides is a basic element of communication and your own role is certainly not to present your report in monologue form!

Successful consultation at this stage will lay the ground effectively for future meetings to review progress and to reassess strategies. Initial discussions with parents are best kept as friendly and informal as possible, without being patronising: they help establish the kind of trusting relationships that are essential if, in the context of larger multi-disciplinary meetings, true partnership between parents and teachers is to be achieved successfully.

CONCLUSION

Ultimately, your aim is to present a well-rounded and accurate picture of the child in his life-situation, with especial reference to his educational difficulties. This requires great care in the selection of those facts that are relevant and in ensuring that your conclusions actually derive from the evidence uncovered through your assessment. Above all, present your findings honestly, and distinguish fact from fiction and firm conclusions from legitimate but speculative hypotheses which require to be tested out through further exploration and the use of different teaching strategies. Assessment is – or should be – exciting and interesting: intuition and empathy are useful qualities for the teacher but piecing together the jigsaw demands, above all, self-discipline, concentration and a methodical approach.

Chapter 4

FORMAL ASSESSMENT

ROSEMARY McGHEE

BACKGROUND

The learning support service in Grampian operates on an area team basis – a team of learning support teachers who cover a Secondary School and its associated primaries. The team implement a 'float' system which enables a learning support teacher within the team to develop an expertise in specific learning difficulties. It is therefore possible for such a specialist to assess pupils in all of the schools covered by the area teams and to either recommend a course of remedial action to a colleague or, if considered more appropriate, to work with an individual pupil of small groups of pupils in any of the area schools. This system is beneficial to pupils with a Specific Learning Difficulty as continuity can be maintained across the P7-S1 transfer and beyond.

HANDLING REFERRALS

The teacher should, in the first instance, gather all the available information about the pupil. Initially this will involve discussion with the referring teacher or parent to establish the areas of concern. Access to school reports and in particular Learning Support reports is vital. Well kept records may show a pattern of difficulty emerging before any formal assessment begins. For example, a history of late language development or involvement with Speech Therapy, letter reversals continuing long after the infant stages and persistent problems with blending, may all be factors which would contribute to a positive identification of a Specific Learning

DIFFICULTY

Diagnosis of a Specific Learning Difficulty may be described as a 'diagnosis by exclusion', in that all other factors which could be the main cause of the child's difficulties must first be discounted. These factors include poor eyesight, poor hearing and social and emotional problems. Much of this information and any evidence of patchy or disturbed school career will be available from records or should be sought from parents. Concerns about eyesight or hearing should be referred to the medical services. Recent tests should not be replicated unless it is anticipated that they will shed new light on the child's difficulties.

THE ASSESSMENT

Once the educational history and other background factors have been established the ground for referral should also be considered before tests are selected which will provide a profile of the pupil's strengths and weaknesses. Once other factors have been ruled out the diagnosis of a Specific Learning Difficulty, at its simplest, is made when there is a significant discrepancy between an individual's ability in non-verbal and/or oral tasks compared to their attainment in basic reading and writing skills.

In a young pupil a discrepancy may be quite easy to identify but delayed development caused by a maturational lag may at this stage be the cause of the difficulty. A policy of 'wait and see' is often adopted. Many professionals are reluctant to make a definite diagnosis at the infant stages because classic signs of a Specific Learning Difficulty, such as letter reversals, poor blending skills and difficulty with letter recognition are present in children who later prove not to have a Specific Learning Difficulty.

It would do no harm, at this stage, to use teaching methods proven to work with children who have a Specific Learning Difficulty even if a definite diagnosis has not yet been made. Early intervention has been shown to be more beneficial than later attempts, particularly if the children are spared the trauma of persistent failure. In older pupils problems of making a clear diagnosis are exacerbated by various compensatory strategies having been adopted by the pupil to cope with or mask their inherent difficulties.

TEST AND TESTING

Tests which provide a Reading Age or Spelling Age when used with tests of ability such as the British Picture Vocabulary Scale or Raven's Matrices may indicate a discrepancy between basic literacy attainments and powers or reasoning and general oral ability. Although there is some doubt in relation to the reliability and validity of these tests, they may provide a useful guide to a pupil's ability. Tests should not be administered solely to provide a score but results should be qualitatively analysed to show skills which have been mastered and those which have not. The teacher should note the child's approach to tasks as well as their performance. A programme can be based, at least in part, on the test results.

Chapter 4

STANDARDISED TESTS USED IN THE ASSESSMENT OF SPECIFIC LEARNING DIFFICULTY

The following list comprises a selection of some of the more commonly used Standardised Tests. They may be substituted by other tests depending on their availability and suitability for the pupil involved.

TESTS	PURPOSE
Tests to establish ability level	
Crichton Vocabulary Scale	To measure Oral Linguistic Ability
Raven's Matrices	Non-verbal test of ability
Reading Tests	
Neale Analysis (Revised)	Reading in context. A Reading and Comprehension Age within an age range is provided.
MacMillan Reading Analysis	As above.
Word Reading Tests	
Burt	Provide a Reading Age but also an indication of the de-coding strategies which the pupil uses.
Spelling Tests	
Vernon	Provide a Spelling Age but can also highlight specific phonic rules which have not yet been mastered.
Schonell	
Arithmetic Test	
Ballard Oral Arithmetic	An arithmetic test is part of the battery of tests which make up Intelligence Tests. Included here to form an overall picture of ability, simple sequencing ability and as a measure of mental agility.
Tests Designed to Diagnose Specific Learning Difficulties	
Bangor Dyslexia Test	Tests areas which researchers have found over the years to indicate a Specific Learning Difficulty. Provides little information which can be of use in planning a remedial programme but seven of the more positive indicators along with other evidence can help in the diagnosis of a Specific Learning Difficulty.

Aston Index — Attempts to provide a profile comparing ability with Reading Age and a profile of the areas of difficulty, i.e. auditory and visual but is poorly constructed and standardised. Recent research (Sutherland and Smith 1991) has suggested that it is unwise to attempt to make a distinction between auditory and visual causes but that a lack of phonological awareness is more likely to be the root cause of a Specific Learning Difficulty. In practice it is unlikely that the whole battery of tests would be administered but selected tests can be helpful in profiling strengths and weaknesses.

Form 2 of the MacMillan Reading Analyses can be used as a Listening Comprehension Test. The teacher reads the passage the pupil is then asked comprehension questions based on the text. A significant difference between Listening Comprehension and Reading comprehension combined with other indications such as auditory processing difficulties, which give rise to bizarre spelling, would more than likely lead to a diagnosis of a Specific Learning Difficulty.

The Daniel and Diack battery of reading tests is useful in profiling reading difficulties particularly in very young children.

Reversals of letters and words in reading and writing, directional confusion and difficulty in copying written work may indicate mixed laterality. While not thought to be a contributory factor in causing a Specific Learning Difficulty mixed laterality can cause confusions which can exacerbate the difficulty. The Laterality Test in the Aston Index can pinpoint whether mixed laterality is in fact present and steps can be taken to ameliorate the problems caused by the directional confusion.

A good working knowledge of a range of tests and a good understanding of the nature of the condition are essential in order to optimise the assessment process.

FEEDBACK OF RESULTS

The results of the assessment may be recorded in a report as well as being communicated through consultancy and discussions with teachers, school

Chapter 4

management and parents. Test results should be set out in a clear style which is easy to read at a glance. The report should refer to the test results and give specific examples, particularly where conclusions are being drawn about the nature of the difficulties the child is experiencing. Indications as to further testing required can be made at this stage. This may help to explore more precisely the nature of the Specific Learning Difficulty or in some cases to suggest that the child's problems are due to some other cause. For example a motor learning difficulty may be at the root of the problem or perhaps a delay in language development due to frequent hearing loss at an early age may be the source of the difficulty. Whatever the conclusions drawn recommendations should be made as to the next step.

There now follows an example of the profile of scores obtained after testing a Primary 7 pupil.

PROFILE OF SCORES

Name: *Andrew*
Date of Birth: *22/2/82*
Chronological Age at date of Assessment: *10 years 8 months*
Assessment date: *2/11/92*

Test results
Schonell Word Reading Test RA *7.6 years*
Bangor Dyslexia Test *7+*
Ballard Oral Arithmetic *Addition* *7 years 7 months*
Subtraction *7 years 7 months*

MacMillan New Reading Analysis
Form A used as a Listening Comprehension
Comprehension Age Equivalents *10:2 to 11:11*
Crichton Vocabulary *Percentile 10*
(below average)

Previous test results
Schonell Spelling (8/9/92) *7.8 years*
MacMillan Individual Reading Analysis *Accuracy* *8.6 years*
Comprehension *8.9 years*

Further tests recommended
Raven's Matrices
Auditory Discrimination from the Aston Index

From the test results and from observation of Andrew's approach to the various tasks it was possible to identify areas of strength and weakness. The conclusions which can be drawn from the test results are that Andrew displays many of the characteristic signs of a Specific Learning Difficulty and that his difficulties would appear to stem from an auditory processing problem. This was evident in his responses to the Crichton Vocabulary Scale. He did not know what 'squabble' meant and kept repeating 'squaggle' despite the target word being presented clearly on several occasions. He also said 'pull' for the meaning of 'brag' suggesting he had confused b/d (drag). The Raven's matrices were recommended to check on Andrew's non-verbal ability since the results of the Crichton Vocabulary Test do not reflect his general ability level. Since an auditory difficulty seemed to be at the root of his problems an Auditory Discrimination Test was also recommended. Andrew's score on the Listening Comprehension Test is in the age range equivalent to his chronological age. There is however, a marked discrepancy between his scores for Reading, Comprehension and Comprehension and understanding of written material is obviously hampered by his reading difficulty. The Bangor Dyslexia test revealed significant difficulties in sequencing especially months of the year and multiplication tables. Andrew had some difficulty with pronunciation of multi-syllabics but was able to say two of them accurately and with ease. The spelling test did not reveal any 'bizarre' spellings but would suggest that there is little visual memory for words. This may mean that with Andrew's auditory discrimination difficulties kinaesthetic methods will need to be adopted in order that success may be achieved quickly in the initial stages of a remedial programme. The word reading test highlighted Andrew's difficulty in segmenting words into manageable chunks. Instruction in how to do this successfully will also have to form part of the remedial programme. A small piece of free writing highlighted Andrew's severe literacy difficulties. He appears to have adopted strategies which allow him to operate reasonably successfully in the primary classroom. The main concern is that he may not cope as well in the secondary situation with a resultant loss of confidence and self-esteem.

Piece of free writing for assessment purposes.

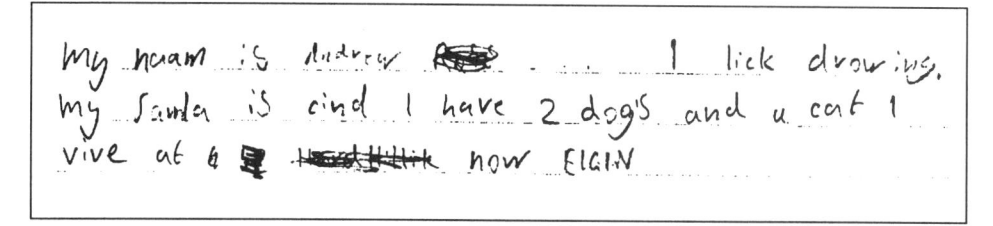

Chapter 4

Sample of writing by the same pupil from a piece of classwork

> We sow lots of raddits and deures foxs and lots of user cnimils me and kirsty yobla rest a heid of the curl— and see how coud get to that tree then to that big then to the top of the hill. I wuing I Sow tipshs geft out of a cart and the hid en horse yack they hid round the corner. I told kirsty to go and get the cutik driver we sow from the top of the hill. I slid down the hill the men were armd with a whip and u n slick then wer danunding munay from father. I got asten in my catiplt meaa from a forgt sap twig and senps gats it hit the mun in the avin I thinek it discolkthd his huad. I pout anuthy ston in my catiplt it hit him in the avin dofos the men dropt there wepnus my multhev hit one of the men over the head with wone of the pams hase foll of poris the mam was carord in poris. kirsey was dack with the cutil driver he seud you neadid help with to tinekers it lont6 lick you didnt nead my help after all.

RECOMMENDED PROGRAMME AND TEACHING MATERIALS

Experts in the field of Specific Learning Difficulty have long recommended multi-sensory approaches to the teaching of children displaying the characteristic signs. The main aim must always be to allow the pupil to achieve success as soon as possible in order that the sense of failure compounded over a period to time can begin to be eroded. In Andrew's case his strength is more likely to be in using visual methods and this should therefore be the starting point. The Charles Cripps 'Hand for Spelling' series combines a handwriting programme with the Look – Cover – Write – Check method of teaching spelling. Drawings on the pages help to jog the memory for specific letter patterns. Blank masters can be used to adapt the method to meet the pupil's needs more precisely. Pupils can make their own mnemonic sentences to aid the memory for particular letter strings.

The vocabulary can be geared to the ability and interest level of the pupil. The kinaesthetic link is added by tracing the word before writing it from memory. There are many computer programmes such as Starspell Plus and Spelltime which have adapted the Look – Cover – Write – Check routine into computer games. They are highly visual and add some variety to the teaching routine. Reading and pelling errors may pin-point the phonic rules which have not yet been mastered. There are many phonics programmes available and an experienced teacher will be able to select the most appropriate one for the age and ability level of the pupil. The Alpha to Omega programme is highly structured and sequential. It need not be followed rigidly but adapted for the pupil's individual needs. Phonic rules are explained, words are grouped according to letter patterns. Sentences are built up using the phonic rules already mastered and suggestions for games are provided. This is a useful resource the teacher. Activity Packs have recently been introduced which provide exercises and activities which run in parallel with the text book. The sentences for dictation are useful and it is recommended that the writing of words and sentences has beneficial effects on reading.

The Simultaneous Oral Spelling (SOS) techniques advocated by Gillingham and Stillman can be used as the pupil repeats the dictated words and writes them down. Pupils with auditory processing difficulties must be encouraged to voice the target words. Awareness of the phonology of words makes the detection of phonemes, particularly in consonant blends and terminal sounds much less of a lottery for the pupil with this kind of difficulty. The Letterland scheme is particularly useful with young pupils in the infant and middle stages. It provides a truly multi-sensory environment in which to learn phonics. Older pupils too enjoy the stories which accompany the phonic rules. It is easier for them if they have started off in the Letterland environment. The 'Reading Direction' is emphasised throughout thus reducing directional confusion. Rhymes accompany the formation of letters and alongside this the character specific to each letter can avoid confusion between similar graphemes like b and d, p and q and m a w. Further recommendations in Andrew's case are to improve his segmenting and blending skills beginning with compound words such as wind-mill, progressing to 2 syllable words such as pillow and then isolating or blending phonemes in a one syllable word. Segmenting and blending can progress in tandem. Some work on sequences would also be beneficial. Mastery of areas which have had repeated failure in the past increases confidence and sequences such as the Alphabet allow participation in an increased number of activities. For example using a dictionary, using an index in a book and looking up the telephone directory.

A degree of repeated learning will be necessary and the teacher must be resourceful in applying different methodology in new and interesting formats to keep the pupil's interest until the sequence has been mastered. Around 3 x 20 minute sessions per week will be required to implement this programme. It is often the recognition of the difficulty and the administration of appropriate measures to ameliorate it that proves to be a turning point in the pupil's attitude and this consequently is reflected in their work.

TRANSFER TO SECONDARY

Consultation with Andrew's parents, Guidance teacher and class teachers will be essential to smooth his transfer. Observation and recording of Andrew's behaviour in class will highlight how he is coping in the initial stages. In consultation with the above group of people it may be felt that a period of withdrawal for small group or individual support may be beneficial to support his subject work, help him to organise homework and respond to subject assessments by alternative means. For example, taped essays and responses to tests rather than written.

INFORMAL ASSESSMENT

The majority of pupils referred to learning support teachers for assessment are likely to be unfamiliar to them. Formal assessment is a way of providing a profile of a pupil's difficulties using a limited amount of time effectively.

Teachers with a good background knowledge of Specific Learning Difficulties may be able to carry out much of their assessment on an informal basis. Keeping careful record of reading and writing behaviours can give valuable information about the nature of the difficulties being experienced by the pupils and enable the teacher to respond more precisely to the needs of the pupil.

Records also help to provide an analysis of the effectiveness or appraisal of the various strategies adopted.

CONCLUSION

Assessment in practice utilises to a great extent skills in diplomacy and communication. Understandably parents in particular are anxious to seek an explanation for their child's inability to progress as they had hoped. Some are relieved to find that there is no constitutional cause for their child's problems, others are even more anxious if no precise cause can be found.

Pupils also can exhibit symptoms of anxiety if they feel they may have a specific learning difficulty and this aspect must be carefully considered. Teachers clearly need help in identifying, assessing and planning programmes for pupils with specific learning difficulties. Consultancy, observation or informal assessment will also have a role to play.

It is important to follow up and monitor the pupil's progress. Assessment therefore is not a 'one-off' analysis of a pupil's progress, but an enduring and inherent component of learning which can help facilitate effective access to the curriculum for children with specific learning difficulties.

REFERENCES

SUTHERLAND M. J. , SMITH C. D. (1991), *Assessing Literacy Problems in Mainstream Schooling: A Critique of Three Literacy Screening Tests* – Educational Review vol. 43, no. 1.

TANSLEY P. and PANCKHURST J. (1981), *Children with Specific Learning Difficulties.* NFFR Nelson.

VINCENT D. de la Mare, *New MacMillan Reading Analysis*. Pub. MacMillan Assessment.

RAVEN J. C., *Raven's Progressive Matrices and Crichton Vocabulary Scale*. Pub. H. K. Lewis & Co. Ltd. London.

MILES T. R., *The Bangor Dyslexia Test*. Pub LDA.

NEWTON and THOMSON, *Aston Index LDA*, Schonell spelling test part of Aston Index.

NEALE ANALYSIS.

NEALE MARIE D, *Neale Analysis of Reading Ability*. Pub. NFER Nelson.

BURT WORD READING TEST, Hodder & Stoughton Ltd. The Scottish Council for Research in Education.

BALLARD ORAL ARITHMETIC – NORMS (P. E. Vernon Scottish Ed. Journal 9.2.40).

WENDON L., *Letterland*. Letterland Ltd.

HORNSBY B. and SHEAR, F *Alpha to Omega Activity Packs* Pub. Heinemann Ed. Boon.

CRIPPS C., *A Hand for Spelling* Pub. LDA.

KEY SOFTWARE, *Spelltime*.

FISHER MARRIOTT, *Starspell Plus*.

XAVIER EDUCATIONAL, *Bangor Hi Spell*.

HORNSBY B. and POOL J. *Alpha to Omega Activity Packs*. Heinemann Educational.

Chapter 5

PSYCHOLOGICAL DIMENSIONS AND THE ROLE OF THE EDUCATIONAL PSYCHOLOGIST IN ASSESSMENT

SIONAH LANNEN and GAVIN REID

INTRODUCTION

Assessment is a multi-dimensional exercise which should consider the child, including the cognitive processes which influence learning; the curriculum, focusing on the content and use of resources; and learning style highlighting the metacognitive aspects of learning. This chapter will examine these three aspects of assessment. It is also important to consider role perceptions between educational psychologists and teachers since such perceptions have clear implications for issues relating to assessment.

ROLE PERCEPTIONS

Some studies have revealed evidence of a mismatch between the perceptions of teachers and educational psychologists regarding the role of the psychologist in assessment (O'Hagen and Swanson 1981, 1983: Reid 1990). The teachers in these studies perceived psychologists as a group of professionals with the skills and remit to provide informative, child focused cognitive assessment. It was felt this could provide additional data in relation to the child's cognitive profile and a clearer explanation of the child's difficulties. The educational psychologist, however, did not perceive the situation in this way preferring to adopt a consultancy and advisory role. Thus a mismatch existed. This in fact may well be related to the shift within the profession of educational psychology from an individual child focus to the broader aspect of the educational context within which the child is functioning (Imich and Kerfoot, 1993). Such a shift has resulted in educational psychologists focusing on whole-school issues, perhaps to the detriment of individual child assessments.

The role of the educational psychologist in assessment therefore may, in fact, reflect the success or otherwise of effectively recognising and addressing both the needs of the individual child and those of the whole-school. How this can be effectively carried out is currently a matter of debate in terms of competing ideologies and restrictive practicalities (Gale 1993).

Related to the issue of role there is the question of function. Irrespective of the role perceived and adopted by the psychologist in the assessment, the actual function, purpose and outcome need to be addressed. Examining these issues can be illuminating. It is usually so when practitioners become introspective and ask themselves, 'Just what exactly am I doing? What is the purpose of this and does the expected outcome justify the cost in terms of time and resources?'

Lannen (1993) attempted to find some answers to these questions when she asked a number of teachers and special needs co-ordinators to comment on the function of the educational psychologist in relation to assessment for specific learning difficulties. The responses from this study indicated that the psychologist can perform a key role in assessment. Some of the statements made by this sample of practitioners included the following:

> 'It is important for the teacher to have some knowledge of the child's level of intellectual ability and underlying cognitive skills indicated by formal standardised assessments'

> 'The inferences highlighted by the psychologist from the assessment can provide a clearer picture of the strengths and weakness of the child'

> 'The consultancy and advice offered by the psychologist informs and highlights practice'

> The outcome of the assessment process involving the teacher and the psychologist can help the teacher develop self supporting strategies for future assessment'

> 'The psychologist, because of access to a range of information from other professionals and parents, can provide a fuller and more objective perspective to the assessment'

This study indicates that the educational psychologist does have a key role to play as part of the multi-disciplinary assessment team. This role varies depending on the situation, but can range from formal cognitive assessment to consultancy and advice on curriculum issues and resources.

Attention needs to be directed, therefore, to the nature and the value of the educational psychologist's intervention in each of these dimensions.

COGNITIVE FACTORS

The importance of cognitive processing in relation to competence in literacy is fairly well documented (Seymour 1986: Snowling 1990: Dockrell and McShane 1993). In relation to dyslexia it has been asserted that an assessment of such processes can help to provide some identification criteria and some definition and explanation of the difficulty (Singleton 1993), Seymour (1986). Seymour provides a useful summary of the psychological processes of learning and their relationship with dyslexia. He discusses three dimensions – the observable behaviours, the cognitive processes and physiological instantiation. He asserts that the level of competence, the observable behaviours in literacy such as the ability to read and spell, should be distinguished from the cognitive function, the underlying psychological processes which influence the 'level of competence'. Seymour's third dimension relates to the physiological instantiation: physiological aspects related to neural tissue and brain structure. This aspect should be considered by paediatricians (see Chapter 6), but the other two dimensions, competence and cognitive processing, should be addressed by the educational psychologist.

The **competence** dimension may be identified by teachers and psychologists using a combination of standardised and diagnostic tests and other materials such as criterion referenced assessment and observational frameworks. The **cognitive** dimension, however, is essentially an interpretation of the observations and data stemming from an analysis of the '**competence**' or performance of the child and Seymour argues this can be defined in three of the processing functions of reading: the recognition of familiar graphemic forms; semantic processing – the system based on comprehension and understanding; and phonological processing – the speech production system which contains the vocabulary store. An analysis of these functions provides some explanation and understanding of the child's competence and performance aspects in the acquisition of literacy. Moreover, Seymour's extensive research in this field in relation to the processing functions of dyslexic readers reveals that there can be impairment within elements of the processing system and that dyslexic children can show individual differences and different patterns of this impairment. Seymour asserts that dyslexic children differ in the strategies they use and in the emphasis they give to each processing route, and suggests that an analysis of these factors provide useful guidance for planning support strategies.

COGNITIVE STYLE

A cognitive style is considered to be a reasonably static characteristic (Riding and Douglas 1993) and can be defined as an individual's characteristic and consistent approach to organising and processing information (Tennant 1988).

Riding and Cheema (1991) highlight the importance of two principal cognitive styles – Verbal-Imagery and Wholist-Analytic. Further research (Riding and Douglas 1993) examined the relationship between cognitive style and mode of presentation of learning materials. This study found, for example, that the 'Imagers' improved their learning performance when the material was presented in a text-plus-picture condition and that learning performance for this group suffered when information was presented in a verbal mode. Interestingly, the 'Verbalisers' performed similarly in both the text only and the text-plus picture conditions. Clearly, therefore a case can be presented for attempting to acknowledge the cognitive learning style of individuals and not assume that all pupils learn in the same way.

The Wholist-Analytic style of learning would result in the learner processing information in wholes or parts while the Verbal-Imagery style of learning would be seen in the learner's processing of information either verbally or in mental images.

Children, however, are persuaded to adopt flexibility in the cognitive strategies they use to compensate for difficulties they may encounter with different modes of presentation of learning material. These strategies are flexible and can be learned and developed with practice. It is important therefore to acknowledge the learners natural cognitive style and furthermore the nature of the learning strategies adopted to accommodate to the learning task.

Dunn and Dunn (1992) have related learning styles to the classroom situation through the use of a Learning Styles Inventory, which has a high validity and reliability and is used most frequently in learning styles research (Dunn, Dunn and Price 1975-1989). The variables identified by Dunn and Dunn which help to differentiate student's learning performances (see Chapter 2) are applicable to the classroom because they focus on key learning issues such as how children process, absorb and retain new information. This clearly has implications for individual differences in learning and in learning conditions, including the learning environment. Furthermore, such a focus on learning styles can help to facilitate the individual taking responsibility for their own learning. This indeed appears to be the essence of one such programme developed to encourage self-knowledge in learning (Given 1993). Given's programme utilises influential concepts such as self-empowered learning, self-managed learning and reflective learning. Clearly an important role for teachers and educational psychologists is to consider the importance of learning styles, which for dyslexic learners can effectively help to provide self-knowledge to assist in the development of cognitive strategies for life-long learning.

COGNITIVE ASSESSMENT

The implication of the above is that cognitive aspects of the child's profile such as attention, concentration, memory processes, organisation, comprehension and phonological processing should be considered during assessment.

PHONOLOGICAL PROCESSING

While there is strong evidence of the link between the above aspects and reading (Dockrell and McShane 1993: Chasty 1990) the area of phonological processing is without doubt of extreme importance in the development of reading skills, particularly pre-reading skills (Dockrell and McShane 1993: Stanovich 1991).

Awareness of the phonemic structure of words can facilitate the essential grapheme-phoneme correspondences which, studies have shown, are essential for tackling new words (Baddeley *et al*, 1982: Szeszulski and Manis 1987). Related to this it has also been shown that awareness of sounds at the pre-reading stage is a good predictor of progress in learning to read (Goswami and Bryant 1992: Bradley 1990), and that a sensitivity to and an awareness of rhyme can be related to subsequent development of reading skills and facilitate competence in using the phonemic structure of words while reading, (Bryant *et al*, 1989). Thus the important aspect of phonological awareness can be assessed at both the pre-reading stage by focusing on children's use of sounds and competence with rhyme, and at the reading stage by analysis of errors. It can be argued that both these processes, that is, pre-reading tasks and the practice of reading, benefit the development of phonological processing and should therefore be taken into account in the assessment.

MEMORY

The role of memory is of considerable importance to reading and to learning and the focus of research has been directed to two aspects in particular: the working memory responsible for processing the information, and the long-term memory in relation to recall. Both processing and recall are important in reading and are areas in which children with dyslexia display difficulties. This is particularly the case on short-term memory tasks in relation to literacy (Jorm 1983: Stanovich 1986: Torgeson 1987). This can be seen in the functioning of the articulatory loop, a component of working memory (Baddeley 1982), which is essentially the verbal rehearsal system and allows material to be processed. This has implications for learning since it has been demonstrated that a competing task can result in 'articulatory suppression' and inefficient use of the working memory.

Furthermore Dockrell and McShane (1993) argue that the link between phonological deficits and memory deficit is significant in the assessment of specific learning difficulties because if there is difficulty in converting the printed word into sounds then it follows that a difficulty will exist in the storing of these sounds in short term, working memory. This implies that the memory difficulty experienced by children with dyslexia is related to the acquisition of literacy and not necessarily related to other non literacy areas. Therefore, it follows that the assessment of this function should also involve literacy related tasks.

COMPREHENSION

It has been shown that the reading comprehension level of dyslexic children is in excess of their decoding ability (Aaron 1989). At the same time it might be argued that the decoding difficulty in itself can restrict comprehension. Slow recognition of words can act as a disruptive and influential factor affecting comprehension (Perfetti and Lesgold 1979). An assessment therefore should not only ascertain the comprehension level of the child's reading ability but also the reasons for either failing or succeeding at comprehension related tasks.

Clearly, decoding skills in themselves can aid comprehension (Curtis 1980), but at the same time there is no guarantee that the skilful decoder possesses parity in comprehension (Aaron 1989; Oakhill and Garnham 1988). In fact Stanovich (1984) argues that as children reach the end of primary education comprehension replaces decoding as the best predictor of overall reading skills. According to Dockrell and McShane (1993), semantic and syntax knowledge at the sentence level are important for comprehension. Thus an assessment should consider the child's ability to use inferences and strategies to facilitate comprehension as well as identifying the child's actual comprehension level.

ATTENTION AND CONCENTRATION

Attention and concentration are implicated in the cognitive processes of the learner in most learning tasks. Other cognitive processes however, such as memory may share a reciprocal relationship with attention. Research in memory, particularly that highlighting sensory memory and the levels of processing model (Craik and Lockhart 1972: Baddeley 1988), supports this view, implying that the actual processing of the information and the level to which it is processed aid retention and recall, and that retention and recall can only be accomplished effectively if sufficient attention and concentration are present. It is therefore of some importance to consider this aspect in an assessment perhaps through recording 'on-task' behaviour or by using a more informal observation technique.

ORGANISATION

In many ways organisation holds the key to a number of cognitive processes related to effective learning. It has been demonstrated that organisation of material during learning can aid retention and recall (Buzan 1984). Organisation in learning can, therefore, have a spin-off effect, enhancing some of the other cognitive aspects of learning. Indeed, many of the successful teaching programmes for dyslexic children display a highly structured pattern and have an organised form of presentation. Organisational ability can be gauged also through observation and by responses in a more formal test, particularly when extended answers are required.

The class teacher can obtain some appreciation of the child's cognitive functioning through observation and the analysis of errors. Thus the child's memory skills, organisational ability, attention and concentration levels are likely to be known to the class teacher or learning support specialist. What additional contribution, therefore, can the educational psychologist bring to this form of assessment? An assertion which may be levelled at the educational psychologist's input is that the information obtained only confirms what is already suspected. Although this chapter asserts that the educational psychologists in fact can extend beyond this, to confirm what the class teacher suspects is not necessarily a futile exercise but can have a worthwhile effect on confidence and morale.

WECHSLER INTELLIGENCE SCALE

Perhaps the most widely known test used by educational psychologists which can provide a cognitive profile of the child is the Wechsler Intelligence Scale for Children. This test which can provide an I.Q. score and consists of 12 sub-tests, (the WISC (III) UK 1993 contains 13 sub-tests) has been the subject of recent criticism concerning its validity and appropriateness (Siegal 1989; Stanovich 1991). The use of such a test, however, does not necessarily imply that the primary aim is to obtain an IQ score. It is fairly well documented that IQ is not a stable measure of cognitive functioning, and indeed there is considerable debate in relation to the notion of intelligence and many different definitions and conceptions of intelligence can be noted (Sternberg and Detterman 1986).

The sub-tests of the WISC, however, can be regarded as a sample of tests focusing on cognitive skills which can provide some indication of the child's mastery of these skills in relation to the task. Such scores should therefore not necessarily be perceived as a measure of intellectual potential (Anastasi 1988). Yet identifying a profile of cognitive skills can be an important aspect of an assessment.

The verbal scale of the test can provide information on the child in relation to general knowledge, comprehension and reasoning, short term memory, concept development, verbal organisation and expression while, visual perception, visual association, spatial and sequencing skills and speed of processing can provide information in relation to the non-verbal (performance) scale. This kind of data, and the accompanying profile, can be of value in the collaborative discussions which take place between teachers and psychologists in relation to assessment. Information highlighting the child's strengths and weaknesses will assist in an explanation of the child's performances in the classroom and can provide guidance for the development of appropriate curriculum materials.

The merits of educational programmes based on the WISC sub-test scores have, however, been questioned and viewed as little more than 'an arbitrary exercise' (Holmes 1985). Some commentators though have successfully provided examples of balanced programmes based on WISC profiles, while acknowledging the need to preserve creativity and individual learning styles (Banas and Wills 1978: Matarazzo 1985).

In relation to children with specific learning difficulties, some evidence exists of a particular cognitive profile based on a child's WISC sub-scale scores (Thomson 1984, 1989). This profile, although subject to some criticism (Pumfrey and Reason 1991), indicates that dyslexic children have difficulties with four sub-tests in particular – Arithmetic, Coding, Information and Digit Span, and is sometimes called the 'ACID' profile. Additionally, the WISC can provide some data in relation to the child's distractability and anxiety level (Kaufman, 1992).

There is also some evidence that the British Ability Scales (BAS), a similar test to the WISC, can produce responses which highlight a sequential processing deficit – a difficulty which can be associated with dyslexia. The scales of the BAS which may highlight this are Information Processing, Recall of Digits, Basic Arithmetic, Immediate Memory for Visual Recall, and Delayed Memory for Visual Recall.

The extracts below highlight some of the information which can be gleaned from standardised and informal assessment. It is good practice both to provide a permanent record of this information in a formal, written report, and to communicate it informally through discussion and consultancy.

Chapter 5

CASE STUDY EXTRACTS: COGNITIVE ASSESSMENT

Fig. 1:

Christopher had a significant strength on the sub-test of Comprehension. This item measures the ability to process and understand incoming verbal information. There was, however, a significant difference between Christopher's performance on this item and the sub-test of Vocabulary which measures the ability to express ideas verbally. It is possible that Christopher's comparative weakness in this area is significant in terms of the way he finds it difficult to formulate his thought processes verbally and consequently organise his written work effectively and systematically.

Fig.2:

The results of the assessment indicate that John is a boy of considerable cognitive ability. He performed exceptionally well on sub-tests measuring both Verbal Comprehension Factor and the Perceptual Organisation Factor.

John's performance on the tasks which indicate the 'Distractability Factor' was weaker. These sub-tests measure the mental manipulation of numbers/symbols in short-term memory and John's performance suggests a weakness in this form of processing. Once information gets into long term memory, however, John shows strengths in both storage and retrieval.

It must be noted that performance on these sub-tests can also be adversely affected by distractability/anxiety. John frequently appears to lose focus resulting in questions having to be repeated or rephrased.

TEACHING AND CURRICULUM DIMENSIONS OF ASSESSMENT

Cognitive assessment, informal assessment and consultancy can also address issues relating to teaching, resources and the curriculum. The following extract, from an educational psychologist's feedback following an assessment, highlights these factors.

Fig.3:

Michael has mixed laterality. At the beginning stages of reading this can cause difficulties with orientation and visual tracking often resulting in reversals, loss of place and lack of fluency.

Perspectives on Practice

Aims of Provision

The following areas therefore need to be addressed:

(a) Reading development/Comprehension.
(b) Spelling/writing skills.
(c) The development of a confident attitude, and independent work habits.
(d) The development of social interaction skills.

Suggested Methods or Approaches:

- Support in a small group within or outwith the classroom situation.
- Individual educational programmes developed and carefully matched to Michael's current attainment levels.
- Close liaison between the learning support teacher and class teacher to ensure continuity of curricula and teaching methods.
- Michael needs to gain more experience in reading. He needs the experience of reading meaningful written material in order to increase his word identification, knowledge of letter/sound combinations and develop mediated meaning. 'Taped', 'paired' or 'reading buddies' are all excellent ways of increasing non-visual information such as language structure and inference. These approaches are also excellent for developing visual tracking skills.
- Michael would benefit from a structured approach to spelling/writing skills. His word recognition and use of context cues can be developed in a meaningful way by presenting 'word families' or bingo games (where the child listens for the sound e.g. 'p' as in pet, and covers up the sound on his/her card).

  The above techniques enable a book higher than the child's actual reading age to be used, helping to overcome the problem of a mismatch between reading ability and interest level.

  'I Spy' is also an excellent game for phonic development and can be used for sounds at the beginning, middle and end of words.

  In terms of developing spelling skills, Michael would benefit from consolidation at the 'cvc' stage before moving on to consonant blends.

  Michael also needs to develop his writing skills. Tracking exercises, mazes, crossing out letters or words in magazines, 'penmanship' and key-boarding will help in this area.

- Social Skills – many of the activities found in social skills programmes would be appropriate. The 'safe' environment promoted in this type of group activity encourages children to listen and respond appropriately and is excellent for developing positive social interaction skills.

Arrangements for Access to the Curriculum

Differentiation of the curriculum may be required in terms of:

delivery e.g. the task may be presented differently.

operations e.g. Michael may required a longer time spent on some areas of the curriculum.

outcomes e.g. Michael may require different arrangements for assessment.

Fig.4:

Reading Development

It is significant that John's listening comprehension is at the 12.5 year old level. Listening comprehension gives an indication of the **reading potential** for an individual so that John's word reading score of 10.0 years suggests that he is under-achieving in this area.

John's reading also lacked fluency. He needs, therefore, to gain more experience in reading. He needs the experience of reading meaningful written material in order to increase his word identification and his knowledge of letter/sound combinations and to develop mediated meaning.

Spelling/Writing skills

John needs a very structured approach to spelling/writing skills.

A hand held spell checker (Spell Master) would also help John to be more confident in terms of using more sophisticated vocabulary in his written work.

John also needs to develop his writing speed. Tracking exercises, mazes, crossing out letters or words in magazines, 'penmanship' and keyboarding will help in this area.

LEARNING STYLES

The whole area of learning styles and the associated metacognitive aspects of learning styles have received considerable recent attention (see Chapter 22). It is therefore essential that this facet is picked up by the educational psychologist and considered during assessment. Examples of how this can be found in the following extracts from a psychologist's feedback from an assessment.

Chapter 5

Fig:5
Learning Style

Connor has a strength in his abilities to reason with words, to learn verbal material and to process verbal information. He has difficulty in processing visual material efficiently.

Because his auditory processing is better developed than his visual processing 'taped' reading would be an excellent way of increasing his sight vocabulary and knowledge of sound/symbol associations and at the same time help to develop the visual channel. 'Taped' reading is also an excellent medium for increasing relevant non-visual information such as language structure and inference. It also means that a book higher than the child's actual reading age can be used which can help to overcome the problem of matching reading age and interest level.

Fig:6

(i) Garth's abilities lie in the areas of verbal comprehension, expression and acquired knowledge. He does, however, lack experience in problem solving. A situation which encourages an adaptive, problem solving approach but which also capitalises and encourages his ability to learn facts as a means of acquiring new knowledge would be the most suitable educational setting.

This would suggest an environment which shapes his ability to figure things out but which frequently gives verbal explanation of various facts and concepts and encourages rote learning techniques as a means of acquiring new information.

(ii) The information gathered suggests that Garth has difficulty remaining 'on task' and is easily distracted from assignments. It is suggested, therefore, that some form of checklist or task completion sheet be used to encourage him to complete his work and to improve his work habits and study skills.

(iii) He also needs help with 'attention' signals and 'task' signals. His perseverence, starting 'on task' signals and attending behaviours all need to be prompted and reinforced consistently.

(iv) In the area of reading it is felt that Garth would manage best with a highly structured, phonic based reading program which addresses his reading sub-skill difficulties of rhyming and letter identification.

(v) Some regular reading sessions should be carried out at home. In these sessions the goal is for Garth to enjoy stories and talk about them. It may be beneficial therefore for stories to be read to him. Garth should be allowed to choose the book (this is an excellent way of fostering interest and motivation), and no attempt should be made to make him read the text unless he really wants to

OBSERVATIONAL ASSESSMENT

Although considerable data can be gleaned from cognitive and formal assessments, observation in the classroom to examine the child's on-task behaviour in the learning context may be as, or more, revealing. Clearly an assessment should consider different facets of learning and there is scope for standardised cognitive and informal observational assessment.

Observational assessment can not only assist in a diagnosis of the difficulty, but also provide an indication of the student's learning style and learning preferences and give some direction to intervention in terms of teaching and resources.

A number of arguments can be put forward to support the use of observation in assessment. These include:

- **Flexibility:** observation schedules need not be rigidly criterion referenced. There are no correct or incorrect responses.
- **Adaptability:** the observation framework or schedule can be adapted to different classroom situations and learning situations.
- **Contextualised:** observational assessment does not only focus on the learner, but the learning context. Thus it provides a more holistic picture than an assessment which is purely child focused.
- **Natural:** one is looking at the actual learning behaviour in the learning situation. Formal tests and testing, whilst useful, may produce an 'artificial' response which needs to be taken into account when analysing the test results.

OBSERVATIONAL FRAMEWORK

It is necessary therefore to develop an observational framework which looks at the broad range of areas which can relate to some of the difficulties experienced by children with specific learning difficulties.

It is important to gather information which relates to the child, the learning situation and context. The aim is not only to find out **how** or **why** the child is having difficulty, but to gain some insight and understanding into the strategies and processes of learning for that child.

Chapter 5

A framework for observational assessment for specific learning difficulties can therefore include the following areas:

- **ATTENTION**
    - length of attention span
    - conditions when attention is enhanced
    - factors contributing to distractability
    - attention/distractability under different learning conditions.

- **ORGANISATION**
    - organisational preferences
    - degree of structure required
    - organisation of work, desk, self
    - reactions to imposed organisation

- **SEQUENCING**
    - able to follow sequence with aid
    - general difficulty with sequencing:
        - work
        - carrying out instructions
        - words when reading
        - individual letters in written work

- **INTERACTION**
    - degree of interaction with peers, adults
    - preferred interaction – one-to-one
        – small groups
        – whole class
    - how is interaction sustained.

- **LANGUAGE**
    - Expressive language
        - is meaning accurately conveyed?
        - spontaneous/prompted
        - is there appropriate use of natural breaks in speech?
        - expressive language in different contexts e.g. one-to-one, small group, class group.
        - errors, omissions and difficulties in conversation and responses e.g. mispronunciations, questions to be repeated or clarified.

- **COMPREHENSION**
  - How does the child comprehend information?
  - What type of cues most readily facilitate comprehension?
  - Use of schema
  - What type of instructions are most easily understood
    - written?
    - oral?
    - visual?
  - How readily can knowledge be transferred to other areas?

- **READING**
  - Reading preferences – aloud, silent, alone, paired.
  - Type of errors: **VISUAL, e.g.**
    - discrimination between letters which look the same – 'O' 'Q' 'B' 'D' 'T' 'I'.
    - inability to appreciate that the same letter may look different 'R' 'r' 'L' 'l' 'A' 'a'.
    - visual segmentation difficulty – either omitting segments of a word or confusing them with similar looking letters.
    - visual sequencing difficulty – altering the sequencing of letters or groups of letters within words.

    AUDITORY, e.g.
    - difficulties in auditory discrimination, with sounds of different frequencies, inability to hear sounds in initial and final position.

- **MOTIVATION/INITIATIVE**
  - Interest level of child
  - How is motivation increased, what kind of prompting and cueing is necessary?
  - To what extent does the child take responsibility for own learning?
  - What kind of help is required?

- **SELF-CONCEPT**
  - What tasks are more likely to be tackled with confidence?
  - When is confidence low?
  - Self-Concept and confidence in different contexts

- **RELAXATION**
- Is the child relaxed when learning?
- Evidence of tension and relaxation

- **LEARNING STYLE**

All learners have a preferred learning style and children with dyslexic difficulties will also have their own individual style of learning. The key phrase is 'individual style of learning', because there will be a variation of learning styles within any group of dyslexic children.

These include the following learning preferences:
- auditory
- visual
- oral
- kinesthetic
- tactile
- global
- analytic

It is important therefore to note in observational assessment the preferred mode of learning. Many children will, of course, show preferences and skills in a number of modes of learning. Multi-sensory teaching therefore is crucial in order to accommodate as many modes as possible.

LEARNING CONTEXT

When assessing the nature and degree of the difficulty experienced by the child it is important to take into account the learning context. This context, depending on the learner's preferred style, can either exacerbate the difficulty or minimise the problem. (Reid, 1992).

Context for Learning:
- Classroom
- Role of Teacher
- Task
- Materials/Resources.

Observation and assessment therefore needs to adopt a holistic perspective i.e.

- To observe components within a framework for learning
- To observe some factors within that framework associated with specific learning difficulties
- To observe preferred styles of learning
- To acknowledge the importance of the learning context and to observe the degree of match or mis-match between the learner and the context.

CONCLUSION

This chapter has attempted to illustrate the importance and the potential involvement of the educational psychologist in the three dimensions of assessment – cognitive, curriculum and learning styles. Such intervention may take the form of formal testing using standardised procedures, informal observation, consultancy over curriculum and teaching issues, and awareness of appropriate resources. Effective assessment therefore should provide for an interaction of these factors in order that a balanced and appropriate assessment can be obtained.

REFERENCES

AARON R. G. (1989) Dyslexia and Hyperlexia. Kluwer Academic Publisher.

ANASTASI A. (1988) *Psychological Testing* (6th ed). Macmillan, New York.

BADDELEY A. D., ELLIS N. C., MILES T. R. and LEWIS V. J. (1982) 'Developmental and Acquired Dyslexia: A Comparison' *Cognition, 11, 185-99.*

BADDELEY A. D. (1982) 'Reading and working memory'. *Bulletin of the British Psychological Society,* 35 pp. 414-416.

BANAS N. and WILLS I. H. (1978) *WISC-R Prescriptions: How to work creatively with individual learning styles.* Academic Therapy Publications, Novats, California.

BRADLEY L. (1990) 'Rhyming connections in learning to read or spell'. In Pumfrey P. D. and Elliott C. *(eds) Children's difficulties in reading, spelling and writing.* Falmer Press.

BRYANT P. E., BRADLEY L., McLEAN M. and CROSSLAND J. (1989). 'Nursery rhymes, phonological skills, and reading'. *Journal of Child Language* 16, 407-428.

BUZAN T. (1984) *Use your memory.* BBC Publications.

CHASTY H. (1990) *Meeting the Challenges of Specific Learning Difficulties in Reading, Spelling and Writing.* (Pumfrey P. D. and Elliott C. (eds). Falmer Press.

CRAIK F. I. N. and LOCKHART R. S. (1972) 'Levels of processing: a framework for memory research'. In *Journal of Verbal Learning and Verbal Behaviour,* 11, 268-94.

CURTIS M. E. (1980) 'Development of components of reading skill'. *Journal of Educational Psychology,* 72, 656-69.

DOCKRELL J. and McSHANE J. (1993) *Children's Learning Difficulties: A Cognitive Approach.* Blackwell.

DUNN R. and DUNN K. (1992) *Teaching elementary students through their individual learning styles.* Allyn and Bacon

DUNN R., DUNN K. and PRICE G. E. (1975,77,78,79,87,88,89). *Learning Style Inventory.* Price Systems, Box 1818, Lawrence, KS 66044.

GALE A. A task analysis of Educational Psychology: Is Educational Psychology up to the Task? *Proceedings of the Annual Conference of the British Psychological Society.* April 1993. Blackpool.

GIVEN B. K. (1993) *Breakthrough: A Holistic approach to learning style.* George Mason University, Virginia, USA.

GOSWAMI U and BRYANT P. (1990) *Phonological skills and learning to read.* Hove, Erlbaum.

HOLMES B. J. (1985) A critique of programmed WISC-R remediations. *Canadian Journal of Studies of Psychology.* June 1985, Vol. 1. No. 1.

IMICH A. J. and KERFOOT S. R. Educational Psychology: Meeting the Challenge of Change. *Proceedings of the Annual Conference of the British Psychological Society.* April 1993, Blackpool.

JORM A. F. (1983) 'Specific reading retardation and working memory: A Review. *British Journal of Psychology,* 74, 311-42.

KAUFMAN A, S. (1992) *Intelligent Testing with the WISC-R.* Joan Wiley, New York.

LANNEN S. (1993) *Perceptions of the Educational Psychologists Role in Assessment.* Unpublished study, Lancashire Psychological Service.

MATARAZZO J. D. (1985) *Computerized clinical psychological test interpretations.* American Psychologist.

OAKHILL J. U. and GARNHAM A. (1988) *Becoming a skilled reader.* Blackwell, Oxford.

O'HAGEN F. J. and SWANSON W. I. (1981) 'Teacher's views regarding the role of the educational psychologist in schools. *Research in Education,* 29, 29-40.

O'HAGEN F, J. and SWANSON W. I. (1983) 'Teachers and Psychologists: a comparison of views. *Research in Education,* 36.

PERFETTI C, A. and LESGOLD A, M. (1979) 'Coding and comprehension in skilled reading and implications for reading instruction'. In Resnick L. B. and Leaver P. (eds) *Theory and Practice of Early Reading.* Vol. 1, Erlbaum, Hillstate, New Jersey.

PUMFRY P. D. and REASON R. (eds) (1991) *Specific Learning Difficulties (Dyslexia) Challenges and Responses.* NFER. Nelson.

REID G. (1990) 'Specific Learning Difficulties: Attitudes Towards Assessment and Teaching'. In Hales G. (ed) *Meeting Points in Dyslexia,* BDA.

REID G. (1992) *Learning difficulties and learning styles – Observational Criteria.* Paper presented at South East Learning Styles Conference, Virginia, USA.

RIDING R. and DOUGLAS G. (1993) 'The effect of cognitive style and mode of presentation on learning performance.' *British Journal of Educational Psychology,* 63, 2, 297-307. June 1993.

RIDING R. and CHEEMA I. (1991) 'Cognitive Styles – an overview and integration' *Educational Psychology,* 11, 193-215.

SEYMOUR P. H. K. (1986) *Cognitive analysis of dyslexia.* Routledge and Paul Kegan.

SIEGAL L. (1989) 'I.Q. is irrelevant to the definition of learning disabilities' In *Journal of Learning Disabilities,* 22, 5, 577-85.

SNOWLING M. (1990) *Dyslexia: A cognitive developmental perspective.* Blackwell.

STANOVICH K. E. (1986) 'Cognitive processes and reading problems of learning-disabled children: Evaluating the assumption of specificity. In Torgeson J. K . and Yong B .Y. L. (eds) *Psychological and Educational Perspectives on Learning Disabilities*. Academic Press, New York.

STANOVICH K. E. (1991) 'Discrepancy definitions of reading disability: Has intelligence led us astray?' *Reading Research Quarterly,* 19, 278-303.

STERNBERG R. J. and DETTERMAN D. K. (eds) (1986) *What is intelligence?.* Ablex, Norwood, New Jersey.

SZESZULSKI P. A. and MANIS F. B. (1987) 'A comparison of word recognition processes for effective use.' *Learning Disabilities Quarterly,* 12, 3-14.

TENNANT M. (1988) *Psychology and Adult Learning* . Routledge, London.

THOMSON M. E. (1982) 'Assessing the intelligence of dyslexic children'. *Bulletin of the British Psychological Society* 35, 94-96.

THOMSON M. E. (1989) *Developmental Dyslexia,* (3rd edition). Whurr, London.

TORGESON J. K., KISTNER J. and MORGAN S. (1987) 'Component processes in working memory'. In Borkowski J. G. and Day J. D. (eds). *Cognition in special children: comparative approaches to retardation, learning disabilities and giftedness.* Ablex, Norwood, N.J.

Chapter 6

A DOCTOR'S PERSPECTIVE

DR ANNE O'HARE

THE ROLE OF THE PAEDIATRICIAN

The doctors who are most commonly consulted with regard to children with specific learning difficulties are those working in Community Child Health and since 1902 local education authorities have been empowered to employ doctors who could periodically examine school children. Obviously the focus at that time was on conditions such as malnutrition and infection which might impair a child's ability to learn and such considerations are rarely encountered now. The doctor in the school maintains, however, a role in the evaluation of children who are experiencing difficulty learning.

LINKS WITH HEALTH PROFESSIONALS

Since 1974, Community Child Health doctors have been employed directly in the National Health Service, and the speciality has become Consultant led. Community Child Health has two major remits:

i) Clinical practice, particularly in developmental medicine, neurology and disability,
ii) Population paediatrics, e.g., educational medicine, which involves health issues relating to the learning environment,

Professional links between Community Child Health and Community Nurses, especially Health Visitors, go back to the latter part of the 19th century.

Links with Primary Care General Practitioners are strengthening, especially since the 1990 National Health Service reorganisation which led to routine immunisations and child health surveillance being conducted largely in general practice, thus releasing Community Child Health doctors to concentrate on other areas such as Special Needs.

Links with hospital services have also increased as a large proportion of community Child Health consultants hold additional hospital appointments over and above their community duties.

Perspectives on Practice

Thus if a child presents in the pre-school years with a risk factor for specific learning difficulties, such as speech and language delay, it may be appropriate to alert the school doctor. If the family consult their General Practitioner, either directly because of the specific learning difficulty, or because of related physical disorders such as migraine, they may be referred to the Community Child Health Department. If a child sustains an insult to the developing nervous system which results in a specific learning difficulty, they may be transferred for further assessment and follow-up from the hospital out to the Community Paediatricians. In addition, paediatric therapists frequently consult with Community Child Health doctors.

LINKS WITH OTHER AGENCIES

In addition to these links with Health Service staff, Community Child Health doctors have long-standing links with Social Services, Education and the voluntary sector. Community Child Health doctors are familiar with the demands of working in the community setting. The community is diffuse and complex as a place to work, and much of the work is interdisciplinary and takes place in working environments such as school and social service nurseries which are not under direct medical or health control. Thus, considerable experience of the locality is also needed to build and maintain personal professional contacts (Rogers 1993).

Taking an appropriate role in the care of children with specific learning difficulties requires skills in communication, assessment and advocacy. Forty per cent of a child's waking life is spent at school and their experiences there contribute to their health and well-being in its widest sense. Where a doctor handles a situation with sensitivity, they have much to offer as part of a team involved in assessing and helping a child with a specific learning difficulty. This can be done productively whilst still recognising that the majority of the intervention for such children is educational.

IDENTIFICATION OF CHILDREN WITH DYSLEXIA

Prediction is not the objective of a school medical examination. The primary purpose is to have a considered clinical overview of the child's health status and to consult with parents and teaching staff in the case of children who may give rise to concern. The doctor may have the task of trying to relate the medical findings to the child's functioning. This can be difficult because a child with, for example, a speech and language delay in the pre-school years, may experience difficulty learning to read, but this is not necessarily so (Bax and Whitmore 1987).

Despite these uncertainties with regard to predicting specific learning difficulties in individual children, there can be a worthwhile contribution from the informed school doctor. Certainly the Dyslexia Association view is that 'the contribution from the Health Services is of the highest importance' (British Dyslexia Association 1992). They highlight risk factors to be considered, which involve features such a slow development of speech and language, perceptual difficulties such as those seen in poor shape copying, difficulty sequencing, poor co-ordination and delayed establishment of literacy with a family history of literacy difficulties. How valid then is this advice?

Certainly, a neurodevelopmental examination incorporating these considerations has a relationship to subsequent school progress. Within this broader picture, particular features such as poor auditory discrimination can have an impact on reading progress.

However, Bax and Whitmore's 1987 study of school entrants showed that none of the sub-scores, which included items such as motor score, speech and language score and visual perception score, on their own predicted reading difficulty.

Indeed, it is important to remember that 77% of their clumsy children at school entry had no academic problems at age 7-10 years. However, of the remaining children with poor co-ordination, one quarter did run into significant academic difficulties despite normal intellectual scores.

Bishop (1990) concludes that it is plausible that the left hemisphere of the brain is poorly developed in dyslexics and provides an inadequate substrate for the development of competence in verbally based skills. Dyslexics as a group have poorer motor skills, which could be a consequence of underlying neurological immaturity. Therefore it may be possible to identify dyslexic children within the broader group of children with these neurodevelopmental immaturities. Although three quarters of children with these feature will have no neurodevelopmental deficit at the age of 10 years, a significant proportion will have under-achieved academically (Gillberg 1988). Some of the simpler interpretations of risk factors in children such as left-handedness have not stood the test of time, but examining the co-ordination of the hands may reveal the child with mild unilateral brain abnormality which renders the contra-lateral hand clumsy and thus leads to a shift of handedness away from that which would have been genetically determined (Bishop 1980).

There are many aspects in a child's history and examination which merit serious reflection. These are expounded in the following sections and allow the doctor to be alert to children at risk of academic failure. The skill therefore required of the doctor is that of arriving at a balanced view and being prepared to facilitate intervention for children where this is appropriate.

DYSLEXIA

For nearly a century there has been intense debate over the mechanisms of dyslexia and whether it exists or not. Initially the disorder was thought to be visual, and certainly in the medical literature it was first described by ophthalmologists and termed 'word blindness'. Subsequently in the 1930's the American neurologist Samuel Orton drew attention to the frequent association between reading disability and an underlying disturbance of language. A more recent formulation of dyslexia as a disorder of phonemic awareness has been supported by a wide range of anatomical, neurophysiolgial and neuropsychological findings (Roseberger 1992).

DOES DYSLEXIA EXIST?

Reading skills vary along with intelligence in the normal population, and in addition dyslexic children fall within the normal distribution of reading skills corrected for ability. That is to say they do not form a hump at the lower end of the normal distribution (Shavwitz et al 1992). However, it cannot be concluded that biologically determined reading disabilities do not exist. A similar distribution is seen for intelligence in the mentally handicapped population and yet there is no doubt that many of these individuals have an organic aetiology.

DYSLEXIA AND THE BRAIN

A small number of neuropathological studies in developmental dyslexics have determined that the brain abnormalities are developmental in nature (Geschwind and Galaburda 1985).

Features include excessive numbers of neurones in the sub cortical white matter of the left parasagittal region of the brain, and also in the left planum temporale and posterior third of the superior temporal gyrus, suggesting a disorder of neuronal migration. These abnormalities generally fall below the resolution of neuroanatomical brain scanning. However, regional cerebral blood flow techniques in developmental dyslexics in adult life who have deficits in phonological processing have revealed differences from controls with greater asymmetry of function (Rumsy 1987). Computerised classification of brain electrical activity has also revealed significant differences in functions in the bilateral media frontal lobes and the left posterior quadrant of the brain in dyslexics (Duffy 1979).

These findings which map function in the brain in dyslexic individuals are compatible with Bishop's theory that dyslexics are characterised by a normal pattern of cerebral lateralisation but that the left hemisphere, which in the majority of people is the language hemisphere, is poorly developed and provides an inadequate substrate for development of competence in verbally based skills (Bishop 1990).

DYSLEXIA AND GENETICS

Many studies relate a genetic predisposition to dyslexia. The prevalence of dyslexia is variably quoted between 5-10%, with a male to female ratio of 3.5-4 to 1 (Pennington 1990). The sex ratio in familial samples is considerably lower, about 1.8-2 to 1 boys to girls. James 1992 presented evidence that boys are more susceptible to dyslexia as opposed to them being more commonly represented in research through a referral bias. The risk of having an affected father for a dyslexic son is 40%, and for an affected mother is 35%. Dyslexic daughters have a lower risk of having an affected parent, around 17-18%. Twin studies have revealed that 30% of the cognitive phenotype in reading disability is attributable to heritable factors and not due to IQ. The pattern of heritable deficits leads to a growing consensus that dyslexics are more deficient in single word recognition and phonological processing skills than other neuro-psychological factors. A minority of families demonstrate significant linkage between dyslexia and chromosome 15 (Pennington *et al* 1987).

It is still unclear whether there is a causal relationship between phonological processing problems and dyslexia. Are the former manifestations of the underlying cause: are they simply correlates of the underlying cause, are they the result of poor reading or are they just incidental to the syndrome?

Certainly, neuro-psychological deficits can be found in adults who have recovered from their difficulties in reading and spelling, and involve deficits in verbal learning and memory, word fluency, temporal order judgments in auditory and visual fields and dexterity in right-sided sequential finger movements (Kinsbourne *et al* 1991).

The cognitive phenotype of inherited learning disabilities is complex. Even when mapped very carefully through an affected family there can be a wide range of findings. Such a family had one child with difficulty with phoneme discrimination but relatively intact linguistic processing, whilst another had severe deficits in phoneme analysis and another had generalised deficits across all visual processing tasks. Yet another child had a very specific written spelling disorder and intact reading achievement. Within this family there were, however, similar difficulties across the generations of affected members, on coding digit symbol sub tests (Elbert and Seale 1988).

THE RELEVANCE OF HEARING, SPEECH AND LANGUAGE TO THE DEVELOPMENT OF READING

The condition of otitis media with effusion (OME) has a part to play in some children who find it difficult to learn to read. This is essentially a process of middle ear catarrh which is very prevalent in pre-school children. Chalmers *et al* 1989 showed that the presence of a conductive hearing loss, associated with OME at the age of five years in children, led to both depressed articulation scores in their speech and depressed reading scores when they were examined at the age of 7, 9 and 11. In addition, teachers reported behaviour problems more frequently in these children. Obviously the paediatrician in the school needs to ensure that the process is no longer active; if there is a continuing hearing loss in association with middle ear catarrh this requires to be treated in it's own right. The more common situation is that there is a lot of past evidence of hearing problems and ear infections, but that at the time that the child presents with problems learning to read the process is no longer active. It is then appropriate for the Paediatrician to advise the teaching staff on this medical background, as it may be pertinent and indicate that the child requires work in the areas which he has missed out on in his pre-school years. He may have poor foundations for his phonological knowledge that he needs to bring to reading.

Dyslexic children are impaired in many language skills to varying extents, and the dominant view is that a central deficit resides at some point in the processes of representing speech sounds and in maintaining and manipulating these phonological representations in memory. Children who can pick odd-one-out words go on to have better reading levels, taking into account their IQ and memory. Children trained in rhyming techniques, particularly if they are linked to the alphabet, do better subsequently in reading and spelling. Many children who are reading deficient have difficulties in short-term memory for linguistic material. Poor readers are less good at repeating a sentence, whereas they are just as good as controls in their comprehension of complex sentences (Shankweiler and Smith 1984).

Many of these language deficits in dyslexic children will not have been apparent in the pre-school years, but there are some children who before going into school display developmental language delay which has an adverse impact on reading (Silva *et al* 1987). Such children are often known to the school doctor when they enter school, and it may be valuable to alert teachers so that they can check whether the child has any difficulties in picking up reading.

PERINATAL CONSIDERATIONS

The Paediatrician seeing a child with a specific learning difficulty may have to consider whether events in the pregnancy, birth and early neo-natal period, might have some bearing on the child's under-achievement at school. Children of low birth weight are known to under-achieve at school, and this is not necessarily associated with a lower intellectual ability (Zubrick *et al* 1988). These specific difficulties may be more pronounced in low birth weight children who experience adverse events such as intra-ventricular haemorrhage within the brain. This type of event is very common in pre-term infants, being present in about 50% of very low birth weight infants.

Even low birth weight infants who had an unremarkable course after delivery have delays in verbal comprehension when compared to term children, and problems in phonology are seen in low birth weight children who have experienced illness in the neo-natal period (Largo *et al* 1986). In addition, some of the children may have poor visual motor skills (Hunt *et al* 1988), and subtle problems in motor development (Marlow *et al* 1989).

It is recognised that as a group, low birth weight children can experience difficulties with attention and concentration which have a neurological basis, and are related to effects on the brain of various perinatal events, when the brain has an immature cerebral circulation. These facets of the child's behaviour can compound their academic under-achievement in the classroom.

The Paediatrician will be in a position to evaluate whether perinatal events have contributed to the child's difficulties in the classroom, by considering all the above points.

THE EFFECT OF AN ADVERSE HOME ENVIRONMENT

Learning to read, like any complex behavioural development, is influenced by the child's environment. The Paediatrician may be in a position to judge whether this has had an adverse impact on the child's academic progress. Children who live in crowded homes which lack amenities have lower attainments in reading and mathematics when examined at the age of 16 (Esson *et al* 1978). In addition, children in care have lower reading and mathematics attainments than children who have similar socio-economic backgrounds but no experience of care (Esson *et al* 1976). Children who are neglected or abused can have more difficulty with speech and language than with cognitive or other development. Auditory and verbal subscales of language tests may be the most adversely affected (Law and Conway 1992).

ACQUIRED DYSLEXIA

Some children experience difficulty learning to read following insults to the central nervous system. These may be quite direct, involving crucial areas for reading such as the left anterior temporal lobe, which leads to deficits in memory skills for auditory-verbal learning (Levine *et al* 1981). In other children there is less direct evidence of damage to the brain, but a clear association may be recognised between their condition (e.g. left temporal lobe epilepsy) and their disability in learning to read. In the rare circumstances where these medical problems are strongly relating to poor progress in reading, the Paediatrician is in a position to assess and advise.

THE ROLE OF MEDICAL MANAGEMENT IN TREATMENT

The Paediatrician can contribute most to meeting the needs of children with specific learning difficulties as part of a multi-disciplinary team. Much of the management and treatment is the province of the education system, but there are several principles which the doctor must bear in mind. These include reducing the child's anxiety, circumventing the handicap, practising areas without disability and direct remedial programme for the disability itself (O'Hare and Brown 1992). By participating in multi-disciplinary working, the Paediatrician can avoid delivering an assessment which is couched in technical jargon, and may not offer advice of a practical nature. Parents of children with specific difficulties can be all too often met with opposition, when all they need is the reassurance that something is being done, and frequent contact with parents is to be encouraged in this multi-disciplinary working. Morris 1989 also stresses the obvious advantages of new technology for children with specific learning disabilities.

Paediatricians have a scientific training and can help parents, teachers and the community at large to evaluate claims in the treatment of specific learning difficulties. Whilst it is important to remain open-minded, the wholesale endorsement of single explanations and treatments for children with clinical disorders as complex as reading disabilities deserve the doctor's outspoken mistrust (Levine 1984).

In many instances, the Paediatrician is well placed to contribute to explaining the nature of the child's specific learning disability to the child and the family, and this can often be therapeutic in it's own right. There are some specific areas which might be regarded as the remit of the doctor, and controversy remains as to how useful these techniques are to promote children's reading.

THE CONTRIBUTION OF THERAPY SERVICES

The Paediatrician may feel it appropriate to refer the child for assessment and therapy from colleagues in speech therapy or occupational therapy. The contribution of the former is being increasingly recognised and is discussed at some length in other chapters. The occupational therapist may have a particular role for children experiencing difficulty learning to write. Some techniques have been subjected to scientific evaluation and been shown to make a worthwhile contribution to improving the child's situation. Oliver (1990) looked at some special populations of children who had deficits in their writing readiness, and considered that they benefited from individualised instruction which emphasised multi-sensory training. This was especially helpful for children with a difference of 15 points or more between their verbal and performance IQ, and the greatest gains were made by the boys. However, she stressed the unique elements of the writing readiness programme, in that there was co-ordination of direct therapy and ongoing classroom orientated remedial programmes, and identified the need for research to evaluate whether other motor components of writing readinesssuch as sitting posture and pencil grip are important treatment modalities.

THE ROLE OF VISUAL TRAINING

This is a most controversial area. Ever since dyslexia 'word-blindness' was first described at the turn of the century people have been attracted to the idea that vision and visual-perceptual problems were the root cause of reading disabilities. Metzger and Werner (1984) reviewed the literature and found no evidence that children with refractive abnormalities and ocular-motor abnormalities were worse readers than children without these features, and also found no evidence that the perceptual capabilities of children with reading disabilities were any different from those of normal readers. There was no evidence that visual-motor perceptual training produced significant improvement in poor readers, and visual-perceptual skills did not predict poor readers. Whilst visual discrimination test results were different in children who had difficulties learning to read, this was restricted to letter stimuli. However, it does seem sensible to include a test of near-visual acuity in a child having difficulty learning to read. Stewart-Brown *et al* (1985) taking intelligence into account, found that only children with mild hypermetropia (long-sight) were underachieving at reading in their total group of children with visual deficits. The prescription of spectacles did not seem to alter reading for any of the groups of visually defective children, apart from a trend which did not reach statistical significance in the hypermetropic children. They suggested that it was plausible that the degree of accommodation of the eyes required by these hypermetropic children to read text might have been sufficient to affect their learning to read, and urged that near-vision in such a child should be checked.

There is even greater controversy around the role of orthoptic management in children with reading problems. Stein and Fowler (1985) suggested that 1/6 of dyslexic children may be helped by developing reliable vergance control through establishment of a leading eye. Their technique of occluded spectacles showed a highly significant improvement in reading over chronological age in such children, but it did not appear to help children who had phonemic errors, e.g., children who found it hard to rhyme with simple words or sequence items such as days of the week.

The most recent developments in this area of visual-perceptual underpinnings of reading have followed the observation that some individuals are subject to perceptual distortion of text, and yet no longer perceive this distortion when the text has a particular colour. The physiological basis for this remains unclear. Wilkins (1992) has developed a system for ophthalmic precision tinting, and is conducting a multi-centre, double blind, cross-over trial to evaluate the contribution of this therapy in children experiencing difficulties learning to read. In his preliminary work most of the children who reported abatement of perceptual distortions, had either migraine or a family history of migraine, and they picked colours complementary to red. After using their tinted lenses and overlays, the children had fewer headaches and a more positive attitude to reading, but they did not always have improved reading attainments.

MEDICATION

Medication must be seen to have a very limited role in the management of children with specific learning difficulties. This approach is far more popular in the United States where some children with specific learning difficulties would be regarded as suffering from the attention deficit disorder. That is to say they are developmentally inappropriately inattentive, impulsive and hyper-active. Whilst claims are made for the role of mega-vitamin therapy and exclusion diets, such as the Feingold diet (excluding artificial additives) there is either no benefit demonstrated or the results do not allow one to exclude the effect of a placebo (Haslam *et al* 1984). Stimulant therapy, such as methylphenidate, does have place in some hyper-active children. However, in a follow-up of young adults treated for at least three years in childhood with such medications, there was no significant difference in academic outcome, although there was a significantly better outcome for social skills, self-esteem and delinquency rates in young adult life (Hechtmann *et al* 1984).

In rare instances, the child with specific learning difficulties may express unusual features which merit further investigation. Such investigations may include neuro-physiological techniques such as electroencephalograms (EEG's), or evaluation of chromosome anomalies. Children with sex chromosome anomalies are frequently intellectually normal, but have an increased rate of problems in auditory perception, receptive and expressive language. Thus a Paediatrician's opinion, when children run into academic difficulties, may be helpful in clarifying the aetiology of their disabilities.

REFERENCES

BAX M., WHITMORE, K. (1987) 'The medical examination of children on entry to school. The results and use of neurodevelopmental assessment.' *Developmental medicine and child neurology,* 29, 40-55

BISHOP D. (1980) 'Handedness, clumsiness and cognitive ability.' *Developmental medicine and child neurology,* 22, 569-579.

BISHOP D. (1990) 'Handedness and developmental disorder.' *Clinics in developmental medicine.* MacKeith Press Oxford No. 110.

DUFFY F. H., DENCKLA M. B., BARTELS P. H., SANDINI G. (1979) 'Dyslexia: regional differences in brain electrical activity by topographic mapping.' *Annals of neurology,* 7, No 5, 412-420.

ELBERT J. C., SEALE T. W. (1988) 'Complexity of the cognitive phenotype of an inherited form of learning disability.' *Developmental Medicine and Child Neurology,* 30, 181-189.

ESSON J., LAMBERT L., HEAD J. (1976) 'School attainments of children who have been in care.' *Child care health and development,* 2, 339-351.

ESSON J., FOGELMAN K., HEAD J. (1978) 'Childhood housing experience and school attainments.' *Child care health and development,* 4, 41-58.

GESCHWIND N., GALABURDA A. M. (1985) 'Cerebral lateralisation biological mechanisms associations and pathology; a hypothesis and a programme for research.' *Archives of Neurology,* 42, 428-459.

GILLBERG I. C. (1985) 'Children with minor neurodevelopmental disorders 111 neurological and neurodevelopmental problems at age 10.' *Developmental Medicine and Child Neurology,* 27, 3-16.

HASLAM R. H. A., DALBY J. T., RADENAKER A. W. (1984) 'Effects of megavitamin therapy on children with attention deficit disorders.' *Paediatrics,* 77 No 1, 103-111.

HECHTMANN L., WEISS G., PERLMAN T. (1984) 'Young adult outcome of hyperactive children who received long-term stimulant therapy.' *Journal of American Academy of Child Psychiatry,* 23, 261-269.

HUNT J. V., TOOLEY W. H., HARVIN D. (1982) 'Learning disabilities in children with birth weights less than 1500 grams.' *Seminars in Perinatology,* 6, 280-287.

JAMES W. H. (1992) 'The sex ratios of dyslexic children and their sibs.' *Developmental Medicine and Child Neurology,* 34, 530-533.

KINSBOURNE M., RUFFO D. T., GAMZU E., PARMA R. L., BERLINER A . K. (1991) 'Neuropsychological Deficits in Adults with Dyslexia.' *Developmental Medicine and Child Neurology,* 33, 763-775.

LAW J., CONWAY J. (1992) 'Effect of abuse and neglect on the development of children's speech and language.' *Developmental Medicine and Child Neurology,* 34, 943-948.

LEVINE D., HIER D., CALVANIO R. (1981) 'Acquired learning disability for reading after left temporal lobe damage in childhood.' *Neurology,* 31, 257-264.

LEVINE M. D. (1984) 'Reading disability. Do the eyes have it?' *Paediatrics,* 73 (6, 869-870)

MARLOW N., ROBERTS D. L., COOKE W. I. (1989) 'Motor skills in extremely low birth weight children at the age of 6 years.' *Archives of Diseases in Childhood,* 64, 839-847

METZGER R. L, WERNER D. B. (1984) 'Use of visual training for reading disabilities.' *Paediatrics.* 73 (6, 824-828).

MORRIS H. (1989) 'Don't Look at the Penguins'. *Special Children,* 29, 7-10.

O'HARE A. E., BROWN J. K. (1992) 'Learning disorders in disorders of the central nervous system' Chapter 14 in Campbell A. G. M., Mackintosh N., Eds. *Forfar and Arneils Textbook of Paediatrics* (Edition 4) Churchill Livingstone, 847-854.

OLIVER C .E. (1990) 'A sensory motor programme for improving writing readiness skills in elementary age children.' *American Journal of Occupational Therapy,* 44, 2, 111-115.

PENNINGTON B. F., SMITH S. D., KIMBERLINGS W. J., GREEN P. A., HAITH M. M. (1987) 'Left handedness and immune disorders in familial dyslexics.' *Archives of Neurology,* 44, 634-639.

PENNINGTON B. F. (1990) 'Annotation the genetics of dyslexia.' *Journal of Child Psychology and Psychiatry,* 31, 193-201.

ROGERS M. (1993) 'The growing pains of community child health.' *Archives of Disease in Childhood,* 68 (1) 140-144.

ROSENBERGER P. B. (1992) 'Dyslexia – Is it a Disease?' *New England Journal of Medicine,* 326, 192-193.

SHANKWEILER (1984) 'Repetition and comprehension of spoken sentences by reading disabled children.' *Brain and Language,* 23, 241-257.

SHAVWITZ S. E., ESCOBAR N. D., SHAYWITZ B. A., FLETCHER J. M., MAKUCH R. (1992) 'Evidence that dyslexia may represent the lower tail of a normal distribution of reading ability. ' *New England Journal of Medicine,* 326, 145-150.

SILVA P. A., McGEE R., WILLIAMS S. M. (1983) 'Developmental language delay from 3-7 years and its significance for low intelligence and reading difficulties at age 7.' *Developmental Medicine and Child Neurology,* 25, 783-793.

STEIN J., FOWLER S. (1985) 'Effect of monocular occlusion on visu-motor perception and reading in dyslexic children.' *Lancet,* 13, 69-73.

STEWART-BROWN S., HASLEM M. N., BUTLER N. (1985) 'Educational attainment of 10 year old children with treated and untreated visual defects.' *Developmental Medicine and Child Neurology* 1985, 27, 504-513.

WILKINS A., MILROY R., NIMMO-SMITH I., WRIGHT A., TYRILL K., HOLLAND K., MARTIN J. (1992) 'Preliminary observations concerning treatment of visual discomfort and associated perceptual distortion.' *Ophthalmology, Physiology, Optics,* 12, 257-263.

SECTION 3

TEACHING AND THE CURRICULUM

Chapter 7

THE ROLE OF THE TEACHER

MARGARET CROMBIE

INTRODUCTION

Provision available to dyslexic children varies widely throughout Britain. There are a few private establishments which offer a very specialised curriculum and teaching geared to meet the needs of a dyslexic population of pupils. At the other extreme there are schools where the very existence of dyslexic pupils is denied (Thomson and Watkins 1990; Singleton 1992). Whether we choose to use the word 'dyslexia' or the term 'specific learning difficulties' is irrelevant to the current chapter. The actual incidence of specific learning difficulties will depend on how we choose to define the problems, but whether we accept a figure of over six per cent (Rutter *et al* 1970; Snowling 1987) or two per cent (Miles 1991), the reality of the situation dictates that most schools will have a handful of such children. For these children, then, the role of teacher is vital and the responsibilities of the teacher extremely demanding. Meeting the everyday special educational needs of children with a variety of different problems can never be easy, but it is the teacher who has an important role in determining whether a pupil will thrive or merely survive.

Just what then is involved in the role of effective teacher where children with specific learning difficulties are concerned? And what should teachers be expected to provide? All teachers have a responsibility to recognise the signs of such difficulties, to know where to turn for help, and to be able to deal competently with the problems in the classroom situation.

THE PATTERN OF DIFFICULTIES

The initial signs of specific learning difficulties (dyslexia) may not be apparent in the child's early days at school. Sometimes the dyslexic child will learn to identify words by their visual pattern using a look-and-say approach, and it is not till the load on memory becomes too great that the 'reading' process breaks down (Thomson and Watkins 1990). Sometimes too, children who do not have specific learning difficulties will show signs, such as b/d confusion, mixed laterality, sequencing difficulties etc., and yet not turn out to be dyslexic (Pumfrey and Reason 1991). However, if the initial signs do exist, then the teacher should exercise caution and take further steps to establish whether there are grounds for recommending further assessment. Many books on the subject will give a list of indicators of specific learning difficulties (Arkell 1977; Blight 1985; Crombie,1992; Hornsby 1984; Miles 1983; Thomson and Watkins 1990). These include poor reading and spelling; left/right confusion; orientation problems; sequencing difficulties; poor short term memory; mixed laterality; confusion over punctuation and grammar; difficulty in naming objects; problems with letter formation and a family history of similar difficulties.

Outwith school the child may be generally quite happy, but difficulties may be apparent when the child is asked to follow a short sequence of instructions, remember a phone number, address or birthday, and the child may be confused over concepts such as yesterday, today, tomorrow, saying, 'I'll do it yesterday'. If there are a significant group of such indicators (six or more), then the role of the teacher at this point is to draw up a programme for intervention in an attempt to accelerate progress and help the child to catch up (Crombie 1992).

EARLY INTERVENTION

There is good evidence to show that early intervention can be extremely effective. Marie Clay's reading recovery programme (Clay 1979;1981), although expensive to implement, has proved successful in many countries. She suggests that the best time for intervention is in the child's second year of formal schooling. It is an extremely unfortunate reality of the situation that a child often has to fail significantly in learning to read and spell before he will be officially recognised as 'dyslexic'. This may mean that a gap of at least two years has to exist between a child's chronological age and his reading and/or spelling ages before he will be considered 'dyslexic' and in need of some kind of special or specialist help. This size of gap between age and achievement cannot usually exist till a child is in his third year of formal schooling at the earliest. By this time bad reading habits, mis-spellings and other problems will have become reinforced to a considerable extent, making remediation all the more difficult.

It is important then for the teacher to take steps to remedy dyslexic-type difficulties even when no actual diagnosis exists. It may be that in cases of only mild difficulties the child will never be assessed as dyslexic. If, however, difficulties are severe in nature it is likely that they will require a full diagnostic assessment later, and that specific learning difficulties will become apparent in spite of the best efforts to avoid this. It may be a comfort to know that the difficulties would have been even more severe without intervention, and that without sympathetic help the child might also have developed emotional and behavioural problems.

PREPARATION OF INTERVENTION PROGRAMMES

If the teacher herself does not feel confident to draw up an intervention programme then it is important for her to recognise this and to draw in all the help available. Within the school there may be others who are qualified or at least have a special interest in the field. The learning support teacher, co-ordinator and/or head teacher may be able to give advice and recommend appropriate materials. If the school can request help from local Support Services outwith the immediate school, then their expertise too should be put to use. The advice given should undoubtedly benefit more than just one child: because of the logistics problems of implementation of early intervention for individual pupils a small group could be targeted. This may include children who have been off ill and missed a significant amount of schooling and children who have come in from other schools or from abroad if they need help in fitting in with the class programme. Any children who are having difficulty in mastering phonic work can be included in the group so long as it is kept small. The most effective intervention programmes for dyslexic children, it has been found, is phonic and multi-sensory (Hornsby and Miles 1980; Pumfrey and Elliott 1990).

While not all the children in the group may actually need multi-sensory teaching, all will benefit from this type of training since it requires the child to use all his available senses to aid the learning process. In effect, this means that the child should learn to look, say, listen, and write whatever he is attempting to learn. Because the difficulties are mainly in processing symbolic information, this method is particularly effective in learning to read, write and spell but it is also effective for mathematical knowledge (writing and learning number facts). A considerable amount of overlearning too will be needed for points to become established (Pumfrey and Elliott 1990).

PLANNING PROGRAMMES

Not all dyslexic children will be spotted early. Often the difficulties only come to light at a later stage. Whether the dyslexic pupil is recognised in the early years of primary school or later, accurate assessment of the pupil's difficulties is essential if his individual needs are to be met (Pumfrey and Reason 1991). The teacher will use this assessment to plan and guide her teaching. A pattern of strengths and weaknesses along with precise details of phonic knowledge and spelling ability will enable accurate teaching honed to individual needs. When the teacher has gathered precise information on the exact points which the child is unsure of she can then start to build on what the child does know, introducing the points of uncertainty one at a time in a structured, cumulative manner. Advice on planning these multi-sensory programmes should be available, when required, through area specialist teachers and/or educational psychologists.

STRATEGIES AND MATERIALS

In word attack and reading accurate assessment will require to take into account exactly which aspects of reading the child knows and understands. It will not be sufficient for the child to recognise each letter on one occasion. If the child is really to master the reading process then responses to symbols must become an automatic process. Digraphs must be recognised as such and not as individual sounds. Blending too has to be practised until it becomes automatic. Often the simplest way to give reinforcement is through the daily use of flash cards or reading packs to reinforce symbol-sound correspondence. There are a number of phonic based programmes which are quite suitable for implementing in the classroom. Alpha to Omega (Hornsby and Shear 1980) is structured to the needs of dyslexic children and flashcards are available ready-made to give the necessary practice. The Letterland material too (Wendon 1985 1987), although it appeals more to the younger age group of children, can be extremely useful at later stages. The approach may require to be adapted slightly so that the older pupil will accept the stories and enjoy them, but for the child who has not experienced Letterland at the infant stage presentation can still be appealing and the learning particularly beneficial to children with different types of learning problems (Bald 1992).

Reading schemes for dyslexic children need to be selected with care. To give a 10-year-old the same reading book as his young brother who has only been in school for six months could be totally demoralising for the dyslexic pupil. The reading book chosen may well be at the appropriate stage for the dyslexic child's reading level, but in this case would be totally inappropriate for the particular child. It is often best for the teacher to try to find a scheme which is unknown to the other pupils in the class. In this way comparisons will not be made and the child will avoid the humiliation of being put on an 'infant book'. There are a large range of different schemes available aimed to suit children whose interest age and reading age are discrepant. Schemes such as Oxford University Press's 'fuzzbuzz' or 'Wellington Square', published by Thomas Nelson & Sons, for younger readers, or for older children the Five Minute Thrillers series from Learning Development Aids, will give the pupils reading experiences at their own level of understanding.

SPELLING

The role of the teacher in helping with spelling is to establish good spelling habits from an early stage (Bryant and Bradley 1985). Learning that spelling is not simply a matter of copying letter by letter is beneficial for all children, but is absolutely essential if the dyslexic pupil is ever to master spelling skills. The use of a LOOK, COVER, WRITE and CHECK routine will encourage the child to think what he is writing as he does so. He must however also learn to say the letters and to rehearse these verbally in his head as he practises the word. Self-checking too has to be carried out very carefully as it is very easy for the dyslexic pupil to miss an error. It is important also to match the spelling tasks to the individuals who are learning (Reason and Boote 1986). Some children may cope with three or four words a day. Others may require to spend a week on two or three words. After the child has learned a word it is important to check that he can remember it, so testing after a few minutes, a day later, and a week later will establish if the word is really known. There is also an aspect that if the child knows he will be tested he will make a greater effort.

However, in spite of all the effort the dyslexic child will sometimes be unable to remember the word or words. There will also be errors that seem to persist for ever. Common ones seem to be *whith* for *with*, *meny* for *many* and *sed* for *said*. It is not always easy to understand why some of the errors persist and why apparently straightforward words prove so difficult for the dyslexic pupil. The teacher should understand that in these cases it is no one's fault that the child has not mastered the words, but with persistence and patience eventually they usually do come right. It might not, however, always be felt worthwhile to expend this amount of effort on each word and the teacher may decide that time spent on dictionary training may be more worthwhile. Often a spelling dictionary or calculator-type Spelling Checker may be more beneficial than the usual dictionary where the dyslexic pupil trying to spell *photograph* may well look under 'f', and wonder why he can't find it. The Pergamon Dictionary of Perfect Spelling (Maxwell 1978) is popular with most dyslexic children and is easy enough for most upper primary pupils to master. If the pupil looks up the word by its sound he will see the word spelled in red ink if it is wrong. Alongside is the correct spelling. For example, the child who requires to spell 'sed' looks it up under 'said' and finds it printed in red. Alongside is the correct spelling in black.

One aspect of spelling which teachers often find difficult is that dyslexic children get words right at one point on the page and get them wrong in different ways at other points on the page. The reason for this is quite simply that the dyslexic pupil does not know that the word is right. In the same way a dyslexic student who is sent back to his desk to look for his own spelling errors and to correct them may well end up with an even worse attempt than the original. For this reason then patience and understanding are essential, as is a realisation that asking the dyslexic pupil to correct his own mistakes without supervision is often impossible. The class teacher needs to try to set aside a few extra minutes regularly throughout the day to ensure that the dyslexic pupil gets the help he desperately needs. This is not always easy to do in a class of mixed-ability children all of whom have their own very special needs.

THE CLASSROOM CONTEXT

Seating arrangements and classroom planning are very important. Always seat a dyslexic child facing the board as children with these difficulties often become disorientated by having to turn round to copy down work. If the teacher's desk is also positioned by the board, this will avoid the child having to turn round to see her and losing track of what he is doing. Grouping arrangements can be such that the dyslexic child is paired with an agreeable pupil who is prepared to help with reading difficult words, or with finding these in the dictionary. Flexibility of groupings needs to be such that the child is not confined to one group for all activities. If, for example, the child were to be in the same group for both reading and topic work he might well become disheartened. Often the pupil's oral skills will greatly outpace the reading skills. In a subject which puts reliance on discussion and wider, more general knowledge the dyslexic child has the opportunity to show his knowledge. This also gives an opportunity to boost confidence and increase self-esteem.

Over recent years there has been great and lengthy debate on the pros and cons of withdrawal for individual or small group teaching (Payne, 1991). In my own mind there is no doubt about the efficacy of the move away from the teaching of a small group outwith the classroom by a teacher who is often unknown to the rest of the class. There does, however, have to be a consideration of what is going to be best for the pupil. Decisions on whether to withdraw or not are sometimes made as a matter of whole school policy. In this situation we are not considering the best interest of the individual child. Teachers, and often this will mean head teacher, class teacher and support teacher, should get together to decide what they are aiming to teach and whether it can be achieved best within class or outwith. Accommodation, staffing level and teacher expertise will all play a part in determining the decision to be made, as should the feelings and needs of the pupil.

For instance, for a child who has difficulty hearing the individual sounds within words, training in auditory discrimination skills will be necessary if he is ever to learn to spell. To give this training in identifying small differences in sounds in a noisy classroom will be almost impossible. In the same way, it might be a matter of considerable embarrassment to an older pupil to be seen to be practising elementary reading skills in the presence of his peer group. There is no easy answer, but it is the role of the child's teachers, in the light of all the facts, to decide what is best and on what occasions a child might be withdrawn.

THE SECONDARY STAGE

Decisions on where structured individual teaching should take place will also have to be made if help is being sought from outwith the school. Support teachers, whether specialists in specific learning difficulties or in the wider range of learning difficulties, should also view the interests of the pupils as being paramount. Often a mixed approach can be best with the support teacher spending some time in the classroom and some time with the child outwith to work on specific skills training.

At the secondary stage, however, where specific help is being given in basic reading, spelling and writing skills, it is generally in the best interests of the child for a specialist teacher to carry this out away from the main classroom. There is no way that such basic skills can be taught in the classroom without some degree of embarrassment to the pupil. It is, however, still extremely important for the secondary pupil to receive the level of help which he needs even when this does mean extraction from another subject. The main difficulty for the specialist teacher, in liaison with secondary subject specialists, is to decide which is the most appropriate subject from which to withdraw the pupil. Is it best to withdraw from the best subject in the hope that the pupil will be able to easily catch up on time missed, or a subject which stresses individualised programmes, perhaps maths, or a subject the pupil is particularly poor at, accepting that he is not likely to make much improvement anyway? Another possibility is to withdraw from non-examinable subjects like social education. Not all pupils however will be able to be withdrawn from the most appropriate subject. Demands on the specialist teachers timetable are likely to be such that compromises will always be necessary. The role of the specialist, however, is to minimise the likely difficulties which might occur through a policy of withdrawing pupils from classes.

Secondary subject teachers do also have an important role in furthering the work of the specific learning difficulties specialists and in promoting alternative strategies for those who are totally unable to cope with the demands of the secondary curriculum. Often, when specific difficulties are severe ,the role of the subject specialist is to look for alternative means of presentation. On occasions too, difficulties will be such that a reader and scribe may be needed to give the pupil a fair chance of expressing his knowledge in exam situations. When this is the case the teacher's role is to give the pupil considerable practice in using these resources, learning to use a reader and scribe to maximum benefit is a skill which has to be practised just like any other. The same applies to the use of tape recorders (Reilly

1991). Pupils will need considerable practice in using the equipment before they reach the degree of efficiency which is desirable for the exam situation. They need to recognise just how much they have to rewind to get back to the section they wish to hear again or say again. They also have to recognise the right keys for running the tape forward, rewinding etc.. All these can be practised and need to be practised if pupils are to master the skills and gain the desired benefits. It is for the teacher to ensure that this is done as often as possible.

The subject teacher can help by providing copies of notes, either by asking a competent pupil to use carbon paper under his work or by photocopying. The use of tape-recorded material too may help in accessing the pupil to novels or other material he might have difficulty in reading. Specialist vocabulary for the pupil's various subjects should be kept handy. If subject teachers write this vocabulary into a pocket-sized dictionary the pupil can refer to this whenever the need arises (Stirling, 1985). For those whose needs are less severe most material can be differentiated to a level which will enable the student to cope. Often symbolic information can be given alongside the written words to help these pupils cope. While there may be difficulties in accessing pupils to all subjects at the secondary stage it is not impossible, and with time and consideration the needs of the pupils can be met by altering or adapting the means of presentation and responding.

WORDPROCESSING

The use of wordprocessors with the facility to correct spelling can be extremely beneficial to dyslexic pupils once they have reached a certain stage. Generally this is when work is sufficiently acceptable for an adult to recognise what the words are meant to say. As the computer has been programmed to recognise mis-spellings, generally it will respond by suggesting various alternatives.

The pupil will, however, have to have reached a stage where he can recognise the correct version when he sees it on the screen. Small portable wordprocessors with a spelling checker are available for well under £200 and for some dyslexic pupils are a reasonably cheap and easy method of vastly improving the standard of written presentation. Pupils should be given a trial on this type of equipment for a few weeks at least to ensure that it will be of use before the equipment is purchased. These cheaper machines are of limited use since they are unable generally to recognise more bizarre spellings, and wrong spellings of homophones such as 'too' for 'to'. For the pupil who has difficulties in producing legible work the wordprocessor is also of enormous benefit. Whatever the quality of the spelling, work will always be legible. The need for redrafting, which can be a nightmare for pupils who are likely to introduce new mistakes with every redraft, is eliminated and the teacher can concentrate on correcting the existing errors. The motivational aspect of these machines cannot be underestimated. They present to the pupil as a non-judgemental aid to the writing process (Singleton, 1992). For pupils who are all too well aware that the standard of their written work falls considerably short of what the teacher would wish they can be invaluable.

PARENTAL INVOLVEMENT

The involvement of parents in the education process has been well researched and found to be wholly desirable (France, Topping and Revell 1993; Hewison and Tizard 1980; Young and Tyre 1983). The role of the teacher in involving parents therefore is an important one (Acklaw and Gupta 1991). Parents must feel that they are able to discuss any points of concern. They must also be helped to know how they can best aid their children. Whether this is in providing moral support, paired reading help, or more detailed instruction will depend on the abilities and previous knowledge of the parents.

The attitudes of teachers towards parents will also determine just how much knowledge is gained. Parents should feel sufficiently comfortable to be able to divulge in confidence relevant information which may influence expectations and increase the teacher's understanding of the pupil and his background. This will only happen if the parents see teachers as being sympathetic and genuinely interested in the learning needs of their children. For example, if parents themselves are unable to read, teachers would want to know this. It would be a pointless exercise to send out letters inviting such parents to attend a paired reading evening at the school. These parents may also need help in interpreting reports and understanding Records of Needs. All parents can help their children in some way. Often with guidance from the teacher parents can prove a tremendous resource in aiding the development of the children we all seek to help (Hornsby, 1984).

INVOLVEMENT OF OUTSIDE AGENCIES

In most areas help is available from outwith the immediate school. This may be in the form of further assessment, advice, direct teaching, support teaching or in-service training, and might involve agencies such as psychological service, support services, colleges or university faculties of education. The type of help provided will vary from area to area, but certainly there should be help in determining the needs of the pupil through psychological services. They will arrange and carry out detailed assessment of needs, and decide in consultation with school staff and parents whether the case is sufficiently severe to warrant the opening of a Record of Needs in order to describe what provision should be available for the pupil and to safeguard the pupil's rights in a legal sense. Psychological services can also determine what level of support is desirable and advise on sources of obtaining this help.

As more and more teachers are becoming aware of the types of difficulties faced by dyslexic pupils the demand for training has increased. Pressure from outside bodies to ensure that pupils' needs are met by staff who have the training to deal with the problems has meant that training agencies are now offering more INSET in response to an increasing demand. Provided the training of pre-service teachers is included we should in time have a much greater awareness of specific learning difficulties and how teachers can best deal with the problems in the classroom situation.

MOTIVATION

An area which deserves separate consideration in any discussion of dyslexic problems is that of motivation. A pupil who has poor motivation is unlikely to gain much from his time in school. All too often where there are dyslexic problems over time the pupil loses interest. This is only to be expected when, no matter how much effort is expended, success is seldom or never achieved. From this point the pupil seems to be on a downward spiral, avoiding where possible any situation which brings negative feelings of self-concept (Pumfrey and Reason 1991).

As reading is likely to bring about such feelings, the pupil will try at all costs to avoid reading. Such pupils need all the support and help teachers can offer to bring about a change in attitude which will reverse the downward trend. It is for the teacher to find the strengths of the pupil and give praise and encouragement whenever possible. Through an increase in confidence the pupil's whole approach to his school work may be altered.

CONCLUSION

The key to the success or failure of teaching for dyslexic pupils undoubtedly lies in the hands of the teachers they encounter as they make their way through our schools. A successful programme for dyslexic pupils will provide them with maximum support, encouragement, and opportunity for achievement by whatever means are available. The demands made on dyslexic children must be realistic. Often this will mean accepting much less than the child seems to be capable of orally. However, by a series of small and carefully graded increments the dyslexic pupil can often be brought to a very acceptable standard of literacy. Where this is

Chapter 7

not always possible an acceptance of the problems and perseverance to keep on trying can be balanced by presenting alternative means of accessing the curriculum. Through careful handling and sympathetic help the dyslexic pupil can then be helped to achieve his potential, however great or humble that may be.

REFERENCES

ACKLAW J. and GUPTA Y., (1991), *Talking with parents of 'dyslexic' children: The value of skilled discussion methods*, Support for Learning, Vol. 6, No. 1, 37-39.

ARKELL H., (1977), *Dyslexia – Introduction – A Dyslexic's Eye View*, The Helen Arkell Dyslexia Centre, Farnham.

BALD J., (1992), *Love and War in Letterland*, Child Education, Vol. 69, No. 5, 40-41.

BLIGHT J., (1985), *Practical Guide to Dyslexia*, Egon Publishers Ltd., Baldock.

BRYANT P. and BRADLEY L., (1985), *Children's Reading Problems*, Basil Blackwell Ltd., Oxford.

CLAY M. M., (1979), *Reading: The Patterning of Complex Behaviour – Second Edition*, Heinemann, Portsmouth, New Hampshire.

CLAD M., (1981), *The Early Detection of Reading Difficulties*, Heinemann Educational, London.

CROMBIE M., (1992), *Specific Learning Difficulties (Dyslexia) – A Teachers' Guide – Revised*, Jordanhill Sales and Publications, Glasgow.

FRANCE L., TOPPING K. and REVELL K., (1993), *Parent-tutored Cued Spelling*, Support for Learning, Vol. 8, No. 1, 11-15.

HARRIS C., (1978), *fuzzbuzz*, Oxford University Press. Oxford.

HEWISON J. and TIZARD J., (1980), *Parental Involvement and Reading Attainment*, British Journal of Educational Psychology, 50, 209-15.

HORNSBY B., (1984), *Overcoming Dyslexia*, Martin Dunitz Ltd., London.

HORNSBY B., and MILES T. R., (1980), *The Effects of a Dyslexia-Centred Teaching Programme*, British Journal of Educational Psychology, 50, 236-242.

HORNSBY B., and SHEAR F., (1980), *Alpha to Omega*, – Second Edition, Heinemann Educational Books Ltd., Oxford.

MAXWELL C., (1978), *The Pergamon Dictionary of Perfect Spelling*, Second Edition, Thos. Nelson.

MILES T. R., (1983), *Dyslexia – the Pattern of Difficulties*, Granada, London.

MILES T. R., (1991), *Dyslexia: Integrating Theory and Practice*, Whurr Publishers Ltd., London.

PAYNE T., (1991), *It's Cold In The Other Room*, Support for Learning, Vol. 6, No. 2, 61-65.

PUMFREY P. D. and ELLIOTT C. D., (1990), *Children's Difficulties in Reading, Spelling and Writing*, The Falmer Press, London.

PUMFREY P. D. and REASON R., (1991), *Specific Learning Difficulties (Dyslexia) Challenges and Responses*, Routledge, London.

REASON R. and BOOTE R., (1986), *Learning Difficulties in Reading and Writing – A Teacher's Manual,* NFER-Nelson, Windsor.

REILLY J., (1991), *The Use of Tape-recorders to Develop Speaking and Listening skills,* in SNOWLING and THOMSON, (Eds.), (1991).

RUTTER M., TIZARD J. and WHITMORE K., (1970), *Education, Health and Behaviour,* Longman, London.

SINGLETON C., (1992), *The Patient Teacher,* Special Children, September, 1992.

SNOWLING M., (1987), *Dyslexia – A Cognitive Developmental Perspective,* Blackwell, Oxford.

SNOWLING M. and THOMSON M., (1991), *Dyslexia; Integrating Theory and Practice,* Whurr Publishers Ltd., London.

STIRLING E. G., (1985), *Help for the Dyslexic Adolescent,* Better Books, Dudley.

THOMSON M. E. and WATKINS E. J., (1990), *Dyslexia: A Teaching Handbook,* Whurr Publishers, London.

WENDON L., (1985, 1987), *Letterland Teaching Programmes 1 and 2,* Letterland Ltd., Cambridge.

YOUNG P, and TYRE C., (1983), *Dyslexia or Illiteracy? Realising the Right to Read,* The Open University, Milton Keynes.

Chapter 8

ACCESS TO THE CURRICULUM

SYLVIA RUSSELL

INTRODUCTION

In the interests of brevity, throughout this chapter I have used the term 'dyslexia' rather than 'Specific Learning Difficulties'. Since the majority of primary teachers are female, I have used the pronoun 'she' and since the majority of dyslexic children are male, I have used the pronoun 'he'.

By differentiation is meant the identification of, and effective provision for, a range of abilities in one classroom, such that pupils in a particular class need not study the same things at the same pace and in the same way at all times. Differentiated approaches should mean that the needs of the very able, and of children with learning difficulties are discerned and met.

SOED (quoted by Mary Simpson, Northern College)

Differentiation is synonymous with good teaching and is the process of assessing the needs of children and adjusting teaching methodology, materials, pacing and expected outcomes accordingly.

The most important feature of successful differentiation is good planning, firstly at whole school level with senior management taking responsibility for curriculum support, and secondly at classroom level with the class teacher involved in a cycle of assessment, curriculum support and evaluation.

ASSESSMENT

Assessment is crucial to the implementation of an effective teaching programme.

Assessment is inseparable from the teaching process since its prime purpose is to improve pupils' performance. It should help teachers to diagnose pupils' strengths and weaknesses; to match the work of the classroom to their capabilities; to guide them to appropriate courses and groups; to involve them in discussion and self appraisal . . .

(D.E.S., 1985, p51, para 134)

Assessment, does not mean full scale examinations, reading and spelling tests

Chapter 8

every other week but a continuous analysis of **what** we are teaching and **why**, an observation of **how** our pupils are learning and the difficulties they are encountering. This will lead on to the devising of alternative strategies to enhance learning.

INTELLIGENCE

Dyslexic children are no more and no less intelligent than non-dyslexic children. You may find dyslexic children who are above average, average or below average intelligence. What will be noticeable will be the discrepancy between the child's expected and actual attainments. (Siegel, 1989)

LEARNING STYLES

Like all children (and adults), individual dyslexic children will have individual preferred learning styles. Some children learn best when lessons are activity based and they 'learn by doing', some like to be teacher directed and use textbooks, some learn best by talking and discussing and some by discovery and problem solving approaches. The good class teacher, through close observation, will have built up a picture of whether the child learns best alone, in a pair, with the teacher or in a reading group; whether he needs to move about or whether he needs to sit quietly without distractions; the time of day that is most suitable for highly concentrated study; the pupil's perceptual strengths and whether he learns best by auditory, visual, tactile or kinesthetic modes. The child's preferred learning style will have implications for the way that teachers teach different groups of children and the type of methodology that works for particular children but may not be appropriate for others. Carbo, Dunn and Dunn (1986).

The variations in ability, learning styles and degrees of dyslexia make it impossible to write a prescription for differentiated teaching for dyslexic pupils. One can only write in the most general terms and the following suggestions will not meet the needs of all dyslexic pupils all of the time. These suggestions are intended to give busy class teachers some practical tips to allow dyslexic children access to the curriculum. The dyslexic child needs a highly structured approach which builds on what he already knows, in this he is no different from the majority of children. The dyslexic child however, because of poor working memory will also need a great deal of practice and revision before a lesson is mastered, and will need to be taught in a multi-sensory way.

IN-CLASS TEACHING OR EXTRACTION ?

Differentiation implies that the child will be taught within the classroom following the same curriculum as the rest of his classmates, but that the way in which he gains access to that curriculum may be different from his classmates. Whenever possible the dyslexic child should be helped **within** the classroom. Withdrawal from the classroom places the child in a 'special' category perhaps leading the class teacher to feel that she is not skilled enough to teach the dyslexic child and that he is therefore someone else's responsibility. That is not to say that extraction may not be necessary from time to time to work on specific skill areas. When this happens it is important for both teachers to liaise closely so that there is a planned programme of learning objectives which both teachers are reinforcing. Time for this liaison is essential if both teachers are to co-operate on a structured teaching programme for the dyslexic child.

READING

Virtually all primary aged dyslexic children will first come to the notice of their teachers because of poor literacy skills. We often forget what a complex skill reading is. It involves the recognition of words, letters, and letter patterns, as well as sequencing, use of context, prediction, grammatical construction, punctuation and comprehension.

READING – EARLY STAGES

Most schools use early reading schemes which are largely 'Look and Say' but may also have a limited phonic element to them. Many dyslexic children have poor visual memories which can make 'Look and Say' approaches to reading very difficult. These children need early reading teaching which has a heavy emphasis on phonics, and makes as light a demand as possible on visual memory skills. The dyslexic child will need much more practice and revision of phonics than the majority of his classmates and should be taught in a highly structured, multi-sensory way to compensate for his poor working memory and organisational skills.

Teachers will find the book, 'Specific Learning Difficulties (Dyslexia) : A Teachers' Guide' by Margaret Crombie, an excellent source of ideas for multi-sensory teaching.

The dyslexic child need not be taught on his own as almost certainly there will be other children in his class who would benefit from joining him in such a structured approach.

Many schools have developed their own worksheets etc. for teaching phonics and some of these are better than others but most of them will not fulfil the criteria for structure and multi-sensory approaches. I would strongly recommend the

Chapter 8

Letterland Teaching Programme by Lyn Wendon which combines the structure, progression and multi-sensory teaching approaches that are so important for mastery learning and does it in a way that is great fun for young children. There are also excellent computer programmes for reinforcing phonics, 'The Animated Alphabet', (Sherston), 'A to Z' (IEC Software). One which I have found very useful is 'Concept Keyboard Matching' (Scetlander) which allows the teacher to make up her own concept keyboard overlays for alphabet matching exercises. This programme is also versatile enough to allow it to be used for any kind of matching exercise at all ages to reinforce vocabulary, number bonds, multiplication tables, foreign languages etc.

It is important that the dyslexic child is using a reading scheme which is appropriate to his age and reading level. It may not be appropriate for him to continue on the class scheme if he is unable to keep up with the other children and is becoming embarrassed by being on a much lower level than his peers. It would make sense to switch him to either an alternative infant scheme which has a graded, structured vocabulary or try one of the many reading schemes aimed at children with reading difficulties. It is difficult to single out one as being better than another as so much depends on the child's preferences, but two which I have found particularly successful are 'Bangers and Mash' (Longmans) and 'Fuzzbuzz' (Oxford University Press). Both schemes have excellent reinforcement activities and are well structured. It is a good idea to reinforce the vocabulary of a reading scheme by preparing concept keyboard overlays. This allows the child to 'write' stories from a very early stage. (Folio, Stylus, Prompt/Writer)

Obviously if you are placing a child on a different scheme you are moving away from a differentiated programme of work to an individual programme. In my experience, it is usually possible to have the dyslexic child work as part of a group of children who are all trying to master early literacy skills.

Many dyslexic children have difficulty remembering the common 'abstract' words such as *the, this, who, why, and, of, does* etc. I have found that playing the 'Crocodile Game' helps them to memorise them. Children usually work in pairs and as it can be rather noisy you may wish them to play in the corridor outside the classroom door. Write the words to be learned in large letters on large pieces of card (at least 25cm x 25cm). The cards are scattered at random over the floor and are stepping stones to cross a crocodile infested river. Each child is given 3 lives and is told to jump on to the stepping stone that says for example 'this' and then to jump on to 'why' and so on until he reaches the other side of the river. Every time he jumps on the wrong word he loses a life. If he loses all three, he is eaten by crocodiles! Children find the game great fun and the large body movements involved in leaping from one stone to another seem to help 'fix' the words in the child's memory. The same game can be played with any sight vocabulary or phonic clusters that are proving difficult to remember.

READING – UPPER PRIMARY

The older dyslexic pupil may present a greater challenge to the busy class teacher. If the child's problems have not been diagnosed at an early stage he may have experienced years of failure and become totally turned off school in general and reading in particular. For such children reading is very stressful and it is small wonder that they start to yawn, fidget and look for any excuse to avoid reading. It is important that the older dyslexic child is made to feel part of the class and work with his peers as much as possible. There is no reason why he should not take part in discussions and follow up work on a novel that is being studied by the whole class. However the teacher must be aware of the difficulties that he is likely to face and make alternative provision for them. It should be possible to tape record the story in advance. This can be done by the class teacher, parent helper or even other pupils. Make sure that the dyslexic child works in a group working at his intellectual level for even though his reading and written work are of a lower standard he will be motivated and stimulated by being in such a discussion/project group.

If worksheets are being used, the teacher must look very carefully at the language used and at the layout. It may be necessary to provide simplified worksheets or worksheets which have the key words marked with a highlighter pen to cut down on the reading load for the dyslexic child. It is also necessary to look at the follow-up work that is expected. The dyslexic pupil may find report writing and essays very difficult because of his poor handwriting and spelling so alternative ways of recording his ideas should be found. This could be done graphically or recorded on a tape recorder to be transcribed or word processed later.

As well as taking part in the 'reading' of the class novel it is important that the dyslexic child continues on a structured reading programme which will improve his reading fluency. This must be handled sensitively with older children who can be very self-conscious about their difficulties. It often helps to be quite open with the rest of the class and explain to them the types of difficulties the dyslexic child encounters and enlist their help. Most primary aged children are incredibly understanding and supportive of children with problems. Choose a reading scheme which is appropriate to the age, ability and interests of the pupil. The final choice is usually down to the child's personal preference and what is available within school or from the peripatetic support teacher. I have found the following schemes to be very useful : Wellington Square (Nelson), Skyways (Collins), Nick Dick Detective Series (Collins), Starpol Series (Ginn & Co.), Trog Series (Nelson), Rescue Readers (Ginn & Co.), Five Minute Thrillers and Tapes (LDA).

To encourage careful, accurate reading I have found two close procedure books to be invaluable, 'False Teeth and Vampires', and 'Astronauts and the Black Death' (LDA).

A Paired Reading approach should be used so that the dyslexic child is not put under pressure. It is also a good idea to let the child read into a tape recorder and then play the tape back while he follows the text in the book and tries to spot for himself any errors he has made.

Older children may still need to work on phonics to develop decoding skills for reading, and also to help with spelling. This can present a problem for class teachers beyond the infant stages who may not have any great understanding of phonic progression and the need to build on what is already mastered. Using a structured scheme such as 'Phonic Code Cracker (Russell, S., Jordanhill College Publications) will give the teacher a package which includes assessments, precision teaching workbooks to encourage mastery learning, and a computer programme for reinforcement and revision. This phonics programme has been devised to need very little teacher time since most of the learning takes place either at home if parents are willing to help or in school through peer tutoring. The teacher is only needed for the 'Fluency Tests' which are timed with a stop watch and should only take 30 seconds or so each day.

As with Letterland for the younger children, phonics for the older children should encourage them to look at the patterns in words and should be presented in a way which is fun.

Much consolidation can be done through the use of games such as Phonic Rummy (Kenworthy Educational Services), Reading Games (Macmillan Educational), Betty Root series of reading games (NES Arnold), Help Games (H.E.L.P. Educational Games).

For children who have developed a real 'hang-up' about reading from books I have found the computer to be a great motivator. There are many excellent programmes to reinforce phonics but teachers seldom consider the amount of on-screen reading a child has to do in order to complete some of the excellent 'Adventure' programmes such as 'Granny's Garden' (4 Mation), 'Flowers of

Crystal' (4 Mation) 'Nature Park Adventure' (Sherston) , 'Dragon World' (4 Mation), 'Fleet Street Phantom' (Sherston), The Worst Witch (Sherston), Sellardore Tales (Sherston) etc.

HANDWRITING

Many Dyslexic children have poor handwriting skills. The letters may be poorly formed, wrongly sized, frequently reversed, interspersed with capitals and unjoined. Dyslexic children are often highly embarrassed by their messy, illegible handwriting and it can act as a deterrent to story writing. In the lower primary stages the teaching of handwriting should be done at the same time as the teaching of the letter sounds and multi-sensory methods should be used.

e.g.: the child **looks** at the letter, **says** the letter sound and letter name, **hears** the sound of the letter. The teacher writes the letter on the blackboard The child, using different coloured chalk, **writes** over the top of the letter and then writes it again. He writes it on the desktop with his finger, he writes it with his finger on sandpaper (or in a sand tray) and finally he writes it on **lined** paper. Because dyslexic children have problems with letter sizes I have found 'Tramline' paper (Philip & Tacey) to be excellent as children can see quite clearly that tall letters go above the line and tails hang down below. By paying close attention to correct letter formation and giving the child practice using large arm movements and 'feeling' how the letter is made it is hoped that the child's muscle memory and kinesthetic memory will help him to retain the letter when his visual memory proves unequal to the task. Correct letter formation is essential if the child is going to join up his writing properly. I would recommend adding, as soon as possible, the necessary ligatures which allow the child to develop a flowing cursive style of handwriting.

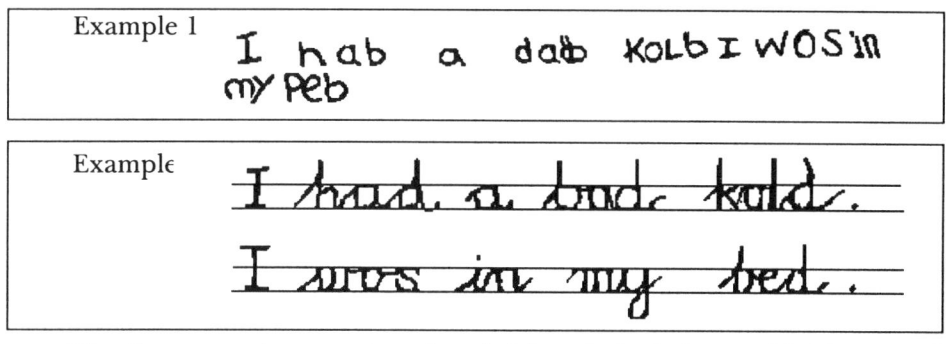

Example 1	I hab a dab kolb I wos in my peb
Example	I had a bad kold. I wors in my bed.

The first example was written by a bright, dyslexic 8 year old. The second example was dictated to him after six months' instruction in cursive handwriting. You will notice that although there are still spelling errors, the reversals have been eradicated and his work is readable.

When copying from the blackboard, make sure the dyslexic child is facing it and not having to turn round which may disorientate him. Teachers should also be aware that some dyslexic children find copying from the blackboard very difficult as they keep losing the place and have to keep re-reading and checking their work from the beginning. If this is the case try to avoid asking the dyslexic to copy and allow him to have photocopied notes instead.

Some dyslexic children hold their pencils in strange, tight grips. This can be helped by sliding a 'Grippy' grip (L.D.A.) over the end of the pencil. This will encourage the child to place his fingers correctly (put it on upside down for left-handed children).

With older children I have found the answer to be to supply them with a script pen and treat writing lessons as art lessons. Once you have broken the initial feeling of failure so that the child can see that he can, on occasions, produce lovely work, it is easier to encourage him to practice this style and to begin to use it for general class work. As with the young children multi-sensory approaches should be used, and tramline paper (with narrower lines) is again recommended.

SPELLING

Handwriting and spelling are very closely linked and many dyslexic children use poor handwriting as a way of disguising their atrocious spelling. In my experience, spelling is generally poorly taught in primary schools with many children experiencing difficulties and being given no real strategies for learning. Children with good visual memories will usually be good spellers since they can visualise the word they want to spell and spot when a word looks wrong but many children, including dyslexic children, have poor visual memories and need to be given a structure for learning. There should be no difficulty in forming a 'spelling support group' in any classroom. This group will certainly need more teacher input than the rest of the class but the extra work should show dividends. The teacher must have a clear idea of what she is trying to achieve and not just present words at random. As a general rule, teach word families which have the same sound pattern in them. Teach prefixes and suffixes and spelling rules since these can cut down considerably on the load of individual words to be memorised ('Logical Spelling' Collins). Teach the common, irregular words such as *done, any, was* etc. as the child will need these for written work. The 'Look, Cover, Write, Check' method advocated by Charles Cripps works well as does Lynette Bradley's 'Simultaneous Oral Spelling' technique. 'Cued Spelling' (Topping, Scoble & Oxley) is another useful teaching method and can be done by children working in pairs and supporting each other in a similar way to paired reading. 'Cracker Spell' (Russell, S., Jordanhill College Publications), uses the Look, Cover, Write, Check approach and also has a computer programme for reinforcement. Using mnemonics can be a great help for children with poor visual memories. Children should be encouraged to think up their own mnemonics for their own 'bogey' words. 'Signposts to Spelling' by Joy Pollok and the series of photo-copiable masters 'Don't Let Spelling Get You Down' (Tregear Publications), are packed with good ideas for this.

Some children will continue to have considerable problems with spelling regardless of the amount of special teaching that they receive. It may be more realistic to accept that they will always have a problem and begin to give them strategies for coping. At the simplest level they should be shown how to use a spelling dictionary such as 'The Pergamon Dictionary of Perfect Spelling' (Nelson) or the 'ACE Dictionary' (L.D.A.). The dyslexic child will need training in alphabetical order before he will be able to use a dictionary successfully. The computer programme 'Dyslexia Aid' (Edsoft), gives practice in alphabetic sequencing.

The 'Franklin Spellmaster' (Venture Marketing) is an electronic spelling aid which is little bigger than a pocket calculator. It will not be of much use if the child's spelling is totally bizarre but it can give a child great confidence when he is beginning to get to grips with spelling.

WRITTEN LANGUAGE WORK

Dyslexic children can be just as imaginative as the other children in the class. However, the teacher must be sensitive to the fact that writing a story follows on from having developed the ability to read, write and spell and these may prove an insurmountable barrier to good story writing. Initially the child should tape record the story for transcribing later. A dyslexic child has the additional problem of sequencing difficulties and will almost certainly need training in working out a structure for his work so that he is able to put his ideas in a logical order. Younger children may be helped in this by giving them a series of pictures for which they have to write captions. 'Picture Writing Books' (Learning Materials Ltd.) are excellent for this or alternatively cut up comic strips and ask the child to stick them in sequence in his jotter and then write a caption for each picture. Older children can be helped by giving them a structure of steps to encourage logical sequencing. At its simplest level this would be three steps – a beginning, a middle and an ending. By the upper stages of primary school most children should be able to cope with a six part structure which includes :–

1	introduce the people	2	describe the setting/place
3	something begins to happen	4	the exciting part
5	things sort themselves out	6	the ending

Children will need encouragement to pad out each section and it is helpful to give them the chance to do rough plans of the sequence of their stories and discuss these with them before they begin to write the actual piece of work. Proof reading is another important skill which should be encouraged by the teacher. Train the child to self-correct his work when he has finished a piece of writing. He should be able to spot some spelling errors for himself and should also be encouraged to look at his sentence construction, at whether the story makes sense, and at whether he has punctuated it properly.

Allowing dyslexic children to use a computer to word process their work improves it considerably. Obviously it is much less of a chore to correct mistakes on the screen than it is to rewrite a piece of work. For children with poor handwriting, the finished piece of work looks much better and the child is able to concentrate on the story rather than on the correct formation of letters and words. I have also noticed an improvement in spelling when a dyslexic's work has been word processed. One dyslexic boy explained this phenomenon to me by saying that the words 'looked wronger' on the screen so it was easier to see the ones he must correct.

Using a computer is also a great motivator for most children and the quality and quantity of their work also tends to improve. Many word processing programmes now include spell checkers which, though far from foolproof especially where homonyms are concerned, undoubtedly help. There are also programmes which will predict the word as the child starts to type ('PAL', for PCs. and 'PREDICTYPE' for the BBC computer, both from Scetlander Ltd., Glasgow). I have found 'STYLUS' (MAPE) a very useful programme for the BBC as it has a 'talk' facility. The child can type in his story and then ask the computer to 'tell' it back. The Dalek sounding voice greatly appeals to children and again, though not foolproof because of phonic irregularities in the English language, can help children to spot words that are obviously wrong. Children quickly become proficient at keyboarding skills and it does the dyslexic child's self-image no harm at all to find that he has become the class expert on the computer. With laptop computers tumbling in price many upper primary dyslexic children are now being given their own laptop with a spell checker which enables them to do all their written work on it without hogging the class computer. When this happens it is important that the child, the class teacher and the parents are given training in the correct use of the laptop otherwise it can gather dust in a cupboard because no one is very sure how to operate it!

MATHEMATICS

The majority of dyslexic children also have difficulty with mathematics. Just as they have difficulty with letter recognition and orientation, dyslexic children will have similar problems with numbers. The same multi-sensory teaching strategies should be used. The mathematical symbols, $+ - \times \div$ also cause confusion as indeed does the language which accompanies each process e.g. $+$, plus, add, count on, total, sum of etc.

These will all need to be carefully taught. It is helpful to give the child a small pack of cards as an 'aide memoire'. The symbol is written on one side of each card and the vocabulary for that process on the other. The cards should be practised frequently and can be used by the child whenever he is unsure of a process. The teacher can help him by talking about what the symbol means and the method involved. The dyslexic child who has directional problems with reading from left to right will be even more confused in mathematics where division is worked from left to right but addition, subtraction and multiplication are worked from right to left. Putting in small direction arrows will help him to remember where to start. Using a jotter with boxes helps the dyslexic child to lay out his work neatly and makes calculations involving place value easier. He should also head his columns with Hundreds, Tens and units and should be encouraged to talk himself through the place value of his answers so that he doesn't inadvertently put the numbers in the wrong columns.

A dyslexic child may have to rely on concrete material for a longer period of time than his peers since he will probably find it difficult to memorise number bonds. Showing him how to use a number line can speed up his work considerably. Many dyslexic children never master the multiplication tables though they can be helped to do so by using tape recordings of tables to music and giving them practice on the various computer software which is available such as 'Best Four Maths' (E.S.M.), 'Funfair' (Northern Micromedia), 'Monster Maths' (AVP) which reinforce 'almost learned tables' in a fun way. It may be more realistic to show them how to use a tables card or a pocket calculator efficiently.

For some dyslexic children, the mathematics presented in class is not a problem but because of poor literacy skills they may be unable to read and understand the instructions in their textbooks. This is the simplest problem to overcome as instructions can either be tape-recorded or the child can be paired with a good reader who can read the questions to him but must be instructed not to tell him the answers!

ORGANISATIONAL SKILLS

Most people appreciate that a dyslexic child has difficulty organising sounds and symbols into their correct sequence for reading and spelling, but it is not always realised that the dyslexic child's untidiness, poor concept of time, inability to remember more than one instruction at a time, and failure to remember to bring P.E. kit, football kit, swimming kit on the correct day are all part and parcel of the same problem. The dyslexic child may not have acquired a concept of time in its widest sense of days, weeks, months and years quite apart from learning to tell the time from a clock.

They find the sequencing of time difficult and may not be able to tell you what day it is, whether it is morning or afternoon. They may be thoroughly confused by *yesterday, tomorrow, next week, last week* etc. Teachers need to be understanding but at the same time must help the child to become more organised. Giving him a pictorial timetable where he can see clearly marked a picture of his football boots in the space for Tuesday afternoon and his swimming trunks on Friday morning can help but it is usually necessary to enlist the support of his parents so that they are reinforcing his organisation at home (see Christine Ostler's book, 'Dyslexia, A Parents' Survival Guide' for further help).

SELF-ESTEEM AND MOTIVATION

Self-esteem and motivation go hand in hand. Many dyslexic children have a very low self-esteem. They feel failures at school. Some may become depressed, some exhibit stress related ailments such as headaches, stomach aches, exhaustion etc. and miss a lot of schooling. Others may, through frustration, begin to be disruptive in class and playground, or try to gain the esteem of their peers by being either the class clown or the 'hard man'.

The late-diagnosed dyslexic child may have experienced years at school of being called lazy, stupid, careless etc. and it is hardly surprising that dyslexic children tend to give up more easily than their peers. Confidence building must be a priority for the class teacher. Explaining the nature of dyslexia to the child and emphasising that it is not his fault and that he is not stupid can be helpful but it is vital to present class work in a way that ensures success. The teacher's maxim must be to minimise failure and maximise success.

Chapter 8

The teacher must be ready to give praise and encouragement whenever possible and must be alert to situations which could prove difficult for the dyslexic. Give him praise for oral responses, mark his written work positively, give him credit for content and point out to him how many words he has written correctly and how many he has nearly got right. It is not necessary to dwell on his errors as he will already be more than aware of them, the teacher should be as encouraging as possible. Lawrence (1973) suggests that counselling in an uncritical atmosphere, providing opportunities for the child to talk about his family, friends, anxieties and aspirations, can build up self-esteem and enhance progress

Using 'Records of Achievement' can be a good approach to building self-esteem as the child is able to keep a record of everything he is proud of, whether related to school work or not. He is then able to look back at the things he has succeeded at, a certificate for swimming 25 metres, a cub scout badge, a page of sums all correct, a good piece of descriptive writing etc.

LEARNING TO LEARN (METACOGNITION)

Explain to the child why he is learning certain things so that he has an understanding of the structure and progression of what he is doing. Too often children do not see the relevance of certain lessons as they don't see where it fits into the big picture of education. Discuss with the child what he finds particularly difficult and ask him to identify what he would like to concentrate on next. Plan his next step with him so that he can see the relevance of his learning programme. If he can see that he is jointly planning his progress with you his motivation will increase. Bringing the child to an awareness of his own mental processes, reflecting on how he learns, how to strengthen memory and how to tackle problems systematically will all help the child to 'learn how to learn' (Nisbet and Shucksmith, 1984). Children will learn more effectively if they have an understanding of how they learn best and have a strategy for organising their learning.

CASE STUDY

This case study is intended to help highlight some of the points discussed in the chapter.

THE PUPIL

Robert, when I first met him, was just beginning primary seven. He had recently been assessed by the Educational Psychologist and was in the average range of intellectual ability with a weakness in verbal skills and a significant

Perspectives on Practice

immaturity in perceptual and motor skills. I assessed his reading using the Neale Analysis and the British Ability Scale Word Reading Test, and his spelling using the Vernon Graded Spelling Test.

His reading and spelling were both two and a half to three years behind his chronological age. His reading comprehension was one year behind his chronological age but when I reassessed his comprehension, having read the stories to him, his comprehension was three months in advance of his chronological age. I assessed his phonological awareness using the Code Cracker Phonic Test and found that he had large gaps in his knowledge and had great difficulty decoding multisyllabic words which he tended to telescope. He needed to follow a highly structured and cumulative programme and particularly needed practice in phonemic segmentation (Bryant and Bradley, 1985). His written work was almost unreadable, partly because of his poor spelling and reversal of letters but also because his handwriting was so poor with letters badly formed unjoined and with no size consistency. His maths, though better than his reading, was being hindered by his difficulty in reading instructions and his inability to memorise multiplication tables.

Most worrying of all was his behaviour. He had become very lethargic in class, yawned a great deal, hardly put pencil to paper and was generally extremely poorly motivated. He was becoming increasingly aggressive with the other children and there were incidents when he tried to injure himself by punching a metal post until his knuckles bled or by banging his head on a wall. He was also receiving medical treatment for migraine headaches and bedwetting.

All in all, what I was seeing was a very unhappy and frustrated boy who had no confidence in himself, hated school and had given up on school work.

ACTION PLAN

After discussions with the educational psychologist, class teacher and mother it was decided that I would work with Robert on a one to one basis for three 50 minute sessions a week. I would use part of one session to liaise and plan with the class teacher so that Robert's individualised learning programme would dovetail with the class work and she would also be reinforcing his programme in class. I also arranged to see Robert's mother, initially once a fortnight and then once a month to keep her informed of progress and to ensure that she was supporting appropriately at home.

I had four main aims :–

1. improve his self image
2. change his attitude to work
3. improve his behaviour with his peers
4. improve his reading, spelling and writing skills

TEACHING PROGRAMME

The first few sessions were very difficult. Robert was totally demoralised over school work and his eyes glazed over whenever a reading book was produced. I decided to abandon formal work from books and use the computer instead. As a first step I presented him with various adventure programmes (see references). I wanted the sessions to be enjoyable and motivating yet challenging.

These were excellent for problem solving and stimulating discussion. Most of the programmes had a great deal of 'on screen' reading, much of it too difficult for Robert but he was so keen to solve the adventure that he worked hard at decoding text on the screen which should have been too difficult for him.

He used the Phonic Code Cracker computer programme to cover the main gaps in his phonic knowledge. (Russell, 1992)

Lawrence (1973) suggests that providing opportunities for the child to talk about his anxieties, aspirations, family and friends can build up self-confidence, self-esteem and enhance progress. By working one-to-one with Robert I was able to give him the opportunity to talk about himself. We discussed dyslexia and what it can mean for children and adults. I told him about other dyslexic people I knew and how they were coping with their difficulties. I emphasised at all times that being dyslexic did not mean that you were stupid (Siegal, 1989) but that you had a specific problem just as some people are deaf or have poor eyesight etc. I used the term 'dyslexia' rather than specific learning difficulties since the mother was happier with the commonly used terminology.

I also used a metacognitive approach to help him become aware of and take responsibility for his own learning (Nisbet and Shucksmith, 1984). Hunter-Carsch (1990) suggests that we should be giving children strategies for learning and that the emphasis in teaching should be on *'de-toning anxiety and building confidence through self-awareness'*.

LIAISON WITH CLASS TEACHER

During my consultations with the class teacher we looked at parts of the curriculum that were causing problems for Robert. I assisted the class teacher in providing differentiated worksheets for various lessons and projects that were being done. These were useful for many more children than Robert and he found some success in class at last and was able to work with a group. The class teacher was very co-operative and was willing to allow Robert to sit beside a 'buddy' who would read instructions for him but not give him the answers to questions; she marked written work for content rather than spelling; she allowed him to tape record his stories for transcription later; he used a multiplication/division table card for maths; most important of all, she tried very hard to find something positive to say about every piece of work that he did.

LIAISON WITH HOME

At our regular meetings I was able to convince mother that she was doing more harm than good by drilling phonics, spelling and tables every night. I encouraged her to be more positive with him and to concentrate on helping Robert to become more organised. She began to encourage him to join clubs such as the Boys' Brigade and a karate club and to socialise more. She bought him a BBC computer for his birthday and most of his homework then tended to be related to that.

REVIEW

After 4 months we reviewed his progress. Everyone agreed that his behaviour had improved and his mother reported that he was wetting the bed and having migraine attacks less frequently. He was also showing more interest in his school work. I was anxious that Robert did not become too dependent on one to one support and I felt it was important that Robert worked on the same curriculum as his classmates as much as possible so for the second half of his primary seven year I dropped one of the individual teaching sessions and worked co-operatively with the class teacher. This was invaluable as I could link his individual lessons more closely to his class work and it also allowed me to work with Robert in a group of children, lessening his dependence on one-to-one support.

CREATIVE WRITING

I now decided to begin more formal work with Robert. Still using the computer he used the 'Keyboard Skills' programme (SCET) to speed up his typing and began to use the 'Folio' wordprocessing workbook package (NCET). Robert was still very reluctant to 'write' his own stories. The breakthrough came after he had been to a computer camp with his class. He was so stimulated by this that I persuaded him to write a report for the local newspaper. His report was published and he glowed for a week. He became a more enthusiastic writer and produced more written work than he had every done before. The quality of his wordprocessed writing was much better than his handwritten stories. He spotted spelling errors more readily and found it easy to edit text when the sequence of his story was wrong.

Chris Singleton (1991) confirms this and states that the editing flexibility of wordprocessing helps dyslexics to overcome their difficulties with organising ideas and structuring written work. He also stresses the motivational value of computer assisted learning which increases the time that children are willing to practice academic skills so that mastery learning can take place.

READING

I wanted him to begin to read from books again. His reading was slow and stilted and he still tended to yawn excessively when asked to read. He lost the place frequently, had difficulty with visual tracking and misread many of the 'little' words. I used the Ann Arbor visual tracking exercises to reinforce left to right tracking. Initially, I used the 'Skyways Readers' (Collins Educational). I stressed that we were reading for enjoyment and the story needed to be read fluently if we were going to enjoy it. We experimented with ways of speeding up his reading. For example using a stopwatch. I would time him reading a page and then he would read it two or three times more, trying to beat his time on each reading. He responded very well to this approach and we then took turn about at reading alternate pages.

He became very interested in the 'Nick Dick the Detective' books from the 'Skyways Series' and another opportunity for writing came when, having read one particular book, he was very annoyed with the ending as he felt there was not enough proof to incriminate the gardener! I encouraged him to write to the author to complain about the weak story line in this particular book. He was highly delighted to receive an apologetic reply from the author enclosing a book from another series as compensation. This meant of course that he had to write a thank you letter as well. By selecting his reading books very carefully he continued to improve in reading fluency and comprehension. He particularly enjoyed the 'Starpol Series' (Ginn and Co.) and the 'Trog Series' (Thomas Nelson). To encourage careful, accurate reading Robert used two close procedure books, 'False Teeth and Vampires' and 'Astronauts and the Black Death' (LDA)

HANDWRITING

As Robert's handwriting was so poor I had to re-teach letter formation using cursive script. Because his letters were poorly sized, I used 'tramline' paper to make it easier for him to see that tall letters go above the top tramline and tails hang down below the bottom tramline. I felt that teaching cursive script would eliminate the b/d and p/q reversals which were such a feature of Robert's written work and would also encourage a more flowing style. Robert was very negative about this to begin with as he complained that it was too slow but after timing me writing a passage in unjoined infant script and then again in cursive script he had to agree that once he had mastered the new script his writing should be much neater and faster. He worked enthusiastically through a set of cursive script workbooks. Within a few months his handwriting improved dramatically and for the first time in his life he had some of his written work displayed on the classroom wall.

SPELLING

Robert's visual memory was very poor. He could spell the same word in three different ways in a short passage of writing. He tended to spell phonetically and had little or no knowledge of spelling rules or common letter combinations. Robert needed to use a multi-sensory approach to spelling and I used a combination of the 'Look, Cover, Write, Check' method advocated by Margaret Peters and the 'Simultaneous Oral Spelling' technique used by Lynette Bradley. Again much work was done on the computer using the 'Cracker Spell' programme (Jordanhill College Publications). Teaching word families and spelling rules using 'Signposts to Spelling' (Heinemann) and 'Logical Spelling' (Collins) helped Robert to see that there was a pattern to language and for words that he just could not remember we devised pictorial mnemonics. As spelling will continue to be a problem for Robert, I thought that it was important that he should develop skills for coping.

Before his transfer to secondary school he was given a Tandy WP2 laptop computer with a spell checker. Much of his individual teaching time during those last few weeks of term was devoted to making sure he could operate the laptop competently as we hoped that he would do most of his written work in secondary on the computer. He was delighted with this and quickly mastered the intricacies of the machine. It was quite a potent status symbol for him as it made him feel grown up and important.

LIAISON WITH SECONDARY STAFF

The principal teacher of learning support was invited to join the class teacher and myself to observe Robert's difficulties and to plan how best to support him when he transferred to S1. It was not felt appropriate to continue with one-to-one teaching but the secondary school made sure that Robert would be in a class that received a great deal of extra support through co-operative teaching. All subject teachers were made aware of Robert's specific problems and were asked to co-operate on using a standard correction code and not penalising Robert for poor spelling or asking him to read aloud.

The use of a 'Buddy' to help him read questions on worksheets or textbooks would continue and the school would photocopy notes for him instead of expecting him to copy them for himself as he found this very difficult. The secondary school was already running a successful paired reading project involving sixth year pupils as tutors for first year children. Robert would be included in this and his 'tutor' would be carefully chosen and given some insight into Robert's specific difficulties. Robert was also given a 'consultation' time with the learning support teacher each week when he would be able to discuss with him any problems that he was facing.

CONCLUSION

At the end of the year when Robert was re-assessed, his reading age had improved by eighteen months and his spelling age by 12 months. His handwriting was neat and well-formed. However everyone felt that the greatest gains were in the three other original aims:

1. his self-confidence was markedly improved, the bed wetting had stopped and the migraine headaches were infrequent
2. He was now well motivated in class and was prepared to 'have a go' at most things
3. His aggressive behaviour had ceased. He was now the class 'expert' on the computer and the other children asked him for help which was a great boost to his self-image.

The success of this intervention was largely due to the holistic perspective adopted. This has been highlighted in this chapter and includes addressing the child's needs, examining the curriculum content, differentiating the mode of teaching and learning, utilising the available resources, and consulting with other professionals and very importantly the parents.

Chapter 8

REFERENCES

BRADLEY L., (1980), *Assessing Reading Difficulties : A Diagnostic and Remedial Approach*. Macmillan Education.
CARBO M., DUNN R. and DUNN K., (1986), *Teaching Students to Read through their Individual Learning Styles*. Englewood Cliffs, NJ: Prentice-Hall.
CROMBIE M., (1990), *Specific Learning Difficulties (Dyslexia) – A Teacher's Guide*. Jordanhill College Publications, Glasgow.
DEPARTMENT OF EDUCATION AND SCIENCE, (1985), *The Curriculum 5 to 16*. HMSO.
HENDERSON A., (1989), *Maths for Dyslexics*. St David's College, Llandudno.
LAWRENCE D., (1973), *Improved Reading through Counselling*. Ward Lock.
NISBET J. and SHUCKSMITH J., (1988), *The Seventh Sense*. SCRE.
OSTLER CHRISTINE, (1991), *Dyslexia, A Parents' Guide*. Ammonite Books.
POLLOK J., *Signposts to Spelling*. Heinemann Education.
SIMPSON M., (1989), *Differentiation in the Primary School : Investigations of Learning and Teaching*. Northern College, Aberdeen.
SIEGEL L. S., (1989), 'IQ is irrelevant to the definition of learning disabilities'. *Journal of Learning Disabilities*, 22, 469-78.

TEACHING MATERIAL

Astronauts and the Black Death and *False Teeth and Vampires*. Learning Development Aids.
Bangers and Mash. Longmans.
CRIPPS CHARLES, *A Hand for Spelling*. Learning Development Aids.
Five Minute Thrillers and Tapes. Learning Development Aids.
Franklin Spellmaster. Venture Marketing.
Fuzzbuzz. Oxford University Press.
Help Games. H.E.L.P. Educational Games, Didcot, Oxon.
LIDDICOAT A., *Don't Let Spelling Get You Down*. Tregear Publications, Ickenham, Middlesex.
Logical Spelling. Collins Educational.
ACE Dictionary. Learning Development Aids Ltd.
Nick Dick Detective Series. Collins Educational.
Pergamon Dictionary of Perfect Spelling. Thomas Nelson & Sons Ltd.
Picture Writing Series. Learning Materials Ltd.

Phonic Rummy. Kenworthy Educational Services.
Reading Games. Macmillan Educational.
Rescue Readers. Ginn & Co.
ROOT BETTY, *Reading Games Series.* NES Arnold.
RUSSELL S., (1992), *Phonic Code Cracker.* Jordanhill College Publications, Glasgow.
RUSSELL S., (1992), *Cracker Spell.* Jordanhill College Publications, Glasgow.
Skyways Series. Collins Educational.
Starpol Series. Ginn & Co.
Grippy Pencil Grip. Learning Development Aids.
Trog Series. Thomas Nelson & Sons Ltd.
TOPPING, SCOBLE and OXLEY, (1988), *Cued Spelling.* Kirklees Metropolitan Council.
Tramline Writing Paper. Philip and Tacey.
Wellington Square. Thomas Nelson & Sons Ltd.
WENDON L., *Letterland Teaching Programme.* Letterland Ltd., Cambridge.

COMPUTER PROGRAMMES

(BBC 'B'/ Master, though many now also available for other machines).
Animated Alphabet. (Sherston).
A to Z. (IEC Software).
Concept Keyboard Matching. (Scetlander).
Cracker Spell. (Jordanhill College Publications).
Dragon World. (4 Mation).
Dyslexia Aid. (Edsoft).
Flowers of Crystal. (4 Mation).
Folio. (ESM) and *Folio Workbook* package (NCET).
Funfair. (Northern Micromedia).
Fun School, (Europress Software).
Games For Dyslexic Children, (IEC Software).
Granny's Garden, (4 Mation).
Fleet Street Phantom. (Sherston).
Monster Maths. (AVP).
Nature Park Adventure. (Sherston).
Phonic Code Cracker. (Jordanhill College Publications).
PAL (predictive adaptive lexicon for PC's). Scetlander Ltd., Glasgow.
Predictype. Scetlander Ltd., Glasgow.
Sellardore Tales. (Sherston).
Stylus. (MAPE).
The Worst Witch. (Sherston).

Chapter 9

DIFFERENTIATION IN THE SECONDARY SCHOOL

DAVID DODDS

INTRODUCTION

Differentiation has become a widely used term for a wide variety of teaching approaches, taking different forms in different subjects, so it is as well to be clear at the outset what is meant by the term.

The SOED defines differentiation as:
'. . . The identification of, and effective provision for a range of abilities in the classroom . . . Differentiated approaches should mean that the needs of the very able and of children with learning difficulties are discerned and met'.

This definition clearly implies that the starting place in planning to differentiate a course or unit has to be the pupils and their abilities. This will determine the contexts and content to a large extent, rather than having the content determine what it is pupils will be expected to do.

ROLE OF THE SUBJECT TEACHER

Considerable skill and expertise exists within learning support departments in direct teaching methods that contribute to improving the language skills of pupils with specific learning difficulties. Equally, in advising subject teachers on appropriate teaching strategies or the suitability of materials, learning support teachers have a great deal to offer in supporting such pupils. Subject teachers on the other hand often feel particularly challenged by such pupils and lack confidence that their training or subsequent experience has equipped them with the skills necessary to teach them.

It is, however, no more appropriate to seek the solution of such difficulties principally within the pupil than it is for pupils with other difficulties. If the curriculum is differentiated to allow for the full range of ability and structured to take account of young peoples' learning needs then pupils with specific learning difficulties will only have difficulty gaining access to the curriculum in the most extreme cases.

In fact the subject teacher has a crucial role to play. The vast majority, if not all of the time spent in school by pupils with even the most severe specific learning difficulties will be spent in subject classes being taught by subject teachers working alone. The subject teacher's expertise is also invaluable for developing the skills, approaches and insights of the subject in all pupils. At a time when the curriculum is crowded as never before, the justification for including a subject is very often its distinctive approach or methodology, and it is therefore of great importance that that approach is embodied in the activities of all pupils.

It should always be borne in mind that the teacher is the most readily available information source in any classroom and the use of a carefully planned class lesson as a stimulus to a sequence of activities should not be underestimated. A short exposition possibly using visual aids, but making full use of tone, emphasis and careful pacing, then developing understanding with open ended questioning and responses to pupil questions remains a powerful tool of the classroom teacher.

As stated earlier different subjects would, and should, approach teaching and learning situations differently with each emphasising the particular skills and methods that characterise that subject, and it is possible that some subject teachers may feel that the approaches suggested here are not particularly relevant to their subject.

The maths teacher might have doubts about the use of discussion techniques but in fact mathematical language is least like everyday language and will pose many problems for learners. The option of removing language completely and presenting the pupil with a page of examples is likely to make the situation worse rather than better as it leads to an all or nothing dependence on algorithms. If these are not recalled accurately there can be no possibility of success. In fact anyone spending time in maths classes, particularly mixed ability, cannot fail to be struck by the high level of 'informal peer tutoring' that arises naturally, with pupils explaining processes to each other quite readily. This is an aspect that can be fostered and developed to take account of the needs of the learners to deploy their own spoken language in attempting to understand a problem. Pupils might not only be encouraged but required to explain what they are doing to their peers. The increasing use of problem solving approaches also lends itself naturally to discussion.

A modern languages teacher might point out that discussion in English is, in fact, counter productive and discussion in a foreign language not possible till late in the development of the language. This may be so but the main factors in learning remain unchanged and need to be taken into account. The kind of vocabulary and situations used to develop the modern language will need to reflect closely the kind of language and situations the pupil is familiar with in his own language. Also critical listening is extremely important in developing spoken language. Where pupils are working in pairs the listener can often be passive. By requiring the listener to identify and correct errors made by the speaker, both partners can be involved throughout the activity. Equally short or closed assignments, with their emphasis on right or wrong answers, can be very discouraging. Pupils are much more likely to respond to more open-ended assignments where absolute precision comes second to genuine communication.

MATERIALS AND APPROACHES

To develop resources for pupils with specific learning difficulties, an appropriate starting point can be an examination of existing materials with a view to adapting them to meet the needs of the pupils concerned. It might be anticipated that this would be a process of simplifying text, providing tape recorded text where necessary, and simplifying written assignments or altering them to provide alternatives to writing. It may, however, be necessary to substantially revise units of work to alter the sequence of activities or to change the emphasis in a particular assignment.

This possible need to substantially redraft can be due to the emphasis on presenting information leading to an individual written outcome as the organising principle of the unit. Although units may certainly cover the topic area it is much less certain that it would be learned. Polling a study of a number of such units I found little evidence of a consistent view about the nature of the learner or how learning took place. The underlying assumption was that exposure to the materials would be sufficient in itself. This appeared to be confirmed by the findings of recent study (Off the Record, SCRE 1991) that subject teachers were concerned to try to ensure that pupils **learned the same content.**

Where the content is the starting point for course design the options for differentiation are likely to be reduced. Differentiation is often attempted either by having all pupils doing the same things but at different rates, e.g. all pupils work through the topics covered in a specific textbook but work individually and with different levels of support, or pupils follow courses at different levels of difficulty but covering the same areas in terms of the topic covered. On this model pupils working on the lowest level might be expected to complete a blank-filling activity or word-search while pupils at a higher level might give single sentence answers to questions and at a still higher level might have to write a paragraph. The information leading to the pupil response would be presented at differing degrees of reading level and complexity

A common approach to course construction that combines both elements is the core plus options model where all pupils in a class work through a common core which is followed by a criterion referenced test. The results of this test determine whether pupils go on to carry out extension or remediation activities before completing another final test. In practice such a course is extremely difficult to construct. Problems tend to arise on what should constitute the core. If the core is limited as far as possible then the time spent by pupils on separate extension or remediation activities can increase to such an extent that it would be difficult to describe pupils as following the 'same' course. If on the other hand a wider view of the core is taken then the possibilities for meeting the needs of the least and most able decrease. Underlying this approach is the concept of mastery learning, and defining mastery for a set of tasks can be problematic as can testing for it. Nevertheless such an approach can offer many pupils the opportunity to work on appropriate texts and at a suitable pace, and there are many examples of departments running successful courses along these lines. The structure in itself is, however, no guarantee that differentiation will occur. Teaching and learning approaches are the key to differentiation, whatever course structure is adopted.

PRINCIPLES OF DISCUSSION

In developing units and courses it is essential to take account of:

(i) pupils' language skills;

(ii) pupils' existing knowledge.

It is essential both to recognise and to capitalise on the highly developed language skills of all pupils, and to bear in mind that even pupils with reading and / or writing difficulties have considerable oral language skills. It is also important to keep in mind that the pupil's understanding will depend on how well he can assimilate new input with what he already knows. The most effective way of allowing pupils to bring to bear both their existing knowledge and their oral language skills is to give a high priority to talk and discussion as part of the learning process. Talking and listening to talk, being able to rehearse and examine ideas using their own language, is the most powerful tool and occasionally the only effective tool that pupils are able to bring to bear in understanding the curriculum.

Chapter 9

ACTIVITY 4

THE PEOPLE OF SOUTH AFRICA

INFORMATION CARD

When it was elected in 1948, the Nationalist Government passed laws to support its policy of APARTHEID. Apartheid means separate development for people of different races. The government thought that it was best for each race to live separately. This would allow them to keep their own language, customs and traditions.

- Look carefully at all the information below. Now complete the graphs on the sheet called, 'SOUTH AFRICA'S PEOPLE: FACTS AND FIGURES.'

TABLE 1: SOUTH AFRICA: POPULATION

Racial group	Population	% of Total
WHITE: People whose ancestors came from Europe. English or Afrikaans (a kind of Dutch)	5.0 million	13.7%
AFRICAN: Blacks who are descendents of the people who lived in Southern Africa before the whites arrived	28.0 million	75.0%
COLOURED: 'Mixed Race.' Descendents of early marriages between blacks and whites	3.2 million	8.7%
ASIAN: The people whose ancestors came from India to work for the British on the railways they built after they arrived in South Africa	1.0 million	2.6%

TABLE 2: INCOME, PENSIONS, SPENDING ON EDUCATION, PUPILS PER TEACHER

	WHITE	BLACK	COLOURED	ASIAN
INCOME PER PERSON (RANDS per year)	15,000	1250	3000	4600
OLD AGE PENSIONS (RANDS per month)	280	180	230	230
SPENDING PER PUPILS (RANDS per year)	1300	500	1300	2600
PUPILS PER TEACHER	19	40	22	20

Chapter 9

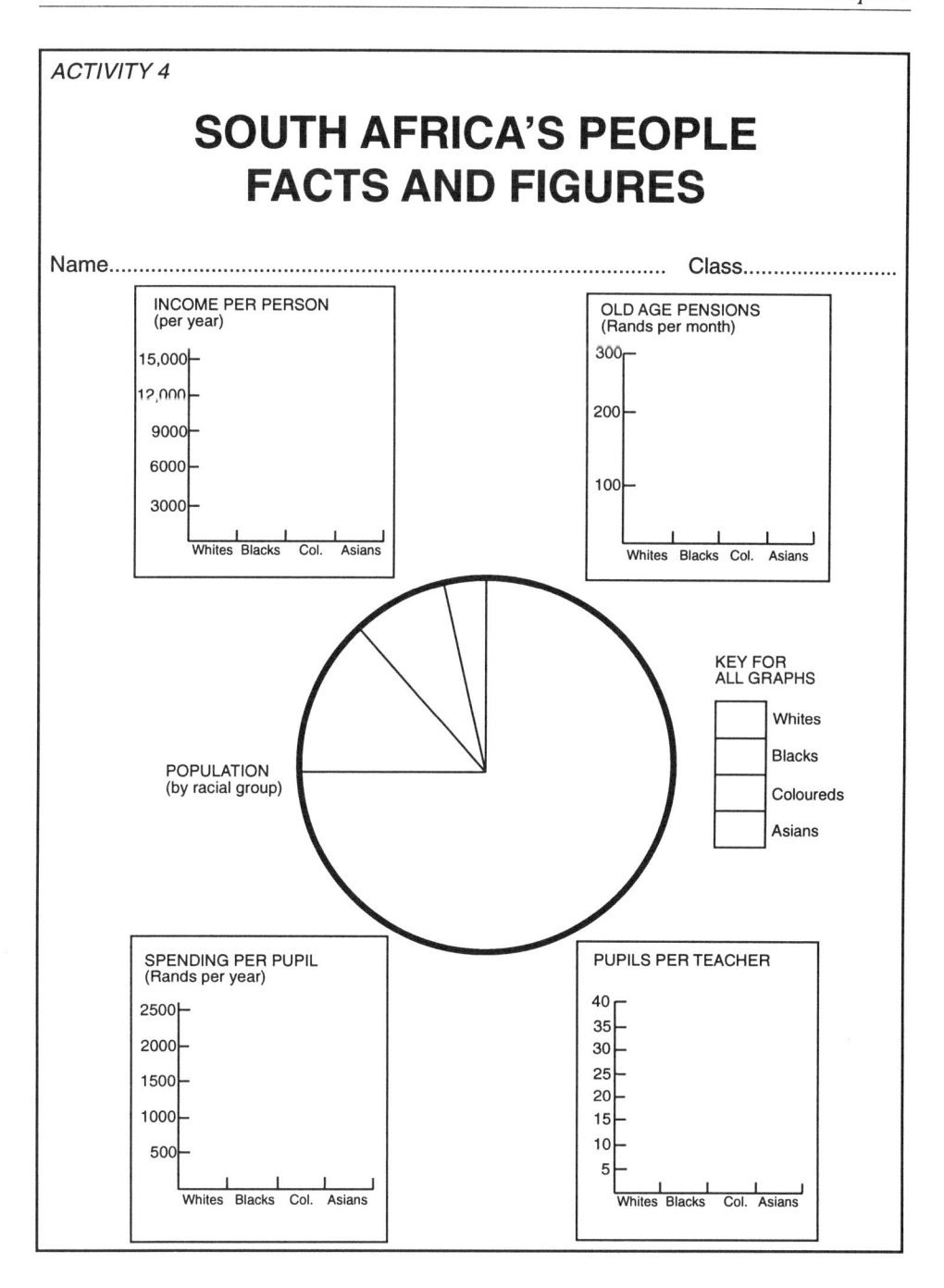

ACTIVITY 4

SOUTH AFRICA'S PEOPLE FACTS AND FIGURES

Name.. Class........................

INCOME PER PERSON (per year)

15,000
12,000
9000
6000
3000

Whites Blacks Col. Asians

OLD AGE PENSIONS (Rands per month)

300
200
100

Whites Blacks Col. Asians

POPULATION (by racial group)

KEY FOR ALL GRAPHS

☐ Whites
☐ Blacks
☐ Coloureds
☐ Asians

SPENDING PER PUPIL (Rands per year)

2500
2000
1500
1000
500

Whites Blacks Col. Asians

PUPILS PER TEACHER

40
35
30
25
20
15
10
5

Whites Blacks Col. Asians

Perspectives on Practice

Chapter 9

ACTIVITY 4   Fig. 1

SOUTH AFRICA'S PEOPLE
GROUP DISCUSSION SHEET

Name.. Class.....................

- Look at your sheet 'SOUTH AFRICA'S PEOPLE: FACTS AND FIGURES'
- In groups of AT LEAST FOUR, discuss the information then complete the following table:

Standard of Living	Racial Group
HIGHEST	
↓	
LOWEST	

- Write the words ASIAN, BLACK, COLOURED and WHITE on four pieces of paper. Fold them up and get each member of the group to pick one.
- How do you feel about your choice? EXPLAIN WHY

- If you could, would you change?
  If YES, which group would you have chosen? WHY?

- In your groups, try to explain why the living standards of the racial groups are so different. Write your ideas in the space below.

GROUP DISCUSSION

Encouraging pupils to work together on discussion tasks in small groups or even in pairs can be a means of providing support for less able group members and allowing groups of differing abilities to tackle complex tasks. An example (fig. 1) taken from an S2 Modern Studies unit on South Africa illustrates how this approach might work in practice. In the original form the sequence was as shown, an information card, followed by completion of the graphs and then the discussion. By altering the sequence so that the discussion activities precede the completion of the graphs the activity becomes much more acessible. The information card is extremely dense, containing a great deal of complex information. For many pupils working individually on this sheet would be a daunting prospect, but taking part in a group discussion, hearing the ideas re-phrased in familiar language, and being required to offer their own understanding of the material to the group allows pupils of all abilities to profit from the process, either in the support it offers or in the demands it makes not only to understand the material but to explain that understanding to others.

Groups are not seen as being fixed but would vary from task to task, on occasions being pupil selected or perhaps teacher selected for a particular purpose, perhaps to group together children who were felt to be hesitant in offering ideas or to ensure a balance between different levels of ability. Where a particular topic or idea is felt to be of central importance the teacher might decide to make use of tutorial groups within the class, either teacher led, or led by a pupil combining a good understanding of the ideas being discussed with the ability to lead a discussion.

In addition to promoting understanding of the topic under discussion the group situation can be used to assess understanding by use of reporting back. Individuals can report back to small groups, or groups to the whole class, orally, perhaps using visual aids.

If group discussion is to play a central role in the learning process it follows that the process itself, rather than just the outcomes of the process, must be taught and assessed within the context in which they are to be used. While many of the processes that shape group discussion, such as the ability to listen critically and to develop an argument, will be common to all subjects the type of task undertaken will vary from subject to subject and should reflect the skills and priorities of that subject. A discussion in Science might well centre on the variables that need to be controlled if an experiment is to be reliable, while a discussion in History might centre on the interests and therefore the reliability of a particular source. In each case the criteria to be used will need to be taught and developed. There will be

Chapter 9

> ACTIVITY 6   Fig. 2A
>
> # THE HOMELANDS
>
> Name.. Class........................
>
> ## INDIVIDUAL WORK
>
> - Get a copy of THE HOMELANDS INFORMATION CARD
> - Read the information and look carefully at the map
> - Complete this passage:
>
> When the Nationalist Government divided South Africa, the areas for black people were
>
> known as .... Where they were sent depended on
>
> the home of their .... Families were often ....
>
> because some people worked for whites in the... These
>
> people lived in ....outside the cities.
>
> An example of a HOMELAND is..
>
> An example of a TOWNSHIP is ....

occasions when a teacher may wish to emphasise only these subject specific aspects of a task and may group pupils by their understanding in that particular aspect of the work to ensure that pupils are able to develop through working with others at a similar level.

While working in groups on discussion based activities will allow pupils of differing abilities to cope more efficiently with information, another important factor in developing understanding is the use to which the information is put.

This example (fig. 2a) from the same Modern Studies unit shows a fairly typical type of pupil activity. The pupil, having read a section of text, is required to fill in the blanks in this paragraph to ascertain whether or not he has understood the original information. A number of points arise out of this activity.

(i) Taking into account what has been said earlier, I would argue strongly that requiring the pupil to deal with the text individually is much less effective than using the text as the basis for group discussion activities.

(ii) Even allowing for the fact that the missing words are supplied and that they all represent key ideas for this topic, a pupil cannot begin to cope with the exercise as a means of checking understanding of the ideas involved unless he can cope with the exercise as a piece of reading difficulties. This type of exercise requires the pupil to understand the context of the missing word as well as the word itself and is always likely to prove problematic for any pupil with reading difficulties even though the words and the ideas behind them are well enough understood. If the pupil realises that the missing word has the same number of letters as there are dashes in the blank, the activity can be completed without understanding either the original text or the comprehension check. (In practice pupils presented with this type of activity will frequently reduce it to a letter count, just as presented with a worksheet giving a text followed by numbered questions they will often begin reading at the first question, using the test only as a 'mine' from which correct answers are to be extracted).

Fig. 2B

GROUP WORK

- In your groups, discuss the HOMELANDS INFORMATION CARD.
- Complete the table below: use ALL the information

THE HOMELANDS	
Advantages to Whites	Disadvantages to Blacks

Chapter 9

(iii) This is a good example of an activity likely to ensure coverage, rather than learning of a group of ideas. The paragraph for completion is similar to the original text in which the terms were presented. All that is really required of the pupil is literal comprehension. Provided the paragraph is understood the missing terms can almost be transposed from the original text. The information does not need to be reorganised in any way. The sequence of activities is intended to introduce information for pupils to read as individuals and to demonstrate their understanding individually before moving to group discussion. In practice the group discussion activity (fig. 2b) makes the blank filling exercise redundant and it would be more effective for the group discussion to be the means for developing the understanding of the ideas in the original text. Individual follow up from the discussion might have required the pupil to re-organise the information or to use it in another context, eg writing a script for a radio broadcast or writing as a black South African to explain to a Scottish teenager what the Homelands mean at a personal level. Compare this sequence of activities with the earlier sequence (fig. 1) where the pupils were required to represent the information in graph form. (Even here opportunities for further differentiation exist by allowing pupils to opt for producing suitable graphs without the templates)

WRITTEN RESPONSES

The nature of individual written responses as illustrated by fig. 2a is extremely important from the point of view of differentiation of the curriculum; in that example or in the type of 'text followed by questions' activity, even where care is taken to go beyond purely literal comprehension questions the room for differentiation of responses is extremely limited. If all that is required is a sentence then the difference between the 'best' possible answer, an adequate answer and an unsuccessful answer is very small. A pupil who has fully understood is denied the opportunity to display the extent of that understanding and the pupil who has not understood may not reveal the nature of source of his failure to understand. Written assignments need to be as open ended as possible to allow pupils to extend their understanding in their completion.

Pupils should be given the opportunity to:

re-organise information, e.g. changing events from chronological order to their order of importance;

re-present information, e.g. present it in the form of a graph or table;

evaluate information, e.g. in history to consider the reliability of a source; in Science to consider the validity of an experiment;

respond imaginatively to information, e.g. to write as one of the protagonists in a situation;

relay information, e.g. to 'teach' a new concept to a peer or group of peers, or to younger children.

This is by no means intended as an exhaustive list. Subject teachers will undoubtedly be able to offer further alternatives for their particular subject, and the balance of activities might alter from subject to subject, but every subject offers opportunities to develop understanding that goes far beyond literal comprehension.

THE USE OF TEXT

The use of printed text as the main or even sole source of information has limitations even when group discussion activities are being used as a means of allowing access to the material. In terms of involving pupils directly in a situation it requires a leap of imagination on the part of the readers even with the highest quality of written text. Much more direct access to information about a problem or situation, can be given by using video-tapes, audio-tapes or indeed talk by the teacher or other individual with first hand experience. In the unit on South Africa already referred to the second half of the unit is organised around a commercial video-tape based on the experiences of four British teenagers living for a month with South African teenagers. This allows complex and often difficult issues to be explored in a very direct and powerful manner. The sequence in the film that contrasts the opulent lifestyle of the white South African family with the black teenager collecting water to wash in from a standpipe illustrates inequality with a power that would be difficult to achieve even with the best of textbooks or worksheets.

In setting assignments we need to allow pupils sufficient opportunity to bring what they already know to bear on the task and to extend their understanding, before setting a task that requires them to rework the input in some way that will allow us to measure how their understanding has grown.

CONCLUSION

In seeking to differentiate the curriculum in the secondary school it has become common to try to provide different levels of printed input or to require different levels of written response while at the same time setting strict limits on the length and nature of the response. In short it has been an attempt to differentiate on paper, to adjust the input and the output. If we are to meet a wide range of learning needs within the same subject class we need to concentrate on the area between the input and output – the learning skills and processes that pupils are expected to develop through the activities on offer. It is here that pupils with specific learning difficulties can develop skills in learning often in collaboration with others, to develop and refine the characteristic skills and perspectives of each subject area.

REFERENCES

ALLAN, BROWN and MUNN, (eds). *Off The Record: Mainstream provision for pupils with non-recorded lerning difficulties in primary and secondary schools.* SCRE.

Chapter 10

A PHONIC ATTACK STRUCTURED SKILLS PROGRAMME (P.A.S.S.)

HELEN CALCLUTH

BACKGROUND

The programme which will be described in this chapter is a multi-sensory structured phonics programme for children with dyslexic-type difficulties. Recognising the limitations of other similar multi-sensory programmes, this programme developed by the author, attempts to overcome these through acknowledging the individual needs of children and in particular the difficulties with auditory discrimination, sequencing and blending displayed by children with dyslexic type difficulties.

The PASS programme, was developed to tackle the problem of Specific Learning Difficulties in reading and spelling in a practical and viable way within the mainstream school setting. It is designed to be used in a whole-class or group situation and if used in the early stages can prevent the specific learning difficulty from becoming severe. Although the programme focuses on the whole-class or small group situation, it can still be tailored to the individual needs of each. Older dyslexic children and adults can also benefit from the Programme.

PROGRAMME

The programme deals only with single syllable phonic words. Reading and spelling skills are taught together through phonics. PASS cards (single letter, blend and digraph cards) are used to make words. The programme is presented in a cumulative, structured, phonic order, with accompanying wordlists at each level. The presentation of the structure highlights auditory discrimination skills.

- **Phonic Structure - main programme**

	Level A	consonant/vowel/consonant words
	Level B	Use of k and c
	Level C	Initial blends
	Level D	end blends

Level E   -ck, -ll, -ff, -ss, -zz
Level F   sh, ch, th, qu, wh
Level G   'magic' -e
Level H   w/wh, f/th/v, ng/nk (auditory discrimination)
Level I   oo, ee, ea, ea, ai, ay, oa, ou, aw, au, oi, oy, ow, ow and vowel digraphs with letter -k.

A Supplementary Programme deals solely with auditory confusions and is used as additional material where a child or group of children have particular difficulty. It deals with:

1   medial vowels
2   endings -t, -d, -k, -p, -b and n/m
3   s blends
4   r/l blends
5   j/d, ch/sh, ch/j, j/dr, ch/tr
6   -ar, -or, -er, -ir, -ur
7   'magic' - e with -re and -ke

- **PASS Cards**

   PASS cards have rounded top corners to facilitate easy arrangement for use. They are colour-coded to help establish vowel/consonant awareness and the development of figure ground discrimination for blends and digraphs. PASS cards are used in a multi-sensory way. The learner therefore is trained to listen to the speaker and vocalise each sound as he sequentially places the letter cards from left to right. This means that the learner is simultaneously **hearing** the sound and **seeing** the letter card as he **places** it in sequence. This procedure helps to integrate auditory and visual skills and develops automatic sequencing skills.

Examples of words at different PASS levels

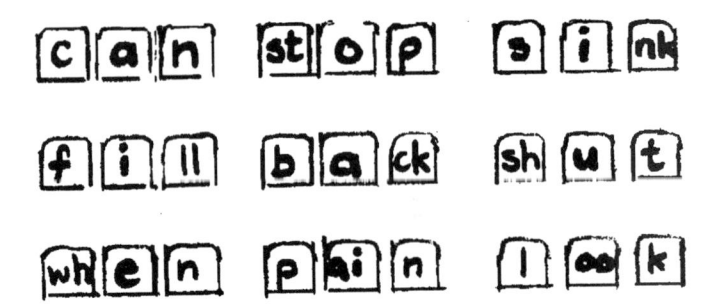

c|a|n st|o|p s|i|nk

f|i|ll b|a|ck sh|u|t

wh|e|n p|ai|n l|oo|k

Magic – e cards

s|a|m|e ch|i|m|e

Single consonants are colour coded in black, vowels and vowel diagraps in green, initial blends in red, end blends in purple, and double letters and consonant diagraphs in blue.

The cards can also be used by the teacher to form words for the learner to decode.

In written spelling, the learner must be trained to use a similar multi-sensory technique. he must simultaneously sound aloud each letter or digraph as he writes it, thus assisting in the integration of auditory, visual and kinaesthetic channels.

- **Implementation**

The programme can be implemented by the class teacher or the school learning support teacher, for an individual child, or a group of children, with specific learning difficulties. It can also be used to advantage in the whole class situation. No specialised knowledge is required to utilise and implement the programme.

In the whole class situation, the programme can be used as an effective intervention programme, at Primary 3 or 4 stage. The class is taught, or reminded of, a simple phonic skill or rule, for example, letter 'x' makes the sound (ks), or double -ll, -ss, ff, -zz comes after a short vowel in a one syllable word. The skills are presented in a cumulative structured order. The class is given a simple spelling test to diagnose difficulty in a particular skill. Those who have difficulty in the particular skill, become a selected group to work on the PASS cards. When the selected group has mastered this skill, the class is taught and tested in the next skill in the structure, and a new group with difficulties in this skill selected to work on PASS cards at this level. Selected groups will be different for each PASS level, although there may be a core group of children who require every level. Children with no dyslexic-type difficulties will not be selected by testing procedures and, therefore, will not receive input.

- **Whole Class**

    If the programme is used in the whole-class situation, it gives all children in the class the same known cumulative framework of phonic knowledge, which the teacher can use as a basis for spelling correction in free writing. This is an important aspect of the programme. An error can be pointed out to the child, and he can use his own learned phonic structure to correct the error.

    In the whole-class situation, the programme is not exclusive, and can be used to complement, any phonic programme in place in the school. It is suitable also for children familiar with Letterland characters.

    In the classroom situation the PASS programme can easily become part of the language programme. To fit in with class organisation, PASS cards can be conveniently used with selected groups of children sitting round a table after group activities in reading.

- **Evaluation of the Programme**

    Although in most cases the PASS programme has been used in conjunction with other programmes, the instances where it has been used as the principal means of dealing with the dyslexic difficulty have been well evaluated. Below is an example of one such evaluation following the use of the PASS programme in a whole-class situation.

- **Whole-class Situation**

    A Primary 3 class, in which about one third of the children displayed dyslexic-type difficulties, was chosen for PASS Programme intervention.

Two of these children had been assessed by the School Psychologist as having severe specific learning difficulties, requiring individual specialist input. I worked with the class teacher, on a cooperative teaching basis, for 15 blocks of one and a half hours, from September 1992 to March 1993. The class teacher taught the appropriate teaching point and administered the relative spelling test before each PASS level. On my visits, I implemented the programme with the groups of children, selected at each level, as having difficulty. Only five children required no input.

The Burt Word Reading Test was used for reading assessment. For calculation purposes, it was assumed that below a reading accuracy of 6 years 4 months, an improvement of two words was equivalent to one month. In the class of twenty four children, tested in reading, before and after the implementation of the PASS Programme, the average increase in reading accuracy was 10.5 months in six months. On analysing the results, it was found that the nine children (Group 1), who had marked specific difficulties, that is those who required six or more PASS sessions, had an average increase of 9.6 months: the ten children (Group 2), who had minor difficulties, that is those who required one to three PASS sessions, had an average increase of 15.2 months; and the five children (Group 3) who had no difficulties and no PASS sessions had an average increase of 7.4 months.

Fig. 1

	No of PASS Sessions	Range of RAs (Sept)	Average Increase in RA (Sept-March)
Group 1	6-13	-6y4m to 6y8m (and 1 RA 7y2m)	**9.6 months**
Group 2	1-3	6y5m to 8y5m	15.2 months
Group 3	none	6y9m to 9y10m	7.4 months

The PASS Programme in the whole class situation achieved its objective by significantly improving the reading attainments of those children with mild to severe specific learning difficulties (Group 1). It also effected an increase in reading accuracy of better readers, whose very minor problems would normally go undetected (Group 2). This significant increase in RA in Group 2 was not anticipated, and the hypothesis that very minor difficulties, such as occasional difficulty with medial vowels or r/l in blends, can significantly impede reading accuracy merits further investigation. The children who required no input (Group 3) made the progress in reading accuracy at the rate which would be anticipated.

Continuous assessment was used to monitor spelling. Most children in Group 1 made significant progress (see Fig.1) and the improvement in spelling in other groups was in line with that expected for the age group.

[Handwritten sample, November '92:]

2 2 i̇ 9 2 0
2 bo 2 o m P l y
     D i P f a g
s i m d a t
2 e m f a t 9 o s
d r i e l a
i a h m i l 2 o t
2 i r m i 2 w m
S i r f a e

Child X has been assessed by the school psychologist as having Severe Specific Learning Difficulties. Above is his PASS test in words with initial blends (Nov. '92) and on the right his attempt at the same words in final assessment (March '93).

[Handwritten sample, March '93:]

SPot   7rip
Stem   pot
brim   flot
brip   glas
pram   twin
Slot   klap
Swim   plug
~~----~~
grac   frog
Stor
flog   Ciff

CONCLUSION

From present evaluation, the PASS Programme presents itself as an effective multi-sensory structured phonics programme which can be used to prevent or remediate specific learning difficulties in the individual, group or whole class situation.

As a multi-sensory programme, it differs from some other commercial programmes, in that the multi-sensory input is implemented only where and when the child requires such input.

As a whole class intervention programme, it differs from other programmes in which initial screening is carried out and a remediation programme developed and implemented for each child. In the PASS Programme **continuous** screening (spelling assessments) for a structured set of difficulties is an integral part of the programme, and children are selected for intervention in a group situation for particular difficulties, rather than an intervention programme being developed for each child. The programme is, therefore, a much more time-effective and cost-effective exercise.

Chapter 11

SPELLING – DIAGNOSIS AND STRATEGIES

CATRIONA COLLINS and JEAN C. MILLER

INTRODUCTION

'I'm not a good speller'

This oft heard statement is made by children and adults from all walks of life including many who are highly articulate and very well educated. Is there then a common denominator in this situation other than the belief that this is an unhappy fact of life which must be accepted? Spelling is undoubtedly an area of the curriculum which has been subject to varying teaching approaches, from the total emphasis on phonics to the opposite end of the spectrum where spelling errors were barely corrected, allowing freedom of expression unfettered by any pressures for accuracy. It is not uncommon for pupils to perceive spelling in a rather negative fashion.

SPELLING DIFFICULTIES

The inability to spell worries many dyslexic children very much and they may have experienced considerable humiliation in the classroom. Frequently their work has been returned liberally marked with red ink and often with comments about their spelling. No wonder they need courage to continue to write! What then is the solution to that negative approach? What we need to do is to tick words that they have spelt correctly and gradually highlight one or two important words which, if given help, they can learn to spell and, hopefully, reproduce correctly in their written work.

How should we tackle the teaching of spelling? To begin with we must recognise that there are a number of reasons for students experiencing difficulty with spelling.

- **Visual Factors**

Poor spellers with weak visual recall have a fairly clear idea which symbol represents which sounds, but they are not always able to remember how the word should look and become confused when they try to write it down.

- **Auditory Factors**

Children suffering from weak auditory analysis are often unable to say which letter symbol represents which sound. They are not able to hear some of the sounds within words and make wild guesses and often miss out syllables. 'Giraffe', for example, can be written as 'girf', 'suddenly' as 'sudnile', 'rescued' as rsood', etc. Before we can begin to work with poor spellers, we must try to decide to which group each child belongs. It is not an easy task – some have a 'foot in each camp'.

DIAGNOSIS OF THE DIFFICULTY

Spelling difficulty may be caused by poor performance in a number of areas. Diagnostic testing and scrutiny of the nature of the errors will pinpoint the problem. Necessary support may be planned using a variety of different strategies to support the student.

Where the difficulty arises from an aural problem it will be important to bear in mind that careful articulation by both teacher and pupil is crucial, and to link aural to visual representation.

More commonly the difficulty arises because the pupil is unable to recall the sequence of letters which go to make a word. A mistake of the type – 'I 'bot' a card' – suggests that a purely phonetic attempt (indeed phonetically correct) has been made but that there was no visual recognition/recall of the word 'bought'. Moreover, 'bot' suggests some recall of the word, but difficulty with the letter string 'ght'.

MULTI-SENSORY ASPECTS

It is now well established in the teaching of spelling that multi-sensory skills are involved in the acquisition of the ability to spell well.

Knowledge of phonics is acquired via a systematic programme and visual skills using word games and most of all by seeing the written word. Many sounds in the English language may be written in two or even more ways, e.g. p(ear: p(are: p(air: and in this situation visual recall is used. It follows then that exposure to spoken language and to the written word are very significant. It is very important that children write correctly right from the beginning those words which are most frequently used in their own work which do not follow phonetic patterns e.g. they, where, their, two, etc., as the more often these are written wrongly the more difficult it can be to correct. Good spelling habits with these familiar words should be encouraged from the very early stages.

Such approaches are employed in, for example, 'Spelling Made Easy' by Violet Brand, published by EPL, with 'Remedial Spelling' aimed at pupils who have difficulty. Much emphasis is placed on the multi-sensory nature of spelling to listen, to say, to write, to look, and to link together common patterns and families of words so that spelling vocabulary can be encouraged and expanded, building on those words which the pupils can comfortably spell.

SPELLING SKILLS

The auditory discrimination of initial sounds, word endings, medial sounds, and rhyming words can be enhanced by means of listening games. Visual discrimination can be developed by means of sorting–matching type activities, motor skills by drawing, and handwriting activities as part of the programme to ensure fluency of writing. Where there is an established mis-spelling identified in a diagnostic test, it is helpful to re-train in the motor aspect of the spelling as well as the visual and aural. The handwriting programme of study can be consciously structured in such a way as to ensure practice in the letter strings or combinations of letters and to concentrate upon the visual and motor knowledge which is to be reinforced.

SPELLING RULES

Pupils should also learn the spelling rules, especially those simple ones which are most commonly seen in use and can be most helpful e.g. i before e except after c, dropping of final e before adding ing, changing y to i to make plurals as in baby – babies. These spelling rules can be taught in a structured way and there are many commercially produced schemes using this approach. Pupils learn groups of words and use them in exercises to reinforce the visual and motor aspects. These rules do cover a great majority of the words in the English Language. For pupils with spelling difficulties these common rules as applied to the most frequently used words can be very helpful.

Spelling rules can be taught but much later than is often considered. Boys and girls in their third year in the Secondary School will ask about and appear to enjoy and understand some of the spelling rules which, to them, are logical.

Chapter 11

The ultimate aim is to help the child to become aware of words, to be unafraid to write, and to use words regardless of spelling. Many children have devised their own way out of their failure. The teacher's task is not to be constantly correcting mistakes but to be helping children not to make so many the next time.

SPELLING AND READING

Spelling is not the same as Reading. It is a different skill and indeed fluent, able readers may be very poor spellers. Spelling has to be taught in a structured way, building upon skills using a variety of approaches to foster confidence in the use of the written word. It must be extremely unusual for a parallel progression to take place in the development of reading skills and of writing and spelling and the majority of pupils can read materials at a much more difficult level than the writing they produce.

Frith and Frith (1980) made an important observation: they argued that there was a difference between reading and spelling. Reading, they felt, was a recognition process, whilst spelling was a retrieval process. Thus reading can proceed using 'partial cues'. In contrast spelling requires the use of 'full cues'. To spell well words must be represented in a detailed way in the mind of the speller and this memory image must be recoverable. In the absence of spelling knowledge an individual will be forced to spell words according to the way in which they sound. In the English orthography reliance on a sound strategy is unsatisfactory (Snowling, 1985).

AIDS AND STRATEGIES

Pupils with spelling difficulties may be helped by work focusing on 'family grouping' of words containing the same letter strings. These letter strings do not necessarily always have the same sound e.g. gone: done: bone.

Another helpful activity is to look for words within words, e.g. **train**ing.

The use of cursive handwriting exercises linked into letter strings e.g. ch: ing: increases fluency in writing these frequently used strings whilst also reinforcing the sequencing of the letters.

The keyboard is another aid found to be useful in reinforcing knowledge of letter strings. Pupils look for the key on the keyboard and then check the printout when using it for word processing or using such programmes as 'Eye for Spelling' or producing lists.

The visual dimension of spelling is further strengthened by means of the look, say, cover, write, check technique (which includes oral and writing aspects) to ensure consistency of the multi-sensory approach to spelling. The oral aspect reinforces work in the listening and phonic skills; the ability, where appropriate, to use the syllables of the word.

For those pupils who may already have built up anxieties about spelling it is very important that correction of work be supportive and positive. Where the error is only one letter or one syllable only that part should be indicated and the pupils praised for what is correct whilst their attention is drawn to the part which is not correct. To a pupil who has difficulties in either visual or aural discrimination it is daunting and discouraging to have to search through a string of letters or syllables to find the error.

A spelling problem is not easy to remedy, despite a range of methods of teaching. Poor spellers are a constant reminder that teachers must continue to devise new ideas. Some strategies which could be considered include the following:

1 **Typing** enables the pupils to work slowly, finding the correct letters as they type, and it reinforces and strengthens their poor visual recall for words. If they have weak fine motor control, using correct typing skills strengthens their fingering and improves their handwriting.

2 **Dividing Word into Syllables** can be a difficult task but some like the challenge of this skill. Finding two words from a compound word can be an excellent activity.

| else where | where ever | be gun |
| hat red | dough nut | news paper |

3 **Fitting Words into Shapes**

(see over).

Chapter 11

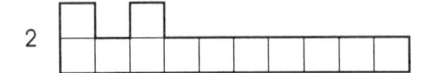

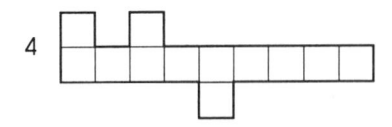

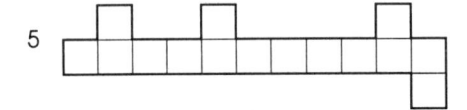

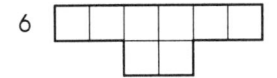

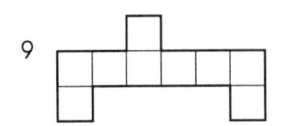

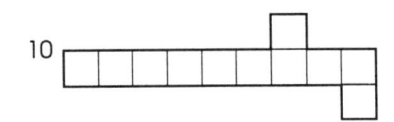

1. **p r o g r a m m e**

laser

computer

microchip

television

kilograms

electricity

oxygen

astronaut

galaxy

programme

140 *Specific Learning Difficulties (Dyslexia)*

4 **Growing words** have a fascination. Inventing patterns, working alone or in pairs, is ideal. Here is one example:

>   new
>   wall
>   link
>   kitchen
>   never
>   reached.

5 **Proof-reading** is a very useful exercise provided the pupils are presented with short sentences and the number of errors is stated. If this work can be linked with spelling just taught it will reinforce the work.

6 **Anagrams** are very successful but must be based on the pupil's own experience. Pupils should be able, if they wish, to work in pairs for this activity.

7 **Crosswords** can be a teaching aid, reinforcing words being taught.

Teachers are often asked about spelling books, but there is no book or list of words that can be used regularly for children with specific learning difficulties. They have to develop their own list, so that for checking purposes they can refer to their own alphabetical indexed books. This enables each child to look up a word quickly when it is needed.

CONCLUSION

It is also important to remember that dyslexia affects areas other than reading and spelling. A child's difficulties with literacy result in anxiety and concern to that child, the parent and the teacher. Society demands a certain degree of competence in reading and spelling and therefore it is essential that, as teachers, we give due consideration to the assessment and the development of strategies in spelling to facilitate the development of literacy skills.

Spelling is a skill which those who have good visual recall, good aural skill and a wide experience of language, including listening, talking and seeing written language, are most likely to acquire easily. For those who have difficulty the school can provide opportunities to experience language, and varied techniques to help and support the learner in the acquisition of skills. Teachers should be positive and encouraging and employ a variety of teaching aids, activities and text.

REFERENCES

BRAND V. (1989) *Remedial Spelling*. Egon Publishers.
BRAND V. (1992) *Spelling Made Easy*. Egon Publishers.
FRITH U. and FRITH C. C. (1980) 'Relationships between Reading and Spelling' in Kavanagh J. F. and Venezky R. L. (eds) *Orthography, Reading and Dyslexia*. Baltimore: University Park Press.
SNOWLING M. J. (1985) *Children's Written Language Difficulties*. NFER, Nelson Publishing Co.Ltd.

Chapter 12

PERCEPTUAL MOTOR AND NEURO-DEVELOPMENTAL DIMENSIONS IN IDENTIFYING AND REMEDIATING DEVELOPMENTAL DELAY IN CHILDREN WITH SPECIFIC LEARNING DIFFICULTIES

SHEILA DOBIE

INTRODUCTION

Many children display severe limitations in their motor abilities. There is much evidence in any classroom of children adopting compensatory measures to cope with the wide ranging demands placed upon them by the school environment. They have failed to develop the physical competencies so essential in the everyday management of themselves and the tasks which comprise the educational process.

Maeland (1992) and Lerner *et al* (1987) identify the mastery of many school subjects and everyday activities as dependent on the acquisition of skilled movement. Lerner indicates that academic and cognitive problems may be due to insufficient motor experiences and gaps in motor learning.

It is further suggested,

> 'One fact remains, motor activity is essential in order to learn; the child must stabilise his body and govern its movements in order to obtain real learning'.
>
> de Quiros and Schrager (1979).

BIRTH FACTORS

Much debate presently focuses on influences which impinge upon children reaching their optimal performance. At risk factors both biological and environmental have been the concern of Garwood and Sheehan (1989). Low birth weight has been identified by Hunt *et al* (1982) and Klein (1988) as a potential risk factor for developmental difficulties.

Studies by Abel Smith and Knight-Jones (1990) confirm previous findings that low birth weight children compared with full term infants, were inferior in intelligence, had significantly lower motor performance, verbal, quantitative and memory scores. In a further study, Astbury *et al* (1990), of 110 children, of whom 57 survived, six children had physical disabilities, five had sensory disabilities and six had developmental delay. Some 47% of the surviving population were found at two years to have evidence of hyperactivity, impulsivity or distractability; and three children were deemed to be withdrawn or passive.

Cotrell (1992) examined 135 cases of learning disabled children and adults, concluding that in every case there was some form of interference at birth. Major contributing factors appeared to be early or premature birth, 35% of the children and 45% of the adults. The second factor was that of precipitate birth, 41% of the children and 22% of the adults. Other factors included late delivery, forceps delivery, caesarean section, breech delivery, foetal anoxia, and induced labour. Associated learning problems were identified as chronic.

Swanson *et al* (1992) confirms the importance of differential developmental profiles of all at risk babies including consideration of ethnic variations, infants with chronic lung disease and the normal pre-term infant or those exposed to drugs or alcohol in utero.

Escalating developmental problems in babies as a consequence of maternal drug use are reported by Cratty (1990) and perhaps understandably, poverty, low maternal education, or age and low support systems are reflected in the concerns of Abraham and Scott (1988). Whatever the origins the difficulties which confront children are both troublesome and diverse.

THE IMPORTANCE OF MOTOR DEVELOPMENT

In consideration of the evidence concerning children who are underachieving, or present behavioural problems, some of the underlying factors frequently reported include limitations in motor skill development, poor coordination, perceptual motor difficulties, clumsiness and visual-motor integration problems. Klein (1988) and Cowden and Eason (1991) advocate early intervention to ameliorate presenting problems and prevent school failure.

It should be noted that,

> '. . . *developmental movement and gross motor deficiencies are a special case for intervention strategies and that movement problems may be more difficult to eliminate than other deficiency classifications*'.
>
> Cowden and Euson 1991.

Sherrill and Pyler (1985) have established that as many as 75% of children with learning difficulties have moderate motor difficulties. Cermak and Henderson (1989) provide an estimation of 60-90% for children with learning difficulties, who also have coordination problems.

Looking at pre-school neuro-developmental disorders and subsequent profiles at ages 10 and 13, Gilberg *et al* (1989) showed that almost 25% of all children with school achievement problems at 10 and almost 40% of such children at 13 had motor perception dysfunction and attention deficit disorders.

A higher frequency of learning difficulties, particularly in spelling, writing and also in reading and maths was identified in a sample of clumsy children than in a comparative group, (Sovik and Maeland 1986). Children with specific developmental language disorders are recognised, Cermak *et al* (1986) and Rintala and Palsio (1993) to have accompanying problems with motor skills.

Motor deviance as a marker for dysfunction in other areas is identified by Capute et al (1981) and studies by Gilberg *et al* (1989), Losse *et al* (1991) and more recently Geuze and Borger (1993); all reflect that contrary to the expectations of many professionals the problems of inept motor performance do not diminish with maturity, and are thought to be associated with a high prevalence of learning difficulties and psychological problems.

> '*Motor learning problems have been shown to be persistent characteristics associated with educational failure, social isolation, anxiety, withdrawal and depression persisting into adolescence*'.
> Russell (1988).

INTERVENTION PROGRAMMES

It is significant that Furth and Wachs (1975) see movement and thinking as interdependent, claiming that many children perform academic tasks inadequately because they have failed to master the contributory movement control which supports learning. Considerable controversy exists in the determination of the efficacy of different interventional programmes and attempts have been made to evaluate their effectiveness.

Kavale and Mattson (1983) examined the most popular perceptual motor training programmes and found that all programmes evidenced small treatment affects. However, from an analysis of 180 studies, the primary findings indicated that, *'perceptual motor training is not an effective intervention technique for comparing academic, cognitive or perceptual motor variables'.*

Kavale and Mattson (1983).

In a study of the effectiveness of a sensory integration therapy programme for children with perceptual motor deficits, Densen *et al* (1989) found no greater gains in language development, in perceptual motor development or in handwriting – than a parallel physical education programme or no treatment at all. In a further study looking at motor treatments and learning disabilities, Humphries (1992), examined sensory integration, perceptual motor and non treatment groups adopted for 133 children with learning difficulties. The findings supported improvement using either of the intervention strategies, including gains in motor planning and gross motor functioning but without any carry over into other functional activities.

Support over time has been afforded various interventional approaches including the development work based on the movement theories of Rudolph Laban, promoted by Veronica Sherbourne and reported in her publication Developmental Movement for Children (1990).

Other interventions include:

> Therapeutic intervention of specific motor therapy following assessment. Godfrey and Kephart (1969).
> Occular-motor integration through visual perceptual skills. Frostig (1970).
> Sensory integration approaches using the basic input systems, visual kinaesthetic, vestibular tactile and auditory. Ayres (1980).
> Goal directed intervention approaches through short term objectives and task analysis. Wessel (1980).
> The generalisation of motor patterns using extensive movement exploration and participation in multiple variations of motor situations. Kiphard (1981).
> Developmental strategies with a remedial approach. McClenaghan and Gallaghue (1982).
> Evaluation of kinaesthetic abilities. Laszlo and Bairstow (1985).
> Early paediatric intervention. Eason (1991).
> Consideration of the learning environment including modification and adaptation of techniques. Cutforth (1991).
> and Adaptation of physical activities. Sherrill (1986).

EVALUATION OF INTERVENTION

Despite all these treatment strategies, the perplexing problem has remained that although many assessments may be made, the root cause of the presenting problems and deficiencies remains unidentified. The programmes may produce improvement for some children but whether this is generalisable and influential in alleviating associated learning has been considered to be uncertain.

It has come to be accepted Capute *et al* (1981) that practice of individual gross and fine motor skills will have no demonstrable influence on cognitive development. Single isolated competencies may improve, but without generation.

In taking cognisance of the reflected reservations and in the general acknowledgement that the problems which underlie the motor, and in many cases, associated learning difficulties, are variable amongst children, professionals have sought informed solutions to the problems. In consideration of why some children regardless of how much they practice never become as skilled as their peers, Sveistrup *et al* (1992) suggest that,

> *'Identifying the system which is dysfunctional rather than the skill the child is having problems with will allow the development of a remedial programme for teaching the underlying deficit versus training the specific task'.*

A process orientated approach of diagnosis and treatment is advocated by Laszlo and Bairstow (1985) who focus on the development of kinaesthetic acuity and perception and memory.

THE ROLE OF REFLEXES

A substantial body of knowledge Rider (1972), Ayres (1972), de Quiros (1976), Blythe and McGlown (1979), Morrison (1985), Auxter and Pyfer (1989), Field (1990), Blythe (1992) and Eichstaedt and Kalakian (1993) point to the influences of sensory integration systems and reflex patterns in supporting efficient movement.

In other circumstances,

> *'Abnormalities in the early modification of primitive reflexes and the development of a broad range of coordinated motor behaviours appear to be causal factors in the learning problems of a variety of children'.*
>
> Morrison, D (1985).

Rider (1972) in an investigation to establish the relationship between postural reflexes and academic performance compared a group of children who exhibited learning problems and who had been referred for a perceptual motor learning programme with a group of normal children. The prevalence of abnormal postural reflexes was compared between the two groups and the children referred for the motor programme were identified as having significantly more abnormal reflex responses than the normal group. An additional factor which emerged showed that within the normal group, those children who exhibited abnormal reflexes were found to score lower on achievement tests than did others in the group who exhibited no abnormal reflexes.

Blythe (1992) asserts that,

> *'the continued presences or absence of a cluster of aberrant reflexes causes writing and copying difficulties, reading and spelling problems, impaired short term memory, the inability to sit still and concentrate, excessive day dreaming, clumsiness and awkwardness and to a lesser degree mathematical problems'.*
>
> Blythe, P (1992).

Furthermore, Morrison (1985) points out that failure to inhibit the primitive reflexes and establish adequate responses to gravity has been constantly associated with varying degrees of behavioural disturbance. Fortunately processes of intervention are possible. Pyfer (1988), Nelson (1988), Fisher and Murray (1991) all point to the potential for change in any individual afforded relevant developmental experiences. Pyfer (1988) supports skilful evaluation of reflexes and sensory systems, followed by intervention.

Fisher and Murray (1991) speculate that enhancement of the function of the nervous system is feasible through tactile, vestibular and proprioceptive inputs. Nelson (1988) sees the central nervous system as an unhappy system,

> *'Just waiting for the message that it needs to activate the normal response that is obscured by the effect of damage or disruption'.*

In alleviating the concomitant difficulties, which may be associated with the vestibular, kinaesthetic, tactile, visual auditory or reflex systems, particularly in those children who exhibit motor control, learning or behavioural difficulties, it is proposed that a systematic neuro-developmental approach should be adopted.

Chapter 12

CONCLUSION

The responsibility for intervention should be cross-curricular and multi-professional with the starting point being derived from the maturational status of individual pupils. Participation in specially individualised and differentiated activities would provide the basis for amelioration of the underlying neurological dysfunctions. Interesting varied physical activities are not in themselves sufficient to ensure functional change which will alleviate motor or other associated problems.

In situations where neuro development is delayed critical control is necessary to compensate for the lack of voluntary movement, therefore directing attention to the motor control rather than the learning process. It is known that,

> '. . . language development, language internalisation, speech, reading, writing and other symbolic processes progress as the child is able to exclude from the conscious or awareness level a great amount of body information or external information transmitted through body receptors'.
>
> de Quiros (1979).

Dysfunctions which prevent the automisation of perceptual skills, impede learning, and dictate a potential vulnerability for distractability and concentration must be of concern to educators.

Neuro-developmental remediation is a viable strategy which allows motor skills to emerge and generalise with practice, thus allowing the child to optimise their full learning potential.

REFERENCES

ABEL SMITH A. E. and KNIGHT-JONES E. B. (1990) 'The abilities of very low birthweight children and their classroom controls,' *Developmental Medicine and Child Neurology*. 32. 590-601.

ASTBURY J. and ORGILL A. A., BAJUK B. and YU V. H. (1990) 'Low Birthweight Survivors. How soon can we tell?' *Developmental Medicine and Child Neurology*. 32 582-589.

AUXTER D. and PYFER J. (1989) *Principles and Methods of Adapted Physical Education and Recreation*. Times Mirror/Morsby Pub. 6th Ed.

AYRES A. J., MAILLOUX Z. and WENDLERE C. (1987) 'Development Dyspraxia – Is it a unitary function?' *Occupational Therapy Journal of Research* 7.93-110.

AYRES A. J. (1972) *Sensory Integration and Learning Disorders*. Los Angeles. Western Psychological Services.

AYRES A. J. (1972) 'Types of Sensory Integrative Dysfunction Among Disabled Learners'. *A J Occupational Therapy*. 26. 13-18.

AYRES J. (1980) *Sensory Integration and the Child*. Western Psychological Services.

BLYTH P. and McGLOWN D. (1979) *An Organic Basis for Neuroses and Educational Difficulties*. Insight Publications.

BLYTHE P. (1992) *A Physical Approach to Resolving Learning Difficulties*. Presented – 4th European Conference of Neuro-developmental Delay in Children with Specific Learning Difficulties. Chester.

CAPUTE A., SHAPIRO B. and PALMER F. (1981) 'Spectrum of Developmental Disabilities.' *Orthopedic Clinics of North America*. No 1 June 1981.

CERMAK S., WARD E. and WARD L. (1986) 'The relationship between articulation disorders and motor co-ordination in children.' *The American Journal of Occupational Therapy*. 40. 546-550.

CERMAK S. and HENDERSON A. (1989) 'Learning Disabilities.' In *Neurological Rehabilitation*. C. V. Mosby.

CHANDLER L. S., ANDREW M. S. and SWANSON M. W. (1980). *Movement Assessment of Infants.*. Rolling Bay, W A.

COTRELL S. (1992) 'The Effect of Obstetric Problems on Neuro-Developmental Delay.' 4th European Conference on Neuro-Developmental Delay. March 1992.

COWDEN J. E. and EASON B. L. (1991) 'Pediatric Adapted Physical Education for Infants, Toddlers and Pre-Schoolers.' *Adapted Physical Activity Quarterly*. (8) 263-279.

CRATTY B. J. (1975). *Remedial Motor Activity for Children*. Philadelphia. Lea and Febiger.

CRATTY B. J. (1979). 'Perceptual and Motor Development 'in *Infants and Children*. 2nd edition. N J Prentice Hall.

CRATTY B. J. (1986) 'Perceptual and Motor Development 'in *Infants and Children*. 3rd edition. NJ Prentice Hall.

CRATTY B. (1990) 'Motor development of infants subject to maternal drug use. Current evidence and future research strategies.' *Adopted Physical Activity Quarterly*. 7. 101-125.

CUTFORTH N. (1991) 'The under-achieving child. Implications for Physical Education.' *Bulletin of Physical Education*.

DENSEN J. F., NUTHALL G. A, BUSHNELL J. and HORN J. (1989) 'Effectiveness of a sensory integrative therapy programme for children with perceptual motor deficits.' *Journal of Learning Disabilities*. 22. 221-229.

de QUIROS J. and SCHARGER D. (1979) *Neuro-Psychological Fundamentals in Learning Disabilities*. Novato, C A Academic Therapy Publications.

de QUIROS J. (1976) 'Diagnosis of vestibular disorders in the learning disabled.' *Journal of Learning Disabilities*. 9(50-57).

EASON B. L. (1991) 'Adapted physical education delivery model for infants and toddlers with disabilities.' *Journal of Physical Education and Recreation and Dance*. 2(6) 41-43.

EICHSTAEDT C. and KALAKIAN L. (1993) *Developmental/Adapted Physical Education. Making Ability Count*. Macmillan Pub Co 3rd ed.

FISHER J. G. and MURRAY E. Chapter 1 in *Sensory Integration Theory and Practice*. F A Davies Co. Philadelphia 1991.

FURTH H. and WACHS H .(1975) *Piagets Theory in Practice. Thinking Goes to School* Oxford University Press.

GALLAHUE D. (1982) *Developmental Movement Experiences for Children*. John Wiley.

GARWOOD S. G. and SHEEHAN R. (1989) 'Designing a Comprehensive Early Intervention System.' *The Challenge of Public Law*. 99-457. Austin TX Pro Ed.

GILLBERG I. C., GILLBERG C. and GROTH J. (1989) 'Children with pre-school minor neuro developmental disorders v neuro developmental profiles at age 13.' *Developmental Medicine and Child Neurology*. 31 14-24.

GODFREY B. and KEPHART. N. (1969) *Movement Patterns and Motor Education* Appleton Century Crofts.

GRAHAM M. A .and SCOTT K. G. (1988) 'The Impact of Definitions of High Risk on Services to Infants and Toddlers.' *Topics in Early Childhood Special Education*. 8(3) 23-38.

GEUZE R. and BORGER H. (1993) 'Children who are clumsy: five years later.' *Adapted Physical Activity Quarterly*. (10)10-21.

HUMPHRIES T., WRIGHT M., SNIDER M., McDOUGALL B. (1992) 'A comparison of effectiveness of sensory integrative therapy and perceptual-motor training in treating children with learning disabilities.' *Development and Behavioural Pediatrics.* Vol 13 No 1.

HUNT J., TOOLE W. R., HALVIN D. (1982) 'Learning disabilities in children with birthweights >1500 grams.' *Perinatology* (6)280-287.

KLEIN N. K. (1988) 'Children who were very low birthweight. Cognitive abilities and classroom behaviour at five years of age.' *Journal of Special Education.* Vol. 22 (No 1) 1988.

KAVALE and MATTSON P. D .(1983) 'One jumped off the balance beam. Meta-analysis of perceptual motor training.' *Journal of Learning Disabilities.* 16. 165-173.

KEPHART N. (1960) *The Slow Learner in the Classroom.* Columbus. O. H. Merrill.

KIPHARD E. (1981) 'Adapted Physical Education in Germany.' Proceedings of International Symposium on Adapted Physical Activity. New Orleans.

LASZLO J. and BAIRSTOW P. (1985) *Perceptual motor behaviour. Developmental assessment and therapy.* Praeger Scientific.

LERNER J., MARDELL-CZUDNOWSKI C. and GOLDENBURG D. (1987) *Special education for the early childhood years.* 2nd ed. Englewood Cliffs. NG Prentice Hall.

LOSSE A., HENDERSON S. E., ELLIMAN D., HALL D., KNIGHT E. and JONGMANNS M. (1991). 'Clumsiness in Children – do they grow out of it? A 10-year follow up study.' *Developmental Medicine and Children Neurology.* 33,55-68.

MAELAND A. F. (1992) Identification of Children with Motor Co-ordination Problems. *Adapted Physical Activity Quarterly.* (9) 330-342.

McCLENAGHAN B. and GALLAHUE D. (1978) *Fundamental Movement. A Developmental and Remedial Approach.* Philadelphia Saunders.

MORRISON D. C. (1985) *Neurobehavioural and Perceptual Dysfunction in Learning Disabled Children.* C. J. Hogrefc Inc. N I Toronto.

NELSON C. (1988) 'Infant Movement. Normal and Abnormal Development.' *Journal of Physical Education Recreation and Dance. September.*

PYFFER J. (1988) 'Teachers don't let your students grow up to be clumsy adults.' *Journal of Physical Education, Recreation and Dance.* January.

RIDER B. (1972) 'Relationships of postural reflexes to learning disabilities.' *American Journal of Development Therapy.* Vol 26 No 5. July/Aug (239-243).

RINTAL A. and PALSIO N. (1993) 'Effects of Physical Education Programmes in Children in Learning Disabilities.' Paper presented at the 9th International Symposium on Adapted Physical Activity. Yokohama, Japan.

RUSSELL J. (1988) *Graded Activities for Children with Motor Difficulties.* Cambridge University Press.

SHERBOURNE Veronica (1988) *Developmental Movement for Children in Mainstream, Special Needs and Pre-School.* Cambridge University Press.

SHERRILL C. and PYLER J. (1985) 'Learning Disabled Students in Physical Education.' *Adapted Physical Activity Quarterly.* 2.283-291.

SHERRILL C. (1986) *Adapted Physical Education and Recreation. A Multi-disciplinary Approach.* Dubuque, I. A .William C. Brown.

SOVIK N. and MAELAND A. (1986) 'Children with Motor Problems. (Clumsy Children).' *Scandinavian Journal of Educational Research.* 30,1.39-53.

STOTT D. H., MOYES F. A. and HENDERSON S. E. (1984) 'Test of Motor Impairment'. London Psychological Corporation.

SUGDEN D. (1991) 'Assessment of Children with Movement Skill Difficulties.' *The British Journal of Physical Education.* Summer.

SVEISTRUP H., BURTNER P. and WOLLACOTT M. H. (1992) 'Motor control approaches that may help to identify and teach children with motor impairments.' *Pediatric Exercise Scheme.* Vol 4(3).

SWANSON M., BENNETT F., KIRKWOOD S. and WHITFIELD M. (1992) 'Identification of neuro-development abnormality at four and eight months by the movement assessment of infants.' *Development Medicine and Child Neurology.* (34) 321-337.

TINGLE M. (1990) 'The Motor Impaired Child.' *Practical Integration in Education.* NFER London.

WESSEL J. A. (1980) 'I Can.' *Primary Skills.* Northbristle, I. L. Hubbard.

Chapter 13

INFORMATION TECHNOLOGY AND SPECIFIC LEARNING DIFFICULTIES

MARIE DOUGAN and GEORGE TURNER

INTRODUCTION

Children with specific learning difficulties are children first and their needs are similar to those of all children. The need to exercise some control over their environment is one of these basic needs. It is this need which gives micro-technology its power. Microcomputers, with appropriate input devices and software although internally complex, can be remarkably simple to control. Furthermore, unlike some of the humans the children come into contact with, they have a consistency in their performance and give feedback on the children's performance in an uncritical way, making their use in presenting educational material highly acceptable.

The last 10 years or so have seen significant advances in the development of microcomputer systems. They are now cheap enough to be accessible to children for educational purposes and powerful enough to meet many of their needs.

USING IT FOR SUPPORT STRATEGIES

IT has a unique contribution to make in the area of support for children with specific learning difficulties. It can provide support for organising of writing, for the writing itself, and for spelling and memory.

IT AND ORGANISING THOUGHTS

Many individuals with Specific Learning Difficulties encounter problems when beginning to commit their thoughts to paper. Apart from any difficulties with handwriting skills, it is often difficult for them to commit their ideas in logical sequences – they are 'all over the place'. There are various planner and outliner packages available for computer systems which will allow pupils to type in their ideas in any order and subsequently link them together and add text to them under 'idea headings'. An example of a useful package in this area is **Thinksheet** [1], which allows 'ideas' to be manipulated on screen and text moved about visually.

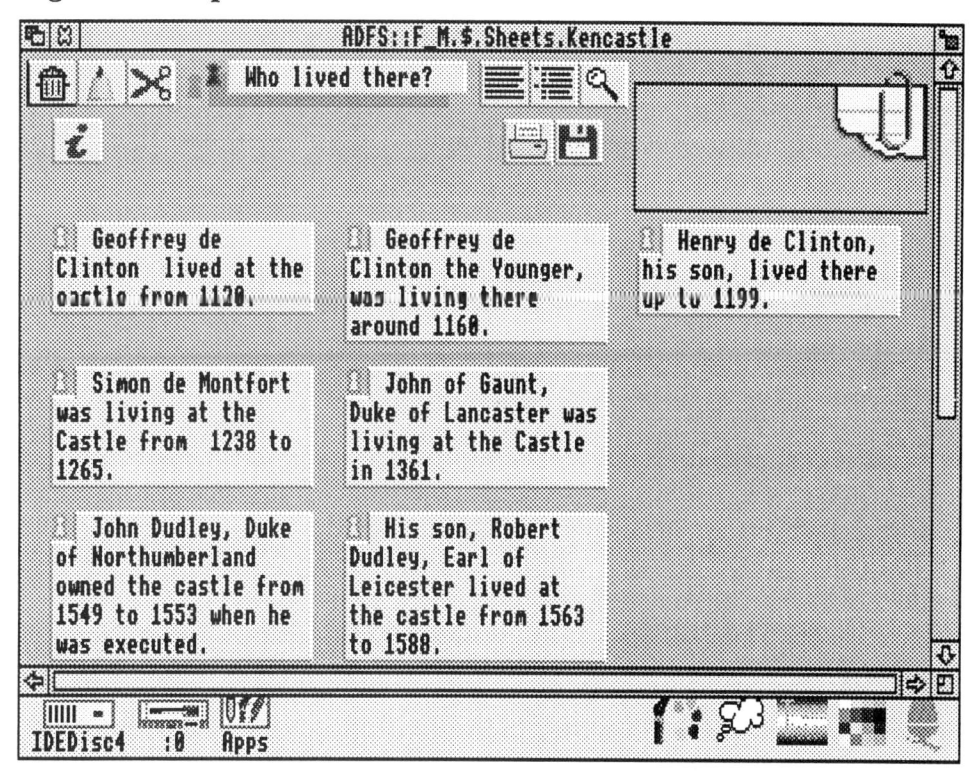

Fig. 1   Example of Thinksheet screen

Many word processing packages also have the added feature of an outliner facility. This is, however, not so easy to manipulate visually because the ideas are being sequenced in a more linear progression. Many people find electronic personal organisers very useful and the memory-jogging and organisation support which they offer can be of immense value to those with Specific Learning Difficulties.

SUPPORT FOR WRITING

Micro-technology offers huge benefits in this area for those with Specific Learning Difficulties. Pupils who have experienced failure in writing throughout their school career often take a very natural step and avoid the process at every possible opportunity. For a large number of pupils it comes as a great relief to be told that they can make as many mistakes as they wish in their writing when using a word processor.

Chapter 13

Pupils using word processors often report feeling less apprehensive or stressed when approaching a writing task. The actual process of forming letters may constitute a block to writing and can be removed by access to a word processor. Word processors are particularly useful for those who have problems in the kinaesthetic-motor area. Often, removing this anxiety will have the effect of freeing them to concentrate on skills of composition, and may in turn lead to work which is of better quality and greater in quantity.

Touch typing skills, although very helpful, are not an essential requirement for using a word processor efficiently. Some keyboard familiarity is however, essential, and opportunities must be provided to practise this activity.

Word processors offer the facility to edit text and move it around within the piece of writing. Some pupils prefer to have their work printed out at a draft stage, and consider the possible changes they make from their paper copy. Others find it easier to edit directly on screen and have no difficulty in moving the cursor around. Whichever technique is employed, there is no doubt that drafting using a word processor is much less laborious than redrafting and rewriting by hand. A good quality printed product gives the pupil a real sense of achievement and provides an opportunity for the work to be shared with others. Indeed, the process also lends itself to providing more opportunities for collaborative work and discussion and this is particularly important for those with Specific Learning Difficulties .

Some pupils find it easier to read through their own work when it is printed rather than handwritten. In fact the same applies to teachers who on seeing a printed copy of a pupil's work have commented 'Now I can see what some of the difficulties are. At last the text is readable.'

There are facilities within most programs to change the typeface (or font) and it is often possible to vary both background and foreground colours. This is discussed in detail later.

Other support strategies may be incorporated within the word processor program. Word processors can be introduced at a very early stage by employing the concept keyboard (a touch sensitive pad) as an alternative input device – **Prompt Writer**[2] Text may then be entered by pressing a picture to enter a word or phrase. There is also the facility to enter the actual text required by pressing the appropriate area on the concept keyboard. The flexibility of many of these programs in allowing the teacher to customise overlays for particular pupils is a great bonus. The overlays may be developed to allow the pupil to progress in small steps by gradually replacing the pictures by text, which can be built up into fairly complex language structures. Sometimes the only support required may be the availability of a wordbank or wordlist, and these are readily available within these programs. In addition, there are some concept keyboard programs which present the user with a sequencing activity resulting in the production of a piece of text. Such programs involve the user in pressing the areas in the correct order – thus providing further practice in sequencing skills as well as the production of text.

Fig. 2   Concept keyboard overlay for use with PromptWriter program

	NCET Kaleidoscope Packs				**Albert's House Support Pack**				Program : Prompt/Writer filename : Albert C.Hopkins & SMurty B.I.T. Team Bristol SEMERC, Dept of Education, Bristol Polytechnic, Redland Hill, Bristol BS6 6UZ		
a	b	c	d	e	f	g	h	i	j	k	l	m	"	'	Caps
n	o	p	q	r	s	t	u	v	w	x	y	z	!	?	•
	Here	There	This	The	Albert	Albert's	afraid	from
I	He	is	hiding	can	see	mouse	has	and
	white	little	big	cat	upstairs	long	a
	hall	house	his	lives	downstairs	of	in
	landing	bedroom	mousehole	lounge	← →	DELETE
	the	garden	kitchen	bathroom	SPACE	↑ ↓	RETURN

Recently more powerful support has become available through the use of predictive word processors. The user typically types in the first letter of the word which they wish to enter. A list of possible words are then offered on screen – based on the particular vocabulary used by the child, and often also based on a set of grammatical rules. Such systems include **PAL**[3] and **Co:Writer**[4].

One advantage of the Co:Writer program is that it may be set up in such a way that the pupil can point to the words offered with a mouse or other pointing device and have the word spoken back through the computer providing auditory feedback. In addition there is flexibility over the way in which the words are

Chapter 13

Fig. 3 Example of Co:Writer

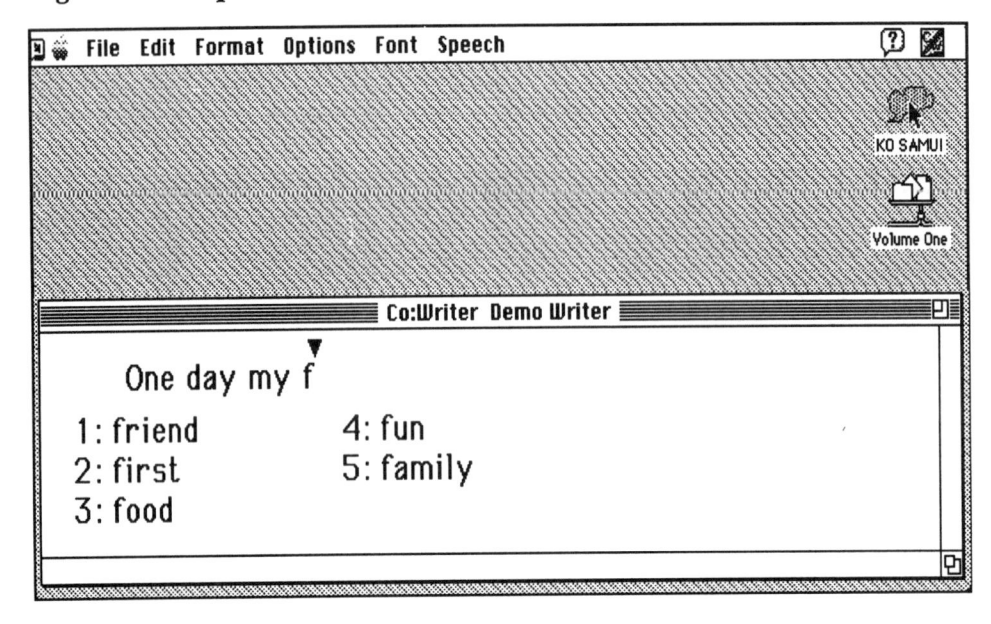

```
File  Edit  Format  Options  Font  Speech

                    Co:Writer Demo Writer

    One day my f
  1: friend        4: fun
  2: first         5: family
  3: food
```

displayed on screen – the size of the letters, the font, whether they are arranged alphabetically or in order of the most likely first.

The computer 'learns' the new words the user types in and will begin to offer these also as predicted words. Great care has to exercised by the teacher over this facility – it is very easy for the pupil to be offered his own misspellings as predicted words. There is usually some facility whereby the teacher can either switch this feature off or edit this new vocabulary and correct the spelling if required. The option of having the words offered according to grammatical rules is a powerful feature, particularly for those who have significant language problems.

The combination of a predictive program together with a talking word processor offers the opportunity for further auditory feedback. Such a combination might be **Co:Writer** with **Write:OutLoud**[5].

SUPPORT FOR SPELLING

Support for spelling can be offered by using a spelling checker to encourage the pupil in independent self-correction. These can be a real boon to some pupils but emphasis should be placed on the word 'some' here. Often teachers and parents clutch at the spelling checker as at a straw whereas, in reality, their use is not always appropriate.

Spelling checkers can be divided into two main groups – hand-held devices and those which are incorporated into a word processor used within a microcomputer. Of the former, the most common in use are probably in the **Franklin**[6] range. Usually these are a cheaper option than buying a microcomputer with spelling-checker built into the software but suffer from the disadvantage that the user must either realise that a particular word has been misspelt or check the spelling of every word. The latter will normally check a complete document, highlighting only possible misspellings, and suggest alternatives. This has the effect of protecting the correctly-spelt words and saving the pupil with Specific Learning Difficulties the frustration of examining correct spellings. In addition, such systems normally allow words to be added to the dictionary set giving a measure of personalisation. Some, like the **Tandy WP3**[7], give an optional audible warning of a possible misspelling.

Some points to bear in mind when considering a spelling-checker:-

> The keyboard on a hand-held device may not be large enough to allow comfortable typing.
>
> The spelling-checker will highlight all words which are not in its dictionary set – including some which are correctly spelt e.g. proper names.
>
> It will not pick out words which are correctly spelt but which are wrongly used in the context e.g. homonyms 'their' and 'there'.
>
> It may suggest too many alternative spellings and create further confusion.
>
> Most spelling checkers are designed specifically to highlight typing errors rather than spelling errors.
>
> Some spelling errors may be too bizarre for the checker to cope.
>
> Some are designed for the American market with, of course, American spelling.
>
> Usually spelling checkers rely upon the user being able to read and recognise a suggested correction – not always possible for pupils with specific learning difficulties.

Software is now available on some systems which offers an option for the computer to 'say' the words which are given as suggested corrections and thus help those with poor reading skills to make a correct choice.

An example of this is the **Write:OutLoud** talking word processing package which is available for the Macintosh range of computers. The words offered can be spoken by the computer and also may be spelled out letter by letter.

Fig. 4   Example of Write:OutLoud

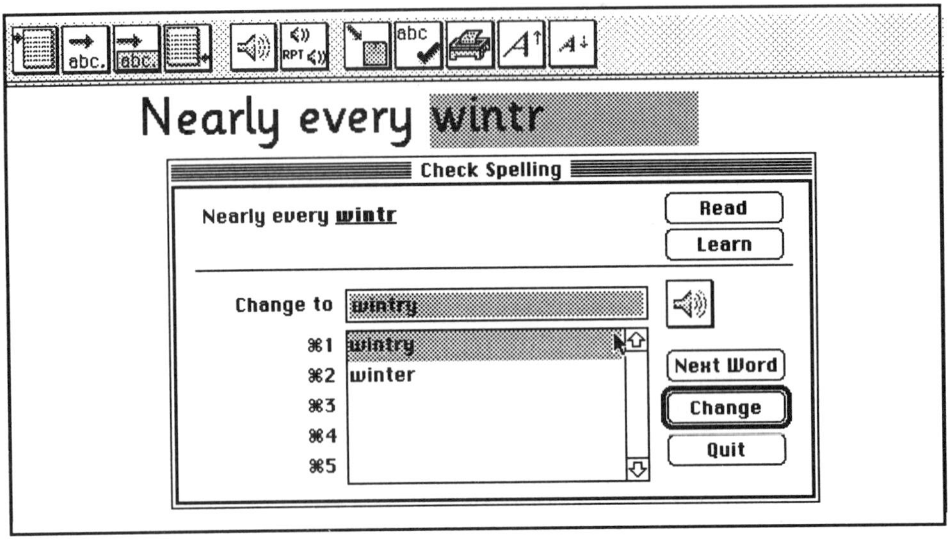

Franklin have also produced a speaking version of the '**Wordmaster**' one of the hand held range of spelling checker devices. Unfortunately, at the present time, this is only available with an American dictionary option.

For a comparison of spellcheck effectiveness, it may be worth consulting **I.T. Support for Specific Learning Difficulties (1992).**

SUPPORT FOR READING

The more powerful systems currently available are sophisticated enough to allow them to produce 'talking books'. Such systems incorporate the facility to display good quality graphics on screen together with good audio output. At the simplest level, this involves pictures being presented on screen and linked to recorded sounds which may be accompanied by highlighted text. It may be possible (noting copyright restrictions) to transfer pupils' reading materials to the computer. At a higher level, text may be scanned electronically and spoken by the computer.

Another strategy which may be employed is the use of programs such as **Developing Tray**[8] which require the pupils to predict letters and words in a hidden passage of text using both context clues and knowledge of the syntax.

SUPPORT IN THE PRESENTATION OF MATERIALS

The technology also permits schools to produce clear, well presented materials for pupil use. Word processors allow teachers to have control over the typeface used and the layout of the text.

Choice of typestyle is also very important when considering the readability of printed materials. Rosemary Sassoon has investigated this problem, spending a great deal of time working with and talking to children. She wishes ' to bring to everyone's attention the need to consider the requirements of different classes of readers, and also to highlight the implications for computer-generated letters in education in general'.

For instance, the ability to justify text is generally used for newsletters and textbooks, but justified text is actually harder to read than text which has a ragged right hand edge. In order for the text to have even margins on both sides, spaces have to be added into the text to make all lines exactly the same length. This causes more problems for those with reading difficulties, since it is more difficult to track easily from the end of one line to the beginning of the other.

A result of her work is the production of a typeface specifically designed for children called the **Sassoon Font**[9].

Fig. 5   Example of Sassoon Font

Nearly every winter my family makes cakes for the old folk. Kevin and my dad made fairy cakes and sponges.

Shorter lines are also much easier to read than lines filling the width of the page – when it is easier for a beginner reader to get lost.

```
This paragraph illustrates the difference in
using a font whose characters are not spaced
proportionally - the letter i takes up the same
width as the letter w.
```

The size of the printed type also has some bearing on the readability of text – small 9 point text is very tiring to read,

but much larger text requires the reader to read a much larger number of lines.

A good range of type size is between 12 and 18 point text.

Care also has to be taken over the **enthusiastic** use of **bold**, <u>underline</u> and *italics*, to avoid the print becoming very <u>***cluttered and confusing.***</u>

Most word processing programs will also allow the spacing between lines to be altered to make the text more suitable for an individual reader.

These techniques can be used to create good quality worksheets for pupils with specific learning difficulties, for example with short lines, and with lists of keywords with phonetic spellings. Technology also allows worksheets to be presented electronically on screen, possibly even with auditory clues attached to some of the keywords.

IT AND REMEDIATION

There are computer programs around for all machine platforms, which aim to provide practice in particular skills. If used carefully, these programs can complement a structured teaching programme very well. Although the microcomputer may simply be offering the same old materials to pupils, they are usually very motivated to use them. A number of the programs have been specifically designed to follow closely a particular teaching programme. Again, many of the programs produced more recently offer a number of additional features such as auditory feedback through both digitised and synthesised speech.

These programs can be used to provide additional practice and training in areas such as :

>   letter recognition – **Fun Phonics**[10] **Hi-Spell**[11]
>   auditory memory – sound pelmanism programs
>   visual memory – **Picture Gallery**[12]
>   sequencing skills – **CK Sequencer** [13]
>   spelling patterns – **Starspell** [14] , **Complete Speller** [15], **Soapbox** [16]
>   reading skills– wordsquare programs, **Developing Tray**
>   keyboard skills – these may be simply keyboard familiarity trainers such as **Keyboard Skills**[17] or typing tutors such as **Mavis Beacon Teaches Typing**[18]
>   directional skills – **Alan Nixon Special Care**[19]

The programs highlighted are examples only.

Details of many other programs useful in these areas are available in **A Software Guide for Specific Learning Difficulties (1993)**.

HARDWARE

At the time of writing, we are in a period of change as far as educational hardware is concerned. This is symptomatic of the over-riding difficulty in dealing with computer hardware – it is in a continual state of flux. No sooner has something been written about it than it is out-of-date. For many years now, schools have relied very heavily on BBC systems. Much of the development work on software has taken place with these systems in mind and many different access methods have been devised for pupils with special needs (e.g. Concept keyboards, switches). Unfortunately such systems are no longer in production but they will continue to give good service in schools for many years to come. It is tempting for developers to turn their attention to exciting new systems with promising new features but it would be a mistake to forget the tried and tested equipment which plays such a useful part in classrooms all over the country.

Hardware can be divided usefully into two main classes – desktop systems and portable systems.

>   Desktop systems
>   Those in common use are:–

BBC – models B and Master
PC's from many different manufacturers
Apple Macintosh
Archimedes
RM Nimbus

Early systems were severely limited in terms of their ability to handle graphics and colour as well as having limited internal memory and this resulted in a plethora of text-based programs or programs with chunky graphics which presented children with pictures which were often difficult to recognise. Where the graphics were good the programs frequently had the disadvantage of being very inflexible.

Clever design and techniques of mass-production have produced (in a price range which makes them accessible to schools) systems which are now better-able to handle the graphic requirements of pupils, and which are still modifiable to meet individual needs. In addition the advent of relatively inexpensive scanners and the ability of systems to make use of video images or still images stored on magnetic disk or CD ROM bring high quality graphics into the realm of educational software. Furthermore, and this may be of particular interest to those working with pupils with specific learning difficulties, modern systems are often capable of allowing the digital recording of sounds. Within appropriate software this opens up the possibility of adding audio-help to passages of text, including screen-based worksheets without having to resort to robotic, synthetic speech. It may be, however, that schools are still unable to afford these additional peripheral devices and this is one area where local information technology support units may be able to provide a helpful service for schools.

PORTABLE SYSTEMS

In some cases a portable system may be appropriate to meet the needs of an individual pupil. This is certainly so in the secondary sector where pupils are required to move from class to class. For some time 'pseudo' portable machines have been available but many of these have, in practice, been too heavy to be readily transportable – especially if they are required to be moved from school to home and vice versa. Others, although truly portable, have been limited in internal memory and processing power. Unfortunately, development of light-weight battery power has not kept pace with the developments in the processors themselves resulting in limited time being available for computer use between battery charges. Furthermore, ignorance of the characteristics of rechargeable batteries has created serious difficulties in the management of power supplies for portable systems – particularly systems incorporating electromechanical devices, such as disk drives, which have relatively heavy power consumption.

Miniaturisation of components and reduction in moving parts should allow the advent of truly portable systems without reduction in processing power. Already systems which rely on memory cards as external storage devices are becoming available at reasonable cost. Some schools are considering the use of portable, laptop machines as standard word-processors for classroom use. This seems to be a sensible idea in these days of financial restraint when perhaps four laptops could be purchased for the price of one desktop. Furthermore, there is usually relatively-easy transfer of files from laptops to desktop systems. This spread in the use of laptops is gradually making it less likely that individuals are being singled out by their peers as pupils with special needs.

WHICH MICROCOMPUTER?

Choosing an appropriate machine can prove to be a frustrating experience. It is worthwhile trying to be as specific as possible about the reasons for investing in a microcomputer system and to be aware of operational difficulties which may occur once the machine is in use. It may be helpful to ask the following questions:–

Who is going to use it?

What are they going to use it for?

What software is available to meet the needs of the users?

Are there any special problems of access that must be addressed?

What training is available in the use of the equipment?

Does it have an understandable and helpful handbook with a good index?

Who will repair it when it fails?

What will happen if a replacement is not available at crucial times and a machine fault occurs e.g. during examinations?

How will the Examinations Board view the use of the machine and software?

Who will be able to give support once the machine has been purchased?

What will it cost to insure against theft accidental damage etc.?

Who is going to be responsible for the equipment?

Is the pupil familiar enough with the keyboard to make effective use of the machine?

In the case of the portable and in addition to the above:–

Chapter 13

- How will it be powered?
- What backup power is available?
- Can the screen be read in different lighting conditions?
- Is the keyboard the correct size for comfortable use?
- Will there be ready access to any additional equipment in the various locations where the machine will be used e.g. printers
- Is the pupil sufficiently literate to make use of a laptop? – If not a concept keyboard and desktop system would perhaps be better option.

Schools are not the only purchasers of microcomputer equipment. Many parents seek help before investing in equipment for their children. In order to deal with such requests for help in choosing a microcomputer the following may be worth considering:–

Which computers are in use at school?

Is extra computing time at home really necessary?

What are the chances that the children will become bored by using programs to which they already have access at school?

Is the pupil sufficiently motivated to make good use of the machine?

If the computer is required for more than one purpose then compromise may be necessary and neither user may get the 'ideal' system.

Whichever item of hardware is ultimately chosen it is important to consider the specific needs of the individual and then to find appropriate hardware and software to meet these needs rather than start with the hardware and look around for a client to fit it. In addition it should be stressed that additional items may be required – items often overlooked. In these days of emphasis on safety in the home and with more stringent rules of safety in the schools a trolley with lockable wheels and fixed power block may be required. A disk storage system may be worthwhile in order to avoid frustrating delay in getting started on a program.

POWER MANAGEMENT AND PORTABLES

As mentioned earlier many portable systems rely upon the use of rechargeable batteries for their power. Those with backlit screens and in-built disk drives may only be able to deliver 2 to 3 hours use between charges so it is important to make the best use of the power available. Some systems will power down automatically if not used within a specified period of time or if the display panel is closed. Some will give an audible or visual warning if low on power. Others offer full power management programs on chip as an integral part of the machine.

Most of the portables make use of Ni-Cad rechargeable batteries which require careful handling and the following should be especially noted:–

The manufacturers instructions should be followed regarding charging (particularly the first charge).

The first charge may take 16 hours and even then may only be charged to 80% capacity.

Two charges may be required to achieve full charge.

If batteries are recharged before reaching the level at which the portable gives a low charge warning then they may develop a 'memory' for full charge which is less than their actual capacity.

In order to correct the condition above the batteries should be discharged as far as possible before going through the procedure of recharging as for a first charge.

CONCLUSION

Although the use of technology is not a panacea for those with Specific Learning Difficulties, it has great potential to assist in teaching and learning. Technology is changing very rapidly and it is important to keep the needs of the children in mind. Great care must be taken in choosing appropriate hardware and software to meet the needs of learners since it is all too easy to be led by the technology rather than by the needs of the pupils.

Chapter 13

REFERENCES

1	Thinksheet	Fisher Marriott, 3 Grove Road, Ansty, Coventry CV7 9JD. 0203 616325.
2	Prompt Writer	NCET, Sir William Lyons Road, Science Park, Coventry CV4 7EZ. 0203 416994.
3	PAL	Scetlander 74 Victoria Crescent Road, Glasgow G12 9JN. 041 357 1659.
4	Co:Writer	Don Johnston Developmental Equipment, Inc. UK Supplier: Fairhurst Apple Centre Chester, Northgate Pavilion, Chester Business Park, Chester CH4 1LN. 0244 680 700.
5	Write:OutLoud	Don Johnston Developmental Equipment, Inc. UK Supplier: Fairhurst Apple Centre Chester, Northgate Pavilion, Chester Business Park, Chester CH4 1LN. 0244 680 700.
6	Franklin	7 Windmill Business Village, Brooklands Close, Sunbury-on-Thames, Middlesex TW16 7DY. 0932 770185.
7	Tandy WP3	Intertan UK Ltd., Leamore Lane, Walsall WS2 7PS. 0922 710000.

8 Developing Tray — North West Semerc,
Fitton Hill CDC,
Rosary Road,
Oldham OL8 2QE.
061 627 4469.

9 Sassoon Font — Dr Rosemary Sassoon,
34 Witches Lane,
Riverhead,
Sevenoaks.

10 Fun Phonics — Pavic Publications,
Sheffield City Polytechnic,
36 Collegiate Crescent,
Sheffield S10 2BP.
0742 665274.

11 Hi-Spell — Xavier Software,
Bangor Dyslexia Unit,
Department of Psychology,
University College of North Wales,
Bangor, Gwynedd LL57 2DG.
0248 351151 x 2616.

12 Picture Gallery — Scetlander,
74 Victoria Crescent Road,
Glasgow G12 9JN.
041 357 1659.

13 CK Sequencer — Ian Singer,
Lothian Region.

14 Starspell — Fisher Marriott,
3 Grove Road,
Ansty
Coventry CV7 9JD.
0203 616325.

15 Complete Speller — Northern Micromedia,
University of Northumbria,
Coach Lane Campus,
Newcastle upon Tyne NE7 7XA.
091 270 0424.

Chapter 13

16	Soapbox	Xavier Software, Bangor Dyslexia Unit, Department of Psychology, University College of North Wales, Bangor, Gwynedd LL57 2DG, 0248 351151 x 2616.
17	Keyboard Skills	Scetlander, 74 Victoria Crescent Road, Glasgow G12 9JN, 041 357 1659.
18	Mavis Beacon Teaches Typing	Software Toolworks Ltd., The Coach House, Hooklands, Scaynes Hill, Haywards Heath, W Sussex RH17 7NG, 0444831761.
19	Alan Nixon Special Care	NorthWest Semerc, Fitton Hill CDC, Rosary Road, Oldham OL8 2QE, 061 627 4469.

BIBLIOGRAPHY

A Software Guide for Specific Learning Difficulties (1993)

    Day, Jill.,   Sir William Lyons Road,
    NCET   Science Park,
                         Coventry CV4 7EZ.

IT Support for Specific Learning Difficulties (1992)

    Ed. Sally McKeown,   Sir William Lyons Road,
    NCET   Science Park,
                         Coventry CV4 7EZ.

Computers and Literacy Skills (1991)

    Ed. Chris Singleton,
    The British Dyslexia Association Computer Resource Centre,
    Department of Psychology,
    University of Hull,
    Hull HU6 7RX.

Computers and Typography (1993)

    compiled by Rosemary Sassoon,
    Intellect Books,
    Suite 2, 108/110 London Road, Oxford OX3 9AW.

The diagram on page (Fig.2) is taken from Alberts House Support Pack by Chris Hopkins published by the NCET and is reproduced here with the permission of the publishers.

Figures 1, 3 and 4 reproduced by permission of the publishers.

Chapter 13

USEFUL CONTACTS

NCET
Sir William Lyons Road, Science Park, Coventry. CV4 7EZ .
Tel 0203-416994.

Publications: A Software Guide for Specific Learning Difficulties – J. Day.
Special Update – Jan 1993.
Dyslexia Information sheet SEN 6.11.
Portable Computers and Special Needs SEN 6.21.

NERIS
Maryland College Leighton Street, Woburn, Beds. MK17 9JD.
Useful source of information on software and publications.

BRITISH DYSLEXIA ASSOCIATION
98 London Road, Reading, Berks., RGl 5AU.

Publications: Computers and Literacy Skills – Chris Singleton (Ed).
Using Computers with Dyslexics – Getting Started Series.

NASEN
2 Lichfield Road, Stafford. ST17 4JX.

SNUG
Jeff Hughes, 3g Eccleston Gardens, St Helens. WA10 3BJ.
Help and advice for users of technology.

BDA COMPUTER RESOURCE CENTRE
Dept. of Psychology, University of Hull, HULL HU67RX.

Northwest SEMERC
– Fitton Hill CDC, Rosary Road, Oldham. OL8 2QE.
A Source of useful software.

Publications: Laptop Computers and Special Educational Needs – L. Mason.

CECC
Prissick Base, Marton Road, Middlesborough, Cleveland. TS4 3R.
A Source of useful software.

Publications: Technology for Specific Learning Difficulties.
A Parent's Guide to buying a computer.

SCOTTISH EXAMINATIONS BOARD
Ironmills Road, Dalkeith, Midlothian EH22 1 LE.
Guidance on the use of technology in examinations.

Chapter 14

INTEGRATED SUPPORT: WORKING ON THE SYSTEM IN THE SYSTEM

ROS HUNTER

INTRODUCTION

This chapter describes the process of supporting pupils with specific learning difficulties through the transition from primary to secondary school. It seeks to highlight approaches and issues that may be useful to the reader in reflecting on their own practice.

The context of the case study is that of a comprehensive High School of around 700 pupils with . . . associate primaries in a highly rural catchment area. The school prides itself on high academic standards. It has a long-established Learning Support Department where the focus has been on support for pupils with moderate and severe learning difficulties. In recent years, increasing emphasis has been placed on support for learning across the mainstream curriculum, with some collaborative work on producing a differentiated curriculum.

FIRST THOUGHTS

In the second term of the academic year prior to the transfer of the pupils focused on here, the Principal Teacher of Learning Support (PT:LS) began planning for the new intake with the Education Psychologist. Together they noted that there were five[1] pupils in various local Primary 7 classes with marked specific learning difficulties – three with Records of Need in process. Although there were some variations, all four had broadly similar dyslexic type difficulties with reading and writing and were of above average intellectual abilities. All four pupils received Learning Support in their primary schools and had made some use of word processing, two using computers supplied on a loan basis by the regional Learning Support Service through the microtechnology support teacher.

It was felt that this unusually high percentage of pupils with SpLD coming into S1 meant that support staff (LS teachers in both sectors; support staff; educational psychologist and regional advisory staff) should work together to

Perspectives on Practice 173

achieve successful transition, with a particular emphasis on offering subject staff the opportunity to extend their repertoire of relevant skills and approaches. This work also informed the development of regional guidelines for parents and for teachers on SpLd which were written by a Working Party and later distributed to **all** teachers.

Staff development took the form of two distinctive but complementary approaches. Firstly, effective communication between key staff in each sector was established to ensure that the appropriate action plans for transition were drawn up for each pupil. This depended principally on setting up carefully planned and well-attended review meetings for each pupil **early** in the summer term, to which parents also contributed. This exchange of information was used to prepare resumés of pupils' needs which were later distributed to **all** staff.

DEVELOPING THE ANALYSIS

One particular idea which emerged from these reviews was the desirability of setting up a system of support which would encourage the pupils to sustain and develop their use of word processing across the curriculum. This in turn promoted further thinking about ways of raising subject teachers' awareness in such a way that would:

- encourage empathy.
- promote positive attitudes.
- develop practical classroom support.

Four strategies were adopted with this purpose:

- Staff were issued with clear non-judgemental information about each pupil: for example, 'copying work from a blackboard/book is possible but slow and not always accurate. She can operate in terms of writing with acceptance of weak spelling. Reading of SPMG Maths material presents difficulty in Primary.'
- At the same time, guidelines were provided for all staff on accessing the classroom curriculum in relation to specific learning difficulties (See Appendix 1 for extracts).
- A support system based on these guidelines was put in place by the PT: LS which focused on support within the mainstream curriculum, whilst allowing up to four periods per week for work on individualised educational programmes for the continued development of

reading writing and spelling skills. Each pupil was also given access to a Tandy WP2 portable word processor based in the reprographics room (secure but accessible) where a printer sharer and printer were also based. Machines were dedicated to each user and could be taken home.

- Senior management bought additional Tandy WP2s and training in the use of these was made available to **all** staff through the LS regional support staff which some 20% of staff chose to attend.
- At an optional workshop a teacher from a nearby secondary school who has dyslexic difficulties spoke to staff about his own educational experiences – of failing his 11+, of being underestimated and understimulated at a Secondary Modern, of receiving help from a concerned teacher and of finally overcoming his difficulties, and of success at university. His talks were attended by more than half the staff as a whole.
- A structured programme to teach the use of the Tandy WP2 was developed by the PT:LS (with the support staff).

Six Months Later:

Six months later a very informal piece of action research looked at the pupils' progress, through interviews with pupils, with a few subject teachers and with the PT:LS. Pupils were also shown a list of possible teacher strategies (Appendix 2) and asked to identify the most important *for them.*

It was apparent that all four pupils were relatively positive about their secondary school experiences to date. There also appeared to be a strong correlation between their attitude to the school environment and their sense of success.

Laura:

Laura – the only girl – at transfer aged 11 had a reading function around 7 years 9 months and spelling around 7 years 6 months, with handwriting difficulties. She was confident enough to describe herself as having dyslexia . . . 'I told my friends this and they were OK.' She was also able to seek help with reading from friends.

Laura had extended her use of word processing, using it regularly in Science and English, and occasionally for History work, especially at home. These were her favourite subjects. She had made positive use of the intensive support teaching and become committed to learning to touch type and to use spell-checking effectively. Her parents had demonstrated their support for Laura and for the school's approach by buying her her own Amstrad Notebook, which had the advantages of disk storage and a touch typing tutor as 'add-ons'.

The aspects of teacher support most important to her were:

- 'making sure I understood the work.'
- 'showing interest and encouraging me.'
- 'not expecting too much reading and writing.'
- 'letting me use computers, tape recorders and calculators.'

She did, however, perceive some subjects as 'too difficult . . . **because** you have to read and write a lot there' whereas it was actually only the print elements which she could not handle. There was a suggestion that she was losing confidence in her intellectual abilities because of her specific difficulties. Asked about her one wish for school, she replied: 'to be brainier . . . well, to be able to do the work faster.'

Alex:

Alex was an interesting case. He was reported as having marked behavioural difficulties at primary school – destructive and dishonest – in addition to his specific difficulties with auditory and visual memory, with spelling (7 years 8 months: CA12.0) and with organisational skills. His initial programme of support therefore included structured monitoring of behaviour by support and guidance staff, together with access to a Tandy and an element of intensive tutorial support in a small group. He described his difficulties accurately: 'I've got problems with putting letters down the wrong way . . . my reading's getting better.'

Very quickly it became clear that Alex was doing well and so the monitoring was stopped and his support reduced to allow more mainstream curricular access.

He made use of the Tandy WP2, mainly in English. Although he found it slow he felt he would continue to use it. In addition his parents sought advice about a dedicated spell-checker and purchased a Franklin spellmaster for Alex.

In his favourite subjects he liked the work and found the teachers helpful. The aspects of teacher support most important for him were:

- 'making sure I understand the work.'
- 'finding extra ways of giving practice.'
- 'showing interest and encouraging me.'

Generally he felt he was doing well and experiencing success.

Colin:

Colin was described to me as difficult and likely to be taciturn. In practice he was neither and was in fact very articulate reflecting his high average performance in WISC tests. His major difficulties were described as organisational and in terms of attention span, but these difficulties appeared to generate aggravation amongst staff.

Interestingly the support which he most valued was that which appeared most relevant to his needs. Sixth year helpers in some subjects who 'stay with you, make sure you do your work properly and don't make mistakes.' He would have preferred shorter periods of tutorial support with 'more variety'. Was it more difficult to cater for Colin's needs in the system?

The type of support he most valued was:

- 'getting time to finish work.'
- 'not being expected to do too much writing which can be hard going.'
- 'teachers being interesting about their subject.'

THE TEACHER'S PERCEPTIONS:

Classroom teachers' perceptions proved interesting. The staff development input had clearly had an impact . . . it appeared to have been sufficiently subtle, interesting and practical to raise staff awareness **positively.** The practical suggestions had been well received as being useful support strategies for a range of pupils experiencing difficulties, not just these pupils. (This now extended to the regional guidelines distributed at that time.) Attitudes to the use of the Tandys varied: generally speaking staff who used more active learning approaches felt the Tandys enhanced pupil work – again more widely than the pupils with SpLD.

The input by the teacher with dyslexic difficulties had been particularly well received as being interesting and enlightening.

At the same time, sympathetic teachers appeared to find it difficult to hold onto the fact that those pupils with specific difficulties did not have general learning difficulties. The superficial appearance of their work appeared to affect teachers' perceptions: 'One thing I would say, they are by no means the least able . . . ' There was a concern that any supporting readers and tapes should not encourage laziness! One sympathetic teacher was committed to marking all spelling mistakes, despite advice to focus on common words and key subject specific terms: 'It can't help not to know they've got it wrong . . . '

One constant theme was the limited extent to which teachers felt it was legitimate to respond to the particular pupil's needs in the interest of equity: 'I feel I owe equal allegiance to all the pupils.' As a result they felt their contribution was limited 'at the end of the day, most of their support comes from other pupils who help them through . . . '

The valued aspects of Learning Support were the provision of support materials, together with the opportunity to consult – flexibly – often when these were being supplied. The Learning Support Teacher had found the introduction of the word processors a useful stimulus to his planning of internal support. It provided a focus for the work done in extraction periods and he had gone on to devise ways of using the machines to motivate pupils in doing routine and repetitive tasks necessary for improvement of basic spelling (and reading, indirectly).

He had become convinced of the value of teaching touch typing to pupils – provided they had the motivation. Ideally he would have done this using the touch typing tutors now available in the newer generation of computers – including the Amstrad Notebook. In the absence of access to this facility he had devised his own touch typing 'course' simplified from material supplied by Business Studies, and developed together with microtechnology support staff.

He had also worked at improving and refining the microtechnology support system. At a basic level the microtechnology support staff had needed to iron out practical operational difficulties between the Tandys and the printer. A simple system of recording use of the Tandys and use of the printer allowed the PT:LS to develop his ideas about refining the system.

At a second level the system had been enhanced by the purchase (by the region) of disk drives which allowed pupils to develop the habit of saving work. It was clear to him that if pupils were going to make more extensive use of word processing as they progressed into S3/S4 they needed to be trained in the process of disk management at an early stage.

The work was time-consuming no doubt. It had, however, generated thinking about teaching pupils with specific learning difficulties in general.

CONCLUSIONS:

Issues and Questions:

- Pupil attitude
- School ethos
- Staff attitude: LS, mainstream
- Back-up staff – support and advice (to parents)
- Practical advice
- Manageable systems
- Management support
- Slow process
- Stimulus to action . . .
- Help support system as a whole
- Communication . . . feeling OK about asking . . .

Tempering the ideal with the manageable; avoiding making staff feel guilty; working on the positive and raising the profile **gently.**

Chapter 14

Appendix 1

. . . Departments are asked to choose those items from the following menu which would most closely fit the rationale of their S1 curriculum.

1. Provide pupils with photocopies of work sheets / work cards and allow them to write answers on the sheets. Accept limited responses to written work where response indicates understanding of content.

2. Provide photocopies of blackboard/OHP notes. (Special photocopying provision will be provided for 1 & 2 – please enter as Special Needs).

3. Wherever suitable encourage pupils to use Tandy Desk Top Word Processors (with spell check facility) for written work or allow use of other word processors.

4. Accept oral answers on tape as substitute for written responses. Two Dictaphones are available.

5. Provide taped recordings of reading matter to enable pupils to follow class work. Three Walkmans are available from Reprographics and the Learning Support Department will get recordings done if approached.

6. Make use of sixth year volunteers as scribes/readers for recording.

7. Use a reader/scribe for assessment elements of a course. Approach Learning Support for scribe/readers.

8. Allow the use of a partner for reading and written work. Provide photocopy of the joint work.

9. Encourage the use of ring folders and the use of A4 lined paper rather than jotters for work. This will allow any photocopied material to be slotted in at appropriate place.

10. Allow the use of calculators or number squares.

11. Encourage use of Homework Diary as a means of communication between class teacher and home.

12. Keep in mind the predicament of these pupils. They may often feel stupid as a result of lack of writing skills.

Appendix 2

How Teacher Might Help

- Show interest and encourage you
- Help you to be organised
- Make sure you understand what you have to do
- Give you TIME to finish work
- Not expect too much writing
- Find extra ways of giving extra practice
- Write clearly
- Give you a chance to use computer, tape recorder, calculator
- Make sure others don't slag you
- Let other pupils help you with work.

[1] One pupil did not transfer as he moved out of the catchment area

Chapter 14

Appendix 3

Carla Fullerton

, all about me.

I am 12 years old, and live on a farm. I love animals and I hat wherking on the farm. My hoday are cook and Swimmi I kleked lots ot thingys and, I have 2 dogs and 2 cat's wich I love.

Greg Moizer

Myself

name is Greg and i live at ... ... i have ... ... Cotastream for 4 yers. I have ... ... she is 9 yers old she liks net... ... ... hors ranin... ... ... for ... howie. My mum wurks in chris... ... is a ... comunity eqacshon wurker. My dad is the regency sals ... of trico they sell wiper blaws... and... hoays are 4x4 driving he cies with Neil Redpath he wurks at Redpath tyers. My hoays are 4x4 driving trayn sets and biding on bikes and then poing theer. When I am older I want my job to be forastry manigmant.

182   *Specific Learning Difficulties (Dyslexia)*

Chapter 15

SUPPORTING LEARNING THROUGH A WHOLE SCHOOL APPROACH

MORVEN BROWN

INTRODUCTION

This chapter focuses on the contribution that can be made by a Learning Resources Centre to the staff and pupils, including those with specific learning difficulties, of a large school catering for pupils of both sexes aged 5 to 18.

The Centre aims to provide not only for pupils with specific learning difficulties but also for any pupil who needs support, and to serve as a whole school resource for every pupil and member of staff. The staff of the Centre includes experienced learning support teachers and an educational psychologist/teacher. This allows the Centre to offer a wide range of services to pupils throughout the school.

If is still too often the case that the facility (no matter how it is named) which exists in a school to support the learning of those who encounter difficulties is seen in a negative light both by staff and pupils. If the facility can provide a wide range of resources, seen as helpful to all pupils and staff, then a positive view should prevail. This can only be of benefit to those who have greatest need of its services.

The Centre is involved in the screening and monitoring of all pupils' progress; in the investigation of persistent difficulties; in the provision of teaching support; in the provision of materials to aid classroom support and differentiation; in the provision of counselling and emotional support; in liaison with parents; in liaison with outside agencies and so on.

Providing a Centre where support exists for learning and teaching (the two being inextricably bound together) across all areas and stages of the curriculum goes far in meeting the needs of many pupils including those with specific difficulties. The needs of pupils with any kind of learning difficulty cannot be met through specialist teaching/learning support alone. There is little point in pupils going to a special teacher if they have difficulties in learning or processing information and returning to an unenlightened classroom where the nature and implications of their problems are not acknowledged or accommodated.

An essential role of the Learning Resource Centre is, therefore, to provide staff in-service training. All teachers need help in acknowledging a fundamental cornerstone of their function, i.e. to support the learning of their pupils. Learning Support teachers and a Learning Support Department are still too often seen as existing to excuse or absolve the class or subject teacher from this essential task.

The functions that the Learning Resource Centre (L.R.C.) aspires to can be summarised as follows:

IDENTIFICATION

A major function of the L.R.C. is to be instrumental in the identification of pupils who require help or support. They fall into a number of categories:

1. Children with specific learning difficulties who:
   - (a) can be anywhere on the range of intelligence from very superior to well below average
   - (b) can be anywhere on the continuum of difficulty from mild to severe
   - (c) can have any number of additional difficulties

2. Children who have other types of learning difficulties:
   - (a) sensory handicaps – visual, auditory, physical
   - (b) mild neurological impairment – for example because of illness, injury, epilepsy, premature birth etc.
   - (c) emotional difficulties
   - (d) maturational delay, immaturity
   - (e) intellectual impairment
   - (f) language disorders
   - (g) behavioural disorders

3. Children with disadvantageous educational history:
   - (a) disrupted schooling
   - (b) inadequate teaching
   - (c) prolonged absence

4. Children from non-English speaking background or whose language is impoverished for other reasons.

Chapter 15

IDENTIFICATION PROCEDURES

L.R.C. staff can use a number of means at their disposal to identify pupils with difficulties:

1   Through objective assessment:
    (a)   school entrance tests
    (b)   annual screening tests carried out on all primary age children from P3 to P7 in reading, spelling and mathematics
    (c)   National Tests
    (d)   internal tests and examinations
    (e)   external examinations

2   Through subjective assessment:
    (a)   teacher observation and concern
    (b)   teacher reports
    (c)   parental concern

3   Through more detailed diagnostic testing by the experienced Learning Support Teachers.

4   Through full assessment by the Educational Psychologist.

REMEDIAL ACTION

Once children are identified a number of measures can be taken:

1   Help can be provided within the classroom:
    (a)   from the class or subject teacher
    (b)   from additional personnel in the classroom (e.g. another class teacher, trained auxiliary, parent or older pupil)
    (c)   from the L.S. teacher in classroom
    (d)   through the provision of additional teaching materials and aids

2   Help can be offered outwith the classroom through:
    (a)   extraction and specialised teaching help from the L.S. teacher
    (b)   tuition outside school

3   There should be a full discussion with teachers and parents of the results of the identification procedure and of future implications.

Perspectives on Practice

This helps to ensure that the classroom situation is an enlightened one where teachers are aware of the nature of the difficulty and of how to support learning. It costs nothing but time and willingness to be flexible and creative – with the teacher as an enabler and a facilitator. Parents, if willing and supportive, can be encouraged to provide appropriate back up and emotional support.

4   Long-term monitoring:

   (a)   regular checks on progress through teacher comment and reports

   (b)   careful record-keeping of L.S. history, reasons for identification and progress

   (c)   regular checks that staff are aware of pupils' difficulties and the implications of these difficulties

   (d)   automatic checking of all 'noted' names before the stage of sitting external examinations.

'HARD' RESOURCES

The L.R.C. offers a bank of resources and materials which can be used by staff for a wide range of pupils ranging from those with specific difficulties and those who are less able to those who are more able and require extension materials.

There is now an enormous range of photocopiable materials which cover extensive areas of the curriculum and a wide range of skills throughout the school age range. Many of these materials, some developed originally for pupils with difficulties, have relevance to the mainstream class and subject teacher. Many can be used effectively to achieve curriculum differentiation. Furnished with a range of such materials the L.R.C. can provide a 'cafeteria' of choice from which 'customised' packages can be built for pupils. Obviously close liaison with and monitoring by the L.S. teaching staff is essential.

The L.R.C. can collaborate with class and subject teachers in developing 'in-house' materials such as back-ups to course text books, audio-taped and video-taped information which can be used repetitively for those whose auditory or visual memory is poor and in building a bank of aids useful in many subject areas.

By combining proprietary materials and those developed in school it is also possible to devise teaching modules to cover many of the areas which need to be addressed when helping older pupils with spelling, written language and number difficulties. This is of value when time is limited, and the curriculum full, but requires the commitment and self motivation of the pupil and support at home.

Close links with the school library and technology centre are essential. Difficulties with learning are difficulties with processing and organising information and an essential role of the L.R.C. is in exploring effective ways of presenting and receiving information which will compensate for, or circumvent, any difficulties which pupils may have. The L.R.C. may be the first point in directing pupils towards back-up materials in the form of simplified texts, illustrated texts, video and audio-taped material, computer-based information sources such as CD-ROM and information about places to visit, outside sources of information and experience to explore.

The L.R.C. also provides a library of reference books and up-to-date catalogues of materials and books on all aspects of learning and teaching for staff, pupils and parents.

'SERVICE' RESOURCES

As well as a provider of 'hard' resources the L.R.C. can also be a repository of information and advice to teachers, pupils and parents about the learning process. Those of us who have the privilege of working with children with learning difficulties perhaps have a greater awareness of and greater opportunity for exploring the myriad range of individual learning and information processing styles used by children. In recent years awareness of learning styles and approaches has heightened and there is an increasing wealth of explicit techniques aimed at enhancing learning. What is remarkable about many of these approaches is, not their diversity, but the common thread which runs through them all (see Table 1) of self-awareness, self motivation and active involvement. Helping all teaching staff to become aware of these recurrent themes in learning theory and how they can be implemented is an important task of the L.R.C.

Knowledge and understanding of these learning and information processing approaches can enhance any learning situation. If such knowledge can be made easily accessible to all teachers and pupils in a school then benefits can be gained, not just for those with identifiable and enduring difficulties, but also for any individual who encounters difficulty in learning. There are few, perhaps none, of us who can claim to have negotiated the educational system completely free of difficulty.

As well as being a place where pupils receive direct teaching help the L.R.C. should be a repository of information about learning and teaching techniques and a source of support for pupils and teachers who require it. It is therefore useful if L.R.C. staff can be involved directly in In-service Training so that awareness of learning/teaching techniques is heightened and teachers are clear about what is relevant for **them** and **their** pupils. There is no clear-cut border between the teacher and the learner or between the giver and the recipient of knowledge and a thorough understanding of the learning process seems a fundamental basis for effective teaching no matter what the subject. The L.R.C. needs to provide an easy partnership with pupils and teachers in achieving this.

TABLE 1

Some Helpful Approaches to Learning and Their Communality:

(This summary is not intended to be comprehensive or definitive and is merely a personal observation of how these different approaches can be drawn together.)

Approach	Useful elements (stressing common threads)
Neurolinguistic programming	**Modelling** – analysing and understanding of successful learning strategies and applying them to new situations. Developing awareness through analytical observation of self and others.
Metacognition	Awareness of one's own thinking and learning processes, of the nature of a task and what is required to master it. Developing self awareness and self knowledge.
Educational Kinesiology (Brain Gym)	'Noticing' and being aware of one's state of mind and how situations affect one. The sensory integrative exercises may be helpful and the notion of balance, goal setting and positive attitude is central. Using the gestalt, creative brain, integrating the senses.
Instrumental Enrichment	Developing the capacity for storing, organising and using information.
DeBono's CoRT Thinking Programme	Developing thinking skills – evaluative and exploratory thinking. Creativity, looking at all aspects, gaining overviews.
Tony Buzan's Mind Mapping	Considering key concepts, overviews, planning using the gestalt.

	Exploring one's own memory and learning processes. Moving out into use of colour, images and representations – away from the restrictions of linear, language-bound learning. Stressing inter-relationships. Awareness of how information is processed, how memory works.
Multi-sensory teaching	Linking all the senses, exploring memory, becoming aware of every method we use to encode and stressing inter-relationships. Awareness of how information is processed.
Active learning	Acknowledgment of how learning occurs – the importance of doing, experiencing. Using all the senses, manipulating concrete materials. Active versus passive involvement.

STUDY SKILLS

One of the most important areas for those with specific learning difficulties, particularly for the older pupil, is the development of good study skills. The L.R.C. has a significant role in contributing to the whole school policy on study skills. Almost every pupil who has had a history of specific learning difficulty will benefit from some explicit help on methods of study, memory techniques, time organisation and management, planning, drafting and redrafting written assignments, revision and note-taking and examination technique. There should be a whole school policy on study skills with its roots firmly established in the middle primary school so that good habits are established gradually. However it is often only in the upper part of the secondary school that pupils develop the necessary maturity and self-motivation to implement advice effectively. Often the pupil with specific learning difficulties needs a 'short burst' of individual help tailored to his/her own needs when faced with the relatively sophisticated demands of the Higher syllabus. It is for this reason that long-term monitoring of those with difficulties is important. Even those pupils who appear to have coped well up to Standard Grade should be reviewed at the stage of commencing their Higher years.

The well-informed subject teacher, who is in tune with the demands of his subject, can be instrumental in ensuring that pupils are directed to appropriate help when required. The role of the L.R.C. in promoting a school climate which will encourage all teachers to be well-informed about learning and aware of subject demands on information processing skills cannot be sufficiently stressed.

Chapter 15

EXAMINATIONS AND ASSESSMENT

We are indeed fortunate in Scotland in having an enlightened Examination Board who now offer a good range of concessions for those with specific learning difficulties affecting spelling and written language. Another important function of the L.R.C. is to identify those pupils for whom concessions should be applied.

The L.R.C. should also provide information to school staff about the nature and implications of specific learning difficulties and advice on assessment, correction and feedback to pupils. Though it may not be entirely desirable, much of our formal educational provision is assessment and examination-driven. If the Examination board is prepared to offer concessions to candidates then it is essential that school staff are made fully aware of these concessions.

The assessment of those who have difficulties in translating their thoughts and ideas into a written form is problematical. To separate evidence of an individual's knowledge, understanding and ability to manipulate information from his/her technical accuracy, presentation and performance under timed conditions is not easy. If, however, those who are teaching and assessing are not aware of the importance of separating these strands then pupils with written language difficulties will be at an unnecessary disadvantage. The role of the L.R.C. in disseminating information about dealing with pupils who have such difficulties is therefore extremely important.

TECHNOLOGY

The importance of using word processors, data-handling programmes, and computer-based instruction and information retrieval facilities cannot be underestimated for individuals with specific learning difficulties. Learning how to use a word processor proficiently may diminish the impact of the difficulty significantly and allow the individual to embark on courses, gain certificates and take advantage of tertiary educational opportunities which might otherwise be beyond his/her reach.

The L.R.C. staff should be able to ensure that all pupils who would benefit are given the opportunity of gaining that proficiency, preferably by having computers at their disposal.

A library of information about technological developments and opportunities with particular reference to special needs can easily be built up and kept current for almost no cost, and made available to teachers, pupils and parents for reference.

Software packages designed to develop skills such as speed reading, reading comprehension, spelling, mathematical skills and so on can provide valuable opportunities for consolidation of skills. A bank of back up and reference, video and audio-taped material can be built up for older pupils to use as required. The provision of audio and video tape players with earphones allows pupils easy and discrete access to information when they require it.

Dictaphones and tape recorders can also be a useful study or note-taking aid and can be borrowed for use in school. Such materials can be kept in the school library or technology centre as well as in the L.R.C. but a catalogue of them has to be kept in the L.R.C. so that L.S. staff can direct pupils to them as required.

VOCATIONAL HELP

Often the pupil with specific learning difficulties needs help in planning his/her course, choosing subjects and investigating appropriate post school placements. The L.R.C. can hold useful information to help in this and staff can discuss subject choices and implications for demands on reading skills and literacy. Advice can be offered about coping with the demands of post-school life, seeking help at college or university, and coping with later examinations and assessments.

EMOTIONAL SUPPORT

Almost without exception pupils with specific learning difficulties need a good deal of psychological as well as educational support. The negative effects of specific difficulties on self image and motivation are well publicised and the L.R.C. has an important role to play in minimising these effects. Providing support for pupils through allowing them to explore their own successful strategies, increasing their awareness of their strengths, celebrating their achievements, and encouraging them to take control and responsibility for their own learning is an integral part of the learning support teacher's job. It should be an integral part of every teacher's job. The desirable progression for all learners is towards independence. The whole process of education should be to promote skills in individuals which will equip them for the rest of their life and allow them to realise their full potential in every area be it intellectual, emotional or psychological.

In an ideal world young people should emerge from their years of compulsory education capable of thinking and functioning in the adult world to the best of their innate ability. Their educational experience should have promoted self awareness and a positive view of themselves. Unfortunately for many pupils, particularly those with specific learning difficulties, their experience is a negative one. Through in-service training L.R.C. staff can have the opportunity of encouraging all school staff to appreciate the importance of promoting a positive self image and encouraging self motivation.

RELATIONSHIP TO THE WHOLE SCHOOL

The relationship of the L.R.C. to the whole school must be a supportive one, beginning at an early stage and continuing throughout the years of education. A major aim of the L.R.C. is to ensure that the classroom settings in which children spend so much of their days are an enlightened ones. The impact of any learning difficulty will be minimised if the educational setting is appropriate.

A partnership between the L.R.C. and the whole school can help in promoting conditions which will be conducive to effective learning for all, particularly for those with difficulty.

I have described above the major functions to which the L.R.C. aspires. I have stressed the benefits of a L.R.C. for a broad range of pupils but a major role is to meet the needs of individuals with dyslexic and specific learning difficulties. The summary below focuses, in more detail, on meeting their needs throughout the school age range

Nursery   **Pre-school identification**
Children who may be at risk because of a number of factors (e.g. language difficulties; poor phonological awareness; immature speech; clumsiness – poor motor control; immaturity at school entry) can be identified and appropriate action taken to minimise future difficulties e.g. through nursery retention, referral to other agencies such as speech therapy, promotion of useful activities within the nursery setting such as those to encourage language development, fine motor control, co-operative behaviour etc.

Primary 1   Helpful approaches can be advocated such as extra activities to develop language and ensuring an integrated presentation of writing and reading.

Awareness of the development of literacy and language skills, of multi-sensory and other compensatory teaching approaches can be engendered. The importance can be underlined for all children, but in particular for those with difficulties, of a structured teaching approach from the beginning – in reading, written language (spelling, punctuation) and mathematics. Children can be helped to understand that written language is another means of communicating and the conventions and rules of written language are there to enhance that communication and need to be acknowledged from the beginning.

A metacognitive approach, awareness of the nature of the task and why things are done in a certain way, is not beyond the young child and can be advocated.

The importance of helping children to develop an easy and fluent hand cannot be over emphasized. On first entering an infant classroom children should be encouraged to hold a pencil properly (there are many pencil grips and specially shaped pencils available to help this). Developing an easy flowing script should be an aim for all children. It is an appalling indictment of the educational system in this country that so many young people are unable to hold a writing implement efficiently and are condemned to a lifetime of writing in a contorted, awkward fashion. Motor habits are difficult to break once established and it is therefore essential to get the grasp correct in the beginning.

The L.R.C. staff can ensure that there is easy access to advice and materials from the Centre and teaching help in or out of class if necessary.

The importance of early identification and appropriate help can be stressed. Pupils can be screened at the end of the first year to identify those with difficulty but staff can liaise with L.R.C. staff at any time if concerned.

Primary 2 A continuation of the above but with more teaching input either from the Early Education Department or the L.R.C. staff within the classroom or through extraction. Close liaison with any others involved with the child e.g. parents, speech therapist, educational psychologist is encouraged.

Primary 3-5 Building on the above but there will be an increasing need for the child with dyslexic or specific learning difficulties to receive an individualised programme tailored to his specific needs.

Close contact between the class teacher and the L.R.C. is, of course, essential and help within the classroom is beneficial but there is no substitute for the kind of help which can be given one-to-one or in a very small group. Working alongside the child with a dyslexic-type difficulty in a relatively quiet and uninterrupted environment is essential if he is to be helped to gain awareness of his own successful strategies. It is essential that he receives positive feedback, experiences of success, credit for what he does well and careful explanation for what he has difficulty with. His teachers need to be fully aware that the way in which information is presented is of fundamental importance. It is so easy for a failing child to switch off and to stop trying. It is easy for the 'dyslexic' label to become an excuse for both the child and the teacher to expect less; for the child to stop trying and the teacher to expect little. Dyslexic children need to learn the unpalatable fact that they will have to work much harder than everyone else if they are to overcome their difficulty.

The correct balance between delivering praise and encouragement and promoting the need to strive and master difficult skills is tricky to achieve – especially for busy class teachers and harassed parents. They, also, need support from the L.R.C.

Primary 6-7 By Primary 6 the demands on literacy and other basic skills are increasing and continue to increase. There is a growing need to gain good reading skills – fluency, information retrieval, skimming and scanning, extracting key words, understanding nuance and style – all these skills which continue to develop throughout the remaining years in compulsory education.

The abilities to read and comprehend accurately, to infer and extrapolate, become increasingly important and without these skills youngsters become more and more disadvantaged in every area of the curriculum. In the same way the skill of planning, drafting, redrafting and presenting a piece of written work becomes increasingly important. The early years should have given the opportunity to practise but few children are given sufficient experience for developing these skills adequately because of the extensive demands on curriculum content. This is difficult for all but disastrous for those with dyslexic-type difficulties. Like all skills – learning to punctuate, spell and express oneself coherently on paper improves with practise. While these skills can be taught in isolation they need to be put to use in a concerted way as often as possible and the end result used effectively as a teaching aid.

Individuals with specific learning difficulties, more than any others, need to overlearn skills and it is the steady, repetitive, 'little-and-often' approach which usually pays off. It must also be noted that the heavy, repetitive slogging which often goes on for years may not bear fruit for some considerable time. As many teachers of children with specific learning difficulties will testify, they often cover the same ground year after year only to find the pupil making the same mistakes over and over again. Maturity may have an effect in that, often, there seems to be a spurt of progress when these seemingly tenuous skills 'gel' and reading, spelling and technical accuracy in written work suddenly improve.

In my experience this often happens around the end of second year in Secondary School but the importance of the earlier groundwork cannot be overestimated. The later help is offered the less effective it will be and the importance of early identification and intervention is paramount.

Qualitatively the teaching requirements appropriate to pupils with specific learning difficulties in the upper primary school and lower secondary school are very similar if they are within the normal range of intelligence and have received adequate teaching in the early stages.

By the last years in primary school, and certainly by the early years of secondary, pupils with specific learning difficulties should be given every opportunity to develop proficiency in the use of word processors and any other technological device which will allow them to cope with the demands of the curriculum more easily – e.g. hand held spell checkers, tape recorders for notes and as a memory aid.

For many individuals learning to use a word processor proficiently will greatly increase their ability to overcome their difficulties in later life.

Senior 1-2   While the needs of pupils with specific learning difficulties in the lower years of the secondary school remain similar to those in the upper primary the demands of a more subject-orientated curriculum are very taxing.

Chapter 15

The need for teachers to be fully aware of the learning process, the importance of how material is presented and the difficulties some of their pupils, particularly those with specific learning difficulties, have in processing information cannot be over emphasized. Close liaison with the learning support department is highly desirable but may be difficult to achieve. Time needs to be made available explicitly for the purpose of developing dual strategies with the learning support staff to provide the sort of support required by children with specific and other learning difficulties in each subject area. Discussion about presentation of information, back-up facilities, support material, addressing particular difficulties and so on is essential in every area of the curriculum. While each subject area has its own intrinsic set of demands the three Rs remain their cornerstone. Only through developing the skills and knowledge of all teachers can the environment for those with difficulty be improved. Learning support can never exist in a vacuum and all teachers need to know how to support learning.

However, the current vogue for learning support only within the classroom is unlikely to meet the needs of the pupil with specific learning difficulties. Individuals with dyslexic-type learning difficulties require help outwith the classroom either on their own or in very small groups (no more than 2 or 3).

Senior 3   This year is a transition between the primary/lower secondary school and the upper secondary school which becomes more and more syllabus-driven. The demands of sitting examinations and coping with written assignments, reading for information and taking notes are very taxing indeed for the pupil with specific learning difficulties. If the arrangements such as using a scribe or reader in external examinations are likely to be required then practise in using them should begin in earnest. The fully implications of using a scribe or reader need to be explored as it is always preferable for the pupil to develop strategies which allow him independence in later life. At this time the development of mature study habits, organisational and planning skills become increasingly important. While the promotion of good study habits should begin in the middle primary school and develop as an integral part of the curriculum youngsters often do not gain the maturity or motivation to approach study in a routine, ordered way until much later.

Chapter 15

The difference between a fifth or sixth year pupil bent on gaining Highers and moving on to tertiary education and a third or even fourth year pupil moving towards Standard Grades can be quite dramatic in terms of attitude and ability to implement advice.

Senior 4 Support during the demands of the examination year can often be extremely important and working through specific problems in any area of the curriculum may be required. The L.R.C. should be a source of support and advice to all pupils with specific learning difficulties – easily accessible to them as somewhere they can drop in and discuss any difficulties or queries.

In the same way staff should be able to, indeed encouraged to, seek advice, help and materials as required. Ideally there should be easy access to advice and materials e.g. word processors, audio and video taped material, practise exercises, back up to syllabus materials, examples of good practice, routes to information sources e.g. through the library or Technology Centre.

Pupils may need to be motivated through the exam years by being encouraged to consider appropriate and realistic post-school goals. The L.R.C. staff can seek appropriate exam allowances and offer help in preparing for the emotional demands of sitting exams e.g. through using self-help techniques like relaxation. Pupils with specific learning difficulties often need the reassurance that exams are not all-important and that there is almost always another route to a suitable post school goal.

Senior 5-6 As well as continuing in the support for examinations there is an ongoing need to help pupils prepare for life after school. While educational input and practical support is always required for the pupil with a specific learning difficulty the importance of nurturing a positive self image can never be over stressed.

Those with specific learning difficulties will have the best chance of achieving their potential if they feel good about themselves, have developed self awareness and the ability to be assertive and are in control of their own learning and thinking. They should not underestimate their potential but should avoid being over-ambitious. Brighter dyslexics who aspire to college or university may need careful support and guidance in seeking an establishment which will offer support for their difficulties and they will often approach the L.R.C. for advice and information about careers. As always it is important to allow them to be in control but to give them the opportunity to make fully informed choices.

CONCLUSION

I have attempted to describe how a whole school resource could be developed to embrace some of the learning, teaching and psychological needs of teachers, parents and pupils. The facilities offered by such a Learning Resource Centre are essential for those with specific or dyslexic-type learning difficulties, but many of the approaches and materials used with pupils who have difficulty in learning in a conventional setting are of benefit to a much wider range of individuals. Meeting the needs of those with specific learning difficulties in a positive setting where more, as well as less, able pupils can take advantage of what is on offer can only be of benefit to their self perception.

If staff, too, can freely make use of support for their teaching and find opportunities to enhance their skills and to develop their understanding of the learning process then the whole school community will benefit.

SECTION 4

READING, WRITING AND MATHEMATICS

Chapter 16

PERSPECTIVES ON READING

GAVIN REID

The research literature on the process of reading can provide useful insights to indicate why some approaches may be successful while others may not. It can also provide some theoretical frameworks which can help to guide the teacher through the morass of programmes and philosophies, and it can help to identify the nature of reading, the fundamental principles and concepts, and the importance of the role of the learner in the reading process.

It may be useful therefore to examine perspectives on reading by focusing on the following:

> Models and Methods
> Principles and Practices
> Skills and Strategies
> Concepts and Comprehension
> Learning and the Learner

MODELS AND METHODS

It has been asserted (Reason et al, 1988) that a dichotomy exists in reading research between cognitive psychologists who focus on the single word and elements of words, and teachers and educational psychologists who appear more concerned with the wider aspects of literacy and in particular those aspects related to instruction. Methods of teaching reading have therefore been of more concern to teachers and educational psychologists. However it should be appreciated that such methods owe their existence to the models which have been devised and developed following extensive and continuing research evident in the field of reading.

Methods of teaching reading lie within a continuum of approaches ranging from the systematic and sequential acquisition of sub-skills of reading at one end to the osmotic enrichment of language experience at the other end. These two approaches broadly represent the 'bottom-up' and the 'top-down' models of processing information and each presents specific methodologies embodied within a theoretical framework.

The 'bottom-up' model implies that the reader processes graphemic information, then moves to individual letters, then larger chunks, and that only after the word has been processed is meaning inferred by the reader (La Berge and Samuels, 1974).

The top-down model on the other hand which gathered impetus from the work of Smith (1979) and Goodman (1967), assumes that readers move from the higher (cognitive) to the lower (perceptual) mental processes. This model therefore implies that good readers do not need to decode and make sense of the shapes of letters because they initially focus on the whole word. It is from focusing on the whole word that readers abstract meaning. The lower, perceptual elements, according to the 'top-down' theorists are used only to confirm the original 'guess'. Goodman (1967) called this model the 'psycholinguistic guessing game' and it clearly places an important function on the role of context and language experience.

There are, however, arguments against both these models (Stanovich, 1984, 1992). It has been asserted that fluent readers do not necessarily rely on context but are more fluent because they are more adept at recognising text. It has also been shown that the rate of reading is affected by the readers' inferences and the use of context, so at least an element of 'top-down' processing is occurring in fluent reading.

Stanovich theorises that reading actually utilises both 'bottom-up' and 'top-down' processes and his 'interactive compensatory approach' implies that readers use compensatory strategies to assist with reading. Readers, therefore, with poor word recognition (decoding) would be more reliant on context than readers with good decoding skills. The implication of this view is that the teaching of reading should promote flexibility and recognition of the child's individual strengths and weakness in addition to the learning preferences.

Stanovich, focusing on the specific difficulties in reading experienced by dyslexic children, provides evidence for cognitive differences between dyslexic readers and other poor readers. This is encapsulated in his 'phonological-core variable difference model' Stanovich (1988). According to this model dyslexic children display a phonological difficulty which is specific to the reading task and does not pervade other domains of cognitive functioning. Stanovich agrees, however, that a continuum of phonological-core difficulties exists from one end of the spectrum where the deficits will be located only in phonological processing to the other end of the continuum where the reader will have 'a host of cognitive deficits' and a cognitively immature profile. He terms the readers at this end the 'garden variety poor readers'. This model helps to explain why dyslexic children often show secondary problems in addition to a phonological processing deficit. All dyslexic children, except those positioned at the uni-dimensional, phonological processing end of the continuum, will show multi-dimensional cognitive difficulties which may affect performance across a range of tasks.

Frith (1985) describes models of reading development as 'stage models'. The initial stage being the logographic phase when children recognise words based on visual features and contextual cues; the reader then moves to an alphabetic phase in which the letter-sound correspondence is the principal feature and finally to an orthographic phase when the reader becomes fluent and can relate his reading skills to the accurate spelling of words. Dyslexic children find the transition from the logographic to the alphabetic stage problematic because a degree of phonological skills are necessary to cope with the letter-sound relationships which are a feature of the alphabetic stage.

Goswami (1993) argues that reading development should be conceived as an interactive developmental process rather than as a series of stages. Progress in reading therefore will in turn affect changes to the child's level of phonological knowledge. She suggests that children develop phonological knowledge through the use of an analogy model of reading by using the 'onset' and 'rhyme' parts of words to help in word recognition. She further argues that dyslexic children may not spontaneously develop analogous reading strategies, but would benefit from being taught such a strategy.

Augur (1990) believes that while a substantial amount of children will not respond to the essentially visually based methods emanating from psycholinguistic theorists such as 'look and say' and 'real books', dyslexic children will almost certainly encounter difficulty. This is because the memory difficulties encountered by the dyslexic child mean that new words are not stored in memory readily and such new words need to be constantly used otherwise they are forgotten. Additionally, according to Auger, dyslexic children often confuse words which look similar such as 'one' and 'once'. She suggests a highly structured phonics approach (Auger & Briggs, 1992) based on the original programme devised by (Hickey, 1977) which teaches children the fundamental concepts of sound, letter and written shape relationship and begins with only a small combination of carefully selected letters to avoid unnecessary confusion.

Reason (1988) attempted to obtain some consensus on the teaching of reading through the formation of an interest group consisting of twenty specialist support teachers and educational psychologists and concluded that the two approaches are not 'mutually exclusive' Most children would usually acquire literacy through the language experience model and approaches such as apprenticeship (Waterland, 1986)—which allows children to benefit from enriched reading experiences through a psycholinguistic orientation and peer and adult assistance. For some children, however, this method may need to be supplemented by a step-by-step method of skill acquisition. The balance of these two types of instruction needs to be examined in the light of the individual child's learning history, current learning context and learning style. The choice is not, therefore, either/or; instead a focus must be placed on the holistic needs of the learner not only to be able to tackle the reading process, but to receive pleasure from the reading text.

PRINCIPLES AND PRACTICES

Although there are a considerable number of reading programmes and strategies available for use with dyslexic students it is now generally accepted that many of those programmes share similar principles. It is recognised that dyslexic students present difficulties in many aspects of phonological processing and in short and long term memory processes. These difficulties deprive the learner of automatic access to the decoding of print. To help overcome these difficulties programmes suggested to help deal with the problem of dyslexia, usually incorporate the following:

- multi-sensory techniques;
- automaticity principles and structured and cumulative over-learning.

The context and form of programmes may vary but the underlying aims of accessing all the senses and attempting to enhance automaticity by the essentially repetitive processes of over-learning can be seen in many programmes which have been developed to deal with dyslexia.

Multi-Sensory

Multi-sensory techniques involve visual, auditory, kinaesthetic and tactile reinforcement. The rationale of such techniques appear to stem from the view that kinaesthetic activities help to establish visual-auditory associations in grapheme and phoneme correspondences, in addition to reinforcing left to right letter progression (Orton, 1966). It is also suggested that multi-sensory activities can help to retrieve words from long term memory (Slingerland, 1971)

The manner in which multi-sensory techniques are utilised appears to vary depending on the programme used. For example Orton believes that individual phonic sounds should be pronounced as the child traces a word, Gillingham feels that individual letter names should be called out, while Fernald argues that words should not be broken up artificially and that whole words should be said aloud while tracing or writing (Clark, 1988).

Why should multi-sensory techniques work? Although there is evidence to suggest the techniques have considerable merit (Clark, 1988) there is no real evidence available to suggest they work, or indeed which specific skills that enable facilitation of the reading process are enhanced by multi-sensory work. Hulme (1981) found that tracing letters helps children with reading difficulties remember words visually. Since poor readers tend to rely on visual memory this kind of exercise helps to reinforce visual memory and could prove beneficial for such readers. It has also been recognised that children benefit from multi-sensory techniques because it strengthens the visual-perceptual area and therefore increases proficiency at recognising letter shapes.

Lane (1990) developed a multi-sensory programme focusing on the following factors: Aural – Read – Respond – Oral – Written (ARROW). This technique utilises the child's own voice replayed through high fidelity recording equipment and this relationship between the child and his voice helps to explain, according to Lane, the success of the programme. Rowe (1987) examined the use of the ARROW technique and noted improvement in clustering skills. A one-year study (Lane, 1987) provided impressive improvements in reading and spelling attainment. There are, however, some considerations to note in accepting such findings, such as the selection of the sample and the acknowledged difficulty in isolating the precise components of the programme which accounted for its apparent successes. There are indeed many variables within the ARROW technique which could account for such successes. For example there is considerable interaction with adults, considerable reading practice, application of the written mode and the provision of withdrawal facilities.

Some hold a view that multi-sensory learning requires a cognitive focus which has to be learnt over time and especially from an early age. Chasty (1990) argues that a teaching strategy which incorporates both visual and auditory modes simultaneously may be unsuccessful because the child's memory systems have not received sufficient practice in using the two modes purposefully and in linking these two elements together and storing them in long term memory as a recallable unit. The implication of this view is that purposeful multi-sensory training should be incorporated from the early stages and particularly in nursery education. This would help the child develop the complex memory processes for efficient multi-mode learning.

Chapter 16

Automaticity

Automaticity is an important aspect of the learning process. After a period of learning, skills usually become internalised and automatized. This is clearly an economy saving device which liberates one's cognitive capacities to concentrate on the organisation and mastering of new skills and not relearning old previously learned skills. In reading at the word level the process of automaticity frees the working memory to allow for more efficient processing at the sentence and passage levels of text (Stanovich, 1984).

Chasty (1990) sees automaticity as a learned process which consolidates the sub-skills in reading, thus freeing the working memory processes to focus on variables other than the mechanics of reading. Chasty argues that children with specific learning difficulties find automaticity more difficult to achieve and it is this which helps to explain their difficulties in mastering reading sub-skills and, as a result, basic literacy.

To help the child master automaticity three aspects should be taken into account: processing time, presentation and consolidation of learnt material and memory training.

It has been recognised that dyslexic students are slower at word recognition than good readers. Reid (1986) showed the importance of instructional time and the pacing of instruction to prevent information overload. Bryant (1990) also identified this aspect of slow speed of processing information as well as difficulty automatizing information learned. Experimental studies (Fawcett and Nicolson, 1990) have confirmed this difficulty of automatization with dyslexic students. Clearly therefore it must be recognised and appreciated that dyslexic students will need more time to process and learn information than other children who may not share similar difficulties mastering automaticity.

The work of Fawcett and Nicolson (1990) illustrates that presentation of learning tasks singularly is more effective in terms of facilitating automaticity than the presentation of simultaneous tasks which may result in competing demands on the memory's resources. There may be some justification therefore for a systematic review of previously learned material at the beginning and end of each lesson. This perhaps repetitive form of consolidation may be necessary for children with dyslexic difficulties to help them achieve some degree of automaticity.

Chasty (1990) argues that automaticity can be achieved by actually teaching the skills involved in remembering information. Thus he argues more focus should be placed on the facility of memory as opposed to the product of reading. There may well be a case for arguing that children will not benefit fully from the experience of reading until they have acquired appropriate memory skills.

Over-learning

Perhaps one way to help to achieve automaticity and improve the memory processes is to adopt the principle of Over-learning. This can be achieved through repetitive presentations of the same material and in fact is a method frequently utilised with dyslexic children. According to Thomson (1990) such a strategy helps to strengthen the memory processes and alleviate some of the difficulties associated with attentional difficulties. Thomson also suggests that teachers should be aware of the variations in performance of dyslexic children from day-to-day and argues that the long-term effects of this may be minimised by structured over-learning. While benefits may be recognised for over-learning, one has to be cautious that this does not result in boredom and monotony, thus making the learning task unexciting and mechanical. Effort should therefore be made to introduce some variety so that the same principles and concepts may well be presented, but the different forms of presentation will vary thus minimising monotony.

SKILLS AND STRATEGIES

Developmental Perspective

It has been recognised that the skill of reading is a developmental one which is acquired over a number of years (Chall, 1983). From a developmental perspective therefore the first stage includes language awareness, recognition of names and letters and reading concepts such as the purpose of books and the relationship between written and spoken words (Chall, 1983). The child then integrates graphic and contextual factors, a developmental stage which may be restricted by limited phonic knowledge, limited experience with language and lack of reading practice. The implication of a developmental model such as the one proposed by Chall is that readers become more flexible in the use of reading strategies as they become more proficient. This emphasises the holistic nature of reading and the necessity to incorporate strategies and techniques which draw on both top-down and bottom-up models. It is clearly, important therefore, that the learner be provided with a broad range of reading strategies since even accomplished readers may need to utilise bottom-up processing when faced with mastering new types of information, perhaps some technical words, or new concepts.

Although developmental models can provide some useful insights into the acquisition of skills it is important that developmental stages should not be accepted too rigidly. It is therefore necessary to adopt a flexible and individual perspective in implementing reading programmes with dyslexic children.

Reading Words by Analogy

Ehri and Robbins (1992) provide evidence which highlight the strategy of analogous reading. This involves decoding new words not by phonemic segmentation but by using 'onset' and 'rhyme' strategies and the familiarity of known words. Thus to read the word 'peak' by analogy the reader will search his memory store to obtain a word which has the same rhyme pattern as 'peak' e.g. 'beak' and will break that word into onset – 'b' and rhyme 'eak'. The widespread use of this strategy has been documented in a number of other studies (Goswami, 1988, 1992, 1993). She found that analogous reading develops earlier than phonological decoding and that the strategy was of particular benefit to non and poor readers. Goswami investigated the recognition of onset and rhyme syllables by beginning readers and found evidence that the ability to divide words into onset and rhyme sub-units may be a crucial factor which will enable beginning readers to read words by analogy (Goswami and Bryant, 1990, Goswami, 1993). If, as the studies by Ehri and Goswami suggest, analogous reading is an important strategy for non and beginning readers, there is a strong case for focusing the early teaching of reading towards assisting children to grasp the inherent patterns in rhyme words and recognising the sub-units of onset and rhyme.

Ehri and Robbins (1992), however, found that although it was easier for beginning readers to process information words by analogy than by phonological decoding, some basic underlying knowledge of phonological decoding was necessary in order for beginning readers to recognise words using the strategy of analogy. Additionally Bruck and Treiman (1992) found that although they learnt words quicker and easier using analogy strategies, they were less able to generalise their new learning. Whilst they acknowledge that rhyme based analogies do have a role to play in teaching children new words, they nevertheless maintain that such instruction is not a 'panacea' and the relationships between individual graphemes and individual phonemes are of fundamental importance.

Ehri and Robbins (1992) suggests that phonological decoding skills can assist beginning readers to read new words by analogy to known words, helping in the process of segmenting words into onset and rhyme sub-units and in forming appropriate connections between graphemes and phonemes. This finding, though important, still leaves the crucial question unanswered in relation to whether analogous reading is a temporary initial strategy for beginning readers which will be complemented or replaced by phonological decoding once this has been mastered, or whether analogy reading actually underlies decoding skills and indeed facilitates the development of phonological decoding skills. The beginning reader may not therefore be blending phonemes when tackling new words but merely accessing from memory already formed sub-units of onsets and rhymes.

There clearly seems to be some value in learning to read words using the 'onset' and 'rhyme' strategy. Wise *et al* (1990) found that beginning readers who learned to read words by segmenting them into onset and rhyme sub-units remembered how to read the words better than readers who segmented the words into other types of sub-units. Ehri, however, suggests that in order for such programmes to be successful it is important for the reader to acquire some phonological skills at the outset in order to appreciate how letters symbolise sound as this would help the reader recognise the onset and rhyme and sub-units in new words.

Phonological Skills

Phonological factors appear to be of considerable importance to the process of reading. Indeed it has been argued (Liberman and Shankweiler, 1985, Pennington et al, 1987) that phonological processing occurs at all levels of reading and that all letter recognition requires letter sound access or phonological recoding. This may not always be apparent, especially in the case of proficient readers. There is, however, considerable agreement among researchers that a certain level of phonological skills is necessary for reading and that most dyslexic children have a specific deficit in phonological reading (Ellis, 1991). The evidence for this comes from studies in phonological awareness, phonological analysis and phonological segmentation as well as studies in analogous reading (Ehri et al, 1992, Goswami, 1993). In relation to phonological awareness (Bradley and Bryant, 1985) found that pre-readers' sensitivity to rhyme and alliteration correlated with later reading achievement. Fox and Routh (1983) studied children tackling tasks which required phonological analysis – asking children to say only part of a particular word – and were able to identify from this children who would have difficulty in reading. Studies in phonological segmentation (Liberman et al, 1977, Fox and Routh, 1980, et al) have found correlations between children being able to tap out the phonemes (sounds) in a word and learning to read.

Although there appears to be a clear relationship between phonological processes and reading there is still some debate as to whether this relationship is causal or reciprocal. For example Bradley and Bryant (1985) and Bradley (1990) displayed evidence of a causal relationship between sound categorisation and reading. This means that phonological awareness must precede reading since it has a direct causal influence on the child's progress in reading. Studies by Ehri and Wilce (1985) and Jorm and Share (1983) show a reciprocal relationship between phonological processing and reading. These studies revealed the linguistic insight which children develop as a result of an awareness of print and from the experience of matching speech to print.

A case can, however, be made that phonological processing and reading have both a causal and a reciprocal function. While it is true that young children who have developed phonological skills are quicker to grasp the alphabetic principle, it is also the case that exposure to print, the growing awareness that written words correspond to spoken words, and the experience of matching letters with sounds help children become competent and familiar with phonological elements in words.

Indeed Ehri et al (1992) suggest a vitally important role for phonological processing throughout the course of reading development. Ehri's model displays a close link between phonological skills and sight word recognition since she believes that the development of sight word recognition is dependent on subject's phonological skills. This would mean that dyslexic readers would encounter problems at all stages of reading development because of their phonological difficulty. Rack, Snowling and Olsen (1992), however, argue that there is a degree of independence between the skills associated with phonological processing and sight word recognitions. Perhaps phonological focusing may well be the central component, but that does not necessarily compromise the role of the other factors. Rack, Snowling and Olsen present the case that many dyslexic children acquire word recognition skills beyond the level that would be predicted from their phonological skills. Thomson (1990), however, believes that teaching the sub-skills of reading – phonetic teaching – is of vital importance because meaning and comprehension appear to develop out of the teaching of sub-skills such as phonic awareness, syllabification and the relationship between sound and symbol.

Strategies

Arnold (1990) presents a case for making reading real and puts forward the view that scanning is a reading skill which can be taught and used effectively by poor readers. She suggests that the use of the strategy of scanning can help release poor readers from the burden of attempting to read every word. This practice of scanning can be developed by the child through scanning exercises and games. Arnold suggests such activities as asking children questions about a reading passage without giving them time to read it fully. This facilitates the selection of easily discernible words. The use of the technique of scanning helps to facilitate meaning through the identification of key words. Arnold also suggests that reading can be made 'real' through talking and writing activities.

Similarly Waterland (1986) proposes a view that reading should be purposeful and meaningful and that a child can read effectively without necessarily acquiring competence in the sub-skills of reading. This apprenticeship approach to reading (Waterland, 1986) assumes that the acquisition of written language is comparable to spoken language. Thus it is important for the child to benefit from enriched reading experience in the same way that an enriched language expression is necessary for the acquisition of language. Adult and peer support and imitation are therefore two important ingredients in the teaching of reading.

Although this approach can be highly commended in its view of reading as a meaningful and pleasurable activity, in its use of language experiences and the use of the adult role model, it can still be argued that the acute decoding problem of children with dyslexic difficulties prevents them from fully accessing the benefits from programmes like the apprenticeship approach. Indeed, Cashdan and Wright (1990) distinguish between the general context of literacy behaviour and the specific context of the sentence and the word and argue that it is access to the specific components of reading which allows the reading skills to develop. This view implies that some focus and attention should be placed in teaching and accessing the components of reading in order that the child gains full benefit from the reading experience. It might also be argued, however, that abstracting meaning from text, possible even with faulty decoding, is an important component of reading and one which the dyslexic child has skills to access.

There are a number of studies which illustrate reading gains through teaching methods focusing on teaching sub-skills and in particular phonological processing skills (Thomson, 1990). In one study Thomson conducted a daily programme aimed at teaching syllables using a syllable analysis training programme, he found significant gains among a group of poor readers with weak performance in multi-syllable words. The gains were particularly significant in their performance in reading two and three syllable words.

Moreover Johnston and Thomson (1989) carried out an interesting piece of research comparing the reading progress of 8-year-old Scottish and New Zealand children. The Scottish sample were taught through a phonics approach while the New Zealand children were taught through a structured book experience approach which used context and language expression. This study suggested that the Scottish children had a significant advantage over the New Zealand group in their abilities to decode words. This may provide strong evidence to support the effectiveness of phonics teaching.

Some programmes analyse the tasks involved in reading and tackle the teaching of reading from a behaviourist perspective (Solity and Bull, 1987). These programmes propose a reading hierarchy of target objectives to be mastered by the reader. The objectives are broken into smaller and smaller steps until a step-size is reached where the child can succeed. Criterion Referenced tests are used to establish the child's level and identify and monitor those areas where the child can succeed. This is basically a record keeping system but by identifying the areas of difficulty it may help the teacher compile a suitable programme. This approach does not specify any particular methods of teaching so therefore the teacher can adopt a variety of methods and approaches to help the child achieve mastery.

It appears that no one approach can be successful for every child. Reason (1988) used the term the 'scattergun approach' to describe reading intervention strategies which draw on a number of approaches and do not attempt to use any specific programme to develop specific sub-skills. Even though there does seem to be some agreement that many dyslexic-type difficulties result from problems in phonological awareness and memory difficulties, there is no real agreement on how to deal with these difficulties in terms of a reading programme. Reason describes the 'scattergun approach' as a balanced reading programme which acknowledges that individual children may respond to different methods and strategies. This view is supported by the extensive research into reading and learning styles (Carbo et al, 1986, Dunn and Dunn, 1992) which acknowledges the individualism of children in relation to the learning task. A balanced reading programme, therefore, should contain elements of programmes aimed to establish enjoyment and meaning from text and language based reading experiences, as well as dealing with the phonetic aspects of reading.

CONCEPTS AND COMPREHENSION

Children with dyslexic difficulties usually display comprehension skills well in advance of their decoding abilities. At the same time, however, there is evidence to suggest that these decoding difficulties restrict the child's competencies and performance in comprehension tasks (Stanovich, 1986). Although one would expect to find a discrepancy between dyslexic children's reading comprehension and decoding skills (Aaron, 1989), a view has been put forward that dyslexic children generally receive little actual training in reading comprehension because the main focus of teaching is placed on the decoding difficulties (Maria, 1986). If it is the case that the child's decoding difficulties restrict competencies in comprehension, as Stanovich suggests, then it is extremely important for the teacher to take account of this and develop teaching approaches aimed not just at improving decoding, but also fostering appropriate comprehension skills.

Important factors which can facilitate the development of reading comprehension are an awareness of the importance of schema activities which facilitate metacognition, and an understanding of the value of the interactive process between teacher and student. These three factors therefore, schema theory, metacognition and student/teacher interaction will be discussed below in relation to facilitating the reading comprehension of students with dyslexic difficulties.

Role of Schema

The development of a set of schema helps the student build concepts and consequently facilitates reading comprehension. The reader embarks on the reading process with a number of schemas based on his or her background knowledge. These schemas can be seen as providing the learner with a framework based on both background knowledge and cognitive development. Echwall and Shanker (1983) describe schema as 'pre-suppositions about the meaning of text'. Thus beginning readers will understand reading material if it can be accommodated to their existing schema even if it requires the schema to be modified or developed in some way. There is, therefore, a reciprocal relationship between the reader's background knowledge and the reading text, since both interact and enhance the other. For example practice at reading will increase the reader's background knowledge and an extended background knowledge will facilitate comprehension of text. It is therefore important for the teacher to ensure that the reading text can be accommodated within the learner's schema and that the reader's schema is a relevant one for the text.

Maria (1986) views the readers' background knowledge as one of the most important aspects of the understanding and interpretation of text, and thus of the development of reading schema. One of the main concerns, therefore, is the necessity to bridge the gap between the reader's background knowledge and the information in the reading text. Many strategies have been attempted to achieve this and there is still considerable debate on the most effective method. Pre-reading discussion, however, is an approach which has been well evaluated in relation to helping to bridge this gap (Au et al, 1985). Such discussion should help to clarify the extent of the reader's background knowledge and help to shape and develop knowledge framework so helping the reader obtain appropriate meaning from the text.

This view is supported by McKeown, Beck et al (1992) who examined the contribution of prior knowledge to reading and reading comprehension. They found that students who were provided with background knowledge as a primer to reading the text recalled more material from the text and significantly answered more questions than students who read the text without the additional background knowledge.

Rumelhart (1980) argues that if the child has no schema the text is not understood and if the reader finds schema other than those intended the text is misunderstood. There is, therefore, sound argument for viewing a 'prior knowledge' lesson before introducing the reading text as having significant importance to the subsequent comprehension of the text, and for dyslexic readers such a lesson would also assist in the decoding process because they would be able to use context more efficiently.

Metacognition

Metacognition has been defined as 'the knowledge and control the child has over his or her own thinking and learning activities' (Baker and Brown, 1984). Baker and Brown see knowledge as an awareness of the demands of the task and control as the ability to plan and monitor one's own activities while reading.

Metacognition is therefore not about teaching individual skills, but rather it is concerned with teaching knowledge and control strategies which can be generalised by the student across other learning tasks in different contexts. A strategy, as opposed to a skill, can therefore be viewed as a 'problem-solving behaviour'. Baker and Brown acknowledge that many of the strategies which can be utilised to enhance metacognitive skills are essentially study skills, but they point out that the main difference is that in teaching metacognitive strategies one is not first teaching the skill but the rationale for applying that skill and how the learner feels about using a particular strategy. Maria (1986) makes the very valid point in relation to reading comprehension that it is more important for the teacher to know how students arrived at their answers than to determine whether or not the answers are correct. Thus the teacher is facilitating the process of understanding.

A number of approaches are documented in relation to building metacognitive skills, some of which are outlined below.

Reciprocal Teaching

The main aspects of reciprocal teaching (Palincsar and Brown, 1985) include generating questions about the text, summarising the text, predicting what will happen next and clarifying what the students have read. An additional overarching component of reciprocal teaching is the interactive dialogue between teacher and student and eventually among the students themselves. During this interaction the teacher guides the students through the processes outlined above. Thus the teacher will ask questions which will generate further questions from the students and perhaps provide the students with additional background information and some predictions about what will happen next. The student and the teacher are, therefore, reciprocating and sharing knowledge by the building of 'scaffolds' to help develop an understanding of the process of learning and comprehension on the part of the student (Edwards and Mercer, 1987). Initially the teacher may well have to feed in more information than will be fed back by the student, but this should diminish as the student takes more control over his own learning.

Main Idea Identification

Williams (1986) has developed some interesting approaches in relation to assisting the students to identify and select main ideas. According to Williams, the principal skill required in selecting main ideas from text is the skill of being able to classify themes, pictures and objects from the text. Hence Williams encourages practice in studying sentences and words to obtain clues which will help to identify main ideas.

Comprehension through Imagery

An interesting piece of research has been conducted by Bell (1986, 1991) using Gestalt imagery as an aid to comprehension among children with decoding difficulties. Students with weak Gestalt imagery are only able to process 'parts' rather than 'wholes' from either verbal or written verbal stimuli. Students with decoding difficulties would be utilising their cognitive resources to decode the actual print and may, by default, find themselves with a weaker Gestalt, unable to process the meaning of the written word. Bell argues that weak decoding can be a primary contributor to weak Gestalt imagery and that a phonological disorder can cause image distortion which interferes with comprehension. Therefore, according to Bell it is crucial that specific Gestalt training is provided to help support comprehension and to overcome the disadvantages of decoding difficulties such as weak vocabulary. Bell provides a Gestalt programme 'Visualising and Verbalising for Language Comprehension and Thinking'. The programme begins with picture to picture exercises which involve the student describing to the teacher a given picture, then the student moves on to describing in detail a picture of the visual images conveyed, firstly by single words, sentences and paragraphs.

The clinical data provided by Bell's study seems promising, although Clark 1988) argues that some students are simply unable to process verbal information visually because of their particular learning style. Nevertheless what does seem convincing is the link between Gestalt imagery and reading comprehension and the adverse effect of poor decoding skills, such as those experienced by the student with dyslexia, on both Gestalt imagery and reading comprehension.

In a similar manner Hunter-Carsch (1990) developed a programme which aimed to enhance visual imagery in reading. The programme is based on a number of steps which aim to facilitate both visual imagery and comprehension in reading. These steps include:

- attending and abstracting, which facilitates the holding on to an idea
- decoding, which involves the discussing of words, spellings and meanings
- encoding, which focuses on the construction of words,
- extending, which utilises phrases and definitions,
- differentiating, which focuses on concepts and finally assimilation,
- communicating and translating, which is directed to the different uses of words.

The key principles of this programme appear to be both its practical nature which involves the child writing out letters and words, and the element of reciprocity between teacher and child which facilitates the child moving through the stages from the initial one of attending to the more complex skill of interpreting and translating.

Niklasson(1993) argues that any stifling of creativity will impede progress in reading. Niklasson's model of teaching is based on the three aspects of expression, experience, and cognition and on developing perceptual awareness

Chapter 16

in children through specific physical exercises. Niklasson argues that these promote openness and confidence, which benefit creativity, concentration and reading.

Interactive Process

The value of the interactive process between teacher and student and indeed student and student, has been encapsulated in the discussions on the approach known as Reciprocal Teaching (Palincsar and Brown, 1984). This approach provides a good example of the facilitative value of the teacher or peer tutor in enhancing the development of schema and metacognitive strategies. Another approach widely used to help develop metacognitive skills is the mediated learning experience, a central component of Reuven Feuerstein's Instrumental Enrichment. This maintains that early learning is very much influenced by parent-child interactions which helps to guide children through problem solving activities (Blagg, 1991).

LEARNING AND THE LEARNER

Chasty (1990) presents a case that more attention should be directed to developing the teaching of skills which can facilitate effective learning and thus competent reading. Some of the skills he outlines as necessary are learning skills including working memory training and visual-auditory perceptual training; language skills including oral language, language organisation, concepts and labelling; and study skills and thinking skills.

A good case can be made for directing teaching programmes to help develop learning and thinking skills. These programmes, however, should also help the learner develop self-awareness skills. Such skills can help learners appreciate the demands of the task and facilitate the selection of appropriate strategies. Some attention must therefore be directed to examining how the student actually learns.

The implication of this for children with dyslexic difficulties is the necessity to broaden one's teaching perspective from one directed to the acquisition of sub-skills to a holistic one which looks at the complete task in the learning context. It is important that a learning framework be developed to help with the teaching of reading. This framework could incorporate aspects relating to the goals of the exercise, skills and information necessary to fulfil the goals, the value of the outcome of the task for the learner, and the degree of transfer of learning to other tasks and contexts. Such a reading programme, which focuses on the development of contextual and appropriate schema, can incorporate and meet the needs of a much wider variety of children's learning styles than to a highly structured specific reading programme which focuses on the acquisition of reading sub-skills as the primary learning outcome. Chasty (1990) believes that by advocating a broader approach to the teaching of reading one is allowing children to be 'active interrogators of the learning and thinking process' as well as the text. Cashdan and Wright (1990) agree with this view that the learning task needs to be analysed rather than the teaching programme.

This view emphasises that children with specific learning difficulties usually find it difficult to acquire mastery of reading sub-skills and this in turn may restrict their learning opportunities. The development of the learning programme should focus on the specific skill content of the task and on the process which is necessary for the learner to acquire that skill. The main aim of such a programme is to teach children to be 'self-running' and to help them acquire control over their own learning.

Recently considerable attention has been directed to children's learning styles and to how teaching styles and programmes can be modified to take children's different learning styles into account (Dunn and Dunn, 1992). Carbo et al (1986) presents an argument that phonic teaching does not work for every child and she identifies three kinds of reading styles –

- those who need phonics to become good readers;
- those who can learn phonics but who do not need phonics to read well, and
- those who are unable to master phonics.

She distinguishes between auditory/analytical and global reading styles and argues that those who need phonics will have a strong auditory/analytical reading style but will not be able to distinguish word patterns unless taught to do so. Children who can learn phonics but do not need phonics to read well are usually competent in both auditory/analytical and global reading styles, and their global strengths, intuitively supported by abilities to learn and master the principles of phonics, will enable them to develop both a sight vocabulary rapidly and a knowledge of word patterns. This group would learn most successfully through activities such as writing stories, listening and talking about stories, and reading books of their own choice. The third group, those who are unable to master phonics, need a carefully planned individual programme which focuses on comprehension, in order that enjoyment of text will motivate the child to read for pleasure. Carbo points out that good readers exist who have never mastered phonics.

Carbo further argues that too much emphasis is placed on decoding tests to indicate the level of a child's reading progress and decoding is only one aspect of reading. Some children who can read fluently and with good comprehension do poorly on sections of reading tests which focus on decoding. Carbo argues that children with strongly global learning styles can learn to read well without mastering any of the sub-skills on which children may be tested in reading tests. She argues that poor readers tend to be tactile and kinaesthetic learners with a global learning style and this should be taken into account when devising a teaching programme.

Rack, Snowling and Olsen (1992), however, examine the role of phonological processing in reading, and argue it is more prudent to talk of levels of phonological processing rather than dividing reading into phonological processing and direct lexical route. This view also underlines the individual differences among dyslexic students rather than discrete subtypes.

CONCLUSION

The important comment which should be made in relation to dyslexia and the teaching of reading is that no one approach can be held up as having an exclusive role for the remediation of reading difficulties. It is, therefore, important to be aware of a variety of approaches and to appreciate the principles underlying these approaches. At the same time one must acknowledge that there are different varieties and degrees of difficulty among dyslexic children which undermine ready access to the reading process.

As with any teaching programme one must identify and access the learners' strengths. Strategies such as scanning can therefore be of enormous value to dyslexic children. Scanning not only makes reading less arduous it also brings more meaning to the text, which in itself reinforces the pleasurable aspects of reading. There is also an important role for fostering comprehension skills to prevent the decoding difficulty experienced by dyslexic children from further disadvantaging them in relation to text comprehension. Thus the building of appropriate sentences and other preparatory pre-reading work are very important in order to provide dyslexic children with a sufficient textual knowledge base, both to aid decoding and enhance the use of context. Therefore, concepts such as metacognition, which focus on the process of learning rather than the product, are of supreme importance since they underline the holistic nature of learning and of reading. Reading is not just 'cracking a code' but appreciating the meaning and purpose of text and the application of this to other situations and contexts. Account must be taken of teaching processes such as reciprocal teaching and other interactive approaches such as paired reading and the apprenticeship model of reading.

In assessing the individual learning and reading styles of dyslexic children it is important to recognise that a 'common core' difficulty lies in the area of phonological processing, and teaching programmes should reflect this, but not to the exclusion of the other factors mentioned such as comprehension, language experience, development of schema, imagery and modelling. One should not be focusing, therefore, on the teaching *of* reading, but on the teaching *about* reading.

It is interesting to note that the key principles of many specially prepared programmes for dyslexic children, multi-sensory teaching and the development of automaticity skills can be recommended for use in teaching programmes for all children. This underlines the important fact that effective teaching programmes for reading should cover a broad range of perspectives and not just coach the learner to acquire some basic, but perhaps essential, sub-skills of the reading process.

REFERENCES

AARON P. G. (1989) *Dyslexia and Hyperlexia*. Kluwer Academic Publishers, Norwell, M.A.

ARNOLD H. (1990) 'Making Reading Real' in *Children's Difficulties in Reading, Spelling and Writing*. P Pumfrey and C Elliott (eds) Falmer Press.

AU K. H. *et al* (1985). 'The role of research is a successful reading programme.' In *Reading Education*, ed. J Osborn, P F Wilson and R C Anderson 275-292. Lexington M.A. D C Heath.

AUGUR J. (1990) 'Dyslexia – have we got the teaching right?' In *Children with Literacy Difficulties*. P Pinsent (ed) David Fulton Publisher. London.

AUGUR J. and BRIGGS S (eds) (1991). *The Hickey Multi-Sensory Language Course*. Whurr, London.

BAKER L. and BROWN A .L. (1984) 'Metacognitive Skills and Reading' In Pearson P D (ed) *Handbook of Reading Research*. Longman, New York.

BELL N. (1986) *Visualising and Verbalising for Language Comprehension and Thinking*. Paso Robles, C A: Academy of Reading Publications.

BELL N. (1991) 'Gestalt Imagery: A Critical Factor in Language Comprehension' in *Annals of Dyslexia*, vol. 4 (1991)

BLAGG N. (1991) Feuerstein's Instrumental Enrichment Programme: A Comprehensive Evaluation of *Can We Teach Intelligence*. Erlbaum, USA.

BRADLEY L. (1990) 'Rhyming connections in learning to read and spell'. In Pumfrey P D and Elliot C D (eds). *Childrens Reading Spelling and Writing Difficulties. Challenges and Responses*. Falmer, Lewes.

BRADLEY L. and BRYANT P. E. (1980) 'Why children sometimes write words which they do not read.' in V. Frith (ed) *Cognitive Process in Spelling*. London: Academic Press.

BRADLEY L. and BRYANT P. E. (1985) Rhyme and Reason In *Reading and Spelling*. Ann Arbor, M.I. University of Michigan Press, USA.

BRUCK M. and TREIMAN R. (1992) 'Learning to pronounce words: The limitations of analogies.' *Reading Research Quarterly*, vol. 27 no. 4 pp. 375-389.

BRYANT P. (1990) 'Phonological Development and Reading'. In Pumfrey, P. D. and Elliott, C. D. (eds). *Children's difficulties in reading, spelling and writing*. Falmer Press, London.

CARBO M., DUNN K. and DUNN R. (1986) *Teaching students to learn through their individual learning styles*. Prentice Hall.

CASHDAN A. AND WRIGHT J. (1990) 'Intervention strategies for backward readers in the primary school classroom' in *Children's Difficulties in Reading, Spelling and Writing*. P Pumfrey and C Elliott (eds)

CHALL J. S. (1983) *Stages of Reading Development*. New York: McGraw Hill.

CHASTY H. (1990) 'Meeting the Challenge of Specific Learning Difficuties' in *Children's Difficulties in Reading, Spelling and Writing.* P. Pumfrey and C. Elliott (eds). Falmer Press.

CLARK D. B. (1988) *Dyslexia: Theory and Practice of Remedial Instruction* York Press, Maryland.

DUNN R. and DUNN K. (1992) *Teaching elementary students through their individual learning styles..* Allyn and Bacon, Massachusetts (1992).

ECHWALL E. E. and SHANKER J. L. (1983) *Diagnosis and Remediation of the Disabled Reader.* Boston: Albyn and Bowan.

EDWARDS D. and MERCER N. (1987) *Common Knowledge: the Development of Understanding in the Classroom.*

EHRI J. C. (1987). 'Learning to Read and Spell Words.' *Journal of Reading Behaviour,* 19: 5-31.

EHRI J. C. and ROBBINS C. (1992) 'Beginners need some decoding skill to read words by analogy.' *Reading Research Quarterly,* pages 12-26.

EHRI L. C. and WILCE L S (1985) 'Movement into Reading: Is the first stage of printed word learning, visual or phonetic?. *Reading Research Quaterly, 20, 163-179.*

ELLIS N. C .(1991) 'Spelling and Sound in Learning to Read'. In Snowling M and Thomson M. *Dyslexia, Integrating Theory and Practice.* Whurr Publishers.

FAWCETT A. and NICOLSON R. I. (1990) 'Automaticity – a new framework for Dyslexia Research' in *Meeting Points in Dyslexia,* Hales G.(ed). B.D.A.(1990).

FOX B. and ROUTH D. K. (1980) 'Phonemic analysis and severe reading disability in children' *Journal of Psycholinguistic Research 9:115-19.*

FOX B. and ROUTH D. K. (1983) 'Reading disability, phonemic analysis and dysphonetic spelling. A follow up study.' *Journal of Clinical Child Psychology* 12: 28-32.

FOX B. and ROUTH D. K. (1984) 'Phonemic analysis and synthesis as word attack skills: Revisited' *Journal of Educational Psychology 76:1059-64.*

FRITH U. (1985) 'Beneath the surface of developmental dyslexia' in *Surface Dyslexia in Adults and Children.,* J. C. Marshall, K. E.Patterson and M. Coltheart (eds). London: Routledge and Kegan, Paul.

GOODMAN K. (1967) 'Reading:a psycholinguistic guessing game' *Journal of the Reading Specialist,* 6. 125-35.

GOSWAMI U. (1988) 'Orthographic analogies and reading development.' *Quarterly Journal of Experimental Psychology* 40: 239-268.

GOSWAMI U. (1992) Towards orthographic analogy model of reading development. Decoding vowel graphemes. In *Beginning Reading.* Submitted to Journal of Experimental Child Psychology.

GOSWAMI U. (1993) Orthographic analogies and reading development. *The Psychologist Vol.6 No.7 July 1993.*
GOSWAMI U. and BRYANT P. (1990). *Phonological Skills and Learning to read.* Hillsdale, New Jersey: Erlbaum Assoc.
HICKEY M. (1977) *Dyslexia:A Language Training Course for Teachers and Learners.* Better Books, Bath.
HULME C. (1981) *Reading Retardation and Multi-Sensory Teaching.* London: Routledge and Kegan Paul.
HUNTER-CARSCH M. (1990) 'Learning strategies for pupils with literacy difficulties. Motivation, meaning and imagery 'in Children's *Difficulties in Reading, Spelling and Writing.* P. Pumfrey and C Elliott (eds).
JOHNSTON R. S. and THOMSON G. B. (1989). 'Is dependence on phonological information in children's reading a product of instructional approach?' *Journal of Experimental Child Psychology,* 48: 131-45.
JORM A. F. and SHARE D. L. (1983) 'Phonological Recording and Reading Acquisitions.' *Applied Psycholinguistics,* 4: 103-47.
LANE C. H. (1987) 'Aiming Arrow at Learning Targets' *British Journal of Special Education,* 14,3,99-101.
LANE C. H. (1990) 'ARROW: Alleviating Children's Reading and Spelling Difficulties' in *Children's Difficulties in Reading, Spelling and Writing.* P Pumfrey and C Elliott (eds) Falmer Press.
LA BERGE D. and SAMUELS S. J. (1974) 'Toward a theory of automatic information processing in reading.' *Cognitive Psychology,* 6: 293-323.
LIBERMAN I. Y. and SHANKWEILER D. (1985) Phonology and the problems of learning to read and write. *Remedial and Special Education 6:8-17.*
LIBERMAN I. Y., SHANKWEILER D., LIBERMAN A. M., FOWLER L. and FISCHER F. W. (1977). 'Phonetic segmentation and recording in the beginning reader' in *Toward a Psychology of Reading* (ed) A. S. Rober and D. L. Scarborough. Erlbaum Assoc.
MAKER L. and BROWN A.L. (1984) 'Metacognitive skills in reading.' in *Handbook of Reading Research,* ed. P.D.Pearson, 353-94. New York: Longman.
MARIA K. (1986) *Adapting the new comprehension techniques for the learning disabled child.* Paper presented to the Thirteenth Annual Conference of the N.J. Branch of the Orton Dyslexia Society. New York.
McKEOWN M., BECK I., SINATRA G. and LOXTER MANN J. (1992) 'The contribution of prior knowledge and coherent text to comprehension.' *Reading Research Quarterly,* pages 78-93.
NIKLASSON M.(1993) *Adding Meaning to Life – A matter of experience.* Paper presented at 5th European Conference of Neuro-Developmental Delay in Children with Specific Learning Difficulties. Chester, England.

ORTON J. (1966) 'The Orton-Gillingham Approach.' in *The Disabled Reader*. ed J. Money, 119-46. Baltimore. The John Hopkins' University Press.

PALINCSAR A. and BROWN A.(1985) 'Reciprocal Teaching: A means to a meaningful end.' In *Reading Education* ,ed J Osborn, P T Wilson and R C Anderson, 199-310 Lexington M D:DC Heath.

PENNINGTON B. F., LEFLY D. L., Van ORDEN G. C., BOOKMAN M. O. and SMITH S. D. (1987). 'Is Phonology by-passed in normal or dyslexic development? *Annals of Dyslexia* 37:62-89.

RACK J., SNOWLING M. and OLSEN R. (1992) 'Reading Deficit in Developmental Dyslexia.' *A Review: Reading Research Quarterly,* pages 28-53.

REASON R., BROWN B., COLE M. and GREGORY M. (1988). 'Does the "Specific" in "Specific Learning Difficulties "make a difference to the way we teach?' *Support for Learning* ,vol. 3 , no. 4.

REID E. (1986) 'Practicing Effective Instruction.' *Exceptional Children* 52: 510-519.

ROWE M. (1987) 'Arrow in Free Flight.' *Teacher of the Deaf,*11,2.pp.42-54.

RUMELHART D. R. (1980). 'Schemata: The building blocks of cognition.' in *Theoretical Issues in Reading and Comprehension,* ed. R.J. Spiro, B. T. Bruce and W. I.Brewer, 33-58. Lawrence Erlbaum Assoc.

SLINGERLAND B. H. (1971) 'A Multi-Sensory Approach to Language Arts for Specific Language Disability Children.' *A Guide for Primary Teachers*. Cambridge M.A.Education Publishing Service.

SMITH F. (1989) 'Conflicting Approaches to Reading Research and Instruction.' in *Theory and Practice of Early Reading,* vol. 2, ed. L. B. Beswick, P. A. Weaver, L. Goodman. Erlbaum Assoc.

SOLITY J. and BULL S. (1987). *Special Needs – Bridging the Curriculum Gap*. Open University Press. Milton Keynes.

STANOVICH K. E. (1984) 'The interactive-compensatory model of reading. A confluence of developmental, experimental and education psychology.' *Remedial and Special Education* 5: 11-19.

STANOVICH K. E. (1986) 'Mathew effects in reading:Some consequences of individual differences in the acquisition of literacy. *Reading Research Quarterly 21:360-407.*

STANOVICH K. E. (1988) 'Explaining the difference between the dyslexic and the garden-variety poor readers:the phonological core model'. *Journal of Learning Disability* 21, 10, 590-604.

STANOVICH K. E. (1992) 'Speculations on the causes and consequences of individual differences in early reading acquisition.' In P. B. Gouch, L. C. Ehri and R.Treiman(eds). *Reading Acquisition* (pp.65-106). Hillshale, N.J. Erlbaum.

STANOVICH K. E., NATHAN R. G. and ZOLMANU. E.(1985). 'The Developmental Lag Hypothesis in Reading.' *Child Development,* 59: 71-86.

THOMSON M. (1990). 'Evaluating Teaching Programmes for Children with Specific Learning Difficulties.' in *Children's Difficulties in Reading, Spelling and Writing.* P Pumfrey and C Elliott (eds). Falmer Press.

WATERLAND L. (1986) *Read with Me: An Apprenticeship Approach to Reading.* The Thimble Press, Stroud.

WILLIAMS J. P. (1986) 'Teaching children to identify the main idea of expository texts.' *Exceptional Children* 53: 163-68

WISE B. W., OLSON R. K. and TREIMAN R. (1990) 'Subsyllabic units in computerised reading instruction. Onset rhyme vs. post vowel segmentation.' *Journal of Experimental Child Psychology,* 49: 11-19.

READING DISORDERS – DO POOR READERS HAVE PHONOLOGICAL PROBLEMS?

RHONA JOHNSTON

INTRODUCTION

There is currently a major debate in research into specific reading disorders – the issue is whether or not the problems experienced by poor readers can be characterised as being due to a phonological disorder. This has led research in recent years to concentrate heavily on the phonological aspects of reading and the phonological skills which underlie learning to read, to the detriment of the understanding not only of the visual processes involved in reading but also of the interaction between visual and phonological processes.

THE DUAL ROUTE MODEL

The dual route model of skilled adult reading has had a major impact on the theorising about developmental reading problems (Coltheart, 1978). This proposes that there are two routes to skilled reading. There is the direct visual route, which gives direct access to a word's meaning or pronunciation. This is similar to the idea of a 'sight' vocabulary. It must operate with irregular words such as 'aisle', and can also operate with regular words such as 'hand'. Regular words, on the other hand, might also be read by the indirect phonological route, which operates by converting letters and letter sequences into sounds. This must occur for unfamiliar words and nonwords, e.g. 'poast', for which the direct route would be ineffective. This route is similar to a phonic approach. The dual route model is intuitively appealing, and seems to fit well with the idea that some children's problems in reading seem to be on the visual side, whereas others seem to have problems on the phonological side. However, the model has had the unfortunate consequence, in developmental studies, of leading us to imagine that learning to recognise words by sight, and learning to 'sound out' unfamiliar words, are two separate processes.

RESEARCH

There are two areas of research which have led to the view that children's success in reading is largely determined by the development of their phonological skills.

The first of these relates to the development of phonological awareness. A number of studies have shown that preschool phonological awareness skills, e.g. the ability to detect the odd word out in auditorily presented sequences of words such as 'hat, hill, hub, rug', were predictive of later reading development (e.g. Bradley and Bryant, 1983). Several studies have been carried out to train preschool and school age children in phonological segmentation tasks to see whether this enhances reading ability (e.g. Bradley and Bryant, 1983; Lundberg, 1988; Hulme et al, 1992). Successful enhancement of reading skill in such studies has led to the view that reading difficulties are due to poor readers having impaired phonological skills. There are a number of reasons for suggesting that this is too simplistic a view.

Firstly, the majority of these programmes have been successful only when the children were taught about sounds in relation to letters (e.g. Bradley and Bryant, 1983; Hulme et al, 1992). The paper by Bradley and Bryant (1983) is probably the best known of these studies, but it is widely misreported. In this study, children who had weak pre-school phonological awareness skills were trained to categorise sounds. In one condition this was carried out purely auditorily, and in another condition the children were shown plastic letters when trained on the sounds. Only in the latter condition was there a significant increment in reading ability. Hulme et al (1992) similarly found that phonological training alone did not enhance reading performance. These studies point to the importance of teaching children with reading problems how to map letters and letter sequences onto sounds; they do not support the view that training in the auditory analysis of words alone is efficacious.

A further problem is the evidence that learning to read itself contributes to phonemic segmentation ability. Morais et al (1979) found that Portuguese adult illiterates who had started to learn to read as adults could do phoneme deletion tasks, e.g. they could say what sound is left if you take the 'f' from 'flat'. However, adults from a similar background who had not learnt to read could not do the tasks.

The idea that all developmental reading problems can be ascribed to a causative underlying phonological disorder is therefore in severe difficulty. There would appear to be a reciprocal relationship between the development of phonological skill and learning to read, not a simple causal one.

The second major area of research which implicates phonological problems as a cause of reading difficulties involves examining the performance of poor readers on reading tasks. For a while, the evidence in this area, based on several case studies describing poor readers with severe phonological problems (e.g. Johnston, 1983; Temple and Marshall, 1983), weighed heavily in favour of the phonological deficit explanation. Case studies, however, do not tell us how typical phonological reading problems are, although group studies in the early 1980's did suggest that such problems were widespread. These group studies asked poor readers to read nonwords in order to assess their phonological reading skill. (This task is a pure test of decoding ability; with real words there is the possibility that the item may be in their sight vocabulary.) The poor readers' performance on these nonwords was compared with that of reading age controls, i.e. younger normal readers reading at the same level as the poor readers. The argument is that if poor readers read nonwords less well than their reading age controls, despite being matched on word reading ability, then this provides evidence of a phonological reading disorder. Studies such as Snowling's (1981) did find poor readers to be impaired in reading nonwords for reading age; however, other studies have failed to find this deficit (e.g. Treiman and Hirsh-Pasek, 1985; Johnston et al, 1987a). This has posed severe difficulties for the hypothesis that most poor readers have problems with the phonological aspects of reading.

THE WAY FORWARD

In an attempt to resolve this issue, Rack et al (1992) reviewed the ten studies which have shown this deficit, and the six which have not. Their approach was to focus on what they believed to be the methodological weaknesses in the six studies which did not find a nonword naming deficit. They suggested, for example, that nonwords of insufficient complexity were used in these studies since Snowling (1981) had found that poor readers' difficulties were most pronounced with complex polysyllabic nonwords, whereas some of the studies failing to find a nonword naming problem used simple one syllable nonwords. However, Rack et al overlooked the fact that some studies which found a nonword naming deficit used the same nonword stimuli as studies which did not find a nonword naming deficit, e.g. Holligan and Johnston (1988) versus Johnston et al (1987a). This suggests that there is variation in the kinds of problems experienced by different groups of poor readers.

Rack et al also failed to deal with the fact that the dual route model predicts that if a phonological approach is being taken to reading, then regular words should be read better than irregular words so that poor readers suffering from a phonological deficit should not show a regular word advantage. However, in most studies poor readers show an advantage in reading regular words. Furthermore, in the study by Holligan and Johnston (1988) the poor readers had problems in reading nonwords but showed a normal regular word advantage compared with their reading age controls. According to the dual route model this should not happen, as the indirect phonological route is said to be responsible for the reading of both regular words and nonwords. If this route is deficient then there should be evidence for this in both tasks.

In trying to resolve these problems in the literature, I have taken the view that we should be examining children's visual as well as their phonological skills, as both of these processes are used in reading and they may well interact. Marjorie Anderson and I assessed both the visual and phonological segmentation skills of poor readers. In order to test phonological ability, we used two tasks. One of them was a version of Bradley and Bryant's (1983) odd word out task, and the other was a phoneme deletion task, where the child is asked to say what sound is left if you take the 'f' sound from the word 'flat'. Visual segmentation skills were measured by asking the children to detect shapes embedded in pictures, e.g. finding a triangle hidden within a clown's face.

So far we have studied 80 poor readers with an average age of 10, comparing them with normal readers aged 10 (the chronological age controls) and normal readers aged 8 (the reading age controls). In addition to the visual and phonological segmentation tasks, we asked them to read regular and irregular words, and one and two syllable nonwords (e.g. 'mip', 'daspog'). The first result to strike us was that the poor readers performed appropriately for reading age on the two phonological segmentation tasks. We therefore had to conclude that there was no evidence that these children were suffering from an underlying phonological disorder which was causing their reading problems.

However, a different picture emerged when we looked at the reading tasks. Although the poor readers showed a regular word advantage, the effect was smaller than it should have been for reading age. Furthermore, the poor readers were impaired at reading both the one and two syllable nonwords for their reading level. There was evidence, therefore, of phonological reading problems. How could this be explained if their phonological skills in the auditory domain were appropriate for reading age?

We found the answer to lie in the poor readers' visual segmentation skills. The poor readers performed normally for chronological age on this task, this skill apparently developing independently of reading ability. We showed that absolute levels of visual segmentation ability were associated with the extent to which a regular word advantage was shown. Those poor readers who were good at the visual segmentation task showed a very small regular word advantage. It was the disparity between visual and phonological segmentation ability, however, which accounted for the nonword naming deficit. Those poor readers who had a strong advantage on the visual task compared to the phonological task had the most difficulty in reading nonwords. Poor readers who did not have this imbalance used a phonological approach to reading.

This suggests that we need to look at the interaction between visual and phonological segmentation ability in order to explain how individual poor readers approach reading tasks. We believe that poor readers with good visual segmentation ability adopt a rather global visual approach to reading, i.e. they read to their strengths. It seems that they find it hard to read by a phonological approach because these skills are relatively weak, not because these skills are deficient in absolute terms. Visual segmentation ability is known to be associated with IQ, so these children are likely to be the most intellectually able children. Less able children do not have this disparity between visual and phonological ability, and are better able to use a phonological approach to reading.

However, this pattern of performance was only found in reading. The approach the poor readers took to spelling was unaffected by the disparity between their visual and phonological segmentation ability, and they produced as many phonologically accurate spelling errors as their reading age controls.

SOME INTERIM CONCLUSIONS

Our current work is focused on trying to find out more about the visual approach to reading that seems to be adopted by the brighter poor readers. However, in the meantime we offer a number of conclusions:

1. Most poor readers' problems are not due to an underlying phonological disorder. Although many bright poor readers do have difficulty with a phonological approach to reading, this is due to relatively good visual skills rather than to impaired phonological skills.
2. Training in sound analysis alone is unlikely to enhance reading skill in poor readers.
3. The teaching method most likely to help poor readers is a multi-sensory, phonic technique which shows children frequently occurring spelling patterns and how they sound. This is not a form of phonological training as such, and should not be confused with going from sound to spelling, as in the Elkonin method advocated in Reading Recovery.
4. The imbalance between visual and phonological segmentation ability in poor readers will be fairly small in the early stages of schooling.

However, visual skills develop with increasing chronological age, whereas phonological segmentation skills are tied to reading development. An imbalance will therefore develop in many of these children as they get older. This would suggest that remedial help of a phonics type should be given as early as possible, as it may reduce the number of poor readers who adopt a global visual approach to reading. At the same time, the phonics approach should also help the less able poor readers, who we found were able to use a phonological approach to reading.

We do not argue that phonological skills are unimportant – children need to be able to use a phonological approach to reading as this enables them to decode unfamiliar words when reading text. It is not surprising therefore that phonological skills correlate with reading attainment. The performance of the lower ability children in our study, however, shows that being able to use a phonological approach to reading does not mean that reading will develop at the normal rate. What, then, is the cause of reading disorders in most poor readers? Clearly we need to look more closely at other areas of difficulty that poor readers are known to have. We know that consistent weaknesses have been found in short-term memory, and that poor readers often performing like their reading age rather than their chronological age controls on these 5 tasks (e.g. Johnston et al 1987b). However, an area worthy of further investigation is long-term memory. We know that one of the major failings of poor readers is that they do not recognise words to which they have been repeatedly exposed. This is clearly a long-term memory failure, which may be related to the short-term memory deficit, yet it is an area which has received very little consideration in the literature.

REFERENCES

BRADLEY L. and BRYANT P. E. (1983). 'Categorising sounds and learning to read – a causal connection.' *Nature*, 301, 419-421.

COLTHEART M .(1978). 'Lexical access in simple reading tasks' in Underwood G. (ed), *Strategies of Information Processing*. London. Academic Press.

HOLLIGAN C. and JOHNSTON R. S. (1988). 'The use of phonological information by good and poor readers in memory and reading tasks.' *Memory and Cognition*, 16, 522-532.

HULME C., HATCHER P., and ELLIS A., (1992). 'Improving literacy skills in poor readers – the importance of integrating the teaching of phonological and reading skills.' *International Journal of Psychology*, 17, 65.

JOHNSTON R. S. (1983). 'Developmental deep dyslexia?' *Cortex*, 19, 133-139.

JOHNSTON R. S., RUGG M. D. and SCOTT T. (1987a). 'The influence of phonology on good and poor readers when reading for meaning.' *Journal of Memory and Language*, 26, 57-68.

LUNDBERG I., FROST J., and PETERSEN O. P. (1988). 'Effects of an extensive programme for stimulating phonological awareness in pre-school children.' *Reading Research Quarterly*, 23, 263-284.

MORAIS J., CARY L., ALEGRIA J., and BERTELSON P., (1979). 'Does awareness of speech as a sequence of phones arise spontaneously?' *Cognition*, 7, 323-331.

RACK J. P., SNOWLING M. J. and OLSON R. K. (1992). 'The nonword reading deficit in developmental dyslexia – a review.' *Reading Research Quarterly*, 27, 28-53.

SNOWLING M. J. (1981). 'Phonemic deficits in developmental dyslexia.' *Psychological Research*, 43, 219-234.

TEMPLE C. M. and MARSHALL J. C. (1983). 'A case study of developmental phonological dyslexia.' *British Journal of Psychology*, 74, 517-533.

TREIMAN R. and HIRSH-PASEK K., (1985). 'Are there qualitative differences in reading behaviour between dyslexics and normal readers.' *Memory and Cognition*, 13, 357-364.

Chapter 18

PARENTS AND PEERS AS TUTORS FOR DYSLEXIC CHILDREN

KEITH TOPPING

INTRODUCTION

What do children with specific reading difficulties need? It might be presumed that by definition all regular methods of literacy instruction have already failed, so whatever is needed must be new, different, exotic and highly technical.

Yet those who work with these children know all too well that the problem is rarely solely within the child's cognitive abilities. In many cases anxiety, poor self-image, poor attention span associated with social or emotional difficulties, lack of confidence, learned helplessness and other affective factors play a large part.

While 'high-tech' methods of remediation may have the virtue of stimulating interest through novelty and can sometimes give the child a sense of importance, dependence on such methods can create major problems of generalisation of skills to everyday life. Furthermore, such methods may require substantial capital investment in equipment, high levels of specialist training and very favourable and therefore expensive teacher-pupil ratios. The result in some areas has been that not all children in need can be helped, with those who fall through the net unfortunately often being children from families of lower socio-economic status.

Attempts to address the non-cognitive aspects of the problem of specific reading difficulty have also been subject to constraints of cost. While Lawrence (1972) has shown that counselling of weak readers can be as effective in terms of raising reading age as some other interventions targeted directly on reading skills, counselling takes time and time is money. In recognition of this, 'counselling' has sometimes been given by low-paid non-teaching assistants, with no less effect than that given by trained teachers.

For some SpLD children, their anxiety, the grinding arduousness of their attempts to read and their all-consuming fear of failure lead them to devote much energy to evading reading – at times almost as much as they would have devoted to reading. Of course, the more they avoid reading the less practice they have, and the less practice they have the slower their progress and the smaller the likelihood of any sense of achievement. The associated learned helplessness leads some children to wait for the requisite skills to be pumped into them in a quasi-medical fashion, rather than attacking texts themselves as best they can and finding their own idiosyncratic pathways to extracting the meaning.

What if a way could be found to increase the amount of reading practice such children have while simultaneously making reading easier and reducing anxiety, giving children more self-confidence and placing them much more in control of their own learning? What if this could be done by some form of supported reading which enabled children to attack texts nearer their own interest level rather than being confined to their current independent reading level, while making reading feel less effortful and creating a sense of achievement by accelerating progress in terms of numbers of books read? What if this could be achieved at very low cost in teacher time and other resources?

The Paired Reading technique sets out to do exactly this.

PAIRED READING

Paired Reading is not any old thing that two people do with a book. It is a very specific structured technique, designed for parents, peers and other volunteers to use when tutoring reading. At first sight it can seem very simple, this being unsurprising in a method designed for use by non-professionals, but in use it proves both subtle and powerful in its effects.

It has been in use since 1976, and is now deployed with mixed ability and reading delayed groups of all kinds, including those with severe learning difficulties and adult literacy students. It is flexible and responsive and ascribes 50 per cent of the control to the tutor and 50 per cent to the tutee, intending to be both democratic and empowering. Most importantly, it is a kind of supported reading which enables the delayed reader to tackle much more mature reading content than would otherwise be the case. In the vast majority of cases it reduces anxiety and promotes greater self-confidence. It also substantially raises the total amount of reading practice undertaken without stressing the tutee.

METHOD

The child (tutee) chooses high interest reading material irrespective of its readability level, from school, the community library or home. Newspapers and magazines are fine. There is no requirement to finish the book, but if children keep changing in midstream maybe they need to take more care choosing.

Pairs commit themselves to an initial trial period in which they agree to do at least five minutes Paired Reading on five days each week for about eight weeks. This time can be found in any part of the day and the frequency of usage enables them to become fluent in the method and is sufficient for them to begin to see some change in the child's reading. Other tutors (grandparents, siblings, friends and neighbours) can be encouraged to help but must all use the same technique – the target child is deliberately asked to quality control the tutoring they receive.

The usual advice about finding a relatively quiet and comfortable place applies. It is important that both members of the pair can see the book equally easily – tutors who get neck-ache get irritable! Likewise, the usual advice about talking about the book (or whatever it is) applies, but in Paired Reading the child is more likely to want to talk about a book **they** have chosen and talk is also more necessary given the (probably) greater difficulty of the text, as a check on comprehension.

A very simple and ubiquitously applicable correction procedure is prescribed. When the child says a word wrong, the tutor just tells the child the correct way to say the word, has the child repeat it correctly and the pair carry on. Saying 'No!' and giving phonic or any other prompts is forbidden. However, tutors do not jump in and put the word right straight away – the rule is that tutors pause and give the child four or five seconds to see if they will put it right all by themselves. (The exception to this rule is with the sprint reader, who five seconds after making an error could be three lines along and have made more errors – in this case earlier intervention and a finger point from the tutor to guide racing eyes back to the error word is necessary).

So how is the child going to manage this difficult book s/he has chosen? Tutors support children through difficult text by **Reading Together** – both members of the pair read all the words out loud together, with the tutor modulating their speed to match that of the child, while giving a good model of competent reading. The child must read every word and errors are corrected as above.

When an easier section of text is encountered, the child may wish to read a little without support. Tutor and tutee agree on a way for the child to signal for the tutor to stop Reading Together. This could be a knock, a sign or a squeeze. When the child signals, the tutor stops reading out loud right away while praising the child for being so confident. Sooner or later while **Reading Alone** the child will make an error which they cannot self-correct within four or five seconds. Then the tutor applies the usual correction procedure **and** joins back in **Reading Together.**

The pair go on like this, switching from Reading Together to Reading Alone to give the child just as much help as is needed at any moment, according to the difficulty of the text, how tired the tutee is, and so on. Children should never 'grow out of' Reading Together; they should always be ready to use it as they move on to harder and harder books.

Praise for good reading is essential. Tutors must **look** pleased as well as saying 'good' and other positive things. Praise is particularly required for good reading of hard words, getting all the words in a sentence right and putting wrong words right before the tutor does (self-correction). Nagging, fussing and complaining are forbidden, but PR does not rely on negative commands for effectiveness – these undesirable behaviours are engineered out by engineering in incompatible positive behaviours.

The framework of the technique is outlined in Figure 1. Of course there is nothing new about it – some elements of long-standing practice have merely been put together in a particularly successful package. A few teachers have difficulty accepting the technique for philosophical reasons. Forget that, just try it. Remember PR does not constitute the whole reading curriculum, but is designed to complement it without interfering with it. Further details will be found in Topping and Wolfendale (1985).

ORGANISATION

PR is widely used with children of all reading abilities and it makes sense to try it out initially on a range of students rather than attempt to solve all your worst reading problems overnight. This will also help to avoid stigmatisation of your first effort. Choose a small group of fairly well motivated tutors and tutees to practise on, but not so small or scattered that there is no sense of group solidarity or togetherness (around 10 would be good). Ensure that the children have easy and frequent access to a wide range of books available for the project.

Invite all potential tutors to a launch or training meeting, together with the children who will be the tutees, since pairs are trained together from the outset. At this meeting, after an introduction designed to create an air of novelty and excitement (some people like to put on a little play about how NOT to do reading at home), training in the technique commences. Tell the group about the basic structure of the technique **and** give a demonstration of how to do it. The demonstration can be on video, live by role play between teachers or by a teacher with user-friendly child, or by a graduate pair from a previous programme. Demonstrate **Reading Together** and **Reading Alone** separately to start with, then in normal alternation. Take especial care to highlight the correction procedure, the four to five second pause and lots of praise.

Now have the pairs go ahead and practise the technique, offering them necessary space and privacy. Remember that to practise Reading Together at all sensibly the pair will need a book above the child's current independent readability level, so it is highly desirable to have the tutees choose books for the practice in school before the meeting so you can keep an eye on this. Left to themselves, the children will choose easy books for the purpose of making a good impression! As the pairs practise, circulate to diplomatically check on technique, offering further advice, coaching or re-demonstration with the individual child where necessary – and don't forget the praise! Remember that you can't advise or coach unless you have tried out the technique yourself on a few tame children.

After the practice, feed back your observations to the group, take questions, outline the day to day operation of the project, and offer refreshments if appropriate. Pairs should keep a PR Diary, noting the date, what was read, for how long, with whom and any comments about how well the child did. Some tutors have trouble thinking what to write in the last column, so some schools provide them with a dictionary of praise – children are always happy to offer suggestions for this. The diary should be checked by the co-ordinating teacher each week, who should add their own positive comment and sign it officially, perhaps also issuing a new sheet for the next week. This is a means for the child to get a double dose of praise – and is also a mutual accountability device, of course.

You will also need to advise pairs about the different places from which they may borrow books. Give pairs an easy read handout to remind them of the technique and to show to other potential tutors (this may need to be in more than one language). Some schools offer Paired Reading badges, balloons, and other such nonsense beloved by children – all helping to advertise the programme. You may wish to have the pairs contract into the programme more or less formally.

When discussing diaries with children in the ensuing weeks, check if all is going well. If it is not, you may wish to call in the pairs for a brief conference about the programme and to see if they are still 'doing it right'. In a parent tutored project, if you can find the time, a home visit is even better. In all cases have the pair show you how they are doing it and check the difficulty level of the books chosen (these may be consistently too hard or too easy).

After the initial period of commitment, gather the pairs together again for a feedback meeting. Tell them how you think things have gone and seek their opinion on the technique and organisation of the project. Some present will say little and some will not attend, so you might also wish to have feedback questionnaires for the participants (see Topping and Whiteley, 1990 for examples). You might wish to test the children's reading before and after the project so you can feed back the overall results to the group, but avoid giving out individual scores as one score is unlikely to accurately reflect the complexity of what has occurred. You might want to offer the group further tangible indicators of the school's approval at this point.

The main purpose of the meeting is to regenerate enthusiasm and group cohesion, since you do not want anyone to think this is 'the end'. Encourage everyone to say where they want to go from here: go on with PR five days a week, go on but only two or three days a week, go on with reading at home but in a different way, or stop for a rest and perhaps start again later. Children may wish to go on keeping the diary and you will have to decide how often you can find time to see this in the longer run.

Further information and advice about the organisation of parent tutoring will be found in Topping and Wolfendale (1985) and about peer tutoring in Topping (1988).

The idea that parent, peer or other volunteer tutors might succeed where professional teachers have failed is challenging. Surely some parents of children with specific reading difficulties are themselves poor readers and would not be able to serve as tutors. Equally, surely some of them would be so anxious about their child's problem that the effect could be negative.

Both of these questions require consideration. Certainly if the parent is extremely tense there is a risk of negativity creeping into the tutoring situation. Yet many such parents cannot avoid trying to do something, whatever the school may advise. Paired Reading is designed so that the opportunity for negativity is engineered out – if the parent is determined to do something, PR may be the safest thing for them to do. In the few cases where the parent/child relationship seems hopelessly pathological, tutoring by other volunteer adults or by peers is likely to be more successful.

Paired Reading is designed for cross-ability tutoring. In other words, the tutor must be a more able reader than the tutee. Remember that the readability level of the books used needs to be controlled only to the level of the tutor, not that

Chapter 18

Figure 1

```
        Tutee chooses reading material
         within tutor's readability level
                    │
                    ▼
         Tutor and tutee discuss book initially
              (and throughout reading)
                    │
                    ▼
         Tutor and tutee read together
              aloud at tutee's pace
                    │
            ┌───────┴───────┐
            ▼               ▼
     correct reading    any tutee error ◄──────────┐
            │               │                      │
            ▼               ▼                      │
         praise      Correction Procedure          │
            │        Tutor says word               │
            │        correctly (and may            │
            │        point to error word)          │
            │               ▼                      │
            │        Tutee repeats word            │
            │           correctly                  │
            │               ▼                      │
            │        Pair continue reading         │
            │           together                   │
            └───────┬───────┘                      │
                    ▼                              │
         Tutee signals non-verbally                │
              to read alone                        │
                    │                              │
                    ▼                              │
         Tutor praises tutee for                   │
         signalling, then is silent                │
                    │                              │
                    ▼                              │
         Tutee reads alone aloud ───► any error or delay
                    │                 not self-corrected
                    │                 within 5 seconds
       ┌────────────┼────────────┐          │
       ▼            ▼            ▼          ▼
correct reading  increasing  self-    Correction Procedure
of hard words    span of     correction  as above and pair return
                 correct                  to reading together
                 reading
       └────────────┼────────────┘
                    ▼
                 praise
                    │
                    ▼
```

238   *Specific Learning Difficulties (Dyslexia)*

of the tutee. Especially in peer tutoring, but also in parent tutoring where the parent's literacy level is low, books must not be used which are too difficult for the tutor to read accurately – we certainly do not want tutees learning errors. However, a differential in ability of only two years of reading age in the pair is adequate, so some parents of restricted literacy are entirely capable of using the method, given the establishment of a choice of books within an appropriate readability ceiling, For these parents, PR with their child gives them a socially legitimate reason to read low readability material and is likely to raise the confidence and skills of the tutors also, through the extra practice involved for both.

GENERAL EFFECTIVENESS

Paired Reading has been the subject of a very large amount of research, starting in the UK and now internationally, and this has recently been reviewed by Topping and Lindsay (1992).

Much of the evaluation has been in terms of gains on norm-referenced tests of reading before and after the initial intensive period of involvement. Published studies do not always reflect the reality of ordinary life in the classroom, but with PR it is possible to compare the results of 60 published (and therefore selected) studies of projects with outcome data from 155 unselected projects operated in one local authority. In the published studies, involving a total of 1012 children, for each month of time passed the average Paired Reader gained 4.2 months in reading age for accuracy and 5.4 months for comprehension. In the 155 unselected projects, involving 2372 children, for each month of time passed the average Paired Reader gained 3.3 months in reading age for accuracy and 4.4 months for comprehension.

Of the published studies, 19 included control or comparison groups, while of the unselected projects, 37 included control groups. Although the control groups often also made gains greater than would normally be expected, the PR groups on aggregate did far better, although the differential was greater in the published projects.

But do these gains last? Published reports on five projects with follow-up data are available, but of the unselected projects 17 included such evidence. In the latter, up to 17 weeks after the initial project intensive period, 102 children in seven projects were still gaining over two months of reading age per chronological month elapsed for both accuracy and comprehension. At longer term follow-up, 170 children in 10 projects were still gaining well over one month of reading age per month elapsed in both accuracy and comprehension. Thus it seems that while the initial startling acceleration does not continue indefinitely, the gains certainly do not 'wash out' subsequently, and follow-up data from control group projects confirms this (Topping, 1992).

The data from the unselected projects further suggested that well-organised projects yielded better test results, that participant children from lower socio-economic classes tended to show higher gains, that home visiting by teachers increased test scores and that boys tended to accelerate more than girls. Also, second language Paired Readers accelerated more than first language Paired Readers in accuracy but less in comprehension (while of course accelerating a great deal more than non-Paired Readers of either type).

Taking another approach to evaluation, the subjective views of parents, children and teachers in the unselected projects have also been gathered by structured questionnaire enabling responses to be summarised (Topping and Whiteley 1990). In a sample of over 1000 parents, after PR 70 per cent considered their child was now reading more accurately, more fluently and with better comprehension. Greater confidence in reading was noted by 78 per cent of parents. Teachers reported better reading in the classroom in a somewhat smaller proportion of cases (about eight per cent less). Of a sample of 964 children, 95 per cent felt that after PR they were better at reading and 92 per cent liked reading more. Eighty-seven per cent found it easy to learn to do, 83 per cent liked doing it and 70 per cent said they would go on doing it.

Paired Reading has also been used in an Adult Literacy context, with spouses, friends, neighbours and workmates acting as tutors. The advantages of being able to use more appropriate and more readily available reading material and receive tutoring on a little and often basis closely linked to everyday life are extremely important, especially for the majority of adults with literacy difficulties who cannot or will not attend a class.

Scoble, Topping and Wigglesworth (1988) reported the evaluation of a six-week project of this type, noting average gains of 10.4 months in reading age for accuracy and 13 months for comprehension for those students who could register on the scale at pre-test. On miscue analysis, most tutees showed a striking increase in self-correction. Once PR is applied in a more complex Family Literacy context, it soon becomes very difficult to evaluate, since there are problems establishing who is doing what and with which and to whom.

Chapter 18

RESEARCH WITH DYSLEXIC CHILDREN

Of 59 PR published outcome studies reviewed by Topping and Lindsay (1992), 45 targeted children whose reading was delayed. However data from multiple-site field trials in one local authority suggested a much higher proportion of mixed ability pupils were increasingly being included in such projects on an equal opportunity basis. In this latter context, there was some evidence that during PR the weaker readers tended to make slightly greater gains on reading tests than the better readers. The method was however originally devised for use with weak readers and has indeed been used successfully with populations with very severe problems, including special school children with physical handicap, severe learning difficulties, moderate learning difficulties and emotional and behavioural difficulties, as well as travelling children and children for whom English was not their first language.

This of course brings us to the thorny perennial – when is a weak reader truly 'dyslexic'? If we take as a definition recognition as such by the Dyslexia Institute, just two studies have reported on such samples. These two will be focused on here, although many other studies of PR with delayed readers might be regarded as relevant.

In 1984 Evans reported a study of six children aged 10 to 13 years whose retardation ranged from 1.5 to 5.5 years of reading age. Parent tutors were deployed and two training meetings were held, with a view to establishing Reading Together before training Reading Alone. During the seven week initial period of commitment, home-school record sheets were used to keep a diary of activity and progress. An initial home visit was made to introduce the project and weekly home visits were made during the seven week period. Some difficulties were encountered with access to appropriate books. Pre- and post-testing on the Neale Analysis of Reading Ability indicated means gains of 2.8 months in reading accuracy and 15.5 months in reading comprehension, while understanding of vocabulary as measured by the British Picture Vocabulary Scale increased by the equivalent of nine months.

Thus, while the reading accuracy increase was less than two months for each month of the project (an indifferent result compared to the outcomes of many other PR studies), doubtless this reflected something of a triumph for the children and parents concerned and other outcome results were much more substantial. The inclusion of weekly home visits is a luxury many teachers will not be able to afford. The wider research picture (see Topping and Lindsay, 1992) suggests that although home visits do tend to improve the effectiveness of a project as measured by reading test gains, nevertheless very good results are obtainable with no home visits whatsoever.

A larger scale project was reported by Young and Tyre (1983) in their excellent book 'Dyslexia or Illiteracy? – Realising the Right to Read.' Fifteen children between the ages of 8 and 13 years took part, all at least two years retarded in reading. Here Paired Reading was used by parents in combination with other approaches in the context of a complete intervention 'package', and it is thus difficult to tease out which aspects of the project resulted in which elements of the overall gains made.

A number of variations of Paired Reading were utilised simultaneously or sequentially according to the needs of individual participants and supported by parent-tutored writing and spelling activities and three one-week 'holiday schools'. Some supportive home visits were incorporated. Over one year, a matched control group advanced on average 0.8 years on reading tests, the dyslexic experimental group 1.8 years and a matched comparison group of reading delayed but not dyslexic children 2.0 years. The authors emphasise that whether or not the children were classified as dyslexic made no difference to the benefit they derived from the project.

There has been no published study of peer tutored Paired Reading with specific reading difficulty pupils under the definition used above (an opportunity for someone here), but there is a great deal of work on PR peer tutoring with reading delayed pupils not so categorised. The general finding is that peer tutoring is as effective as parent tutoring in the short term while the tutoring takes place, but there is less certainty regarding longer term gains once the tutoring is discontinued than is the case with parent tutoring (see Topping, 1992).

ALTERNATIVE APPROACHES

Of course, Paired Reading is just one of the techniques which have been used by non-teachers to remediate reading delay. A review of research on 'Parents as Reading Tutors for Children with Special Needs' will be found in Topping (1989). Techniques referred to include various versions of 'Shared Reading ,' the Pause Prompt Praise technique, parent workshops, token reinforcement procedures, precision teaching methods and Direct Instruction programmes. Some of these have also been delivered by peer tutors in some circumstances. These are described in more detail in Topping and Wolfendale (1985) and a review of progress in parental tutoring of reading over the last decade will be found in Wolfendale and Topping (1993).

Methods similar to Paired Reading have been devised for other areas of the curriculum, and user-friendly but structured techniques such as Cued Spelling and Paired Writing have been successfully used by both parent and peer tutors (see Topping, 1993 for details). Extension to other areas has included the development of Paired Maths and Paired Science, although these latter are very much intended for dissemination on a mixed-ability basis.

Accepting that children with specific reading difficulties can often seem an intractable group with which to work, there are clearly methods and techniques here which merit exploration. Parents and peers can be made part of the solution instead of being regarded as part of the problem. Solutions need to be more simple rather than more complex. In terms of cost-effectiveness in an era of shrinking resources, this represents a viable way forward.

REFERENCES

EVANS A. (1984). *Paired Reading: a Report on Two Projects*. Division of Education, University of Sheffield (unpublished paper).

LAWRENCE D. (1972). *Counselling of Retarded Readers by Non-Professionals*. Educational Research 15, 48-51.

SCOBLE J., TOPPING K. and WIGGLESWORTH C. (1988). 'Training Family and Friends as Adult Literacy Tutors.' *Journal of Reading* 31 (5) 410-417.

TOPPING K. J. (1988). *The Peer Tutoring Handbook: Promoting Co-operative Learning*. London: Croom Helm; Cambridge, MA: Brookline.

TOPPING K. J. (1989). 'Parents as Reading Tutors for Children with Special Needs'. in: Jones, N. (ed.). *Special Educational Needs Review*, Volume 1. London: Falmer Press.

TOPPING K. J. (1992). 'Short- and Long-Term Follow-up of Parental Involvement In Reading Projects.' *British Educational Research Journal* 18 (4) 369-379.

TOPPING K. J. (1993). *Techniques for Family Literacy*. Viewpoints (ALBSU) 15, 22–33.

TOPPING K. J. and LINDSAY G. (1992). *Paired Reading: A Review of the Literature*. Research Papers in Education 7 (3) 1-50.

TOPPING K. J. and WHITELEY M. (1990). *Participant Evaluation of Parent-Tutored and Peer-Tutored Projects in Reading*. Educational Research 32 (1) 14-32.

TOPPING K. J. and WOLFENDALE S. W. (eds.) (1985). *Parental Involvement in Children's Reading*. London: Croom Helm; New York: Nichols.

WOLFENDALE S. W. and TOPPING K. J. (eds.) (1993). *Parental Involvement in Literacy*. (forthcoming)

YOUNG P. and TYRE C. (1983). *Dyslexia or Illiteracy? Realising the Right to Read*. Milton Keynes: Open University Press.

Note

The Paired Reading and Paired Learning Bulletins are available on microfiche from ERIC (1985 ED285124, 1986 ED285125, 1987 ED285126, 1988 ED298429, 1989 ED313656), as is the Ryedale Paired Reading Adult Literacy Training Pack (ED290845). A Teacher's Manual and NTSC training video titled 'Paired Reading: Positive Reading Practice' is available from the North Alberta Reading Specialists' Council, Box 9538, Edmonton, Alberta T6E 5X2, Canada, and is also distributed by the International Reading Association. Details about the Paired Science Pack are available from the author at the address in the notes on contributors

Chapter 19

THE SKILLED READING EXPERIENCE

JANET HUNTER

INTRODUCTION

'Within the covers of a book is an adventure of the spirit – something that can speak to that child alone and lead her or him into a wider world.' (Waterland 1988).

This chapter is about helping children, and particularly those with Specific Learning Difficulties to experience reading with a partner as an enjoyable, enriching and motivating activity; an activity which at the same time will accelerate their progress towards skilled independent reading.

THE TURNING POINT

Margaret Meek in her book 'Learning to Read' (1982) proposes that seven to eight years is a crucial age for the young reader. Reading has either become 'a varied and exciting affair for those who have learned how to make books serve their purposes' or sadly, and for many pupils with SpLD, it is at this point that they 'are deciding that their interest lies elsewhere and some are still threatened by print and reading lessons.' This can apply regardless of how beginning reading was approached: core readers, apprenticeship reading, or a mixture of both.

SKILLED READING

An American Commission on Reading, Anderson *et al* (1985), identified several factors which are necessary in combination for skilled reading. These included rapid, accurate and automatic decoding of the text allowing attention to be focused on the writer's meaning, linking this meaning to existing schemae, and being motivated to read through seeing it as a useful and enjoyable activity. In addition other writers such as Bradley and Bryant (1983,1985) stress the need for an underlying phonological awareness of the structure of language and Weiner (1979,1985) points out the necessity for the child to perceive himself as a reader.

THE INCOMPETENT READER'S EXPERIENCE

The incompetent or struggling reader in the middle and later stages of primary school will almost certainly not see himself as a reader. If he is asked to read silently and independently, perhaps in class silent reading time, although he may well bring, as is often the case with SpLD children, a well developed knowledge of his world and an ability to comprehend, his lack of accuracy and automaticity in decoding mean that he quickly loses the thread of meaning in the text of a book at his interest level. He will quite rightly feel that being asked to read a book at his reading ability level is a boring and useless activity. Reading aloud adds to this frustration the stress of the motor involvement required in producing speech, along with the embarrassment of knowing that he cannot conceal his incompetence. Bakker (1990) describes two types of dyslexic readers: those who read slowly, accurately and in a fragmented way and those who read hurriedly with many errors. Neither read fluently.

The dyslexic child may well find great pleasure in listening to someone else reading, but even if he is encouraged to follow the print this is still primarily a listening activity. Often his direct reading experience is of being asked to read the same few pages several times before moving on. The passage will be prepared in school, read again at home, and the more conscientious and anxious his parents, the more time he is likely to spend doing this. He then reads it again to his teacher the following day.

The reading experience inherent in this overlearning, where the focus is on improving 'bottom up' skills, is far removed from the skilled reader's experience of dealing with the printed word. For them print falls into place as the medium through which the author communicates and reading becomes as Reason (1990) says, 'visually guided thinking'.

PAIRED READING

In the search for a way to help these children bridge the gap between incompetence and skill why look further than Paired Reading? This is a method which has a proven track record in improving reading accuracy and through that, comprehension. Certain of its features, such as its interactive and supportive nature and the child's control of the process, form a sound basis for any technique, but other aspects for the present purpose of helping children to experience skilled reading need some modification.

Chapter 19

POINTS TO CONSIDER

INTERACTIVE LEARNING

Bruner (1986 and 1990) believes that most learning is 'a sharing of the culture' and as such is necessarily 'social and interactive'. A short time each day with the individual support of an interested adult modelling the integration of all the components of skilled reading is worth hours of reading practice for the child where the adult takes a more passive role. Following books on tape is also no substitute for human interaction.

SIMPLICITY

From a teacher's perspective simplicity is also a key consideration. It can take a great deal of effort and commitment, often of their own time and in addition to perhaps already stretched resources, to organise and train tutors in Paired Reading. The technique itself can be difficult for the tutor to implement accurately given that the tutor has to time their reading to the child's, be alert for miscues and give constant and positive feedback while coping at the same time with the reading process themselves. In doing all this the adult is modelling several skills for the child, but not necessarily that of listening to and interacting with the author as the skilled reader does.

ADVICE TO PARENTS

It is necessary for teachers to provide as effective and clear a method as possible for parents to use in helping their children with reading at home, since much parental anxiety stems not only from an awareness of their child's problems but also, as the Plowden Report (D.E.S. 1967) brought out, from not knowing how to help constructively. Pumfrey and Reason (1991) refer to Young and Tyre (1983) and Miller (1987) in saying that 'the effectiveness of parental help with literacy is dependent on the warmth and intimacy created between the parent and the child' and continue 'If parents and children are not clear about what they are to do or cannot perceive progress, then . . . tensions and anxieties . . . easily become exacerbated.'

THE SCHOOL'S RESPONSIBILITY

At the same time schools cannot rely on parents to help bring reading experience to their children. Partnership with parents is the ideal but not always the reality, so an experiential reading technique to be used as a strategy in school must be not only simple but highly effective in use of time spent either by teachers or other adult helpers.

SUSTAINABILITY

The technique also needs to be easily sustainable. Whatever causes may be attributed to a child's specific learning difficulties, the effects of those difficulties mean that the dyslexic child will probably need a great deal more support compared with his peers, and over a longer period of time, before he can move into skilled independent reading. It follows that, to be sustainable until this point comes, the method used must be highly motivating – 'Reading should lead to enjoyable, interesting, exciting, pleasurable and useful experiences for the individual' Pumfrey (1991) – and the motivation for both child and adult must be inherent within the reading activity itself and not due largely to a Hawthorn effect created by initial additional attention, since this may well fade as the weeks go by.

SELF IMAGE

In addition the child should be helped to understand that the enjoyment and satisfaction he experiences in this reading is due to his own developing skill and not external factors such as luck or his partner's input. Butkowsky and Willows (1980) point out that negative self appraisal is common among poor readers and an example of this type of self perception is seen in the reaction of a child who turned to her adult partner after their first session of reading together and said, 'Look at all those pages you've read!'

STRESS FACTORS

Finally, the process must be rendered as stress free as possible for the child. Hodges (1985) indicates that when students are taught in a compatible learning environment they feel more relaxed and can perform better. Carbo (1986) recognised that, compared to good readers, poor readers tend to need softer lighting and are more likely to benefit from reading while sitting in an informally designed area. These factors are generally recognised and whatever kind of reading the child is doing parents, for example, are usually recommended to sit comfortably with their child and at a time when there is unlikely to be other distractions.

This awareness of the need for comfort and a relaxed atmosphere is doubly important for the dyslexic child, since his difficulties such as lack of automaticity, entail that achievement is usually arrived at through effort; a tiring process. Any anxiety engendered in the activity also effectively reduces working memory or processing capacity. (Eysenck M. W. 1979, 1982; Darke 1988).

READING ALOUD

It seems logical therefore to propose that the child should not be asked to read aloud, indeed Pumfrey and Reason (1991) identify reading aloud as one of the stressors inhibiting successful learning. As well as motor involvement adding to the complexity of the reading task, attention tends to focus towards the medium and how it is being dealt with, rather than the message inherent in the text. The possibility arises that, while outwardly aware of the need to praise and give positive feedback, the adult partner is inwardly evaluating the child's performance in a negative way, particularly if the child lacks any measure of fluency and the adult is anxious about their progress. This could convey an underlying message to the child at odds to the overt positive one. 'Parents report much more relaxed and enjoyable reading with their children when the story itself rather than the child's reading performance, is the issue.' (Obrist and Stuart 1990).

SKILLED EXPERIENCE READING

The following technique takes into account these pointers to success. There are three requirements for the child and his partner.

1   *THE CHILD IS INSTRUCTED TO READ SILENTLY, WHILE HIS PARTNER READS ALOUD.*

BENEFITS

As previously discussed, reading silently frees the child from any negative evaluation, his own or his partner's, about his performance and it shifts his attention, particularly for the plodding reader, from over-focussing on the decoding process. In addition, if some form of motor insecurity or impairment is a cause of lack of automaticity (c.f. Fawcett 1989; Dobie 1993), and this is an area for every dyslexic child which requires careful attention, he will benefit from not having to produce speech on top of integrating all the other skills involved in reading.

THE CHILD'S RESPONSIBILITY

There is no question of this being an easy option or a lazy way out for the child; in this method he is required to take responsibility for the reading process and give his full attention to the text.

Chapter 19

READINESS FOR READING ALOUD

Felicity Craig in 'The Natural Way to Learn' (1990) advocates this approach with struggling readers, but suggests at the end of each silent supported reading session that the child should go back and read aloud a section of the text just covered. In practice what seems a sensible idea is not met with enthusiasm by either children or their adult partners. The children are usually so interested in the book that they do not want to waste time re-reading instead of reading on and the adults are thrown back into the role of performance evaluator. What does often happen, however, is that once the child has moved confidently into independent reading he will volunteer to read out loud, an example being the P4 boy who discovered the delights of Roald Dahl books and started appearing regularly in front of his parents saying, 'listen to this bit!'

MODELLING

The adult in reading aloud acts as a model for the child, demonstrating not only fluency and flexibility in reading style to suit the text, but also the cohesive nature of the text. Pumfrey (1991) explains how important it is for comprehension that the child has an underlying awareness of the cohesive ties linking elements of the text. He quotes Roberts (1989) in saying that, in developing this awareness in children, 'the fundamental basis of such teaching must lie in reading to the children so that they become familiar with the connections that are made across the boundaries of sentences and clauses.' It seems reasonable that the child who habitually misses or misreads grammatical words and word endings, ignores punctuation or reads each word as an individual unit will begin to understand and attend to the structure of the text through his partner's example.

2   *THE CHILD IS INSTRUCTED TO FOLLOW THE WORDS WITH HIS EYES, WHILE HIS PARTNER RUNS HER FINGER ALONG BENEATH THE TEXT. IF THE CHILD LOOKS AWAY FROM THE TEXT, THE ADULT STOPS READING AND WAITS UNTIL HE LOOKS BACK.*

REINFORCEMENT

The adult holds the book so that the child can see it comfortably, allowing the child to be as relaxed as possible. In pointing to the words the adult is reinforcing all the elements she is modelling. Her finger movement, corresponding to her oral reading, is a visual representation of her fluency and attention to the cohesiveness and sense of the text, pausing at full stops for example, or at the end of a clause.

This obviously has quite a different effect to reading slowly, pointing to each word one at a time.

TRACKING

Children's directional awareness of print (Clay 1979) may be affected by problems with motor co-ordination and it has been noted, for example by Zangwill and Blackmore (1972), that dyslexic children are more likely to have a natural preference for right to left tracking across print with the attendant difficulties arising from this. The adult partner therefore is reinforcing a correct tracking movement for the child's eyes from left to right across the page, with the right eye leading.

SCOTOPIC SENSITIVITY

Certain children will benefit from even a brief assessment of scotopic sensitivity and the option of using a coloured overlay which can alleviate effects such as glare, flickering or disappearing print etc.. Some children will only want to use their overlays when they are tired or otherwise stressed, others each time they read.

ATTENTION TO PRINT

It is perfectly acceptable for the child to look away from the print. He may want to assimilate information before reading on, or to look at a related picture. When the adult is aware of the child looking away she just waits for the child to look back before continuing. There is no need to make any comment to the child, unless of course he wants to discuss a point. Adult partners have noted that if looking away frequently is due more to the child's short attention span, this is something which usually improves rapidly, with the child paying attention and wanting to read for longer as each session passes.

3   THE CHILD IS INSTRUCTED TO LISTEN 'INSIDE HIS HEAD' TO WHAT HE IS READING.

PHONOLOGY

Thomson and Watkins (1990) summarise current thinking on aetiology when they say 'Reviews of eye movement research indicate that eye movement and eye sequencing difficulties are secondary to the primary problem in decoding the visual symbols into sound . . . The eye is but a receptor.' Research, for example by Bradley and Bryant (1983, 1985), indicates the importance of adequate auditory categorisation or phonological awareness in developing skilled reading. With the instruction to 'listen inside his head' the child is being asked to pay attention to, and increase his awareness of, a vital component of the reading process. 'The best practice of "articulatory encoding of visual stimuli" (naming) may be provided by the activity of reading itself.' Pumfrey and Reason (1991).

AUDITORY PATHWAYS

It is interesting to speculate whether there may be an advantage in the modelling adult sitting at the right hand side of the child. Pinkerton, Watson and McClelland (1080) suggest that in the normal child there is a dominant auditory pathway between the right ear and the left cerebral hemisphere where language is normally processed, but that the dyslexic child has a more efficient left ear to right hemisphere pathway. It is possible that feeding the sound of language more directly into the child's right ear compared to the left can improve phonological awareness in the same way as eye tracking can be trained to be more efficient. If this is the case then using a Philips AAC 5000/AT Tutor (a component of the ARROW approach to language) in the direct communication mode may also significantly enhance this effect.

ASSESSMENT

If the child is reading silently how is it possible to judge progress? Apart from normative testing at intervals (even in a short space of time such as three weeks it is possible to find a marked difference in listening comprehension as well as reading accuracy and comprehension), the following observations involving motivation, self esteem, interaction, comprehension and prediction have all been noted as frequent indicators of success in using this method. They have all been spontaneous reactions by children in response to the activity.

- The child asks to continue reading for longer at the end of a session.
- He reacts to the text by, for example, laughing and turning to his partner.
- He does not want the book to end and checks to make sure there are no more pages to read.
- As his partner turns the page the child predicts the next word.
- The child evaluates the plot or the characters and predicts a possible outcome.
- He looks relaxed and happy when reading.
- Parents report the child voluntarily picking books up to read at home, something which he avoided doing in the past.

Chapter 19

FINDING READING MATERIAL

To find well written and satisfying material to offer these children necessitates time spent in reading and sifting through available books bearing in mind the particular child's intellect and interests. This can be a time consuming exercise, but necessary for success, particularly at the start.

THE PUBLIC LIBRARY

There is an advantage in using books from the public library, whose staff are usually very helpful and delighted to liaise with local schools, in that both children and parents see that the books they are enjoying are not special 'school' books but 'ordinary' ones easily accessible to all.

FINALLY . . .

It is worth remembering two points made by Goodman (1976a, 1976b). 'There is no hierarchy of skills in learning to read. The learner must use all skills simultaneously' and 'Children learn to read largely by reading'. Skilled Experience Reading takes account of both of these premises in the reading environment it creates for the child, helping him towards competence and a motivation to read.

REFERENCES

ANDERSON R. C., HEIBERT E. H., SCOTT J. A., WILKINSON I. A. G. (1985) *Becoming a Nation of Readers: The Report of the Commission on Reading.* US Government Printing Office.

BAKKER D. J. (1990). *Neuropsychological treatments of dyslexia.* In: HALES, G., with HALES M., MILES T., SOMMERFELD A., (Eds) Meeting Points in Dyslexia: Proceedings of the First International Conference of the British Dyslexia Association. B.D.A.

BRADLEY L. and BRYANT P. E. (1983). *Categorising sounds and learning to read: a causal connection,* Nature, 301, 419-21.

BRADLEY L. and BRYANT P. E. (1985). *Rhyme and Reason in Reading and Spelling.* University of Michigan Press.

BRUNER J. S. (1986). *Actual Minds, Possible Worlds.* Harvard U.P.

BRUNER J. S. and HASTE H. (ed) (1990). *Making Sense.* Rutledge.

BUTKOWSKY I. S. and WILLOWS D. M. (1980). *Cognitive-motivational characteristics of children varying in reading ability; evidence of learned helplessness in poor readers,* Journal of Educational Psychology, 72, 3, 408-22.

CARBO M., DUNN R., and DUNN K. (1986). *Teaching students to read through their individual learning styles.* Englewood Cliffs, N.J. Prentice Hall.

CLAY M. (1979a). *The Early Detection of Reading Difficulties.* Honeymoon.

CRAIG F. (1990). *The Natural Way to Learn, Book 1 – Reading.* The Self Publishing Association Ltd.

DARKE S. (1988). *Anxiety and working memory capacity,* Cognition and Emotion, 2, 145-54.

DOBIE S. (1993). *Perceptual motor and neuro developmental dimension in identifying and remediating developmental delays in children with specific learning difficulties.* Paper presented at 5th European conference of neuro-developmental delay in children with specific learning difficulties. Chester, England.

EYSENCK M. W. (1979). *Anxiety, learning and memory: a reconceptualisation,* Journal of Research in Personality, 13, 363-85.

EYSENCK M. W. (1982). *Attention and Arousal (Cognition and Performance).* Springer Verlag.

FAWCETT A. (1989). *Automaticity: a new framework for dyslexic research.*

GOODMAN K. S. (1976a). *Miscue analysis: theory and reality in reading.* In MERRITT, J. (e) New Horizons in Reading. I.R.A.

GOODMAN K. S. (1976b). *Reading: a psycholinguistic guessing game.* In SINGER, H. and RADIAL, R.B. Theoretical Models and Processes of Reading. I.R.A.

GREAT BRITAIN. D.E.S. (1967). *Children and their Primary Schools* (The Plowden Report). HMSO.

HODGES (1985). *An analysis of the relationships among preferences for a formal / informal design, one element of learning style, academic achievement and attitudes of seventh and eighth grade students in remedial mathematics classes in a New York city junior high school.* Doctoral dissertation, St John's University, 1985. Dissertation Abstracts International 45, 2791A.

IRLEN H. (1983). *Successful treatment of learning disabilities.* Paper presented to the 91st Annual Convention of the American Psychological Association.

LANE C. (1990). *ARROW: alleviating children's reading and spelling difficulties.* In: PUMFREY, P. D. and ELLIOT, C. D. (ed) Children's Difficulties in Reading, Spelling and Writing. Farmer Press.

OBRIST C. and STUART A. (1990). *The Family Reading Groups Movement.* In HUNTER-CARSH *et al.*, Primary English in the National Curriculum. Blackwell Education.

MEEK M. (1982). *Learning to Read.* Bodley Head.

MILLER A. (1987). *Is there still a place for paired reading?*, Educational Psychology in Practice, 3, 1, 38-43.

MORGAN, R. (1986) *Helping Children Read: The Paired Reading Handbook.* Methane.

PINKERTON F., WATSON D. R. and McCELLAND R. J. (1989). *A neurophysiological study of children with reading, writing and spelling difficulties,* Developmental Medicine and Child Neurology, 31, 569-71.

PUMFREY P. D. (1991). *Improving Reading in the Junior School: Challenges and Responses.* Casual.

PUMFREY P. D. and REASON, R., et al. (1991). *Specific Learning Difficulties (Dyslexia).* NFER-Nelson.

REASON R. (1990). *Reconciling different approaches to intervention.* In PUMFREY, P. D. and ELLIOT, C. D. (Eds) Children's Reading, Spelling and Writing Difficulties. Farmer Press.

ROBERTS G. R. (1989). *Teaching Children to Read and Write.* Blackwell.

THOMSON M. E. and WATKINS E. J. (1990). *Dyslexia: a Teaching Handbook.* Whurr.

WATERLAND L. (1988). *Read with Me: An Apprenticeship Approach to Reading.* Thimble Press.

WEINER B. (1979). *A theory of motivation for some classroom experiences,* Journal of Educational Psychology, 71, 3-25.

WEINER B. (1985). *An attributional theory of achievement, motivation and emotion,* Psychological Review 92, 548-73.

YOUNG P. and TYRE C. (1983). *Dyslexia or Illiteracy? Realizing the Right to Read.* O.U.P.

ZANGWILL O. L. and BLACKMORE C. (1972). *Dyslexics reversal of eye movements during reading,* Neuropsychologia, 10, 371-3.

Chapter 20

HANDWRITING – SKILLS, STRATEGIES AND SUCCESS

MARY KIELY

INTRODUCTION

Handwriting

Every craftsman, whatever his trade, needs a tool. If the tool is less than satisfactory, the end result can never fulfil the original aim in its entirety. Handwriting is the tool with which the writer presents his ideas. It is important to write legibly and at speed. It is a skill that can be taught to practically all children and will be of enduring benefit to them. Many children including those with specific learning difficulties find it extremely difficult both to write legibly and at an appropriate speed. These skills can be taught and need to be seen as an important area both in primary and secondary school.

There has also been a tendency to regard the teaching of handwriting as the prerogative of the primary school – the secondary school it seems has more important things to attend to and 'it may be too late anyway'. There may also be some confusion as to who carries the responsibility for improving a pupil's handwriting, since it crosses all subject boundaries.

The cause of the apparent reluctance to do much about bad handwriting in the secondary school, apart from the occasional admonition to 'tidy up your handwriting', has probably lain in a lack of appreciation of the effect of bad handwriting on the pupil himself. Whereas most teachers would agree that poor presentation of work has a bad effect on the self esteem of the child, it would appear most unlikely that any significant number appreciate the sheer magnitude of the destruction of self esteem that can ensue; there may even be a feeling that, if pupils were so worried, they would do something about it – showing also a lack of appreciation that some pupils, such as those with specific learning difficulties, are unable to do anything about it themselves and need considerable help to effect any improvement.

When a pupil's handwriting has improved his self esteem can soar often helping him successfully to tackle much more of his other school work with greater zeal and determination.

AN AGENCY FOR CHANGE: THE WRITING ROOM

A major obstacle to the improvement of handwriting in a secondary school is that there is usually no one with specific responsibility for it and there may be no specific policy on handwriting. At Dumfries Academy, the writing room was introduced to remedy deficiencies in basic English such as sentence structure, punctuation, spelling and handwriting. Pupils were released for periods of approximately 20 minutes per week to attend and they were extracted at different times each week so that their absences were not always from the same subject. Initial referrals were by members of staff.

Much of the work in the writing room focuses on handwriting and the successes achieved encouraged a major influx of self referrals from pupils. Peer recognition of success was responsible for much of this. The considerable increase in morale and self esteem amongst pupils consequent upon the dramatic improvement in the presentation of their work is worthy of note. It is on the results achieved in this writing room that the present chapter is largely based.

PRE-PROGRAMME CONSIDERATIONS

While it may be possible to take children for handwriting instruction in small groups, handwriting is such an individual process and the errors which a pupil has acquired are so particular to himself that it is only through highly individual tuition that these errors can be fully eliminated.

When I first see a pupil, the main requirement is that he should be well motivated. He must be keen to improve his handwriting. That is why I am so much encouraged by the fact that so many of my pupils are self referred. Such motivation, however, can never be taken for granted; it must be nurtured and enhanced together with the confidence and self esteem which are so closely related to it.

Therefore when I see a pupil initially I must convince him that his handwriting can be improved comparatively easily. I show him specimens of 'before and after' handwriting and tell him that such improvements have been effected in a short period. I try to ensure that the process consists of a large number of short term gains so that the pupil is continually meeting success.

Initially, I photocopy a sample from the pupil's normal class-work and I ask him to write a short piece for me in order to observe his writing action closely. Together, we look at these samples of his handwriting; I praise wherever I can and then we discuss aspects of it that he would like to change so that the pupil is very much involved in his own learning.

PLANNING THE PROGRAMME

Having identified the areas of concern in the pupil's handwriting, I plan an individualised programme for him; I decide on which difficulties to concentrate and allocate my areas of priority accordingly. I begin by making a few specific suggestions for improvement and get the pupil to concentrate on these, practise them and incorporate them in a piece of writing. The pupil immediately sees an improvement, albeit on the small side, but this motivates him sufficiently to go away and practise this assiduously during the following week so that it becomes automatic. He is expected to practise every night and to incorporate the teaching points made into the writing of his ordinary class-work. By the time he next attends the writing room the improvements are so noticeable as to encourage and motivate him further; this facilitates the repetition of the process. After a number of such visits to the writing room the improvement is normally large enough to discontinue tuition. A few months later, the pupil's progress is reviewed. In the majority of cases the improvement is sustained, in the few regressions which occur, they can normally be remedied comparatively easily by repetition of the tuition; is some cases, there is further improvement, usually where the pupils' own style has developed. The key to success here is undoubtedly the number of short term gains that are continually built into the learning process to sustain motivation which allows the pupils own natural style to develop.

HANDWRITING SKILLS

It is not the purpose of this chapter to provide a detailed treatise on handwriting but rather to indicate how, within the context of the modern comprehensive school, bad handwriting can be comparatively painlessly improved to an acceptable (not necessarily perfect!) standard, within a space of time so short that the pupil's motivation can be easily maintained. However, it is appropriate to explain briefly the main faults which I attempt to eradicate.

- **Pencil Grip**

    Firstly, it soon becomes obvious if handwriting is an effortless relaxed activity for the pupil. One prime inhibiting factor is a faulty grip on the pen or pencil. A faulty grip can cause tiredness, tension or even pain when

Chapter 20

having to write at length and too much or too little pressure can obviously effect the handwriting; a faulty grip can also prevent good letter formation. It can be difficult to change and can be time consuming but it is very important to do so. Pupils have told me how they hated writing and subjects involving a lot of written work because of this problem. To change the grip, experimenting with different types of pens or pencils to see which suit the pupil best will probably be necessary. Pupils tend to enjoy this and the element of choice involved.

I encountered one pupil who had no problems with handwriting until he was required to write at speed or length, which he resisted, and it became obvious that he tired easily because of his faulty grip. A three sided pencil instead of the usual barrel shaped pencil, produced no improvement; however, the 'GRIPPY', a simple unobtrusive rubber device to attach to the pencil or pen (readily available on the market) which is shaped and slightly hollowed, proved effective and after practising with the 'GRIPPY' for several weeks, he was able to discard it, hold an ordinary pencil correctly and write effectively at speed or length. It should be mentioned, however, that if a child has an unorthodox grip with which he is managing to write legibly, quickly and effortlessly then no attempt is made to change that grip.

- **Positioning**

   Whilst sitting comfortably is obviously important, the correct positioning of the paper is perhaps less evidently so. However, it can be very inhibiting to have the paper squarely in front of the writer as this can restrict movement. To ensure fluent, speedy handwriting the paper should be positioned on the same side of the body as the writing hand and, for right handers, it should be suitably slanted slightly to the left with the left hand on the paper for steadying purposes (and vice-versa for left handers).

- **Paper**

   Lined paper provides a structure of base lines to which the pupil can relate his letters and gauge their size, and also keep his writing straight. Some pupils have to be constantly encouraged to make this appropriate use of the lines. When unlined paper is in use, heavily lined paper underneath can be used as a guide.

- **Spacing**

   One of the notable features of the writing room experience is the pupil's participation in his own learning, an invaluable ingredient for maintaining motivation. When we initially examine the pupil's handwriting together, an obvious error often becomes apparent in our discussion, that of bad spacing; this has the virtue of being easily remedied and making a considerable transformation so quickly that the pupil feels he is really making progress. Poor or little spacing between words is a very common fault and is easily corrected by comparing a model of good spacing with the pupil's own work and asking him to copy the former. Once a pupil becomes aware of this error he normally has little difficulty in eliminating it from his own class-work. Similarly, when uneven spacing occurs between letters in words, the pupil is again shown a correct model to compare with his own; he is asked to write words with and without appropriate spacing and observe the difference, thus heightening his awareness. Once this has registered, the pupil has little difficulty in practising and reinforcing this in his on-going writing.

- **Letter Formation**

  Good letter formation is of prime importance. Pupils have to be taught to form letters correctly, practising together letters which are similar in size and shape. Groups in which letters can be conveniently taught and practised together can be as follows:

  - letters which have a rounded pattern

    c   o   a   d   g   q   s

  - which seem to cause more difficulty

    e   f

  - letters which are more linear

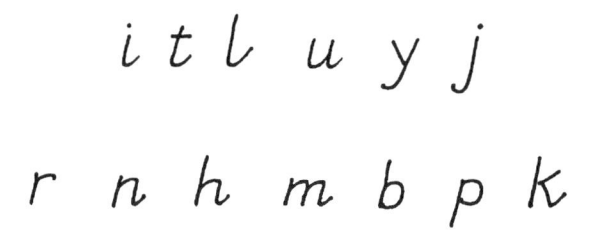

    i t l   u   y   j

    r   n   h   m   b   p   k

- letters which are more zig-zag

k v y w x z

There can be a certain overlap between these groups.

- Letters need to be of the correct height and certain ones need to be practised.

b d f h k l t

- Similar practise has to be given to letters which go below the line:

g j p q y

Capital P and small p frequently cause some difficulty.

It has to be stressed to pupils that letters have to be fully completed so that it can be seen where one letter ends and another begins. In particular

a b d e g o p q

are completely closed. It is especially important to complete 'o' 'a' and 'd' completely, otherwise 'o' can look like 'u;' 'a' can look like 'u' and 'd' can look like 'c l.'

Attention should also be paid to reversals of letters, 'b' and 'd' being particularly important. It should be pointed out that only the letters d and e begin in the middle, all others start at the top. It should be emphasised that 'b' begins at the top with a vertical line. If 'o' is incorrectly formed in a clockwise direction it causes problems for joining; a similar problem arises with 's' if it is started in the wrong place.

It is essential that pupils acquire proper letter formation and a knowledge of where letters should start and finish before joining begins. At the secondary stage, some children have developed their own system of joining which will correspond to a greater or lesser extent with the generally

Chapter 20

accepted methods, and these can be modified to suit their particular requirements.

Letters can then be grouped into those joined horizontally and those joined diagonally

LETTERS WHICH CAN JOIN HORIZONTALLY

for example: o v w

oo oc od oi oy

LETTERS WHICH CAN JOIN DIAGONALLY

a c d e h i k l m n t u

There are the following types of diagonal joins:

1. Diagonal joins to letters of similar heights, for example:

   am an im in ip is

2. Diagonal joins to taller letters, for example:

   ah it il ik

3. Diagonal joins to 'e' for example:

   ae de ce me ee le

4. Diagonal joins which help to form the next letter. These are the most difficult and need particular emphasis and practice, for example:

   ad ca ma na ag ng ao co

Perspectives on Practice

With letters that are traditionally difficult to join or even with letters that the pupil finds difficult to join for some reason of his own, the best course is not to join them but to put the two letters close together so that they appear to be joined. I would also do this where capital letters are involved.

Letters which my pupils found difficulty in joining are:

b g j p q r s x y z

Other points which have to be attended to are the size of the writing, which should not be too large or too small, with adequate definition, the development of a consistent forward slant and the evolution of a smooth flowing, rhythmic style.

- **Writing at Speed**

    Even when the pupil has been taught to write correctly and legibly, there is the question of writing at speed to consider. As far as the slow writer is concerned, problems of grip, comfortable seating and appropriate positioning of paper have been already discussed. If these have been attended to, the key to development of writing at speed is to practise spacing, letter formation and joining so that their correct implementation becomes automatic and the writer can transfer his thoughts to paper without giving attention to the writing process. It is essential to encourage a smooth steady progression across the paper with minimal lifting of the hand. I find it is helpful to have ligatures (ticks) at the end of words where appropriate because this promotes a flowing progression to the next word. Experience has also shown me that a forward consistent slant helps a pupil to introduce a rhythmic and fluent progression across the paper. After these points have been dealt with, the development of writing at speed will usually come naturally with practice. However, if an unsuitable style has been acquired this might have to be changed. In handwriting, as with many other skills, it is often the simplest that is the best. Occasionally a pupil's handwriting can be illegible because of writing too fast. In such requirements as good letter formation, joins, slant and spacing are fulfilled a simple reduction in speed is often enough to effect considerable improvement.

Chapter 20

CASE STUDIES:

Having summarised the main principles of good handwriting it is instructive to consider how these principles can be applied to transform bad handwriting, at the secondary school stage into something that is legible, reasonably attractive and can be written fluently with some semblance of style. It should be emphasised that this is not an attempt to produce near perfect handwriting but just to produce something that will serve as an effortless, expeditious tool for the expression of the written word in an attractive manner, enabling a pupil to take justifiable pride in his presentation of work. Improvements have to be effected quickly in a way which will facilitate a continuous series of successful outcomes for the pupil so as to maintain the initial motivation and to encourage him to undertake the considerable amount of practice required.

- **Barry (aged 12)**

Initial Sample:

Final Sample:

Barry's initial sample shown was given me as typical of his class-work. Barry was unhappy about his writing but did not know how to improve it. His spacing, both between and within words, was poor. His letter formation was inconsistent and the sizing of his letters needed attention. He wrote the letter 's' in reverse. The

Perspectives on Practice

writing had no joins except for a few diagonal ones. He wrote in staccato, jerky movements with the paper straight in front of him.

On his first visit we concentrated on spacing and on improving his letter formation, which was not too bad. Some practice was given on letter sizing with particular reference to ascenders (tall letters) and descenders (letters partly below the line). Barry practised these points at home during the following week and in his class-work and had made a marked improvement by the time of his second visit. At Barry's second visit and for the following few weeks we concentrated on different joins. At the second visit I also introduced the correct positioning of paper and we started to develop a smooth fluent rhythmic style, paying particular to ligatures (ticks) at the end of suitable letters which added to the fluency of movement. Barry practised diligently at home and incorporated the suggestions into his class-work. His regular and marked improvement sufficed to motivate him greatly and the final sample of handwriting was produced on his fifth visit to the writing room.

- **Peter (aged 13)**

    Initial Sample

    [handwritten sample: The witches is told by the boy is is on holiday with his gran. When he is caught up in a meeting of witches. The witches plan to turn all the children in the world into mice. he is caught by them and turned into a mouse.]

    Sample on the sixth visit

    [handwritten sample: Lonnie Zamora was chasing a speeding car when he heard a roar and saw a blue flash in the sky. The flaming ball was slowly coming down not far away.]

Due to his bad handwriting Peter had difficulty in completing assignments, not because of lack of ability for the task, but because his hand became easily tired and he had difficulty writing at length.

As the specimen shows, his writing slanted in different directions and he had difficulty in keeping to base lines. Spacing was irregular and some of his letters, such as 'd' involved loops.

His writing was punctuated by sudden bursts of speed at the end of a line and he seemed to have difficulty moving across the page. Besides rectifying the usual errors, the first priority with Peter was to modify his grip. His wrist movements were also very restricted. The vital development of more flexible movement was greatly facilitated by positioning his paper slightly to the right, angling it to suit him, and positioning his non-writing hand on the paper. Because his writing went up and down so much, Peter also had to practise positioning his writing relative to the base lines. He retained some of his loops, for example in 'y' and 'g' but discarded them in 'l' and 'h'. Achieving a smooth writing movement across the page necessitated a large amount of practise but eventually Peter got into his rhythm and, with a sudden breakthrough, achieved the second sample illustrated on his sixth visit to the writing room. Peter has maintained this improvement and is much more confident in his work across the curriculum.

- **John (aged 14)**

    Original Sample:

    The only difference between the two experiments is that in one the magnesium is being added to a diluted hydrochloric acid and the other is being added to Hydrochloric acid. which is more concentrated

    Second Sample:

    An M.P. can reply to letters and enquiries from his constituents. He represents his constituents by doing such things as investigating complaints about income tax or social security.

Chapter 20

Review Sample:

> *Hundreds of travellers who vanished without trace in the sixteenth century Galloway sparked of one of Galloways most baffling mysteries.*

John is a pupil with considerable academic potential but it was considered that he would be handicapped, particularly in external examinations, by his handwriting. He was keen to improve it and particularly to join his handwriting. In the original sample John was able to form his letters confidently and well, although the letter 'f' needed attention and the letter 'd' could look like 'cl'. Spacing, the relative sizing of letters and joining all needed some attention, whilst assistance with the flow and speed of writing was also required. John worked very hard at remedying these defects with the main priority on joining. Because of his lack of experience of this, it took about four weeks for it to become automatic without having to think about it. It was at this stage that the second sample was produced. This shows that John had then improved his letter formation, mastered cursive writing to some extent and developed a slant. John was now anxious to develop a style, and, although he did not attend the writing room again until two months later, when the third sample was taken, he continued to practise hard and this third sample shows further improvement and development of his writing with adequate speed and fluency. This improvement in his handwriting, favourably commented on by many of his teachers, gave John much more self confidence overall and his grades have improved in subjects across the curriculum.

- **Andrew (aged 15)**

Week One

> *What you were trying to do, how you went about it eg and what your solution was like. you may like to get your parents to read drafts of your report*

Week Two

trying to do, how you went about it and what your solution was like. You may like to get your parents to read drafts of your report.

Week Three

His soul flew from him betrayed and unwanted, replaced by the blackness, sucked in through the pores, draining his very lifeblood. None could quench his burning rage, only the power of the gauntlet could relieve this burden.

This case study is provided to show how a pupil, with a small amount of guidance, can, in three weeks, transform his handwriting to a much more mature style. The initial sample shows an immature style, lacking in slanting and definition. On the first visit to the writing room attention was paid to the following letter formations in the sample. In the first line the letter 'o' has no horizontal join and is not joined to the next letter. Nor is the letter 'u' completed with a ligature (tick). In the word 'went' the letters 'e' and 'n' are incomplete and just merge. In the second line, in the word 'and' the GRAPHIC 'a' is not closed and looks like the letter GRAPHIC 'u'. Also the 'a' and 'n' merge. The formation of the letter 'd' in the third line also needs attention. Discussion also took place on the development of slant and of the smooth movements of the writing hand across the page to develop a rhythmic pattern and abandon jerky movements. All the teaching points were practised and reinforced at home and applied in the normal class-work until the end of the following week, when the next visit produced the much improved second sample.

As well as emphasizing original teaching points it was suggested that the writing could be made smaller and a further week's practice produced the third sample, a fluent acceptable style, produced at a good speed with free and flowing movement. Andrew is delighted with the improvement in his handwriting and is particularly proud of the much more mature impression it conveys.

Chapter 20

CONCLUSION

It is to be hoped that this chapter has firmly established the importance of commitment and motivation in the improvement of handwriting. The key to success is undoubtedly pupil motivation, which is necessary to undertake the considerable amount of practice involved. The process is basically a partnership. There is much discussion and the pupil is encouraged to assess his own work and discuss suggestions for improvement. He does, in fact, take a great deal of responsibility for his own learning, thus cultivating the more mature approach in which the pupil recognises his own difficulties and then attempts to do something about them.

It is only when the effects of improved handwriting are seen, that one begins to comprehend the full extent of the problems created by bad handwriting., When a pupil's self esteem and morale are vastly enhanced, his written work takes on a much greater appearance of maturity, and his whole attitude to school changes for the better, one really begins to appreciate what must have been missing before, and how much greater priority secondary schools should give to the improvement of handwriting.

Where handwriting has improved, teachers tend to value a pupil's work more highly and pay greater attention to it. Improved handwriting also tends to make weaknesses in spelling, punctuation and sentence construction more easily detectable.

The handwriting samples in this chapter typical of many on record show the extent of the actual improvement of handwriting achieved. Perhaps the last word on evaluation should be with those most intimately associated with improved handwriting, the pupils themselves.

> 'The writing room has helped me to rejuvenate my writing technique. This was vital as I am sitting my final exams soon and it could improve my grade as much as from a grade 3 to a grade 2'.

> 'Changing my handwriting really allowed me to express my personality on paper as well as giving me more self confidence'.

> 'Some people see writing as sort of eyes because if you see untidy writing you think that person is untidy and not trustworthy'.

> 'When my writing was bad I didn't like other people to read it'.

'To me better writing means a better job and hopefully further education'.

'I find it easier to revise my notes because I can now read them'.

'Looking back on what I used to write like and what I write like now shows you what you can achieve with a bit of help and a lot of work'.

However, improved handwriting can also be a disadvantage!

'I had to bring an extra I.D. to the bank to prove my identity because my signature had altered so much'.

REFERENCES

ALSTON J. and TAYLOR J. (1985). *The Handwriting File: Diagnosis and Remediation*. LDA Wisbech.

ALSTON J. and TAYLOR J. (1987). *Handwriting: Theory, Research and Practice*. Croom Helm.

PUMFREY P. D. and REASON R. (1991). *Specific Learning Difficulties (Dyslexia) Challenges and Responses*. NFER Routledge.

SASSOON R. (1986). *Helping your Handwriting*. Arnold Wheaton.

COMMITTEE ON PRIMARY EDUCATION (1986). *Report of the Project: Foundations of Writing. Consultative Committee on the Curriculum*.

RABAN B. and POSTLETHWAITE K. (1988). *Classroom Responses to Learning Difficulties*. MacMillan Education.

Chapter 21

SPECIFIC DIFFICULTIES AND MATHEMATICS

CHARLES WEEDON

SPECIFIC DIFFICULTIES

A specific difficulty is one that stands out in contrast to the apparent potential of the individual. Sometimes it may be more precisely labelled – for example, the terms 'dyslexia', 'dysgraphia' and 'dyscalculia'. These carry with them an implication of neurological origin, and a certain intransigence in the face of intervention – but by no means all specific difficulties come into such categories. There may be a range of other, non-neurological explanations, and there is never any reason why intervention should not be successful, at least to some degree.

Difficulties can be highly specific, affecting in an obvious way only one area of activity; they can be specific, but manifest themselves in a wider range of activities; or they can be quite general difficulties. This last grouping, of quite general difficulties, tends often to be equated with an overall low level of intellectual functioning – but often these general difficulties are a function of specific difficulties that affect a range of activities wide enough to give an impression of a generally low level of 'intelligence'.

There can be difficulties that are specific to any human activity – use of written language is one, Mathematics is another. Any sophisticated activity demands access to a wide range of skills and processes, in complex interaction. Every activity draws upon and builds from certain clusters of skills and processes. A localised dysfunction anywhere in the prerequisite skills network, unless successfully circumvented, may finally lead to a specific disability in that area of endeavour.

The degree to which the resulting disability is specific to certain areas of activity will depend upon how task specific is the skill or process concerned. If very specific, it may lead to a disability that manifests itself on a very narrow front. But if the skill is one that is needed in a wider range of activities, then it seems likely that there will be some difficulty manifested, in some form, in each of these activities.

REACTIONS TO SPECIFIC DIFFICULTIES

The most discussed and written about specific difficulties are those that manifest themselves mainly in the area of language. Not surprisingly – language is arguably mankind's most powerful tool, rendered many times more powerful still when made permanent by means of writing.

The tension a specific difficulty creates is proportional to the perceived importance of mastery in that area. At one end of the continuum a particular weakness can be easily dismissed: poor performance as a pole vaulter would not upset most of us; and while we might regret an inability to sketch well we have little difficulty in rearranging our lives around that shortcoming. At the other end no-one laughs off an inability to read or write or spell – it does matter so very much. And somewhere in between the two lie Mathematics and number manipulation: it's common enough to hear people declare, with a kind of perverse pride, that they 'could never do Maths', but there is a certain amused defiance in the declaration – because it does matter. The handling of number, shape and quantity does pervade a great many human activities and any specific weakness in this area is disabling in that it closes many doors, shuts off many areas of activity.

SPECIFIC DIFFICULTIES AND MATHEMATICS

There is a range of specific difficulties that might contribute to difficulties within Mathematics. Dyslexia, dysgraphic-type difficulties, spatial and organisational difficulties, and sensory or motor disabilities may all have implications for Mathematics performance. There may, too, be difficulties whose centre of gravity seem to be primarily mathematical or arithmetical (Lewis, Weedon 1992). Where these are deemed to be neurological in origin, the syndrome may be termed 'dyscalculia' (Kosc, 1986, Sharma and Loveless 1986, Sharma 1979, 1986).

There is little doubt that there are learners who are competent elsewhere in the curriculum, sometimes highly competent, while finding Mathematics or Arithmetic difficult (Share *et al* 1988, Lewis, Weedon 1992). Among children otherwise competent in the classroom, Arithmetic disability is quite commonly a correlate of reading disability, but certainly may exist on its own (Share *et al* 1988). From the sparse research to date, however, no typical cross-curriculum performance patterns can be identified among such pupils. They appear to share little more than their unexpected weakness in Mathematics: their strengths are quite various (Weedon 1992).

SOURCES OF DIFFICULTY WITH MATHS

Those competent with Mathematics and numbers have long been bewildered by the incompetence of others: an HMI in 1876 felt it was 'a subject . . . beyond the comprehension of the rural mind' (McIntosh, in Floyd 1981).

Difficulties with Mathematics are not rare. They can stem from a number of factors, separately or together; social and educational factors, the individual's cognitive performance, neurological make-up, personality and learning style, all interacting with each other and with factors intrinsic to the nature of the subject.

In the same way that explanations of dyslexia tend to draw upon a neurological aetiology, so must a dyscalculic explanation of difficulties specific to Mathematics depend upon the exclusion of contending explanations, and rely upon congenital inheritance. As will be seen, the contending explanations are many and convincing.

Webster's Dictionary includes the entry (perhaps significant when considering why people might find it so hard): 'Mathematical: . . . rigorously exact, perfectly accurate . . . being beyond doubt or question'.

Its rigour combines with its abstraction. Mathematics is inherently abstract. The processes of abstracting and classifying are central to it (Skemp 1971), and the very essence of Mathematics is that it abstracts to a stage beyond words. Mathematical thinking exists as a distinctive entity partly because it explores areas of thought beyond the easy control of words. It has developed and makes use of a whole different symbol system to express ideas and relationships that cannot easily be put into words, in a very compressed and precise way.

The purpose and essence of Mathematics is to solve problems. It demands the acquisition of, organisation of and access to knowledge, rules, techniques, skills and concepts with the aim of providing solutions to novel situations. It is both an organised body of knowledge and a creative activity. For some learners this may imply an internal tension: creativity involves independence, judgement and a readiness to take risks. School Mathematics with its apparent logical certainties pays little attention to these features (Polya 1957, Lansdown 1978, Plunkett 1979, Giles 1981).

'Algorithms' play an essential and central part in this. These are the formal routines that we learn and depend on so much, the 'rules, techniques and skills'. They are the mathematicians tools, his way of compressing and of providing a short cut.

As will be seen, algorithms are essential to success in Mathematics, but probably contribute more than anything else to confusion and lack of understanding. Too often the algorithm tends to take central place, a tool wielded by someone with little understanding of its function. The underlying meanings are left behind: 'the smaller number goes on the bottom line'; or in later years, 'turn it upside down and multiply'. In Ausubel's terms (1968), learning has become rote. It is not meaningful and the learner's mind quickly becomes a cluttered mess of confusing rules.

It is helpful in other ways to see mathematical thinking as having two main strands. Crudely these might be summarised as the distinction between skill and knowledge, between procedures and concepts (Polya 1957, Floyd 1981, Hiebart 1986). Hiebert and Lefevre (Hiebert 1986) think of mathematics in terms of 'procedural knowledge', dominated by rules and algorithms, and 'conceptual knowledge', a connected web of knowledge where the links themselves are as important as the pieces of information they link together.

The question of which of these two kinds of knowledge is most important, and what should be the appropriate balance between them, lies at the heart of most debates about Mathematics teaching.

'MATHEMATICAL ABILITY'

In Mathematics perhaps more than in other subjects there is a feeling that you need to be born with the right **kind** of intelligence, 'and plenty of it' (Giles 1981).

Cluster analysis, however, suggests that Mathematics ability is not a single ability, but a cluster of several. That they are gathered together under the purely convenience heading 'school mathematics' is an arbitrary function of school organisation (Joffe 1980).

Often, the skills needed in Mathematics are seen as forming two main groups. For example, verbal abilities may be contrasted with visual abilities or spatial with linear (Joffe 1980). For Joffe, spatial skills are needed in understanding shape, symmetry, and relative size and quantity, while linear skills contribute to understanding the kind of sequential and ordered symbols and representations found in the number system and algebra.

Recent factor-analytic studies have yielded separate factors for mathematical inference and mathematical knowledge independent of general intelligence or verbal skills, suggesting that mathematical ability is, statistically at least, an independent cognitive entity (Spiers 1987).

Spiers goes on to consider a question important to a neurological perspective of Mathematical ability: whether calculation is a higher cortical 'function' that can be localised within the cortex, and if so, where; or whether it is better seen as a 'performance', a secondary process based upon other more fundamental functions? He suggests that in the sense that we regard language as a higher cortical function, so should we define calculation.

DIFFICULTIES CAUSED BY SCHOOLS AND TEACHERS

It is a frequently recurring theme that Mathematics failure is school induced (e.g. Ginsburg 1977, Plunkett 1979, Giles 1981, Dickson *et al* 1984, Liebeck 1984, Larcombe 1985).

Certainly success levels in Mathematics are generally very low. If teachers test a skill taught and practised some time ago, probably they do not expect a generally high level of competence. Given our recognition of the rigorously linear nature of Mathematics, we teach with a remarkably high tolerance of failure, often even an expectation of failure.

With failure built-in in this way perhaps it is not surprising that Mathematics is associated with varying degrees of boredom, dislike, anxiety, alarm, fear and other emotions that accompany expectation of failure (Giles 1981, Allardyce and Ginsburg 1983, Orton 1987).

These institutional features stem from trying to convey a great deal of highly abstract content in a relatively short space of time and are the factors that cause us to rely so much on the short cuts provided by formal algorithms.

It may be that much failure is due to learning tricks in place of conceptual understanding. Children sometimes seem to think of mathematics as an isolated game with peculiar sets of rules and no evident relation to reality (Ginsburg 1977). Many writers (e.g. Ginsburg 1977, Plunkett 1979, Giles 1981, Allardyce and Ginsburg 1983, Dickson 1984, Liebeck 1984) suggest that standard algorithms are short cut devices introduced before the child has any real grasp of what is involved. As such they conceal the underlying logic, specially from the less able. Any initial glimpses of reason will be lost through this process of mechanising. Seen this way schools are suppressing an intuitive mathematical ability, rather than building on it.

LANGUAGE BASED DIFFICULTIES

These have received a lot of attention from researchers (e.g. Floyd 1981, Cockcroft 1982, Harvey *et al* 1982, Dickson *et al* 1984, Shuard and Rothery 1984). Quite apart from any other reading difficulties the extensive and significant, but often subtle, differences between Mathematical English (ME) and Ordinary English (OE) have been identified as the source of considerable difficulties. They have been well explored, and need not be documented in detail here.

DIFFICULTIES DERIVING FROM PERSONALITY FACTORS

Probably there are aspects of Mathematics that appeal to one individual while repelling another, functions perhaps of preferred styles of study and personality. The affective and the cognitive interpenetrate.

It has been seen that skills and abilities are not evenly or uniformly distributed. Within one individual certain clusters of skills may dominate, and this can sometimes be seen in terms of distinctive learning styles (e.g. Pask 1976, Chinn 1992), applicable to Mathematics as well as other areas: for example those who prefer to build their understanding step by step contrasted by those who prefer a more holistic approach.

Certainly school Mathematics tends to be a socially-isolated activity and one that does not demand the revealing of emotions in the way that other subjects may. Further, it is an area of certainties, with all the sense of beauty and completeness this can bring to some. It is often viewed as highly competitive, satisfying to some and unpleasant for others. Similarly some like the fact that answers are 'right' or 'wrong'; while those who thrive on discussion and debate may not find this aspect pleasing.

It seems helpful to see a personality continuum relevant to Mathematics success or failure, ranging from the very impulsive, through the reflective, to the ultra-reflective (Orton 1987).

On the left the impulsive learner is too ready to take risks and will not be consistently successful. In the middle the reflective learner is prepared to take limited risks and is more likely to be successful. On the right is the far too cautious learner, terrified of failure and unable to take any risk, again leading to lack of success.

The 'right/wrong' nature of most responses to mathematics makes it easy to damage the self esteem of the learner, and many writers suggest that this happens again and again to too many of us (e.g. Allardyce and Ginsburg 1983, Dickson *et al* 1984, Orton 1987).

A HEMISPHERIC PERSPECTIVE

The hemispheric construction of the brain has been widely discussed in relation to mathematics. (Krutetskii 1976, Wheatly 1977, Sharma 1979, DeLoche and Seron 1987).

Sharma identifies two types of Mathematics learners: the Quantitative and the Qualitative mathematics learning personality (Sharma and Loveless 1986, Chinn 1992). Those with a left hemispheric orientation are good in language, verbal expression, problem solving bit by bit, quantifying, quantitative operations, and anything that builds up sequentially, such as counting, addition, multiplication. When given a word problem, they look for a familiar algorithm.

Those with a right hemispheric orientation look at problems holistically and explore global solutions. They are good at identifying patterns, both spatial and symbolic. They are creative and faster at solving 'real-life' problems.

As well difficulties that might arise from uneven hemispheric performance of this kind, there may be a problem in moving information from one hemisphere to other during processing. Further, there may be a problem in overall control by the left hemisphere (Sharma and Loveless 1986)

DYSCALCULIA

There is ongoing interest in neurological explanations of learning difficulties (e.g. Krutetskii 1976, Farnham-Diggory 1978, Sharma 1979, Joffe 1980, Orton 1987).

Gonzalez and Kolers (1987) distinguish between the cognitive and neurological approach by suggesting that while the neuropsychologist is most interested in associating particular impairments with particular lesions, the cognitive psychologist is concerned with the mental operations that underlie particular performance. As the debate between 'function' and 'performance' implies, however, the two disciplines interpenetrate.

There are many ways a learner can encounter difficulties that cannot be attributed to his or her school experiences. While they may be seen as cognitive, they imply a congenital, neurological origin. They include (Bley and Thornton 1981) visual and auditory perception problems, spatial and temporal disabilities, or motor deficits. There may be memory deficits, in working memory or long term. Visual deficits may make copying difficult, while auditory deficits lessen the ability to learn from oral drills. When dealing with word problems memory deficits impede easy retention of items in order to operate on them especially for longer problems. There may be sequencing deficits – much Mathematics involves sequencing; or there may be integrative deficits, a difficulty in pulling information together. In all of these the cognitive/neurological borderlines are not clear and probably not important.

The principles used to define dyscalculia are similar to those used to define dyslexia: developmental dyscalculia is a special difficulty with numbers not due to poor teaching or low IQ. Allardyce and Ginsburg 1983, Sharma 1986). A neurological cause is implicated.

Developmental dyscalculia is neurologically defined as a disorder of the maturation of mathematical abilities which has its origin in a congenital or genetic disorder in a specific area of the brain (Kosc 1974). When there is a pronounced inability for mathematics a low level of functional maturity of the inferior parietal region of the cortex and its connections with other sections of the brain is observed (Krutetskii 1976, Sharma 1986).

Studies of acquired and developmental dyslexia have provided each other with valuable data and insights, while illuminating too the normal functioning of the unimpaired user of language. There has been less interpenetration in the area of mathematical cognition (DeLoche and Seron 1987), and apart from Kosc's work (1974) the neuropsychological studies that have taken place provide much of the sparse empirical evidence available in this field.

LINKS BETWEEN LANGUAGE DIFFICULTIES AND MATHEMATICAL DIFFICULTIES

While there is no clear evidence yet that arithmetic processing can be functionally localised in the brain (Spiers 1987), calculation can best be conceptualised in terms of a network of several component processes, each perhaps with a distinct localisation in a certain site, and mediated at different levels within the nervous system. Such a 'network model' allows explanation of why language and calculation deficits sometimes overlap and coexist while in other cases clear dissociations are established (Spiers 1987).

Often a pupil identified as dyslexic will manifest mathematics problems: the characteristic signs of dyslexia include such things as an inability to subtract, unless with concrete aids, and difficulty with tables (Joffe 1980). Mycklebust and Johnson (1962) placed dyscalculia in sixth place on their list of common features found among their sample of 200 dyslexics.

Joffe's study of dyslexics' Mathematics performance (1980) suggested that 60% of the dyslexic sample were retarded in arithmetic to some extent, the problem being severe for 50%. However, 10% excelled in all aspects of school mathematics, apparently by adopting alternative strategies to cope with numbers and problems. She found that calculation tended to be the major area of weakness, particularly multiplication and division, and attributed this to the dyslexic's characteristic difficulty with verbal labelling and using short term memory. Spatial aspects and concept understanding she found to be usually unimpaired.

Joffe points up a range of extrinsic factors that might exacerbate the mathematics difficulties of a dyslexic: apart from the obvious need for reading skill considerable emphasis may have been put on improving language skills, at expense of other skills; or to avoid putting extra stress on the dyslexic learner mathematics may not have been emphasised.

INCIDENCE OF SPECIFIC DIFFICULTIES IN MATHEMATICS OR ARITHMETIC

The data is sparse and sometimes ill-defined. While referring often to 'mathematics' it tends to focus upon difficulties in arithmetic and calculation.

While acknowledging that most Mathematics difficulties arise from other factors Kosc's influential Bratislavia study (1974) suggests that more than 6% of normal 11 year olds show signs of development dyscalculia.

Kosc's study does not, however, supply data upon the reading abilities of the pupils concerned. Rourke and his colleagues (1978, 1983) considered pupils with arithmetic problems, reading problems, and arithmetic-and-reading problems, and suggested that arithmetic disorders fall into two categories: specific arithmetic disabilities where pupils showed visuo-spatial and tactile-perceptual skills relatively poorer than their verbal skills; and arithmetic-and-reading disabilities where non-verbal skills were better than verbal skills. However, their population of children referred for learning difficulties gave no indication of incidence in the general population.

Epidemiological data is available from a new Zealand study reported by Share *et al* (1988), suggesting that while 6.4% of children show an arithmetic-and-reading disability, 4.8% have a specific arithmetic disability.

A recent study by Lewis, Hitch and Walker (unpublished at time of printing) used a population of over a thousand 9-10 year olds to explore the incidence of arithmetic disability within the general population in UK. Their rigorously defined criteria of pupil performance indicated that 3.9% of their sample had a reading-only disability, 2.3% an arithmetic-and-reading disability, and 1.3% on arithmetic only disability.

SPECIFIC DIFFICULTIES AND MATHEMATICS: HOW THEY AFFECT THE LEARNER

As can be seen specific difficulties do manifest themselves in Mathematics, for a range of reasons and in a range of ways. Certainly there are learners whose performance elsewhere should imply significantly greater success in Mathematics (Share *et al* 1988, Lewis, Weedon 1992).

To date there has been very little close analysis of the classroom performance of such pupils. While studies such as those of Share and Lewis and their colleagues (*op. cit.*) sought to measure typical incidence through paper-and-pencil testing, Weedon (1992) sought to access the perceptions of teachers. It was felt that their experience represented a considerable and relatively untapped source of understanding. In addition their perceptions drew upon long term and typical performance rather than providing the kind of single episode and perhaps atypical analysis that is offered by paper-and-pencil testing.

Weedon's project sought to explore the existence and nature of difficulties specific to Mathematics, and to consider the extent to which provision reflected adequately the learning needs thus exposed.

The resulting data contained patterns of sufficient clarity to allow answers of some confidence to the questions posed:

(i) Teachers' experiences and understanding did suggest quite clearly that pupils who are otherwise competent may experience significant difficulty in aspects of Mathematics; and

(ii) The needs stemming from these difficulties can be met only in part by the types of provision and delivery currently in common usage.

Chapter 21

The research questions were operationalised into a number of more focused strands of investigation.

First, teachers were interviewed to explore in some detail how they perceived and understood mathematical difficulties. The resulting picture suggested that while teachers recognised the unnecessary pitfalls and hindrances caused by social, pedagogical and institutional factors, the main difficulties arise from the ways in which some fairly fixed attributes of the learners (e.g. their memory, certain personality traits, their ability to relate the abstract to the actual) interact with demands that stem from the intrinsic nature of Mathematics (e.g. its abstraction, its linearity). From this wide range of experienced practitioners there was a clear sense that, for most pupils experiencing significant long-term difficulty in part or all of their Mathematics, their level of performance probably offered a fair reflection of their level of potential.

Secondly, teachers' understanding of difficulties specific to Mathematics were explored. It emerged quite clearly that relatively few were sceptical of their existence, attributing them to a range of factors centred about the pupil, again fairly fixed factors stemming from the interaction between the nature of Mathematics and the attributes of the particular pupil. Most conspicuously, many teachers emphasised the distinction between difficulties with Mathematics and those with Arithmetic: number-based difficulties, dysfunctions with calculation and with the very understanding of numbers, were seen as separate from difficulties with other areas of Mathematics, and often more severe and more widespread. It is difficult to provide a precise definition that distinguishes comprehensively between Arithmetic and Mathematics – but evidently there are distinctions that are clear enough in teachers' minds to see difficulties in the two areas as separate phenomena.

The profiles of identified pupils confirmed the existence of these difficulties specific to Mathematics, suggesting not a unitary phenomenon but the kind of variable, multi-factor syndrome that we expect with dyslexic learners. Performance patterns and descriptions confirmed that while different kinds of difficulties may often overlap and interpenetrate they may too exist independently: for example, pupils may have specific difficulties in language alone, in language and Mathematics, or in Mathematics alone. While the project did not seek to quantify incidence the data gave the impression of a relatively low level of incidence.

Throughout there was a pervasive sense that these difficulties relate to pupil attributes that are relatively fixed – as with dyslexia there was a sense that specific difficulties with Mathematics tend to be relatively intransigent and inherent features of the pupil's profile as a learner of Mathematics. They might be lessened or coped with – but probably they will not be eradicated.

Given the picture that emerged it was not easy to be optimistic that provision currently available in schools could maximise the mathematical potential of these pupils. There was a strong sense that individualised schemes had been developed quite rigorously and effectively as the only means of curriculum delivery that might hold out hope – but that even at their best it would be hard for them to provide adequately for pupils with specific difficulties in Mathematics.

IMPLICATIONS FOR OUR CURRICULUM PHILOSOPHY

The project claimed access to no objective realities – only to those insights to be gained from accessing the extended experience and understanding of teachers. These were, however, felt to be of considerable ecological validity: teachers alone, among all other education professionals, have an intimate and continuous experience of both the delivery of the curriculum and the ways in which pupils respond to it. Their views should carry some weight.

The views gathered during this project, expressed in the quite extensive interviews, left an abiding impression of measured pessimism: teachers saw these difficulties as enduring and unlikely easily to be righted. Such a view has curriculum implications: where difficulties seem deeply rooted and intransigent, be they specific or otherwise, then our emphasis upon common curricular goals for the whole mainstream population may need some reconsideration. While the views emerged from the consideration of specific difficulties in Mathematics it seems likely that their implications apply equally to specific difficulties of other kinds too. It may be that, for a small number of pupils under some circumstances, two of our most important current curriculum orthodoxies may be unhelpful. Both are valid and both have been powerful agents for beneficial change. But both have limits beyond which they become unhelpful.

The first concerns the concept of a continuum of difficulty. Since Warnock (DES 1978) it has been argued, with good effect and for obvious reasons, that it is unhelpful to categorise and label. Instead we think of difficulties as lying along a continuum, from the very severe to the less severe. The Specific Mathematics Difficulties project demonstrated, however, something long apparent to those concerned with dyslexic-type difficulties: that there is no single continuum; that serious intellectual difficulties in one or more areas may be balanced by adequacy or even excellence in others. A single continuum can in no way represent this – it seems likely that for these learners, and perhaps others to a lesser extent, a complex mesh of overlapping continua would be needed. Such a model becomes too complex; and whatever the dangers of labelling, the right label, at the right place, may allow a very real difficulty to be identified and responded to.

The second and related concept is that of the curriculum deficit model of learning difficulties. Like Warnock's continuum it has been a powerful and helpful concept. Its implication, that all pupils are able to move in the same direction, albeit at different speeds and by differing pathways, has allowed positive and responsive curriculum development with effective and realistic differentiation. The notion of an intellectual ceiling is rejected, as is the idea that some pupils need to be extracted — removed from their peers and provided with experiences that are essentially different in some respects. It too has been a powerful agent for change. But taken too far it too can become, for a probably small number of learners, thoroughly counter-productive. Where learning difficulties are both specific and severe it may be necessary sometimes to adapt and modify the curriculum, to divert sometimes from the mainstream direction. We have learned to be suspicious of a pupil-deficit model of difficulties, usually rightly so – but if 'pupil-deficit' means to take as the starting point the pupil and his difficulty, then for these pupils that may sometimes be the only way forward.

Any change, however, needs to be undertaken with great care – these curriculum orthodoxies have been powerfully successful and have succeeded in diminishing the ill-effects of institutional labelling and segregation. But both can become absurd if taken to an extreme for which they were not designed.

There are no alternatives that are immediately obvious. The ideal of extended one-to-one tuition is not a realistic option; nor would extended extraction be helpful or appropriate.

The challenge is to find ways of building upon the hard-won strengths and advantages of our current provision while developing, at the same time, an organisational and curricular flexibility where it is needed.

Where there are serious specific difficulties, then certainly it does seem that it is needed.

REFERENCES

ALLARDYCE B., GINSBURG, H., (1983) 'Children's Psychological Difficulties in Mathematics' in *The Development of Mathematical Thinking*, (ed) Ginsburg, H., Academic Press.

AUSUBEL D., (1968) *Educational Psychology: A Cognitive View*, Holt, Rhinehart and Winston.

BADIAN N. A., (1983) 'Dyscalculia and non-verbal disorders in learning' in Myclebust. H. R., (ed) *Progress in Learning Disabilities*, Vol. 5, New York.

BLEY N. S., THORNTON, C. A., (1981) Teaching *Mathematics to the Learning Disabled*, Aspen Systems Corporation.

CARPENTER T. P., MOSER J. M., BEBOUTH. C., (1988) *Representation of Addition and Subtraction Word Problems*, Journal for Research in Mathematical Education 19 (4) 345-357.

CHINN S. J., (1992) 'Individual Diagnosis and Cognitive Syle' in Miles, T. R., Miles, E., (eds) *Dyslexia and Mathematics*, London, Routledge.

CHOAT E., (1978) *Children's Acquisition of Mathematics*, NFER.

COCKCROFT W. H., (1982) *Mathematics Counts*, HMSO London.

CRITCHLEY M., (1970) *The Dyslexic Child*, London, Heinemann.

DELOCHE G., SERON, X., (eds) (1987) *Mathematical Disabilities: a Cognitive Neuropsychological Perspective*, Hillsdale, N.J., Erlbaum.

DEPARTMENT OF EDUCATION AND SCIENCE (1978) *Special Educational Needs* (The Warnock Report), London, HMSO.

DESFORGES C., COCKBURN A., (1987) *Understanding the Mathematics Teacher*, Falmer.

DICKSON L., BROWN M., GIBSON O., (1984) *Children Learning Mathematics*, Schools Council Publications.

FARNHAM-DIGGORY S., (1978). *Learning Disabilities*, London: Fontana/Open Books.

FLOYD A., (ed) (1981) *Developing Mathematical Thinking*, Open University Press.

GILES G., (1981) *School Mathematics under Examination: Part 3, Factors Affecting the Learning of Mathematics*, University of Stirling, Department of Education, DIME Projects.

GINSBURG H. P., (1977) *Children's arithmetic: how they learn it and how you teach it*, Austin, TX:PRO-ED, 1982.

GONZALEZ E. G., KOLERS P.A., (1987) 'Notational Constraints on Mental Operations' in G. DeLoche, X. Seron (eds) *Mathematical Disabilities: a Cognitive Neuropsychological Perspective* Hillsdale, N.J., Erlbaum.

HARTJE W., (1987) 'The Effect of Spatial Disorders on Arithmetical Skills' in G. DeLoche, X. Seron (eds) *Mathematic Disabilities: a Cognitive Neuropsychological Perspective* , Hillsdale, N. J., Erlbaum.

HARVEY R., KERSLAKE D., SHUARD H., TORBE M., (1982) *Language Teaching and Learning: 6 Mathematics,* Ward Lock Educational.

HIEBERT J., (ed) (1986)*Conceptual and Procedural Knowledge: The Case of Mathematics*, Lawrence Erlbaum Associates.

JOFFE L., (1980) *Dyslexia and Attainment in School Mathematics: Part 1,* Dyslexia Review Vol. 3, 1 Summer.

JOFFE L., (1980) *Dyslexia and Attainment in School Mathematics: Part 2,* Dyslexia Review Vol 3, 2 Winter.

JOFFE L., (1990) 'The Mathematical Aspects of Dyslexia: a recap of general issues and some implications for teaching,' *Links,* Vol. 15, No. 2. Spring 1990.

KOSC L., (1986) *Developmental Dyscalculia,* Journal of Learning Disabilities 7,3, 164-77.

KOSC L., (1986) 'Dyscalculia – a special issue on the work of Dr. Ladislav Kosc' in *Focus on Learning Problems in Mathematics,* Summer/Fall 1986, Vol. 8 nos. 3 and 4.

KRUTETSKII V. A., (1976) *The psychology of mathematical abilities in schoolchildren,* University of Chicago Press.

LANSDOWN R., (1978) *Retardation in Mathematics: a consideration of multi-factorial determinant,* Developmental Medicine and Child Neurology 20.

LARCOMBE T., (1985) *Mathematical Learning Difficulties in the Secondary School,* OUP, Milton Keynes.

LEWIS C., HITCH G., WALKER P., (unpublished at time of printing) *The Prevalence of Specific Arithmetic Deficits and Arithmetic-and-Reading Deficits in 9-10 year-olds,* University of Lancaster and Lancaster Polytechnic.

LIEBECK P., (1984) *How Children Learn Mathematics,* Penguin.

LUMB D., (1987) *Teaching Mathematics 5 to 11,* Croom Helm.

McCLOSKEY M., CARAMAZZA A., (1987) 'Cognitive Mechanisms in Normal and Impaired Number Processing' in G. DeLoche, X. Seron (eds) *Mathematical Disabilities: a Cognitive Neuropsychological Perspective,* Hillsdale, N.J., Erlbaum.

MYKLEBUST H. R., JOHNSON, D., (1962) 'Dyslexia in Children,' *Exceptional Children 29, 14-25.*

NEWTON M. J., THOMSON M. E., RICHARDS I. L., (1979) *Readings in Dyslexia,* Wisbech: Learning Development Aids.

NISBET J., SHUCKSMIT J., (1984) *The Seventh Sense,* SCRE, Edinburgh. (1987) *Learning Mathematics: Issues, Theory and Classroom Practice,* Cassell.

PASK G., (1976) 'Styles and Strategies of Learning,' *British Journal of Educational Psychology* ,46, 128-148.

PLUNKETT S., (1979) 'Decomposition and all that rot,' *Mathematics in Schools* 8, (3), 2-5.

POLYA G., (1957) *How to solve it*, Doubleday Anchor

PRITCHARD R. A., MILES T. R., CHINN S. J., TAGGART A. T., (1989) 'Dyslexia and Knowledge of Number Facts,' *Links*, Vol.14, No. 3, Summer 89.

ROURKE B .P., FINLAYSON M. A. J., (1978) 'Neuropsychological Significance of Variations in Patterns of Academic Performance: Verbal and Visuo-Spatial Abilities' *Journal of Abnormal Child Psychology*, 6, 121-123.

ROURKE B. P., FINLAYSON M. A. J., (1978) 'Neuropsychological Significance of Variations in Patterns of Academic Performance: Motor, Psychomotor and Tactile-perceptual Abilities' *Journal of Paediatric Psychology*, 3, 62-66.

ROURKE B. P., STRANG J. D., (1983) 'Subtypes of Reading and Arithmetic Disabilities: A Neuropsychological Analysis' in M. Rutter, (ed) *Developmental Neuropsychiatry*, New York, Guildford Press.

RUTTER M., YULE W., TIZARD J., GRAHAM P., (1966) 'Severe reading retardation: its relationship to maladjustment, epilepsy and neurological disorders' in *What is Special Education? Association for Special Education*, pp. 280-94.

SCHAEFFER B., EGGLESTON V. H., SCOTT J. L., (1974) 'Number development in young children' *Cognitive Psychology*, 6, 357-379.

SHARE D. L., MOFFITT T. E., SILVA P.A., (1988) 'Factors associated with arithmetic-and-reading disability and specific arithmetic disability' *Journal of Learning Disabilities*, 21, 313-320.

SHARMA M. C., (1979) 'Children at risk for disabilities in Mathematics,' *Focus on Learning Problems in Mathematics*, Vol. 1, (2), 63-64.

SHARMA M. C., (1986) 'Dyscalculia and other Learning Problems in Arithmetic: a Historical Perspective' in *Focus on Learning Problems in Mathematics*, Summer/Fall 1986, Vol. 8 nos. 3 and 4.

SHARMA M. C., LOVELES, E. J., (eds) (1986) 'Dyscalculia – a special issue on the work of Dr Ladislav Kosc' in *Focus on Learning Problems in Mathematics*, Summer/Fall 1986, Vol. 8 nos. 3 and 4.

SHUARD H., ROTHERY A., (eds) (1984) *Children Reading Mathematics*, John Murray.

SKEMP R. R., (1971) *The Psychology of Learning Mathematics*, Penguin Books.

SPIERS P. A., (1987) 'Acalculia Revisited: Current Issues' in G DeLoche, X. Seron (eds) *Mathematical Disabilities: a Cognitive Neuropsychological Perspective*, Hillsdale, N.J., Erlbaum.

SUTHERLAND P. (1988) 'Dyscalculia, Acalculia, Dysgraphia or Plain Innumerate? – a brief survey of the literature' *Journal of the Education Section of the British Psychological Society*, Vol. 12, No. 1.

SUYDAM M. N., WEAVER J. F., (1977) 'Research on Problem Solving: Implications for Elementary School Classrooms' *The Arithmetic Teacher*, 25 (2), 40-42.

TANSLEY P., PANCKHURST J., (1981) *Children with Specific Learning Difficulties*, NFER Publishing Company.

WEEDON C., (1992) *Specific Learning Difficulties in Mathematics*. Report to the SOED, University of Stirling and Tayside Region.

WEINSTEIN M. L., (1980) 'A neuropsychological approach to Mathematics disabilities' in *Learning Disabilities: old dogmas – new directions*, (Update 1980), Boston University School of Medicine.

WHEATLY G. H., (1977) 'The right hemisphere's role in problem solving,' *Arithmetic Teacher* 25, (2), 37-38.

SECTION 5

METACOGNITION

Chapter 22

THE LEARNER – METACOGNITION IN READING

PATRICIA BROWN

INTRODUCTION

'Learning is a process which starts at birth, continues in school and extends through life'.

This short statement from an article by Simpson (1988) is neither contentious or novel. In fact educationalists generally would agree with these aspirations. It does, however, simplify the underlying complexities of this variable concept of learning which has been the focus of much research over the years.

Historically, psychologists have attempted to formulate general laws of learning valid for all humans. The ultimate aim has been to improve teaching and classroom learning but this has remained an elusive goal. No single generally acceptable model has been developed for analysing learning effectiveness and the contributing factors. Contrasting explanations of classroom learning have been developed by different psychologists holding different philosophical positions. Each of them, whether they be behaviourist, psychometric or humanistic, contain important and correct explanations of some aspects of certain kinds of learning, but all are partial in that each theorist has concentrated on a limited range of learning situations and so has utilised a restricted range of evidence (Entwistle 1987). Gradually, therefore, research has shifted to an acceptance that it is important to understand learning from the pupil's perspective within the context of the classroom. Psychologists appear to have accepted the importance of this social context and the significance of the complex interaction between pupil, teacher and task.

There is little doubt that children especially in their pre-school years are able to acquire considerable knowledge and skills as a result of 'incidental' learning. This learning takes place in the context of everyday occurrences and interactions. However, with the transition into formal schooling the emphasis changes to 'intentional' learning and problems may arise. Pupils are now expected to learn for the purpose of recall and are subsequently expected to apply that information in the context of some problem-solving activity. Intentional learning contrasts with incidental learning. As Palincsar and Klenk explain (1992), it is an achievement which results from 'the learner's purposeful, effortful, self-regulated, and active engagement'. They outline three requirements for successful learning in this context. Firstly the pupil must possess the ability and awareness to monitor and control learning activities. Secondly it is necessary for the pupil to access a repertoire of appropriate strategies, and finally the pupil requires motivation through success and feelings of self worth.

The concept of 'self-regulation' which occurs when a pupil monitors and controls the active process of learning is a major component of metacognition and is central to this chapter. As children mature they acquire self-regulatory skills. However, these skills develop at different rates and to different degrees. They form the basis for success across the curriculum in a variety of learning contexts from mathematical problem-solving to reading and are crucial for 'adaptive, planful learning'. Unfortunately they are not always easy to acquire and are not generally explicitly taught in classroom situations (Borkowski 1992).

The aim of this chapter, therefore, has been to present a balanced view of metacognition, one which is relevant within an educational setting and which pinpoints the strengths and identifies the limitations. Although the concept of metacognition has consistently been described as abstract and elusive by a variety of researchers, it has generated an abundance of innovative research which has an intuitive appeal to teachers. From this research it has become apparent that those learners who have poor metacognitive skills are at a disadvantage in all subject areas and as a result practical classroom applications have developed. Initially the research focused on reading comprehension skills which are central to the curriculum but the research field has now widened to include for example mathematical problem-solving (Montague 1992).

METACOGNITION IN READING

Metacognition, as Brown, Armbruster and Baker (1986) point out, plays 'a vital role' in reading. The term is a relatively new label for a large amount of theory and research which considers learners' knowledge and their directed use of their cognitive abilities. Recently those involved in educational research have appreciated the importance of metacognition in helping to describe the reading process. Garner (1987) explains the reasons behind this. Firstly the theory and research can help explain the differences in performances of readers of various ages and secondly this theoretical framework can be used for devising instructional interventions to promote greater strategy use among readers.

The work of Flavell, who is credited with first using the term metamemory (that is knowledge about one's own memory), has been fundamental in shaping research into metacognition. He developed a model of cognitive monitoring (1979) in an attempt to capture the complexities of metacognition as well as clarify a concept which he himself indicates could be 'fuzzy'. The components of his model, metacognitive knowledge, metacognitive experiences, cognitive goals (or tasks) and cognitive actions (or strategies) interact and cause the monitoring of a wide variety of 'cognitive enterprises'.

Flavell differentiates between metacognitive knowledge and metacognitive experience. For example metacognitive knowledge would be child's belief that he or she is better than another at reading or spelling while metacognitive experiences would be as Flavell explains 'conscious cognitive or affective experiences that accompany and pertain to any intellectual enterprise'. An example could be a sudden feeling that you do not understand something that has been said or which you have read. Garner describes clearly the links between these concepts by explaining that metacognitive knowledge can serve as a base for metacognitive experiences which in turn trigger strategy use. All are influenced by the goal or task which is the objective of the cognitive enterprise.

Flavell has studied metacognition and cognitive monitoring in a variety of situations, especially in relation to oral communication skills. His model has been influential and his research is constantly referred to by many working in the field of reading. Most of the studies discussed in this chapter use the work of Flavell and/or his terminology when describing metacognition.

RECENT RESEARCH INTO METACOGNITION IN READING

There are many examples of research into the reading process which focus on these metacognitive aspects. The terminology varies but terms such as metacognition, cognitive monitoring and comprehension monitoring are often used interchangeably by researchers. However, some researchers differentiate between these terms and claim they are hierarchically related concepts. For example Baker and Brown (1984) maintain that comprehension monitoring is one type of cognitive monitoring while cognitive monitoring itself is a component of metacognition.

The research field has divided into two main areas. In one the focus is on children's *metacognitive knowledge* about reading, especially their verbalised knowledge of various aspects of reading. The other area studies the *regulation and control of this knowledge* while reading for different purposes. As Baker and Brown comment, each of these two perspectives, although not conceptually exclusive, has developed its own research approach. The former employs interviews while the latter investigates regulatory behaviour across a variety of tasks.

The problems associated with interviews are clearly and fully discussed by Garner (1987) who states, 'Because of limited language skills, confusion about general processes being queried, or inability to speculate about hypothetical events, young children may be at a disadvantage in responding to interview probes.'

Her concerns are that the interview can either underestimate or even overestimate the stable knowledge a child has about person, task and strategy aspects of a wide variety of cognitive processes. She does offer alternative methods to collecting data which may eliminate some of these problems. One alternative method for example is cross-age tutoring where older learners without adult supervision are encouraged to externalise their knowledge to assist younger children to read and answer detailed questions about a text. The externalisation allows observers to assess the metacognitive knowledge displayed by the tutor.

In spite of the inherent problems researchers have experienced with interviews, two main results have emerged consistently from such studies. The first, proposed by Baker and Brown (1984), is 'Younger and poorer readers have little awareness that they must attempt to make sense of text; they focus on reading as a decoding process, rather than as a meaning getting process.' The second is detailed by Garner (1987) when discussing a study she carried out in 1981 with Reis: 'Younger children and poorer readers are unlikely to demonstrate that they notice major blocks to text understanding. They seem not to realise when they do not understand.'

Greater understanding of children's metacognitive knowledge is only one important facet of metacognition in reading. Bearing in mind the interactive meaning – getting model of the reading process, the other (already briefly mentioned) consists of the self-regulatory mechanisms used by an active learner during reading. They include planning, checking the outcomes of any strategy used, and monitoring the effectiveness of any attempted action, as well as testing, revising and evaluating one's strategies for learning (Armbruster and Brown 1984).

Brown has tried to capture this complexity in a tetrahedral model of learning. According to this model, four major variables enter into the learning situation:

1   *Text:* the nature of the material to be learnt.
2   *Task:* the purpose for reading which learners commonly meet in school.
3   *Strategies:* the activities learners engage in to understand and remember information.
4   *Characteristics of the learner:* prior experience, background knowledge, interests and motivation.

The goal of an effective learner is the control or self-regulation of these four variables. He or she must co ordinate their complex interaction to be successful.

This model provides a useful framework for studying the research into the regulation and control of metacognitive knowledge. In the next few paragraphs, therefore, pertinent examples using the model will be included. They illustrate both the developmental and performance differences (Brown, Armbruster and Baker 1986).

- **Text**

When considering the text, readers must be able to distinguish between the central ideas in a text and those that are peripheral. Even young children at primary school are commonly asked to concentrate on main ideas when reading. A study by Brown and Smiley (1977) highlights the problems that may arise. Although young children may be able to identify the main character and sequence of events in a simple story they experience difficulties in more complex texts. In their study Brown and Smiley asked 8, 10, 12 and 18-year-olds to rate the ideas of complex folk stories according to their importance to the theme of the passage. Only 18-year-olds could reliably distinguish four levels of importance or centrality to the theme. Eight-year-olds could make no reliable distinction between levels of importance. Even 12-year-olds had difficulty deciding on the relative importance of text elements. This has important implications for learning. It is not sufficient to simply be aware of the necessary knowledge; a child must be able to apply the knowledge where and when appropriate to achieve a successful outcome.

- **Task**

The fundamental task, however, for any reader is knowing that the primary goal of reading is to understand the content. As stated earlier, the novice reader can have problems even with this basic notion. If children are unaware that reading is supposed to lead to understanding rather than simply decoding they will find great difficulty adjusting their behaviour depending on the task at hand. A simple strategy such as slowing down when encountering difficulties and speeding up when the material is trivial may not be applied when necessary.

Skimming, for example, is one activity again often demanded within classroom contexts which reflects a pupil's understanding of adjusting the reading rate depending on the purpose of the task in hand. A study by Myers and Paris (1978) concluded that 12-year-olds understood concluded that the purpose of skimming was to pick out the informative words. The 8-year-olds, however, thought that skimming was reading all the easy words. One possible interpretation of this result may be that it is a reflection of their conception of reading as meaning getting and word decoding respectively, which in turn affects their ability to control their behaviour.

- **Strategies**

According to Brown's model, reported in an article by Brown, Armbruster and Baker (1986), the crucial variable is 'strategies'. She claims that when comprehension fails the child must make several important strategic decisions and he or she must choose from the following options: 'store the problem in memory as a pending question in the hope that clarification will be forthcoming; reread the text; look ahead in the text; or, if necessary, consult another source.' These strategies, which have been called 'fix-up' strategies (Alessi, Anderson and Goetz 1979), are critical for efficient reading.

- **Characteristics of the learner**

The final variable in Brown's tetrahedral model is possibly the most influential and least susceptible to manipulation in the learning environment. It is the 'characteristics of the learner'. This particular variable appears to have received the least attention in Brown's work because of the inherent problems associated with attempting to design instruction aimed at altering these characteristics. Motivation, for example, clearly plays an important role when reading. Paris *et al* (1984) express this succinctly when they explain that strategies have components of 'both skill and will'. Therefore unless a learner wants to succeed in a task and attain the goals, he or she will never spend the time and energy to engage in metacognitive strategies. In the short term external incentives can produce effort but it is doubtful whether they will continue and have long lasting effects.

Another crucial influence on successful reading is the background knowledge which a reader brings to the task. The child may lack the requisite knowledge of the world to understand texts that presuppose adequate background experience. As Baker and Brown (1984) explain: 'If the text deals with topics unfamiliar to the reader, it will be difficult for her to understand the significance of the material, to select main points, and to disregard trivia.'

One solution is to select texts which deal with familiar material and gradually increase the introduction of new knowledge. However, this would be difficult to implement in the practical everyday life of the classroom when children are constantly exposed to a great wealth and variety of reading materials. Another solution detailed by Baker and Brown is to 'increase the reader's store of information'. This can be achieved by a programme of enrichment although this again may prove difficult since every programme would need to be devised to meet the needs of each individual child.

In conclusion therefore much of the research into the self-regulatory mechanisms of children reading for meaning can be accounted for within Brown's model of learning. The four variables are interdependent and children differ in their control of text, task and strategies depending on their own characteristics. The research itself illustrates the differences in control between learners of differing ages and differing reading achievement. The convergent findings from recent research into metacognition generally, whether it be knowledge or control, have been summarized by Garner (1987) when she states, 'Young children and poorer readers are not nearly as adept as older children and good readers, respectively, in engaging in planful activities either to make cognitive progress or to monitor it.'

Therefore, poorer readers are clearly at a disadvantage in school because of deficiencies in their knowledge and application of metacognitive strategies. They are not nearly as resourceful in completing the variety of reading tasks necessary in academic settings.

STRATEGY TRAINING IN READING

In the last section of this chapter I have indicated some of the problems which children may experience when reading and which can result in a poorer understanding of text. Awareness of these difficulties can be the preliminary step to attempting some form of remediation. Three main ways of improving comprehension have been detailed by Oakhill and Garnham (1988). Firstly, additions or changes can be made in the text to enhance comprehension without requiring any active effort by the reader. For example, the addition of pictures, titles and summaries. Secondly, activities such as note-taking, underlining and writing summaries can all improve comprehension. These are often referred to as 'study aids'. The third set of aids to comprehension are processing strategies which children can be taught to apply as they are reading. They can help children think about the text and whether they understand it. These strategies mainly attempt to enhance comprehension and they differ from the first two types of aids in that they rely entirely on what goes on in the reader's head rather than on 'external' aids to comprehension.

Research has focused almost exclusively on training these processing strategies for two main reasons. Firstly, if successful these procedures can be applied to any text, and secondly poor readers cannot easily provide their own illustrations or text organisation or even make effective use of traditional study aids. The aim is therefore to give poor readers the skills that better readers naturally use. There is also evidence (Garner 1987) that poor comprehenders' problems arise partly because they fail to monitor their comprehension, or at least they make less use of monitoring strategies. In consequence, therefore, a great deal of research has been devoted to identifying then training these strategies. According to Garner, the strategies taught have been 'academically fundamental' (all children appear to need them) and 'differentially exercised' (some children appear not to use them spontaneously).

Success has been measured against three criteria which were identified by Belmont *et al* (1982):

1. Was there an immediate improvement of performance?
2. Were the instructional effects durable?
3. How successful was the transfer of the instructed activity to new situations?

For example, immediate improvements in performance can be evident either in qualitative changes or in quantitative changes. Durability of effects can be measured by maintenance of acceptable performance over a time interval without further instruction. Successful transfer demands acceptable performance in situations that are related but still different from the original training sessions. These three criteria are clearly dependent on each other and essential for successful strategy training.

Brown, Armbruster and Baker (1984) discuss three general types of training studies to illustrate the need for readers to be actively involved. They maintain that this is essential for training to be effective.

'Blind training' instructs children to perform particular activities but without explaining the significance of such activities. They are told what to do but not why. Although these procedures are sufficient for some children because they can infer the significance of the strategy, poorer readers especially are at a disadvantage. For example, rereading is an effective aid to comprehension but for children to use the strategy they must believe in its effectiveness and efficiency. The consequences of this type of instruction for poor readers are detailed by Paris and Oka (1986): 'Passive inattention in the classroom or obedience rule-following are negative tactics that students often use to appear involved in tasks, yet these approaches avoid learning altogether.'

The other two types of training studies detailed by Brown, Armbruster and Baker have added metacognitive supplements. They are 'informed training' and 'self controlled training'. Both have met with success but the latter is viewed as superior in addition to including information about the strategy readers have been instructed to use, there is explicit instruction in how to monitor and evaluate the strategy used.

DIRECT CLASSROOM APPLICATION OF STRATEGY TRAINING IN READING

One particular procedure to improve comprehension which incorporates both 'informed' and 'self-controlled' training is Reciprocal Teaching. It has developed into a flexible instructional approach which has direct applications in a variety of learning contexts. Reciprocal Teaching which takes place in a group or paired situation features guided practice in the application of four concrete strategies aimed at comprehending a section of text (Palincsar and Klenk 1992). The four strategies identified by Palincsar and Brown in their initial study in 1984 were questioning, clarifying, summarising and predicting. According to Palincsar and Brown these four activities serve a dual purpose, they are both comprehension fostering and comprehension monitoring. That is they enhance comprehension while allowing the pupil to check whether it is occurring.

The hallmark of this form of instruction is that it is interactive in nature, with each pupil and adult taking turns to be 'teacher'. No passive inattention here! The text can be read aloud in sections, depending on the decoding skills of the pupils, following which the 'teacher' leads discussion by asking questions. Other participants respond to the questions and generate additional questions if necessary. The 'teacher' then asks for clarifications which encourages further discussion on ambiguous sections of the text. Then the 'teacher' summarises the section and if appropriate generates predictions regarding upcoming content in the text. Finally a new 'teacher' is selected who leads the discussion on the next section of text.

The results from their first study in 1984 were impressive. The three criteria for success outlined earlier had been met. Firstly there was an improvement of performance. The children involved, aged 12, who were at least two years behind in comprehension, made gains quantitatively in daily tests of comprehension and in a standardised reading test. They also made qualitative gains in the content of their daily dialogue with the researchers. An analysis of the dialogue showed main idea questions increased during the period of reciprocal teaching and main idea summaries increased substantially. Secondly the effects were durable. The children involved maintained their improvements at the final follow up visit eight weeks after the study had finished. Finally the skills generalised to other areas of the curriculum such as social studies and science classes.

Moore (1988) identified four main theoretical elements of reciprocal teaching which he considers were instrumental in its success.

The first and most influential is that of 'scaffolding' (Palincsar and Brown 1984) which has been derived from Vygotskian developmental theory. It refers to the support given to a novice by an expert through the use of dialogue to model and explain cognitive processes. The amount of scaffolding is varied to suit individual differences. As Brown and Palincsar explain: 'The teacher should model the desired comprehension activities, thereby making underlying processes overt, explicit and concrete.'

Garner (1987) outlines the work of Vygotsky (1978) which she suggests is a solution to the problem of low durability in some strategy training. She details his notion of 'zone of proximal development' by which Vygotsky suggested that cognitive functions appear first on the social (inter-psychological) level and only later on the individual (intra-psychological) level. This zone of proximal development is the distance between the level of independent problem solving and the level of problem solving in collaboration with an expert. Vygotsky explained: 'What children can do with assistance of others might be in some sense more indicative of their mental development than what they can do alone.'

The second element described by Moore is 'fading' of the expert's role in modelling these reading comprehension strategies. This allows the learner to take over more responsibility slowly while gaining confidence, and has been shown to be an important feature of successful strategy training.

The third element is 'active involvement' which within reciprocal teaching means the learner has to assume an active teacher role. The 'passive inattention' detailed by Paris and Oka (1986) which they describe as 'avoiding learning altogether' is not possible when the learner is forced into such an active role.

The final element is the 'provision of feedback' to the learner regarding the efficiency of the strategy and the value of using a strategy in that context. It is important to know the utility of a strategy. For example when to use it, how to use it and how to monitor the success. Moore concludes by stating, 'In short, reciprocal teaching demonstrates that through active involvement in real reading contexts, strategies can and do make a difference.'

The success of the Palincsar and Brown studies (1984) is not an isolated phenomenon. There have been other training studies which have demonstrated that metacognition can be promoted through direct instruction in the classroom. One such study which appears both relevant and practical in an education setting was reported by Paris, Cross and Lipson (1984). This involved 8 and 10-year-olds in an experimental curriculum of 'informed strategies for learning' (ISL) which was designed to increase children's awareness and use of effective reading strategies.

Fourteen comprehension strategies (e.g. skimming, locating main ideas, monitoring comprehension, making inferences, etc.) were taught over a period of four months. The strategies were taught using concrete metaphors such as 'Be a reading detective', 'Stop – say the meaning in your own words' and 'Dead end – go back and read the parts you don't understand.' The three modes of instruction were classroom lessons which included modelling of a particular strategy as well as how, when and why to us it; the bulletin board which colourfully illustrated the metaphors, included questions that focused on how, when and why and served as a reminder during normal class work; and suggestions for classroom teachers on how to use the strategies within their every day work.

The children who participated in ISL made gains in cloze and error detection tasks compared with a control group. In interviews they also revealed a greater understanding and awareness about reading strategies and the goals of the task. Paris *et al* (1984) concluded, 'The theoretical value of this study lies in the demonstration that group instruction can be used to transmit information about reading strategies and more importantly that children can be convinced to use the strategies on their own.'

However, strategy training in reading has not been without its critics and it is wise to be aware of the more important cautions which have been expressed. Firstly, the basic assumption made by most researchers is that poor readers will benefit from being taught to use strategies that skilled readers use naturally. Although this may appear fairly obvious, the fact that poor comprehenders have not acquired these strategies may indicate they are, in some cases, unable to acquire them. As Oakhill and Garnham (1988) state, training children to ask questions about cause and effect should enhance comprehension because it helps children to find connections between events. But if some readers are not capable of identifying those connections, they will not benefit from such training. It therefore cannot be assumed that poor comprehenders will automatically become good ones if they are 'taught' the skills.

Another realistic caution expressed about strategy training has been outlined by Garner (1987) and is based on research by Peterson and Swing (1984). They point out that children have to carry out cognitive processing 'in real time'. This means that given the nature of the activity flow in most classrooms, pupils cannot work slowly enough to incorporate unpractised metacognitive strategies. In consequence pupils who are worried about 'being left behind' in task completion often revert to less mature, more rehearsed routines. Garner emphasizes, therefore, the need for plenty of guided practice so strategies become 'more personalized and more routinized'.

There is one danger, however, which must be considered when attempting strategy training and that is the problem of being too prescriptive. We do not yet know enough about skilled reading generally or reading strategies specifically to state with any confidence the 'right' way to read or for that matter the 'right' strategies children should adopt to be successful. Research by Pask (1976) for example, has identified two distinctive styles of learning – holist and serialist – which represent consistent preferences for using certain learning processes while other research on cognitive styles has differentiated between convergent and divergent thinking. Differences in styles of learning will in turn affect children's approaches to learning and this needs to be taken into account so that strategy training is not implemented too mechanically. Ultimately children must be encouraged to be flexible in their approach to reading in order to satisfy the task in hand whether it be educational or social. As Palincsar (1986) claims: 'In conducting metacognitive instruction, one aspires to teach students to plan, implement and evaluate strategic approaches to learning and problem solving. Students, therefore, assume control of their own learning.' This 'control' by the pupils themselves must be the ultimate goal of strategy training.

CONCLUSION AND DISCUSSION

This chapter has set out to describe the recent research into strategy training which has its basis within the wider context of metacognition. The literature has illustrated that the training of cognitive skills to enhance comprehension can be successful with poorer readers. Consequently there are educational implications for all teachers. They are in an ideal position to foster metacognitive skills within the context of their everyday teaching. Strategy instruction can be intertwined with subject area instruction and has been successful when applied over a continuous period of time (Garner, 1987). As well as the structured programmes described, such as Reciprocal Teaching and ISL, there are many ways teachers can assist pupils to improve their metacognitive skills and become more successful learners. For example, while completing tasks teachers can make covert metacognitive processes overt by thinking aloud and modelling appropriate strategies. They can demonstrate that the same strategy can transfer successfully to a variety of learning situations and importantly provide pupils with opportunities to practise strategies so they become personalised and routine. The classroom can be a place where cognition is discussed.

Some pupils with specific learning difficulties may also be at risk from poor metacognitive knowledge and strategy use. Their obvious difficulties in acquiring the necessary literacy skills have resulted in intensive direct instruction over prolonged periods of time to develop competence. This, however, may result in failure to utilise self-regulatory skills flexibly or spontaneously. As Wright and Cashdan (1992) explain, 'although the approaches are essentially well-designed there may be more to successful reading and spelling remediation than appropriate skills acquisition alone.'

Bearing this in mind they designed a pilot study aimed at 'young backward readers with poor decoding abilities' which attempted to address this problem by combining phonological skills training with explicit instruction in the meta-linguistic, metacognitive aspects of reading and spelling. The skill component incorporated a direct teaching model adapted from the Simultaneous Oral Spelling method advocated by Bryant and Bradley (1985), while the metacognitive element included the development of concepts about reading and spelling and strategy development as well as self-regulation and monitoring of thinking. Although the formal test results were inconclusive, Wright and Cashdan observed improvements in phonological abilities as well as the ability to approach reading/spelling tasks strategically through co-ordination of plants, strategies and verbalisation. They claimed that, 'during the intervention period the children moved from passive, anxious, unsystematic learners at baseline to keen active participants in the teaching sessions.'

It is interesting to note the choice of words used by the researchers to describe their learners. 'Passive and anxious' at the beginning of this intervention while becoming 'keen, active and interested' as the study progressed. This change in behaviour which can readily be observed when pupils are involved in Reciprocal Teaching (Brown 1992) is essential for success learning. Pupils who have a specific learning difficulty are often characterised as 'passive' and are without doubt 'anxious'. They may have negative motivational attributes and beliefs which in turn influence their approaches to learning.

Metacognitive strategy training does have important motivational consequences. Reciprocal Teaching, for example, through guided practice and scaffolding can control frustration and decrease the risk inherent in problem solving. Among other things it reduces the numbers of steps in the process to a manageable amount and relies on the teacher to make overt any mismatch between the pupil's response and more appropriate strategy use. Therefore pupils gradually gain independence in a supportive learning situation.

As Borkowski (1992) explains, 'Teachers do not merely deliver content to students but rather model strategic processing.' He himself advocates that Reciprocal Teaching could be extended into the realms of motivational retraining in order to provide pupils with the 'energizing factors necessary for independent reading and thinking.' Borkowski also claims that teachers who are consciously aware of metacognitive skills are 'in a good position to reshape self-defeating beliefs, enhance feelings of self-efficiency, foster interests in learning for its own sake and associate such changes in the motivational-self systems with the emergence of independent self-regulatory skills.'

This may seem a formidable challenge, but learning has to be seen as both cognitive and emotional in content and it is wise in a chapter devoted to the learner that this important aspect is not overlooked. Teachers have a crucial role to play in encouraging pupils to become more successful learners in the classroom. The awareness and positive fostering of metacognitive skills is indispensable.

REFERENCES

ALESSI S., ANDERSON T. and GOETZ E. (1979). An Investigation of Lookbacks during Studying. Discourse Processes, 2, 197-212. Cited in Garner R. (1987) *Metacognition and Reading Comprehension*. Norwood, NJ: Ablex Publishing Corporation.

ARMBRUSTER B. and BROWN A. (1984). Learning from Reading: The Role of Metacognition. In R. Anderson, J. Osborn and R. Tierney (Eds.), *Learning to Read in American Schools*. Hillsdale, NJ: Lawrence Erlbaum Associates.

BAKER L. and BROWN A. (1984). Metacognitive Skills and Reading. In P. D. Pearson (Ed.), *Handbook of Reading Research*. New York: Longman.

BELMONT J., BUTTERFIELD E., and FERRETTI R. (1982). To Secure Transfer of Training Instruct Self Management Skills. In D. Determan and R. Sternberg (Eds.), *How and How Much Can Intelligence Be Increased*. Norwood, NJ: Ablex.

BORKOWSKI J. (1992). Metacognitive Theory: A Framework for Teaching Literacy, Writing, and Math Skills. *Journal of Learning Disabilities, 25,* 253-257.

BROWN A., ARMBRUSTER B. and BAKER L. (1986). The Role of Metacognition in Reading and Study. In J. Orasanu (Ed.), *Reading Comprehension: Form Research to Practice*. Hillsdale, NJ: Lawrence Erlbaum Associates.

BROWN A. and SMILEY S. (1977). Rating the Importance of Structural Units of Prose Passages: A Problem of Metacognitive Development. *Child Development, 48,* 1-8.

BROWN P. (1992). Reciprocal Teaching: An Approach to Improving Reading Comprehension by Training Metacognitive Strategies. In F. Satow and B. Gatherer (Eds.), *Literacy without Frontiers*. Great Britain: UKRA.

BRYANT P. E. and BRADLEY L. (1985). *Children's Reading Problems*. Oxford. Markwell.

ENTWISTLE N. (1987). *Understanding Classroom Learning*. London: Hodder & Stoughton.

FLAVELL J. H. (1979). Metacognition and Cognitive Monitoring. *American Psychologist*, Oct., 906-911.

GARNER R. (1987). *Metacognition and Reading Comprehension*. Norwood, NJ: Ablex.

MONTAGUE M. (1992). The Effects of Cognitive and Metacognitive Strategy Instruction on the Mathematical Problem Solving of Middle School Students with Learning Disabilities. *Journal of Learning Disabilities, 25,* 230-248.

MOORE P. (1988). Reciprocal Teaching and Reading Comprehension: A Review. *Journal of Research in Reading, 11,* 3-14.

MYERS M. and PARIS S. (1978). Children's Metacognitive Knowledge About Reading. *Journal of Educational Psychology, 70,* 680-690.

OAKHILL J. and GARNHAM A. (1988). *Becoming a Skilled Reader.* London: Basil Blackwell Ltd.

PALINCSAR A. (1986). Metacognitive Strategy Instruction. *Exceptional Children, 53,* 118-124.

PALINCSAR A. and BROWN A. (1984). Reciprocal Teaching of Comprehension Fostering and Comprehension Monitoring Activities. *Cognition and Instruction, 1(2),* 117-175.

PALINCSAR A. and KLENK L. (1992). Fostering Literacy Learning in Supportive Contexts. *Journal of Learning Disabilities, 25,* 211-225.

PARIS S., CROSS D. and LIPSON M. (1984). Informed Strategies for Learning: A Programme to Improve Children's Reading Awareness and Comprehension. *Journal of Educational Psychology, 76,* 1239-1252.

PARIS S. and OKA E. (1986). Self Regulated Learning Among Exceptional Children. *Exceptional Children* 53, 103-108.

PASK G. (1976). Styles and Strategies for Learning. *British Journal of Educational Psychology, 46,* 128-148.

PETERSON P. and SWING S. (1983). Problems in Classroom Implementation of Cognitive Strategy Instruction. In M. Pressley and J. Leven (Eds.), *Cognitive Strategy Research: Educational Applications.* New York: Springer-Verlag.

SIMPSON M. (1988). Improving Learning in Schools – What Do We Know? A Cognitive Perspective. *Scottish Educational Review, 20,* 22–31.

VYGOTSKY L. (1978). *Mind in Society: the Development of Higher Psychological Processes.* Cambridge, MA: Harvard University Press. Cited in Garner (1987).

WRIGHT J. and CASHDAN A. (1992). Training Metacognitive Skills in Backward Readers: A Pilot Study. *Educational Psychology in Practice, 7,* 153–162.

Chapter 23

STRATEGIES FOR EFFECTIVE LEARNING

VICKY HUNTER

INTRODUCTION

What makes learning effective for children? Many writers recently have considered different kinds of learning and their effectiveness. For example, the idea of deep, surface or strategic learning (Entwistle, 1987).

Surface learning is quickly forgotten; deep learning has more lasting effects because it has relevance for the learner; strategic learning is what is often called for in school, namely learning for an ulterior objective, usually that of passing exams. It is not the purpose of this chapter to explore these aspects of learning but simply to acknowledge their existence and set the following ideas in that context.

The fundamental premise is that for learning to be effective it must be relevant to the learner and must fit in with his or her learning style.

Generally the best way to achieve this is to listen to, observe and respect the pupil. Having stated these preliminaries, the following observations and strategies are offered as suggestions that help us to help children to learn more effectively. The context is that of mainstream secondary schools.

READING

(a) **Decoding**

There are many class teachers (and parents) who consider that the only way to ascertain whether a pupil is coping with reading is to listen to him reading aloud. In fact, oral reading and silent reading are rather different skills. Although pupils often share the view that the only true test of reading ability is to be able to read in front of one's peers, they become incredibly frustrated with their own inability to do so. They are so nervous the words get all jumbled up; the teacher corrects a mistake and makes them feel even more conspicuously incompetent; other pupils start reading over them. In order to escape from this humiliation they attempt to get the whole thing over in record time – with even more disastrous consequences. The annoying thing is that they often understand the passage. Why else do they sometimes read 'high' for 'low' or 'up' for 'down'. That is not a decoding error. It is amazing how children can stutter and stumble over the detail of a passage and yet somehow have a fuller understanding of the content than the teacher who has been intent on conducting an error analysis and has studiously noted omissions, hesitations and repetitions while failing to take in the substance of the story.

(b)   Comprehension

There are some pupils who rely heavily on context clues and comprehension skills rather than decoding skills. Many are adept at the strategies of gleaning information and predicting the likely progress of a story. Unfortunately, if a pupil's decoding skills are too poor, he can construct a story on a completely wrong premise – e.g.. the pupil who read 'peat bog' as 'pet dog' had great difficulty in then getting the rest of the passage to make any sense at all.

Some pupils have become masters of reading the teacher's face. They know the nod and the smile that mean everything is correct and the frown that means a word is wrong. Their tactic, then, is to guess at a word and then check the teacher's face for the signal. When they return to the text they have lost the place and a great commotion of wriggling, sniffing and coughing ensues while it is found.

STRATEGIES

The first strategy, as always, is to observe the pupil, note how he is behaving and discover what kind of learning is currently being effective for him. The kinds of situations outlined above should be explored in order to help the pupil adjust his learning to a more effective mode. Often the pupils who are nervous and embarrassed about reading aloud in the class are the same ones who feel stigmatised because the teacher never asks them to read!

Strategies which could benefit **all** pupils include:

(a)   Decoding
   (i)   Group reading

Pupils can be arranged in social or ability groups and encouraged to find the way of reading that best suits them. They may choose to read silently; or to read in unison; ask their best reader to read; take turns; ask for teacher support. (Group work is often facilitated by the presence of a learning support teacher or, in secondary schools, by the recruitment of senior pupils to assist in this way). This strategy enables them not only to handle the reading, but to develop effective strategies for determining their own favourite way of learning.

(ii) Listening to tapes

Commercially produced tapes or (good) home-made ones. Pupils can sit at a listening centre together, but another strategy is to use Walkman-type tape players. Although this requires multiple tapes it does get rid of the potential for sabotage with a centre. The existence of taped material is also useful if a pupil has been absent and finds difficulty in catching up if reading on his own.

(iii) Teacher and pupil reading

Teacher reading aloud and pupils reading part silently. It is important in this case to summarise what has been read and/or check out comprehension.

(b) Comprehension

(i) Discussion

In pairs or groups, pupils can discuss topics such as:
how did the main character feel
has anything like this ever happened to you
what happens next, etc.

(ii) Illustrations

Pupils can be referred to the appropriate page to draw pictures of the setting, the characters, a plan or a map of the area etc. They can look through magazines to find pictures of people to represent the characters in a poster. This activity leads to discussion e.g.. No, that girl's too young/too pretty/too posh to be that character.

(iii) Written answers
       True/False: Yes/No variety.

       A selection of summaries with the task being to select the correct one – again discussion makes this work even better, a list of events to put in the correct order; close passages.

(iv)   Spidergrams / key word diagrams e.g.

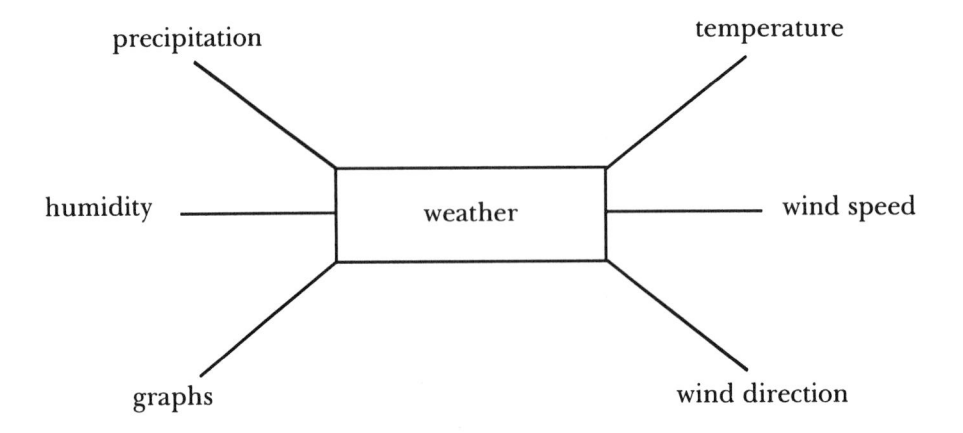

```
   precipitation                    temperature
            \                      /
             \                    /
   humidity ———————[ weather ]——————— wind speed
             /                    \
            /                      \
       graphs                    wind direction
```

(v)   Flowcharts

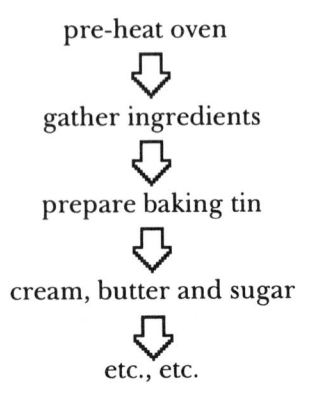

       pre-heat oven
            ⇩
       gather ingredients
            ⇩
       prepare baking tin
            ⇩
       cream, butter and sugar
            ⇩
       etc., etc.

WRITING

A boy wrote on the topic of 'My Best Friend':–

'He's not very briny but niram I sow that's OK.'

(He's not very brainy, but neither am I, so that's OK)

What is writing? It is about communicating one's ideas on paper and this is what children need to be encouraged to do. By secondary school many of them have restricted their output because they are weary of being corrected for spelling, handwriting and punctuation.

The aim must always be to continue to develop these technical skills while continuing to value content and creativity.

(a) **Handwriting**
By secondary school handwriting is a very difficult thing to change. Many pupils have developed personal styles and idiosyncratic pencil grips which have become ingrained over a number of years. Many able pupils face problems when they are required to do more and more writing as they face exams and the style that served them well enough when younger becomes inefficient for lengthy writing sessions.

STRATEGIES:

(a) **Changing handwriting grip and/or style**
If a pupil really wants to change he can be offered pencil grips, specially designed pencils and lessons showing the correct way to form and join letters. However, in my experience, not many pupils have the motivation or determination to do this, particularly as the demands on them in general are constantly increasing. I would, however, stress that the best solution is to get everything right at the start if at all possible.

(b) **Take the pressure off**
Many pupils appear to have been nagged about their handwriting all their school career. Parents complain about it, teachers go on about it. Some youngsters feel that they could submit an investigation unravelling the mystery of the universe and it would be returned with

'Your handwriting requires attention' scrawled across it by teachers who incidentally, often do not present very positive role models.

(c) **Set realistic standards**

For some pupils, particularly early in secondary school, all that is needed is a reminder that neat handwriting is called for. Many Primary teachers are horrified at what their Secondary colleagues appear to be accepting, while the Secondary Staff are simultaneously commenting on the poor standard of handwriting in the new intake. The pupils are just trying it on!

(d) **Alternative solutions**

(i) Use of a word processor/lap top computer

This is not generally the panacea some people think it will be. First of all pupils need practice in key-boarding skills and in the operation of the computer. Even with this, their output is generally slower than that of their peers and of their own written attempts.

Then there is the fact of being different by using this aid. Some children, of course, revel in the kudos, but others feel stigmatised and conspicuous. These aids are useful for finished work but may have limited value on a day-to-day basis.

(ii) Use of a scribe

This, too, is a skill which needs to be practised, particularly if it is to be used for external exams. Again, individual pupil needs and feelings need to be taken into consideration. Some love the sound of their own voice and the freedom to express themselves fully, others are mortified at having to articulate ideas that they are not too sure about anyway.

(iii) Use of tape recorder/dictaphone (for later transcription)

Again, depending on how a pupil feels about speaking into a machine, this can be a useful tool. If it is to be used in class it can be disturbing to other pupils and so arrangements have to be made to overcome this. Transcribing the words is a time consuming task for someone.

SPELLING

There are plenty of books offering advice on ways of teaching spelling and a number of diagnostic tests to help teachers determine the nature of a pupil's difficulty – e.g. poor visual memory, poor auditory memory, lack of phonic knowledge, lack of knowledge of serial probability etc. Self-image as a speller can also be assessed (NFER Nelson Diagnostic Spelling).

It is undoubtedly the case that by secondary stage the view of oneself as a poor speller is one of the major stumbling blocks to improvement. Many dyslexic pupils deliberately restrict their output to the words they can spell or restrict the quantity of their written work to minimise the number of corrections they will have to make at the redrafting stage. For some the self-image problem is so great that they hate the idea of using error analysis as a vehicle for learning spelling. They prefer the objectivity of using spelling books or programmes.

It is thus important to find ways of improving spelling while also encouraging creativity and depth in written work.

STRATEGIES

(a) **Error Analysis/Personal Word Bank**

Provided the pupil is not like the few described above who find the process threatening, this can be an effective way of valuing the pupil. The pupil is asked to highlight words in his own writing that he thinks are wrong and attempt corrections. If the word is still wrong or he is unsure, that word is added to the word bank. It is important to go through this self correction process. If it is just left to the teacher to find the words the pupil will be quick to say it was just carelessness/laziness which led to the mistake.

(b) **Other Methods**

Looking at the word with meaning; look, cover, write check methods; (Peters) building up letter strings; using computer programs; combining handwriting with spelling; using a dictaphone to practise spellings . . . the list of strategies goes on and on. Whatever method is used, it is important to value the pupil's own learning style and offer myriad opportunities for success.

(c) **Alternatives**

As with handwriting, in order to maintain the depth and creativity of response, use can be made of techniques such as scribing and taping where the need for correct spelling can, for the moment, be forgotten.

Chapter 23

MOTIVATION AND LEARNING STYLES

Bearing in mind the maxim that in school 'no-one ever learns nothing' it is interesting to consider how much pupils with learning difficulties have learned in terms of developing coping strategies. Unfortunately for some of them these strategies are destructive – disruption, truancy, detachment. Some coping strategies are conventional and approved of by teachers on the whole – e.g. using pictures to aid understanding, asking the teacher for help. However, many pupils in our classrooms are investing an enormous amount of time and effort first in devising strategies and then in concealing them from the teacher.

The most obvious strategy in this category, of course, is 'asking your pal'. For some teachers this is still beyond the pale but fortunately many more are now accepting that peer discussion is a most effective learning tool. The student doing the explanation has his own understanding deepened by the very process of having to make something clear to another.

Children have several spelling strategies that they try to conceal. If they are having to transfer a word from one context to another they scribble it on their hand, their desk, their folder in order to copy it down later. Because this process is surreptitious the word is often illegible anyway. All these pupils need is permission to use scrap paper to conduct this exercise – and praise for having thought of it.

This piece of scrap paper can also be used for trying out the spelling of a word. This is an effective strategy used by successful adult spellers, but for some reason many pupils are ashamed of their need to test themselves in this way. Again permission and praise are required.

Another example of this phenomenon was the pupil whose method of working out number problems was effective for her because she simply could not remember number bonds. She spent hours of her life in the Maths class flicking her jotter backwards and forwards as she concealed her nefarious practice:

$$13 - 7 = 6 \qquad 1 \; 2 \; 3 \; 4 \; 5 \; 6 \; \cancel{7} \; \cancel{8} \; \cancel{9} \; \cancel{10} \; \cancel{11} \; \cancel{12} \; \cancel{13}$$

She wrote down the numbers 1-13 and then crossed off 7 numbers from the right hand side. She was helped by having her jotter ruled off to allow working; by being valued for her ability to work out this strategy; and of course by being given an addition/subtraction square and a calculator!

For many pupils with specific learning difficulties school is one long experience of failure and frustration. And when they do finally master something they are pushed on to the next task, the next challenge. We can help them by setting smaller, achievable targets and by giving them the chance to enjoy their success. Ten new spelling words learned thoroughly and then tested achieving full marks is more motivating than twenty words half learned and a test score of ten.

Alongside the processes of teaching, there must go genuine respect for the pupil and understanding of his feelings.

CONCLUSION

Effective learning always relies on matching the task to the learner. This requires careful thought as to the level and type of learning experience to offer, but it also requires that teachers value pupils and seek to construct learning situations which enhance their self-esteem and develop in them the belief that they can do it.

> 'When I got up this morning
> I thought the whole thing through
> Say, who's the master, the king of the universe?
> *   Christopher, it's you.
> *   (substitute the name of your pupil).

REFERENCES

ENTWISTLE N. (1987) *Understanding Classroom Learning*, Pub. Hodder & Stoughton.
DENIS V. and CLAYDON J. (1992) *Diagnostic Spelling Test*. NFER, Nelson.
PETERS M. (1985). *Spelling: Caught or Taught*. Routledge.

SECTION 6

SPEECH AND LANGUAGE

Chapter 24

SPECIFIC LANGUAGE IMPAIRMENT: EXPLANATIONS AND IMPLICATIONS

JENNIFER REID and MORAG L. DONALDSON

WHAT IS SPECIFIC LANGUAGE IMPAIRMENT?

A child who fails to develop language[1] normally while making otherwise unexceptional developmental progress may be said to have a specific language impairment (SLI)[2]. Diagnosis of this condition is usually carried out by excluding other conditions associated with language and/or communication difficulties, that is, if the child cannot be shown to be suffering from general learning difficulties, physical disability, hearing loss, emotional or behavioural disorder, autism, environmental deprivation or any other condition which could explain the language problems, then a diagnosis of 'specific language impairment' is made.

The unsatisfactory nature of a definition which refers only to the absence of a clear aetiology has inspired much research over the past 20 years or so involving children with SLI. However, the search for features which are uniquely characteristic of children with SLI has not been particularly successful (Bishop, 1992; Miller, 1991). While such children, by definition, show grossly normal development in non-linguistic areas, when compared to normally developing children, they nevertheless show subtle difficulties and differences in some aspects of non-linguistic ability, especially when assessed in experimental conditions. However, as we will argue in the following section, it is not always clear whether such non-linguistic difficulties are causes or consequences of the linguistic problems.

Language not only fulfils a variety of important communicative functions, but it can also be a powerful cognitive tool, serving as a means of mental

---

1 We use the term 'language' to refer primarily to spoken language, and 'language development' to the ability to both understand and produce spoken language. Spoken language ability involves the integration of knowledge at a number of levels, namely speech sound system (phonology), grammatical system (syntax and morphology), word and sentence meaning (semantics) and communicative functions (pragmatics). We prefer 'language production' or 'expressive language' to the term 'speech' which tends to be more closely associated with the speech sound system rather than the other levels.

2 Other terms may be used to refer to the condition. 'Developmental language disorder' is a term widely used, particularly by practising speech and language therapists. 'Developmental dysphasia' or 'developmental aphasia' were terms widely used in the past but, although still popular in continental Europe, they have largely passed out of favour among practitioners in the UK.

representation and hence influencing children's thinking, memory and learning. Non-linguistic skills which are usually acquired with the help of language may be less well developed in children with a language impairment. Thus the consequences of SLI will not necessarily be restricted to the area of communication.

RESEARCH DESIGN ISSUES

One problem with some of the extensive literature on possible causes of SLI concerns issues of research design. These issues are neither trivial nor restricted to research in this area, therefore we consider some discussion to be relevant here[3].

In the search for an underlying cause for language impairment, the abilities of language-impaired children have been compared with those of normally developing children of the same age[4]. However, caution is required in interpreting the findings from such comparisons. For example, if we observed that language-impaired children tended to be more socially immature than normally developing children of the same age, we could not use this finding to argue that social immaturity causes language impairment. When a child has poor language skills, it is likely that the ability to communicate verbally with other people will be affected. Lack of experience in communicating verbally with other people may lead to a degree of social immaturity. Thus the social immaturity of the SLI group may be the result of language impairment rather than a cause.

In order to overcome this problem with research designs which compare on the basis of chronological age, some studies compare the performance of the SLI children with younger, normally-developing children whose language development is at a similar level (NLD children). Such designs are not without their own problems, not the least of which lies in the choice of language measure. The measure chosen may be one of language comprehension, language production, or a composite measure. Since many children with SLI will have widely discrepant receptive and productive language, the choice of a measure for language matching will have a very significant effect on the nature of the NLD group, and therefore also on the results of any comparison of the two groups.

SLI: A SINGLE UNDERLYING CAUSE?

If there is a single cause of SLI, we might begin by asking whether the source lies within the child or within the child's environment. A common lay assumption is that failure to develop language at the normal rate in the early years comes about because of some inadequacy in the child's communicative environment. There are

---

3 Methodology is discussed by Bishop (1992), and similar issues are discussed with reference to research in reading by Bryant and Bradley (1985) and Gathercole and Baddeley (1993).
4 Studies which use such comparisons are referred to as having a 'chronological age-matched design', in the terminology of experimental psychology. The comparison group of children is referred to as the 'control group', hence 'chronological age-matched controls.'

Chapter 24

two main variations of this argument, both of which are sources of parental anxiety and guilt well-known to practising speech and language therapists.

The first is that a child with a language delay does not talk because s/he has no need to. The home environment does not provide the opportunities or motivation to communicate, or other people 'talk for' the child. The second account comes in several guises, but typically assumes that language input to the child is lacking in some respect, either in quantity or in quality.

There is no doubt that children who experience extreme environmental deprivation suffer adverse consequences for language as well as other abilities (Skuse, 1992) On the other hand, it seems that the ability of the young child to develop language is extremely robust, even in settings which in terms of adult input may appear relatively impoverished. Research studies have produced no evidence that all, or even the majority of children with language impairments, have significantly adverse communicative environments. This literature is reviewed comprehensively by Leonard (1987).

Adults modify their language when they talk to young children. There is an extensive literature on the characteristics of this 'child directed speech', or 'motherese', which, it is hypothesised, serves to facilitate language learning (Snow, 1986). The characteristics of child directed speech include modifications at a variety of levels, such as voice quality, intonation, vocabulary and grammatical structure. In particular, utterance length and complexity appear to reflect the child's current language level.

A number of studies have demonstrated differences in the communicative behaviours of parents of SLI children compared to those of parents of NLD children of the same age[5]. However, a different picture emerges when comparison is made with NLD children of similar language levels. Very few studies using language-matched controls show any differences at all in the language and communicative behaviours of the two groups of parents. It seems that the parents of SLI children, like other parents, are sensitive to their children's language comprehension and production abilities[6]. Even if we find that for some language-impaired children, environmental factors have influenced their developmental progress, there is little case for arguing for an environmental cause for SLI.

The alternative position is that factors underlying SLI are intrinsic to the child, and that environmental factors serve to influence the effects of the condition

---

5 See the review in Leonard (1987), pp 2-10.
6 For a discussion of some of the bi-directional influences on conversation with language-impaired children, see Conti-Ramsden (1985, 1991).

on individual children's histories. There have been several proposed theories of SLI which fit this general position. We shall sketch out a couple of the more influential theoretical positions, but the interested reader should refer to the more detailed reviews presented in Leonard (1987), Miller (1991) and Bishop (1992).

AN AUDITORY PERCEPTUAL DEFICIT?

Eisenson (1972) was an early attempt to present a unitary account of SLI, or 'developmental aphasia', as he called it. He hypothesised that SLI resulted from a fundamental difficulty in auditory (speech) perception. Expressive problems were construed as resulting from inadequate processing of linguistic input Different varieties of SLI arose from varying degrees of severity of the underlying impairment. He proposed a continuum of severity ranging from mild phonological or grammatical difficulties to profound receptive aphasia.

The notion of a fundamental auditory perceptual disorder has fared rather better as a result of research findings than many other theoretical accounts. The work of Tallal and her colleagues[7] has been particularly influential. A central finding is that SLI children are at a disadvantage in tasks requiring the perception of brief or rapid acoustic events, and this has been replicated in a number of forms in many studies and using different groups of children. Unfortunately, most of this work has been conducted using chronological age-matched controls and is therefore insufficient evidence of a causal link from auditory perception to language.

The basic design of the experimental task in the above studies is one in which children are required to distinguish and sequence two complex tones which are presented with varying time intervals between them. It is not immediately obvious how limited language might influence the development of the ability to perform this task. However, one might ask if the SLI children performed as younger, NLD children. This appears not to be the case. Tallal, Stark and Curtiss (1976) presented some evidence of qualitative differences in the performance of SLI children and younger NLD children. However, they also found that NLD children under 4;6 years were not very successful on the experimental task. This finding makes it difficult to interpret the findings from the SLI children, given that in many instances, their language abilities fell below this developmental level.

Despite these findings of interesting qualitative differences in the perceptual abilities of children with SLI, we are left wondering what it means. To date, the verdict on a causal link between the two must remain not proven.

---

[7] There are several important papers, see, for example, Tallal, Stark and Mellits (1985), but this work is also comprehensively reviewed in Bishop (1992).

Chapter 24

A MORE GENERAL COGNITIVE DEFICIT?

Another line of research has been the investigation of non-verbal cognitive abilities in children with SLI. Given that SLI children have by definition non-verbal abilities within the normal range, it is perhaps surprising that investigations have uncovered apparently significant differences and difficulties in non-linguistic activities.

Piaget viewed language acquisition as one aspect of the development of the ability to use symbols (Piaget and Inhelder, 1969). Early symbols usually resemble the real object, such as when a child uses bricks as food while pretending to cook. As children's symbolic understanding develops, they are able to use more arbitrary symbols, which have no physical resemblance to the object or event they denote. Words may be viewed in this light as symbols, the meanings of which are shared by speakers of the language, but essentially arbitrary. Poor symbolic function has been proposed as the cause of language difficulties, but research in this area has also resulted in a mixture of contradictory findings and unconvincing evidence. For example, some investigators have suggested that children with SLI show rather impoverished symbolic play compared to their peers. However, Terrell, Schwartz, Prelock andMessick (1984), using a comparison group matched on expressive language ability, found that the SLI children showed a higher level of symbolic play than these younger NLD children. Poor symbolic play may therefore be the result of language impairment.

Other postulated theories have involved, for example, deficits of short term memory, sequencing or hypothesis testing. In a review of research in this whole area, Johnston (1988 p. 705) concludes,

> 'Research on the cognitive abilities of language-disordered children presents a convincing picture of substantial impairment. At many ages, across visual, auditory and tactile stimuli, across many domains of knowledge, in symbolic and non-symbolic activities, in tasks with little to no explicit verbal demand, language-disordered children perform below age expectations.'

A few years later, the same author urges a move away from research designed to 'document low performance in yet another mental task...' (Johnston, 1991 p. 300). In her view, we need to know what distinguishes children with SLI from children with more general, or other sorts of learning difficulties, in other words, their strengths as well as their weaknesses. Those working with SLI children quote anecdotal evidence for such strengths, such as 'overdeveloped visual skills' or 'compensatory learning strategies', but hard evidence of such strengths across numbers of children is lacking as yet.

It is perhaps rather odd that most of the theories of SLI discussed so far have postulated underlying deficits in non-linguistic abilities. In much of the research to date, despite a general consensus that SLI children present a range of different sorts and severities of linguistic impairments, the linguistic characteristics of individual or groups of children, have been relatively neglected. Children with SLI are treated as a relatively homogeneous group, whose difficulties result from some, as yet undiscovered, common, underlying deficit. To therapists and teachers working with SLI children, this assumption may seem quite unreasonable in the face of so much evidence of individual differences. The only common factor for lumping these children together seems to be the existence of some significant degree of language impairment. Is this sufficient evidence for homogeneity?

UNTANGLING THE LINGUISTIC CHARACTERISTICS

In clinical and educational practice, most of the advances of the past 20 years or so have come, not from searching for elusive causes, but from detailed attention to the particular language difficulties faced by individual children. In the 70's and early 80's, the seminal work of Crystal and colleagues (Crystal, Fletcher, andGarman, 1976) on grammatical disability, and of Ingram (1976) and Grunwell (1982) on phonological disability brought about a revolution in the conception and remediation of disorders of language structure, and the appearance of a new field of academic endeavour, clinical linguistics (Crystal, 1981; Grundy, 1989). More recently, attention has shifted away from structural aspects of language towards the communicative context of language use, the 'pragmatic' aspects of language. The 'pragmatic revolution' was fuelled particularly by the work of Prutting in the USA (Gallagher and Prutting, 1983) Two volumes on clinical pragmatics have recently appeared in the UK (McTear and Conti-Ramsden, 1992; Smith and Leinonen, 1991).

Such developments have had a major impact on the assessment and remediation of language impairments in children. They have opened up new possibilities for dealing with individual and group differences among children with SLI. Not only this, but the focus on pragmatics and issues of language use has led to the 'discovery' of a new type of language impairment, that of pragmatic disorder.

---

8 This impairment may also be referred to as 'articulatory dyspraxia', or just 'dyspraxia', but the latter should perhaps be avoided since it may be confused with conditions affecting non-speech motor systems such as limb or eye movements.

Chapter 24

HETEROGENEITY: DIFFERENT TYPES OF SLI?

The general consensus now seems to be that SLI may be nothing more than a convenient umbrella term, bringing together a range of types of impairment which may or may not be mutually exclusive. The most influential work in this area has been that of Rapin and Allen in the USA (Rapin and Allen, 1983; Rapin and Allen, 1987). Their clinical typology is probably the one to which most frequent reference is made. Their categories include:

verbal auditory agnosia (or 'word deafness' as described originally by Worster Drought and Allen in the 1930s), characterised by inability to comprehend language presented to the auditory channel.

verbal dyspraxia[8], characterised by dysfluent, effortful speech, short utterances with defective phonology in contrast to adequate or even normal comprehension.

phonologic programming deficit syndrome, characterised by speech which is more fluent than in verbal dyspraxia, with longer utterances but poor intelligibility (usually called phonological disorder in the UK).

phonologic-syntactic deficit syndrome: these children have dysfluent speech, phonological deficits and speak in short utterances with grammatical deficits affecting closed class words and morphology, (phonological-syntactic disorder in the UK).

lexical-syntactic deficit syndrome: these children are late to begin talking but have normal phonology for their age. They are characterised by severe word retrieval deficits, immature syntax and language formulation difficulties, (lexical-syntactic disorder).

semantic-pragmatic deficit syndrome, characterised by deviant language processing and use in the context of fluent, well-formed language with adequate speech intelligibility. These children are often verbose and have large vocabularies, yet have comprehension deficits for the meaning of verbal messages, particularly questions and non-literal language. They have pragmatic deficits seen as impaired ability to obey the rules of conversation, such as in turn-taking and topic maintenance. They may perseverate and chatter incessantly. They may be echolalic and use overlearned scripts rather than language which is appropriate to the context. In the UK, this impairment tends to be called 'semantic-pragmatic disorder' (Bishop, 1989)

These potted descriptions pay only lip service to the natural history of SLI, i.e. how the profile of a child with SLI (or an other condition) changes with age, and the effects of differential severity. They are clinically derived, that is, derived from careful observation of large numbers of children with language impairments. Their validity in terms of unique and/or mutually exclusive characteristics has not been systematically tested. However, they appear to have some ecological validity, for they have found favour with many clinicians.

INTERVENTION ISSUES

To be effective, intervention strategies must be geared to the needs of the individual child and therefore must be closely integrated with thorough, ongoing assessment procedures. Few would disagree with this statement, although there is less agreement about exactly how information from diagnostic assessments should be translated into intervention strategies. For example, should the main aim be to develop a child's strengths so as to compensate for her/his weaknesses, or should the emphasis be on developing the skills in which s/he is weakest? Whatever the answer to this question, it is clear that the more general question of 'What is the best intervention strategy for SLI?' is too simplistic. Instead, we need to ask a series of more specific and more complex questions concerning the effectiveness of particular intervention techniques in achieving particular goals, for particular types of children, with particular types of language impairments, in particular sets of circumstances. The following sections aim to give a flavour of some approaches to intervention for children with SLI and to consider some of the evidence which can be used in addressing questions of effectiveness. (For a more detailed review, see Donaldson (1992)).

Intervention strategies vary along several dimensions, including those corresponding to the following questions:

(1)   What should be taught or developed?
(2)   How should the intervention be carried out?

In other words, there is variation in the goals of intervention and in the techniques used to achieve these goals.

GOALS OF INTERVENTION

An intervention will usually have a variety of goals, ranging from very general goals to more specific goals or objectives. Typically, goals are arrived at through assessment procedures which are rather different to those through which the initial diagnosis of SLI was made. Assessment for the purposes of diagnosis will probably be made using norm-referenced, standardised tests, which involve comparing the child's performance with that of a representative sample of other (usually normally-developing) children and the assignation of an age-equivalent or other standardised score. Such norm-referenced assessments are not usually sufficiently detailed or informative for the purposes of planning intervention. For this purpose, clinicians may turn to criterion-referenced procedures, in which the child's performance is compared to a more detailed set of criteria or goals. These are typically organised as developmentally-sequenced levels, and the child's abilities are matched to a developmental level or other standard, either through observation or through testing (which may be informal or standardised). Examples of assessments used for planning treatment would be the Detailed Test of Comprehension, from the Derbyshire Language Scheme (Knowles and Masidlover, 1982), which is an unstandardised test and the Pragmatics Profile (Dewart and Summers, 1988), in which information on developmental level is gained through a structured interview with the child's parents or carers. Linguistic profiles (Crystal, 1982) are derived through the analysis of elicited speech samples, and these are used in particular by therapists working with children who have more complex and persisting impairments and who are receiving intensive remediation, for example, in a language unit.

Developmental goals are selected to help a child achieve those aspects of language which would be the next to appear according to some generally agreed developmental sequence, based on the literature on language development in normal children. This approach works rather better for those aspects of language about which there is a large literature, such as the acquisition of grammatical tense inflections, but can be problematic in areas about which less developmental information is available, such as the acquisition of conversational rules. In fact, developmental goals may not be particularly functionally relevant to a given child in her/his own circumstances. The selection of appropriate goals may therefore be influenced by functional considerations, so that the language skills acquired suit the individual needs of the child and are more likely to lead to pragmatic gains.

Although different types of intervention goals are far from mutually exclusive, there has been a historical shift away from an emphasis on the structure of language towards an emphasis on language as a tool for communication. The relative emphasis on these two types of goal also varies according to the nature of a child's language problems. For instance, for a child with a phonological-syntactic disorder, intervention is likely to focus on language form, although not in isolation from function, whereas for a child with a semantic-pragmatic disorder, intervention is more likely to focus on the communicative functions of language, although not in isolation from the linguistic tools required to achieve communicative goals.

At a more specific level, intervention may target phonological, syntactic, semantic or pragmatic aspects of a child's language, or non-linguistic skills which are felt to provide some of the relevant underpinnings for more efficient language learning, such as attention to sound, turn-taking, representational play or matching and sorting. Within each of these aspects even more specific goals will usually be formulated to guide intervention (Fey, 1986; Harris, 1990; Lees and Urwin, 1991).

In reviewing studies evaluating the effectiveness of language intervention, Nye, Foster and Seaman (1987) found that the largest improvements occurred for syntactic characteristics and the smallest for pragmatic characteristics (although the difference was not statistically significant).

INTERVENTION TECHNIQUES

A vast range of intervention techniques are used with children who have SLI, since most clinicians devise individualised programmes based on the needs of the particular child, combined with their own experience of what has proved successful in the past. Nevertheless, these techniques can be grouped into three broad categories: behavioural approaches, naturalistic approaches and 'compromise' approaches.

Behavioural approaches to language intervention are based on the principles of learning theory and hence on the assumption that language can be learned through such processes as imitation, reinforcement, shaping, modelling and prompting. For example, if the goal is to teach a child to use personal pronouns (such as 'he' and 'she') appropriately, exercises might be presented in which the child is shown a picture (e.g. of a girl swimming) and is asked a question (e.g. 'What is the girl doing?'). The question could then be followed by a prompt ('Say "she is swimming"') to encourage the child to imitate the appropriate response. A correct imitation could then be reinforced by praising the child. Modelling is similar to imitation, but the child is not asked to reproduce the therapist's utterance immediately. Instead, the child is asked to listen carefully to the therapist producing utterances containing the linguistic forms which are the target of intervention. Then the child is given a turn at speaking in a context similar to the one in which the therapist has modelled the relevant linguistic forms. For instance, the therapist and child may take turns at describing a set of pictures.

There are a number of studies indicating that behavioural techniques can be effective in improving the production of various linguistic forms in children with a specific language disorder (for a review, see Leonard, 1981). However, children often experience difficulties in generalising what they have learned to related linguistic constructions. Hegde, Noll and Pecora (1979) taught children to use 'is' in sentences beginning with 'he' and found that although the children successfully generalised their use of 'is' to other sentences beginning with 'he', they failed to generalise to sentences beginning with 'she'.

Problems can also arise in generalising to situations which differ from the training situation. Leonard (1981) outlines four of the ways in which situations may differ from the training situation: in terms of the visual stimuli talked about (e.g. real situations versus pictures), in terms of the verbal stimuli used as prompts (e.g. open-ended versus explicit questions), in terms of the setting (e.g. home versus clinic), and in terms of the co-conversationalist (e.g. parent versus therapist). On the basis of several studies investigating generalisation effects, Leonard concludes that use of a trained linguistic form is usually successfully generalised to situations which differ from the training situation in only one or two of these respects, but that problems in generalising tend to arise when situations differ in three or four respects. It is therefore important for behavioural training to be conducted in a variety of contexts.

Naturalistic approaches to language intervention are based on the assumption that children will learn language best in situations where it is being used to serve genuine communicative purposes and where it is closely integrated with real life activities. This assumption is often accompanied by the assumption that children's language problems can be resolved through incidental learning. Thus, the role of the therapist or teacher is not to improve the use of particular linguistic behaviours through explicit teaching, but rather to facilitate incidental learning of linguistic behaviours in meaningful communicative contexts by providing appropriate linguistic input and opportunities for use of the targeted linguistic behaviour. One way of making communicative contexts meaningful is to base them around activities and topics which are of interest to the child and which relate to her/his experiences. Therefore, naturalistic intervention programmes need to be tailored to the interests of individual children, as well as to their need for an emphasis on a particular type of linguistic input. Another way of ensuring that interventions occur in meaningful, relevant contexts is to carry them out within real-life settings, such as the classroom, playground or home, rather than withdrawing the child to a separate room or to a speech therapy clinic. This, in turn, encourages collaboration with significant people in the child's life, such as parents, siblings, peers, class teachers and nursery nurses. (Of course, collaboration with at least some of these people can also be encouraged in a clinic setting, but in a more contrived way.)

Advocates of naturalistic approaches include McLean and Snyder-McLean (1978) and Lahey (1988).

Since the naturalistic approach involves intervening either in everyday settings or in settings designed to mimic everyday settings, problems of generalising what is learned from the therapeutic situation to real-life situations are avoided or substantially reduced. Bochner et al. (1980) present two case studies which highlight typical differences between the naturalistic approach and the more traditional behavioural approach. One 5 year old who had a language disorder and suspected mild mental retardation received language intervention based on the behavioural approach, whereas another 5 year old who had similar problems received intervention based on the naturalistic approach. Both children made progress in language skills, but the nature of this progress differed between the two children. The child who had received behavioural intervention acquired the skills she had been drilled in, such as labelling pictures and objects and answering direct questions, but she did not succeed in generalising these skills to normal conversations with her teachers and peers when she moved from a special education class into a mainstream class. In contrast, the child who had received the naturalistic intervention did acquire spontaneous language skills which generalised to the new setting of a mainstream class. Bochner et al. see their findings as evidence for the claim that 'children learn what they are taught' (1980: p. 100). Although this conclusion is based on a qualitative study of only two children, it is broadly consistent with the conclusion reached by Leonard (1981) on the basis of more extensive evidence (from a review of studies). He concludes that training which focuses only on particular linguistic forms tends to yield effects limited to the child's use of these forms, whereas training with a more general focus usually results in broader linguistic gains.

When considering issues of generalisation, it is important to remember that the contexts in which children are likely to have to deploy linguistic skills are not restricted to low-structure, informal contexts in which language is closely linked to their own immediate purposes and concerns. It is true that such contexts predominate in the life of a young child, but if the child is to progress successfully in the educational system, s/he will also have to cope with more formal contexts in which language is 'disembedded' from immediate purposes (Donaldson, 1978). In particular, the ability to use and understand language in disembedded contexts, and perhaps also to reflect on the formal properties of language, is likely to be crucial to the acquisition of literacy. Such considerations become especially significant in the light of the evidence indicating that children with spoken language disorders are at risk of encountering reading problems (Silva, 1987).

The naturalistic approach has considerable intuitive appeal since it is consistent with contemporary theories of normal language acquisition. Although such theories differ in whether they emphasise innate knowledge of the structural properties of language ((Chomsky, 1986)) or the acquisition of language within supportive social contexts (Bruner, 1983) , they have in common an eschewal of the role of explicit language teaching by adults. However, despite the superficial plausibility of the argument that intervention procedures for children with language disorders should aim to mimic the processes by which language is normally acquired, some caution is called for. It does not necessarily follow that the 'normal' developmental route is the best route for all children. The very fact that children with language disorders have not made normal progress in acquiring language 'naturally' suggests that an alternative approach may be beneficial or even necessary.

Of course, most naturalistic intervention approaches are alternative approaches in the sense that they aim to adapt normal interactions to the child's needs, by for example providing extra opportunities to observe and practise linguistic forms or functions which are posing problems. However, as Conant et al. (Conant, Budoff, Hecht, and Morse, 1984) point out, a potential difficulty is that opportunities to work on particular problem areas may not arise sufficiently frequently in natural situations. Furthermore, considerable skill and ingenuity on the part of the teacher or therapist is required in order to exploit naturally occurring opportunities for intervention.

Conant et al devised an intervention programme which aimed to combine the advantages of traditional behavioural approaches with those of incidental learning approaches. Their programme consisted of a set of communication games in which particular features of syntax, vocabulary or articulation could be focused upon, but in which these features served the same pragmatic functions as in normal conversation. In these games, the roles of speaker and hearer were alternated between the child and the teacher. For example, hiding games were used in which the child and the teacher took turns at guessing where an object was hidden. The materials for this game could be constructed in such a way as to encourage the use of particular linguistic forms in the guesses. The feedback which the child received related not to arbitrary standards of 'correctness' but to the communicative adequacy or inadequacy of his messages (e.g. whether the child succeeded in communicating his guess to the adult so that she could look for the object in the place the child had intended). Conant et al. found that children who received their intervention programme over a period of four months made more progress (in terms of the quality of their spontaneous speech) than an untreated control group. This effect applied to children whose language disorder was accompanied either by a moderate cognitive delay or by no cognitive delay. It did not hold for children who had a severe cognitive delay. Conant et al.'s findings illustrate the effectiveness of 'compromise' approaches which combine features from the behavioural and naturalistic approaches to intervention. Similar approaches have been devised by several other authors. For example, the Metaphon approach to treating phonological disorders (Howell and Dean, 1991) also employs communication games as a means of focusing intervention on particular phonological contrasts within pragmatically appropriate contexts. Howlin (1969; 1984) reports that in recent years behavioural approaches to intervention have become less artificial and that behavioural techniques are now usually employed in communicatively meaningful contexts. She further suggests that the degree of structure which is appropriate in a language intervention approach will depend on characteristics of the child. In particular, she proposes that more highly structured programmes may be best suited to children with very limited linguistic skills or those with limited motivation to communicate (e.g. severely autistic children).

In summary, most of the available intervention techniques have been shown to produce some positive effects, but no particular technique stands out as being more effective overall than other techniques (Leonard, 1981; Nye et al., 1987). The literature also suggests that different techniques produce different types of positive effects and that different techniques are probably appropriate for different types of children. However, clear and detailed evidence is lacking on which techniques are best suited to which children.

AN ILLUSTRATIVE CASE HISTORY

The eclectic approach which is preferred by the majority of practising clinicians is perhaps best illustrated with a potted case history. J. was referred by her health visitor to a speech and language therapist at the age of 2;10 years. She was reported to be a healthy child, the youngest of three children of professional parents. At that time, she showed little interest in verbal communication with her family, spoke very little and then only in single words or stereotypical phrases, her play was poorly developed and she showed a rather unsettling independence for her age. She attended for her first block of intervention from just after her third birthday (6 weekly 45 minute sessions of individual therapy with J. and her mother.) The goals for this period of intervention included both pre-linguistic and early language behaviours such as response to sound, attention to speech, turn-taking in a simple game, selecting everyday objects by name and carrying out simple commands. A number of the more behavioural techniques such as modelling, shaping and chaining were employed, particularly as her attention span for any one activity was relatively short at this stage. However, attention was also paid to providing opportunities for J. to experience success in simple communicative functions, such as requesting desired, but out-of-reach objects or otherwise influencing the actions of adults through the use of language.

J. made rapid and sustained progress during and immediately after the period of therapy, and on review at age 3;6 years, she was noted to be a much more communicative child, whose play and social interaction had matured to a near age-appropriate level in many areas. Not only was she responding to other people's communicative attempts but she was also initiating conversations with others. However, her language comprehension and production were still well below age-appropriate level, therefore she attended for a second block of weekly intervention, this time with much more specifically linguistic goals. Structured activities were selected in order to build up J's ability to make sense of longer and more complex sentences. New vocabulary, particularly in the area of verbs and adjectives, was taught by focused stimulation during therapy sessions and follow-up consolidation activities at home. Although comprehension of new vocabulary items was primarily targeted, production was also stimulated as encouraging J to produce new words appeared to aid learning (Connell, 1987). New grammatical forms were introduced using 'old' vocabulary, in order to allow J to focus attention on the targeted structure without competing demands from the need to process less well-established vocabulary. While some turn-taking was always preserved, it was often felt necessary to minimise any communicative element to the activity, again in order not to overload J's linguistic system. Consolidation of new words and forms was facilitated by gradually increasing the linguistic or communicative demands during the activity. She received a total of between 6 and 8 hours of therapy over a 3-4 month period.

By the age of 4;6 years, J's comprehension was within the normal range for her age on standardised testing, and the focus of attention shifted to language production. She spoke in largely well-formed sentences but made little or no use of complex, multi-clause structures. She also had persistent problems with some of the language of space, in particular the prepositions 'behind' and 'in front of', despite previous work in this area. This time, intervention took the form of paired therapy with another child of the same age and with similar difficulties. Most of the activities during the sessions were 'communicative', that is, they were devised to provide opportunities which led to successful communication if the targeted linguistic form was used (or failure if it was not used). For example, barrier games (Bunce, 1989) were used, in which one child had to describe a scenario using miniature toys, or one picture from a set of highly similar ones, for the child on the other side of the barrier to copy or select. Instant feedback on the success or not of the communication is achieved merely by removing the barrier. Such activities provide enormous motivation for children of this age and older, and success is inherent in the activity, allowing the child to take responsibility for monitoring her own language.

An interplay of both developmental and functional goals, and a variety of therapeutic techniques is evident in this intervention history, and it serves to illustrate the eclectic yet principled approach which is aimed for in therapy for children with SLI.

CONCLUSION

Specific language impairment is something of a paradox. On the one hand, the problems encountered by children who have a specific language impairment are by definition specific to language, in the sense that they cannot be adequately explained in terms of a single underlying cause such as low general intelligence. On the other hand, these children's linguistic difficulties are sometimes accompanied by more specific and subtle non-linguistic difficulties, for example with auditory processing or symbolic play.

One possible explanation for this paradox may be that the non-linguistic difficulties are at least in part effects (rather than causes) of the linguistic problems. Since language is an important cognitive and social tool, it would not be surprising if language impairments in the developing child interfered with some other aspects of development. However, on the basis of the available research evidence it is difficult to distinguish between the causes and the effects of specific language impairments. Indeed, it may well be that the causal relationships will prove not to be simple unidirectional ones, but rather that a complex pattern of two-way influences and interactions between linguistic and non-linguistic difficulties will be found in future research.

The elusiveness of a single underlying cause for specific language impairment may be partly attributable to the heterogeneity of the linguistic problems which are covered by the diagnostic label 'SLI'. The linguistic problems which characterise children with SLI vary not only in severity but also in whether they affect comprehension, production or both, and in terms of which linguistic levels (i.e. phonological, syntactic, semantic or pragmatic) they influence.

The picture which we have presented of the nature of SLI has several implications for intervention. First, since the problems encountered by children with SLI are primarily linguistic and since the nature of these problems varies across children, assessment procedures should aim to identify which specific aspects of language are problematical for a particular child, so that appropriate goals of intervention can be formulated. Second, despite this emphasis on linguistic goals of intervention, it is also important to recognise that various types of non-linguistic difficulties may be associated with SLI (either as causes or as effects), and that these may need to be taken into account in planning intervention. Third, in view of the heterogeneity of the problems associated with SLI, the goals of intervention will vary from child to child and should be used as a basis for devising individualised programmes of intervention. Finally, regarding intervention techniques, we advocate a compromise approach which combines features of the behavioural and naturalistic approaches. Such an approach is useful in targeting those specific aspects of language which are posing problems for an individual child, while at the same time retaining an emphasis on the communicative and cognitive functions which language fulfils in the child's everyday life.

REFERENCES

BISHOP D. V. M. (1989). 'Autism, Asperger's syndrome and semantic-pragmatic disorder: Where are the boundaries?' *British Journal of Disorders of Communication,* 24(2), 107-121.

BISHOP D. V. M. (1992). 'The underlying nature of specific language impairment.' *Journal of Child Psychology and Psychiatry,* 33(1), 3-66.

BOCHNER S., PRICE P., SALMON L., YEEND G. and ORR E. (1980). 'Language intervention: a classroom report.' *British Journal of Disorders of Communication,* 15, 87-102.

BRUNER J. S. (1983). *Child's Talk: Learning to Use Language.* Oxford. Oxford University Press.

BRYANT P. and BRADLEY L. (1985). *Children's Reading Problems.* Oxford. Blackwell.

BUNCE B. H. (1989). 'Using a barrier game to improve children's referential communication skills.' *Journal of Speech and Hearing Disorders,* 54, 33-43.

CHOMSKY N. (1986). *Knowledge of Language.* New York. Praeger.

CONANT S., BUDOFF M., HECHT B. and MORSE R. (1984). 'Language intervention: a pragmatic approach.' *Journal of Autism and Developmental Disorders,* 14, 301-317.

CONNELL P. J. (1987). 'Teaching language form, meaning and function to specific-language-impaired children', in Rosenberg S. (ed.), *Advances in Applied Psycholinguistics: Disorders of First Language Development* (Volume 1). Cambridge. Cambridge University Press.

CONTI-RAMSDEN G. (1985). 'Mothers in dialogue with language-impaired children.' *Topics in Language Disorders,* 5, 58-68.

CONTI-RAMSDEN G. (1991). 'Mother-child interactions with language-impaired children and their siblings.' *European Journal of Disorders of Communication,* 26, 337-354.

CRYSTAL D. (1981). *Clinical Linguistics.* Vienna. Springer Verlag.

CRYSTAL D. (1982). *Profiling Linguistic Disability.* London. Edward Arnold.

CRYSTAL D., FLETCHER P. and GARMAN M. (1976). *The Grammatical Analysis of Language Disability.* London. Edward Arnold.

DEWART H. and SUMMERS S. (1988). *The Pragmatics Profile of Early Communication Skills.* Windsor. NFER-Nelson.

DONALDSON M. (1978). *Children's Minds.* Glasgow. Collins/Fontana.

DONALDSON M. L (1992). *Children with Language and Communication Disorders: A Review of the Literature.* Edinburgh. Edinburgh Centre for Research in Child Development.

EISENSON J. (1972). *Aphasia in Children.* New York. Harper and Row.

FEY M. E. (1986). *Language Intervention with Young Children.* London. Taylor and Francis.

GALLAGHER T. M. and PRUTTING C. A. (eds.) (1983). *Pragmatic Assessment and Intervention Issues in Language.* San Diego. College Hill Press.

GATHERCOLE S. E. and BADDELEY A. D. (1993). *Working Memory and Language.* Hove, East Sussex. Lawrence Erlbaum.

GRUNDY K. (ed.) (1989). *Linguistics in Clinical Practice.* London. Taylor and Francis.

GRUNWELL P. (1982). *Clinical Phonology.* London. Croom Helm.

HARRIS J. (1990). *Early Language Development: Implications for Clinical and Educational Practice.* London. Routledge.

HEGDE M., NOLL M. and PECORA R. (1979). 'A study of some factors affecting generalisation of language training.' *Journal of Speech and Hearing Disorders,* 44, 301-320.

HOWELL J. and DEAN E. C. (1991). *Treating Phonological Disorders in Children: Metaphon-Theory to Practice.* Kibworth. Far Communications.

HOWLIN P. (1987). 'Behavioural approaches to language', in Yule W. and Rutter M. (eds.), *Language Development and Disorders.* Oxford. Blackwell/MacKeith Press.

HOWLIN P. (1989). 'Changing approaches to communication training with autistic children.' *British Journal of Disorders of Communication,* 24, 151-168.

INGRAM D. (1976). *Phonological Disability in Children.* London. Edward Arnold.

JOHNSTON J. R. (1988). 'Specific language disorders in the child', in McReynolds, L and Yoder, D (eds.), *Handbook of Speech-Language Pathology and Audiology* (pp. 685-715). Philadelphia. B.C. Decker.

JOHNSTON J. R. (1991). 'Questions about cognition in children with specific language impairment', in Miller J. E. (ed.), *Research on Child Language Disorders* Austin, Texas. Pro-Ed.

KNOWLES W. and MASIDLOVER M. (1982). *Derbyshire Language Scheme* (Revised ed.). Ripley, Derbyshire. Educational Psychology Service.

LEES J. and URWIN S. (1991). *Children with Language Disorders.* London. Whurr.

LEONARD L. B. (1981). 'Facilitating linguistic skills in children with specific language impairment.' *Applied Psycholinguistics,* 2, 89-118.

LEONARD L. B. (1987). 'Is specific language impairment a useful construct?' in Rosenberg, S (ed.), *Advances in Applied Psycholinguistics: Disorders of First-Language Development.* Cambridge. Cambridge University Press.

McTEAR M. M. and CONTI-RAMSDEN G. (1992). *Pragmatic Disability in Children.* London. Whurr.

MILLER J, F. (1991). 'Research on language disorders in children: a progress report', in Miller J. F. (ed.), *Research on Child Language Disorders: a Decade of Progress.* Austin, Texas. Pro-Ed.

NYE C., FOSTER S. H. and SEAMAN D. (1987). 'Effectiveness of language intervention with the language/learning disabled.' *Journal of Speech and Hearing Disorders,* 52, 348-357.

PIAGET J. and INHELDER B. (1969). *The Psychology of the Child.* London. Routledge and Kegan Paul.

RAPIN I. and ALLEN D. (1983). 'Developmental language disorders: nosological considerations', in Kirk, U (ed.), *Neuropsychology of Language, Reading and Spelling* (pp. 155-184). New York. Academic Press.

RAPIN I. and ALLEN D. A. (1987). 'Developmental dysphasia and autism in preschool children: characteristics and subtypes', in *Proceedings of the First International Symposium on Specific Speech and Language Disorders in Children,* (pp. 20-35). University of Reading. AFASIC.

SILVA P. A. (1987). 'Epidemiology, longitudinal course and some associated factors: an update', in Yule W. and Rutter M. (eds.), *Language Development and Disorders.* Oxford. Blackwell/MacKeith Press.

SKUSE D. (1992). 'The relationship between deprivation, physical growth and the impaired development of language', in Fletcher P. (ed.), *Specific Speech and Language Disorders in Children.* London. Whurr.

SMITH B. R. and LEINONEN E. (1991). *Clinical Pragmatics.* London. Chapman and Hall.

SNOW C. E. (1986). 'Conversations with children', in Fletcher P. and Garman M. (eds.), *Language Acquisition.* Cambridge. Cambridge University Press.

TALLAL P., STARK R. and CURTISS S. (1976). 'Relation between speech perception and speech production impairment in children with developmental dysphasia.' *Brain and Language,* 3, 305-317.

TALLAL P., STARK R. and MELLITS D. (1985). 'Identification of language-impaired children on the basis of rapid perception and production skills.' *Brain and Language,* 25, 314-322.

TERRELL B., SCHWARTZ R., PRELOCK P. and MESSICK C. (1984). 'Symbolic play in normal and language-impaired children', *Journal of Speech and Hearing Research,* 27, 424-429.

Chapter 25

LANGUAGE AND LITERACY: CONNECTIONS AND IMPLICATIONS

MARYSIA NASH

INTRODUCTION

This chapter explores the relationship between literacy and language disorder and considers both theory and practice. This relationship is important to teachers and speech and language therapists because some children with language disorders have significant difficulties with reading and spelling and some with dyslexia have language difficulties. The chapter is divided into three sections.

1. Language disorders as precursors to problems with literacy
2. The relationship between the type of language disorder and type of literacy difficulty
3. Language deficits in dyslexia

LANGUAGE DISORDERS AS PRECURSORS TO PROBLEMS IN LITERACY

Children learning to read and write need a reasonable foundation of verbal language skills. Stackhouse (1988) suggests that an 'intact facility for speech and language development appears to be a necessary prerequisite for satisfactory reading and spelling development.'

Webster and McConnel (1987) state that many children with early spoken language difficulties will go on to have problems with literacy while those at the severe end of the spectrum will undoubtedly face problems.

EVIDENCE FROM RESEARCH STUDIES

Longitudinal studies such as Fundudis *et al* (1979), Richman *et al* (1982), Silva *et al* (1983) as reported in Howlin and Rutter (1987) provide evidence that the spelling and reading scores of language delayed children were much lower than those of controls.

Making predictions for children with specific language disorders on the basis of these findings is difficult, however, because the research did not differentiate children with specific developmental language disorders from those with global cognitive delay. It is therefore impossible to know how much of the educational differences were as a result of the earlier language deficit and how much as a consequence of low IQ.

Data from a study by Aram *et al* (1984) reported in Howlin and Rutter (1987), who followed up a small group of children identified as language disordered preschool, suggested a greater incidence of poor educational attainments even in children who did not have a low IQ.

Children with both language problems and low IQ had the worst educational outlook.

More recently, Bishop and Adams (1990) longitudinal study investigated the reading attainments of children identified as having specific language impairment preschool.

The children's language had been assessed at $4\frac{1}{2}$ years and again at $5\frac{1}{2}$ years, Bishop and Edmondson (1987). At eight years six months, in addition to other tests, reading and writing were also assessed.

Among the results was the finding of a link between early language difficulties and later problems with literacy. The authors were surprised to find however, that the children whose language impairments had resolved by five years six months, continued to progress well and had no significant impairments on language or literacy measures and that their use of phonics to read and spell non words was as good as other $8\frac{1}{2}$ year olds.

Children with persisting language impairments were poor readers at $8\frac{1}{2}$ years but this was not an isolated difficulty. Problems with reading occurred in the context of widespread verbal deficits and poor non-verbal skills. Reading comprehension was much more of a problem than reading accuracy.

While it seems that language impairment is related to success with literacy, it is clearly not the whole story.

Magnusson and Naucler (1990) also make this observation. They state, in relation to children with language disorders, 'Even if a majority of them have reading and writing problems, some of them seem to acquire written language in much the same way as linguistically normal children. Furthermore the children who seem to have the most serious speech problems are not necessarily the ones for whom reading and writing will be the most problematical, while children whose language problems are not particularly severe may have grave difficulties in learning to read and write.'

To investigate this paradox, Magnusson and Naucler (1990) undertook a longitudinal study to look at the importance of, and relationships between, linguistic, meta-linguistic and non-linguistic factors for reading and spelling. Initial findings were reported for language disordered children and normal children on linguistic and linguistic awareness tasks, one year before starting school and the beginning and end of the first grade. Performance on reading and spelling tasks was measured at the end of the first grade.

Their study allowed them to consider:

1. The role of linguistic competence in general for reading and spelling development.
2. The role of certain aspects of linguistic awareness as a possible prerequisite for reading and spelling acquisition. Tasks included, rhyming, segmentation of syllables and phonemes, identification of phonemes and also a task requiring judgment of syntactic acceptability.
3. The possibility of predicting reading and spelling achievements in the first grade from pre-school data.

Results suggested that **as a group** the language disordered children had poorer language, linguistic awareness and reading and spelling abilities than the normal children. However, some individual language disordered children performed better than their matched normal peer group on some measures. For example, some language disordered children performed better on one or more of the linguistic awareness tasks than the matched normal, and some were better readers and spellers.

Furthermore, even when some of the disordered children's reading and writing scores were compared to an absolute standard, there were language disordered children not only at the lowest reading and spelling level but also among the best. In addition, some normal children were among the poorest. This does not mean that language competence is irrelevant for reading and writing development, because the study found that both the language disordered children who were good at reading and spelling and the normals who performed well gained high scores on language comprehension and syntactic production tasks and, most importantly, high scores on linguistic awareness tasks.

Conversely, the normals who performed poorly were similar to the other poor performers, who were language disordered, by having low scores on these tasks.

Thus, these authors concluded that both linguistic abilities and also linguistic awareness are required for the development of reading and spelling.

Syntactic competence seemed the most important linguistic prerequisite, while rhyming and the ability to identify phonemes are the most important aspects of linguistic awareness and the best predictors for reading and spelling **at least in the first grade.**

While the findings of this study are interesting, the authors acknowledge some children assigned to the normal group may have had language problems that were overlooked. This, together with importance of certain linguistic abilities and linguistic awareness for attainments in literacy, may have accounted for the difference within and between the two groups.

IMPLICATIONS FOR PRACTICE

Research has highlighted the importance of language levels and linguistic awareness for learning to read.

The following suggestions are offered in relation to practice.

Children with persisting language impairment entering school should have their progress in literacy monitored. Liaison between speech and language therapist and teacher is particularly important in the early years to discuss management should problems occur.

An Educational Psychologist's assessment of the child's non verbal ability will help ascertain to what extent any lack of progress is compatible with IQ.

The importance of linguistic awareness for literacy should be recognised. We need to be more aware of the status of these skills in language impaired and normal children and to consider ways in which they can be assessed.

Stackhouse (1988) considers that the speech and language therapist has a critical role with pre-school children in identifying the 'at risk' child and promoting pre-reading and pre-spelling skills since she claims that some of the dyslexics of the future are in speech therapy clinics now.

Nursery teachers should consider whether there is a case for screening 'normal' children's linguistic awareness. Mann (1984) suggests that skills which may predict first grade reading ability might be tested as part of a kindergarten screening battery.

Whether a decision is made to target all children, or to identify and intervene with those who have problems, it seems that developing these skills is important.

Bryant (1985), suggests that skill with sounds can and should be fostered in young children can be an enjoyable activity. He says that young children love nursery rhymes etc and that this kind of activity which happens naturally should be encouraged to help children's progress with literacy at a later stage.

Similarly, Stackhouse (1990) suggests that speech therapy intervention should address the link between spoken and written language problems and that activities can promote pre-reading and pre-spelling skills as well as improvements in verbal language. For specific suggestions see Stackhouse (1985). Mann (1984) feels most optimistic about remediating deficiencies in phonological sophistication. She suggests that phonological awareness may be helped, if not brought about, by some experience which encourages the child to manipulate phonological structure. Some children may need some systematic training in order to achieve the level of sophistication about phonemes and phonological rules that is required for skilled reading. She makes a number of suggestions for indirect methods such as teaching nursery rhymes and poetry or encouraging secret languages like talking backwards, and at a later stage for direct awareness training.

It seems that encouraging linguistic awareness is important for all children, language disordered, normal or dyslexic. Perhaps teachers and therapists should be co-operating to develop this skill in children at both the pre-school and early school stage.

THE RELATIONSHIP BETWEEN THE TYPE OF LANGUAGE DISORDER AND THE TYPE OF LITERACY DIFFICULTY

Children with language disorders are not a homogenous group and they may experience varying difficulties with literacy.

There have been a number of attempts to classify language disorder into different sub-types, Rapin and Allen (1987) and Bishop and Rosenbloom (1987).

Three of the sub-types from the Bishop and Rosenbloom (1987) classification, viz: Developmental apraxia of speech, Phonologic – syntactic syndrome and Semantic pragmatic disorder will be considered in relation to literacy.

DEVELOPMENTAL APRAXIA OF SPEECH (VERBAL DYSPRAXIA)

This is a pronunciation disorder which can vary in severity but where children have a motor programming deficit for speech. The main symptoms are summarised by Tate (1991), as follows:

- Inconsistent articulatory production.
- Difficulty in selection and sequencing of phonological and articulatory movements.
- Increased difficulty with increased complexity of sequences.
- Altered prosodic features.
- Difference between voluntary and involuntary movements.
- Possible concomitant expressive language disorder.
- Possible concomitant learning disability and general motor problems.

With regard to literacy, Stackhouse (1985) states that in dyspraxia there may be no systematic relationship between sounds and meaning. Pronunciations of words may be very variable. Reading and spelling difficulties are to be expected as a result of such inconsistency, since written language will be laid down onto a faulty spoken language base.

Stackhouse looked at the nature of the reading and spelling processes of children with dyspraxia aged 7 - 11 years and found that in reading they were unable to utilise a sound by sound approach to reading unfamiliar words. Their errors e.g. 'canary' read as 'competition' seemed to be guesses prompted by individual letters in the word. It appeared that they were increasing their reading age by relying on a visual reading strategy without phonological skill.

Their spelling errors were bizarre and did not follow the normal processes identified in spelling development.

In another study, Snowling and Stackhouse (1983) noted that in dyspraxic children there was not a direct relationship between pronunciation and spelling. However, great difficulty was observed in segmenting a word prior to spelling. It appeared that mistakes occurred early in the spelling process when speech sounds were analysed prior to sound – letter translation.

Although not all children will be so severely impaired, the case of Michael, Stackhouse and Wells (1991), illustrates the range of difficulties which can be experienced.

Michael 11 years
Verbal Dyspraxia and language problems

Marked phonological processing difficulties.

Reading was at seven year level and the approach to written language tasks indicated that Michael relied on visual strengths to overcome his difficulties with auditory processing. He had great difficulty with phonological strategies, he made visual errors in reading and was unsuccessful in applying phonics. His spelling age was six years eight months and here his difficulty with phonological strategies was even more obvious. He made predominantly bizarre or non phonetic errors.

The authors presumed that his difficulties with making progress beyond a visual approach to reading and spelling were a consequence of his marked phonological processing difficulties (his auditory discrimination, rhyme and segmentation skills were all poor). His inconsistent speech output compounded the problem.

PHONOLOGIC – SYNTACTIC SYNDROME

According to Bishop and Rosenbloom (1987), this is the most common type of developmental language disorder.

Severity varies. Characteristics include:

- Pronunciation errors arising from problems learning the rules of the English sound system and resulting in a spectrum from complete unintelligibility to occasional mild immaturities. (Problems confined to pronunciation of this type are commonly labelled phonological disorder).
- Syntactic structure may be behind age level.
- Possible concomitant comprehension difficulty.

There is some evidence, Bishop and Adams (1990), that isolated phonological problems in pre-literate children were not predictive of reading difficulties at eight years six months. Children with severe and persistent phonological problems may have a different outlook however. Certainly for the children in the Bishop and Adams' study it was difficult to ascertain the severity of the phonological impairment at five years six months and the stage at which it resolved. (The data suggests that almost all the children had no phoneme problems by eight years six months). This may mean that generalising the findings to all children with isolated phonological disorders may not be appropriate.

Robinson Beresford and Dodd (1982) suggest that children with phonological disorders are at risk for dyslexic difficulties.

They compared the spelling of 11 children with phonological disorder with a group or normal children matched on age, sex and reading ability and found that the phonologically disordered children made significantly more errors and unlike the control group did not find the spelling of regular words easier than irregular words. The two groups were also qualitatively different. Unlike the control group, the phonologically disordered group made non-phonetic spelling errors.

Furthermore, the speech disordered children made as many spelling errors on words they pronounced correctly as on words they mispronounced.

It is interesting that the spelling difficulties described are reminiscent of those described in dyspraxic children and it appears that some of the children in the study may also have had symptoms of dyspraxia.

SEMANTIC PRAGMATIC DISORDER

This subtype of language disorder was first described by Rapin and Allen (1983) and is one where children have problems with language use and content but relatively little problem with language form (grammar and pronunciation). Often other behavioural and cognitive abnormalities co-exist with the language difficulty, many of which resemble mild forms of the deficits found in autism.

In relation to literacy, Bishop and Rosenbloom (1987) observe that 'Unlike other language disordered children, a few of these children learn to read at the normal age or even earlier. However, their comprehension for what they read tends to be poor.'

Rapin and Allen (1986) also suggest that this group may have problems with reading comprehension.

Two research studies give some insight into the development of literacy in this group. The first, a single case study by Conti Ramsden and Gunn (1985), describes a boy, Tony, with a conversational disability/semantic pragmatic disorder.

The longitudinal study describes how Tony between the ages of four years four months and four years nine months enjoyed reading and had a small sight vocabulary. This may not seem surprising until we consider that his verbal comprehension as measured by the Reynell Developmental Language Scale was two year two months and his understanding of vocabulary was below a 1.5 year level. At a later stage, between four years nine months and five years two months, and still with very poor scores on verbal comprehension tests, Tony had a sight vocabulary of about 40 words and could write simple sentences without help. The discrepancy between verbal comprehension and mechanical reading ability persisted so that aged five years seven months, and with a verbal comprehension of one-two years behind his chronological age (depending on the test), Tony was observed to have a mechanical reading ability well above his chronological age. The way in which Tony made progress in literacy is not clear, however, and it is not possible to know whether his was a predominantly visual approach or whether he was using phonics.

A slightly larger study, Spence *et al* (1989), looked at the reading of seven children (mean age 12 years five months) with high level semantic difficulties which might also be referred to by some as Semantic Pragmatic Disorder. These authors did not feel, however, that all their children had pragmatic problems.

In addition to their verbal language difficulties the children displayed a discrepancy between their reading accuracy and their reading comprehension, with accuracy better than comprehension.

In the study the children were given a reading passage followed by a series of questions. The passage was read aloud easily and many of the children did so with normal prosody. This, the authors felt, could create the impression that what was read was also understood. However, although their response to the standardised questions was better than expected and superficially correct, with further probing it appeared that the children had not grasped the precise meaning.

Furthermore their scores on the Neale Analysis of Reading Ability were interesting in that although comprehension was well below their chronological age the mean score for accuracy was also depressed, albeit to a lesser extent. In response to this observation the authors suggest that there is a need for further investigation into 'whether mechanical reading skills eventually plateau, because poor comprehension adversely affects the use of predictive strategies'.

IMPLICATIONS FOR PRACTICE

While some language disordered children may be more at risk for reading comprehension problems, others have problems with decoding text and great problems with spelling.

The more severely affected children with Semantic Pragmatic Disorder tend to have marked difficulties with verbal comprehension. These may still be apparent when they start school and they are likely to be placed in language units. While many have great problems with attention they may show a considerable interest in numbers, letters and reading. Nishio (1981), as quoted in Rapin and Allen (1986), suggests that in some reading can be used as a means for improving the comprehension of oral language. It may therefore be possible to use the written word to focus attention on language you may wish to teach using for example either Language Through Reading Level 1 and/or ideas based on it.

At a later stage Language Through Reading Levels two and three, which specifically target the comprehension of 'Wh' questions, pronoun reference, inferencing etc. may be useful as these children often have problems in these areas.

Throughout their reading development it will be necessary to monitor comprehension carefully as this is likely to pose greater problems than accuracy.

Helping the child to identify areas where comprehension is a problem coupled with strategies by which the child addresses this may be helpful for older children, and ideas based on the work of Dollaghen and Kaston (1986) and applied to reading may be useful.

Children with dyspraxia and phonological disorders who have problems decoding and spelling because of poor phonological processing skills may be helped to progress from the visual approach to the alphabetic phase of literacy development. Intervention aimed at strengthening auditory processing skills may be helpful. (See Stackhouse (1985)).

For many language disordered children, including those with semantic pragmatic disorder or phonologic syntactic disorder, the choice of reading scheme/book is important.

When comprehension is impaired significantly it is important to assess the level of understanding required – whether the book requires understanding at sentence or discourse level. Where comprehension relies on understanding discourse (i.e. several sentences linked together to form a bigger unit of meaning such as a story) some children may have considerable difficulty.

In addition it is important to note the extent to which inference is required so that problems may be avoided or overcome. During inference world knowledge is brought to bear in comprehension to 'fill in' information which is not explicitly stated. Children with semantic pragmatic disorder may find this process of inference particularly difficult.

The vocabulary is also important. Children who have poor receptive vocabulary may have reading comprehension difficulties as a result of their failure to understand certain words and figures of speech such as 'fell out' etc. Knowledge of vocabulary will also affect the child's ability to make predictions to assist in decoding.

For the child with very delayed grammar the choice of a reading book/scheme should involve consideration of the grammar in the text. For example, a book may require him to read sentences considerably outwith his grammatical competence. As a result, his ability to use 'top down' processes, i.e. knowledge of language to assist decoding, may be considerably reduced. A text with structures more at his grammatical level, may be more helpful for developing reading and reinforcing language work.

LANGUAGE DEFICITS IN DYSLEXIA

Although not all dyslexics have speech and language problems a proportion have subtle undiagnosed language difficulties that may only become recognised if the child is also seen by a speech and language therapist.

Stackhouse (1991) describes how some dyslexics may have had speech therapy in the past but have been discharged and are then re-referred with a query as to whether their earlier spoken language problems are relevant to their lack of progress with literacy. Other dyslexics despite having some degree of language difficulty may never have been recognised as such, perhaps because their problems went unrecognised or there was a lack of opportunity for referral.

Some children are referred to a speech and language therapist, when the educational psychologist identifies a verbal-performance discrepancy on IQ tests with the verbal score significantly poorer than the performance score.

Whatever the reason for the eventual referral to speech and language therapy, on assessment the following deficits may be identified:

Receptive vocabulary – Some children with specific learning difficulties score at or in advance of their age on tests such as the British Picture Vocabulary Scale while others may score below, Klein (1985)

This author also suggests that higher level comprehension may be affected and that there may be problems understanding age appropriate syntax or with absurdities, puns, proverbs etc.

Naming difficulties are common. Findings from a study by Snowling *et al* (1988) suggested that dyslexics perform more poorly on object naming tasks than their age and intelligence suggests and their difficulty was not associated with inadequate knowledge of word meaning. It appears that the dyslexics may have some difficulty acquiring precise phonological representations for words.

Because the children may possess faulty or impoverished representations of some words, these will tend to be mispronounced and/or be difficult to access. The authors quote an error which illustrates this: 'ack, ac, aquarine, fishtank' for aquarium.

A study by Stirling and Miles (1986) showed that dyslexic children distorted words more frequently than controls when they tried to say them e.g. buckle – buttle, bustle, bucker etc., and these errors seem in keeping with the explanation put forward by Snowling *et al* (1988) and cited above.

Klein (1985) states that dyslexics may have difficulty communicating in a fluent, creative and interesting manner and suggests ideas for assessment and management. Stirling and Miles (1986) investigated dyslexics' fluency when asked to explain the meaning of a particular word. Among other ways, the dyslexics differed from the controls by producing more incomplete sentences and more frequent use of 'um', 'er', and 'well'.

Verbal Memory Deficits may also be apparent and Klein (1985) suggests a number of areas where problems may arise including learning sequences such as the days of the week and months of the year, retaining a sequence of verbal information such as the rules of a game, learning tables etc.

In addition a reduced digit span and difficulty with repetition of, in particular, polysyllabic words can occur.

Stackhouse and Wells (1991) describe how a dyslexic child may have problems with unclear speech due to speech sound omissions together with imprecise articulation. Difficulty may no longer be in pronouncing individual consonants but at a less obvious level. Full assessment of speech by the speech and language therapist may therefore be appropriate.

Poor auditory skills may be present in dyslexia, Stackhouse and Wells (1991), and the following areas should be assessed: auditory discrimination (including complex non-words), rhyme detection and production and syllable and phoneme segmentation.

The child's ability to apply alphabetic skills to reading and spelling tasks should also be assessed. For a case study of a dyslexic boy with a range of higher level language problems, the reader is referred to Stackhouse and Wells (1991).

IMPLICATIONS FOR PRACTICE

The recognition that dyslexics often have some degree of language difficulty suggests that there is a role for the speech and language therapist in their assessment and management. See Robinson (1993), this publication. (Chapter 26).

Stackhouse (1991) states that it is important to use appropriate psycholinguistic tests in investigating older children with subtle speech and language difficulties and that there is a need to develop better assessments for the more subtle speech and language deficits in older children. Furthermore there is a need for teachers, therapists and educational psychologists to collaborate in assessment and intervention.

The work of Snowling *et al* (1988) provides insight into dyslexics' naming difficulties which may be usefully generalised to children with more obvious language disorders.

Naming deficits, often described as word finding difficulty, are recognised in the language disordered population. These difficulties have been so called because the child is unable to provide a word he very often understands. The exact reason for the difficulty and hence the most appropriate remediation for it are still not fully understood.

The research with dyslexics suggests that impoverished or faulty phonological representations may affect accurate naming even when there is good semantic knowledge. This emphasises the phonological aspects of word learning, a neglected area in therapy. Assessment of any child with vocabulary problems should therefore consider both phonological and semantic knowledge in order to target remediation as appropriately as possible.

CONCLUSIONS

Research indicates that language disordered children may be at risk for problems with reading and spelling, that different types of difficulty may be experienced, and that dyslexics may have high level speech and language disorders. In the light of these relationships the need for speech and language therapists to collaborate with teachers in assessing and managing such children is desirable.

REFERENCES

BISHOP D. V. M and ADAMS C. (1990). 'A Prospective Study of the Relationship between Specific Language Impairment, Phonological Disorders and Reading Retardation.' *Journal of Child Psychology and Psychiatry.* 31(7)

BISHOP D. V. M. and EDMUNDSON A. (1987). 'Language Impaired 4-year olds: Distinguishing Transient from Persistent Impairment.' *Journal of Speech and Hearing Disorders,* 52, 156-173.

BISHOP D. V. M. and ROSENBLOOM L. (1987). 'Childhood Language Disorders: Classification and Overview.' In Yule W. and Rutter, M. eds. *Language Development and Disorders.* MacKeith Press.

BRYANT P. (1985). 'The Question of Prevention.' In Snowling, M J. ed. *Children's Written Language Difficulties.* NFER-Nelson.

CONTI RAMSDEN G. and GUNN M. (1986). 'The Development of Conversational Disability: A Case Study.' *British Journal of Disorders of Communication* 21(3).

DOLLAGHAN C. and KASTON N. (1986). 'A Comprehension Monitoring program for Language Impaired Children.' *Journal of Speech and Hearing Disorders,* 51, 264-271.

GILLIES M. and HUTT E. (1985). *Language Through Reading, Parts I, II, III.* Developed by John Horniman School Staff.

HOWLIN P. and RUTTER M. (1987). 'The Consequences of Language Delay for Other Aspects of Development.' In Yule W. and Rutter, M. eds. *Language Development and Disorders.* Mac Keith Press.

KLEIN H. (1985). 'The Assessment and Management of Some Persisting Language Difficulties in the Learning Disabled.' In Snowling, M.J. ed. *Children's Written Language Difficulties.* NFER-Nelson.

MAGNUSSON E. and NAUCLER K. (1990). 'Reading and Spelling in Language Disordered Children-Linguistic and Meta-linguistic Pre-requisites: Report on a Longitudinal Study.' *Clinical Linguistics and Phonetics.* 4(1).

MANN V. A. (1984). 'Longitudinal Prediction and Prevention of Early Reading Difficulty.' *Annals of Dyslexia.* 34.

RAPIN I. and ALLEN D. A. (1983). 'Developmental Language Disorders: Nosologic Consideration.' In U. Kirk ed. *Neuro-psychology of Language Reading and Spelling.* Academic Press. New York.

RAPIN I. and ALLEN, D. A. (1986). 'Communication Disorders in Early Childhood.' In Flemhig, I and Stern L. eds. *Proceedings of the 2nd European Symposium on Developmental Neurology.*

RAPIN I. AND ALLEN D. A. (1987). 'Developmental Dysphasia and Autism in Preschool Children: Characteristics and Sub-types.' In *Specific Speech and Language Disorders in Children*. AFASIC.

SNOWLING M. J. and STACKHOUSE J. (1983). 'Spelling Performance of Children with Developmental Verbal Dyspraxia.' *Developmental Medicine and Child Neurology*, 25, 430-437.

SNOWLING M. VAN WAGTENDONK B. and STAFFORD C. (1988). 'Object Naming Deficits in Developmental Dyslexia.' *Journal of Research in Reading*. 11.

SPENCE L., FLEETWOOD A., GELIVT J., WRENCH B., EARLES L. and SEARBY C. (1989). 'A Descriptive Study of a Subgroup of Moor House School Children with High Level Semantic Difficulties.' In Grunwell, P and James, A. eds. *The Functional Evaluation of Language Disorders*. Croom Helm.

STACKHOUSE J. (1985). 'Segmentation, Speech and Spelling Difficulties.' In Snowling, M. J. ed. *Children's Written Language Difficulties*. NFER-Nelson.

STACKHOUSE J. (1988). 'Relationship between Spoken and Written Language Disorders.' In Mogford, K and Sadler, J. eds. *Child Language Disability: Implications in an Educational Setting*. Multilingual Matters Ltd.

STACKHOUSE J (1990). 'Phonological Deficits in Developmental Reading and Spelling Disorders.' In Grunwell, P ed. *Developmental Speech Disorders*. Churchill Livingston.

STACKHOUSE J. and WELLS B. (1991). 'Dyslexia: The Obvious and Hidden Speech and Language Disorder.' *Speech Therapy in Practice* 7 (1).

STIRLING E. G. and MILES T. R. (1986). 'Oral Language of Dyslexic Adolescents.' *Child Language and Teaching Therapy*. 2 (2).

TATE M. (1991). 'Developmental Dyspraxia – a sibling case study.' *Speech Therapy in Practice*. Vol. 7 No. 1 1991.

WEBSTER A. and McCONNEL C. (1987). *Children with Speech and Language Difficulties*. Cassell.

Chapter 26

ROLE OF THE SPEECH THERAPIST

NICOLA ROBINSON

INTRODUCTION

A community speech therapist provides a service in a local area to all those suffering from a variety of communication disorders. This includes young pre-school children with slow development of speech and language through the whole age range to elderly people with acquired problems following neurological damage. Our job is to offer assessment, to attempt a diagnosis and to suggest appropriate treatment and management. The involvement of a speech therapist with dyslexic children is appropriate if it can be shown that there are links between written and spoken communication. This involves consideration of how the human brain is functioning during language development, whether there might be a neurological cause of dyslexia and whether speech is an important foundation for written language. It is also necessary to review the skills which will normally have been learnt by the time a child is ready for reading and writing, to look for evidence that may indicate that particular kinds of early spoken language difficulty are predictors of later literacy failure and to discover the extent of spoken language problems among children with dyslexia.

THE ISSUES

In considering whether it is justifiable to involve a medically trained and employed speech therapist in the management of a learning disordered child whose problems appear to lie in the realm of reading and writing rather than in speech (Fig 1), a number of questions can be asked:

- What type of links exist between verbal communication and written communication and is there any reason for one type of disorder to coexist with or affect the other?
- Is there any evidence that the child with dyslexia may suffer verbal or oral language problems as well as literacy difficulties?
- Does the child with dyslexia have a hidden verbal deficit which only becomes obvious once more complex language tasks are tackled?

- Is there evidence that children presenting early on with spoken language problems then go on to have problems with literacy?
- Is it possible that dyslexia is a distinct and special kind of language disorder?
- Are the speech disordered and the reading disordered population one and the same?
- Are there faulty underlying processes accounting for failure in both types of language function?
- Do all speech and language disordered children develop dyslexia or only those with specific difficulties in translating visual experience into speech, i.e. those with verbal coding problems?
- Does the condition of dyslexia involve complex difficulties with the auditory processing channel as well as the visual?
- Is it therefore possible to identify a distinct group of children with both spoken and written language disorder who justify particular lines of treatment?
- If so how can these children be identified and what help do they require and when?
- If dyslexia is caused by an underlying pathological process in the development of the central nervous system, is it helpful to include a speech therapist in the team, bearing in mind that speech therapy is normally a health service based profession?

Speech Therapists with their training in medical neurology, child development, speech and language pathology, and linguistic and phonetic analysis, should be able to provide a service to a learning support team. They may be able to provide relevant information on the child's early language development. By using their assessment techniques they should be able to identify any underlying processes which are faulty, and so to help in the planning of remedial treatment.

Chapter 26

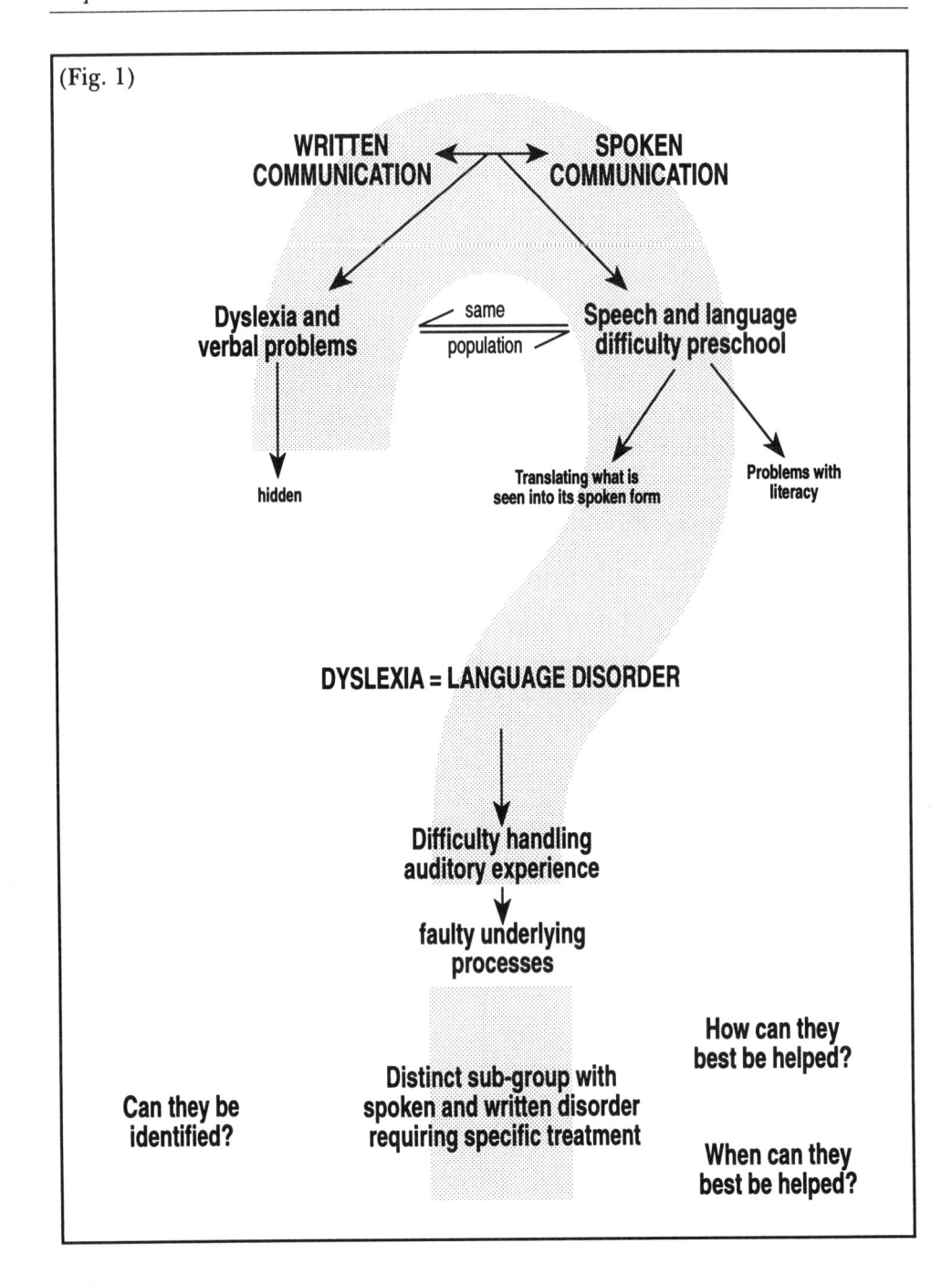

(Fig. 1)

WRITTEN COMMUNICATION ⟷ SPOKEN COMMUNICATION

- Dyslexia and verbal problems ⟷ (same population) ⟷ Speech and language difficulty preschool
  - hidden
  - Translating what is seen into its spoken form
  - Problems with literacy

DYSLEXIA = LANGUAGE DISORDER

↓

Difficulty handling auditory experience

↓

faulty underlying processes

Distinct sub-group with spoken and written disorder requiring specific treatment

Can they be identified?

How can they best be helped?

When can they best be helped?

Chapter 26

LANGUAGE AND LITERACY

Crystal (1986) tells us that language is the most complex piece of behaviour a human being ever learns. Spoken English has over 40 sounds used in over 300 combinations to produce over 7000 syllables. These are used in a vocabulary of around 50,000 reasonably common words. These words are combined into sentences by over 1000 grammatical rules along with several dozen prosodic patterns of intonation, pitch, stress and volume – all of which will be used in a variety of social and educational settings.

Spoken language is a genetically determined faculty evolving historically nearly 60,000 years before written language was invented, a skill dependent on learning from older members of the group and so more vulnerable to personal or social disruption.

For language processing to take place, both in understanding and in responding, the brain must receive, interpret and organise information adequately in order to connect what we see with what we hear.

Complex associations must take place between adjacent parts of the brain within the language area if the functions of speech, understanding, reading and spelling are to take place (see fig. 2).

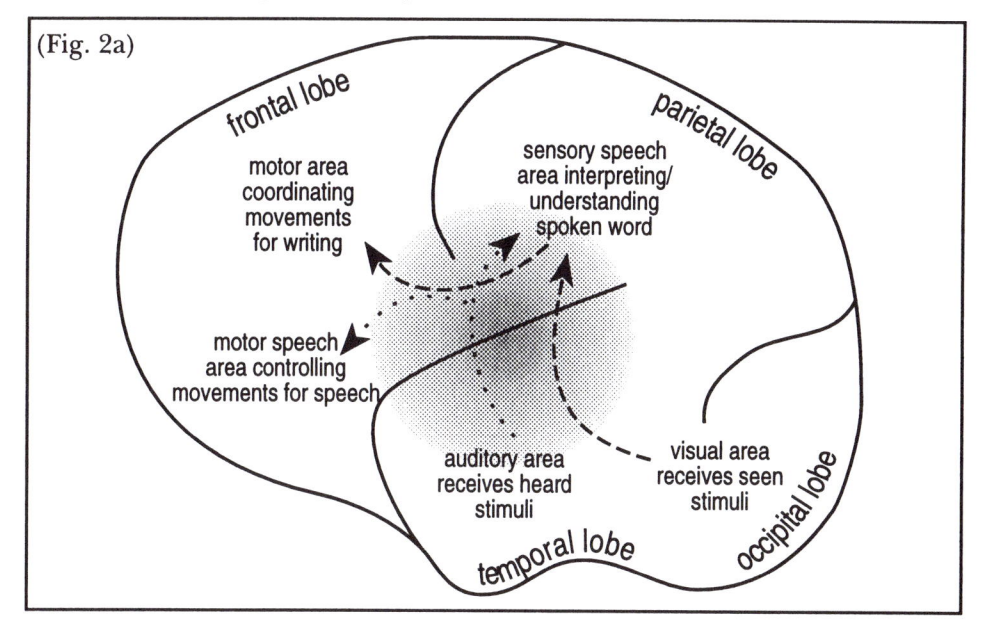

(Fig. 2a) — frontal lobe; parietal lobe; temporal lobe; occipital lobe
- motor area coordinating movements for writing
- sensory speech area interpreting/understanding spoken word
- motor speech area controlling movements for speech
- auditory area receives heard stimuli
- visual area receives seen stimuli

Perspectives on Practice

Reading a written text and spelling out written words both relate to the representation of language. When reading aloud we convert visual symbols into spoken language and when spelling we convert speech into visual patterns. We can therefore predict that such correlated behaviour will share common brain mechanisms (Duane 1991) and problems with both are likely to share a common base.

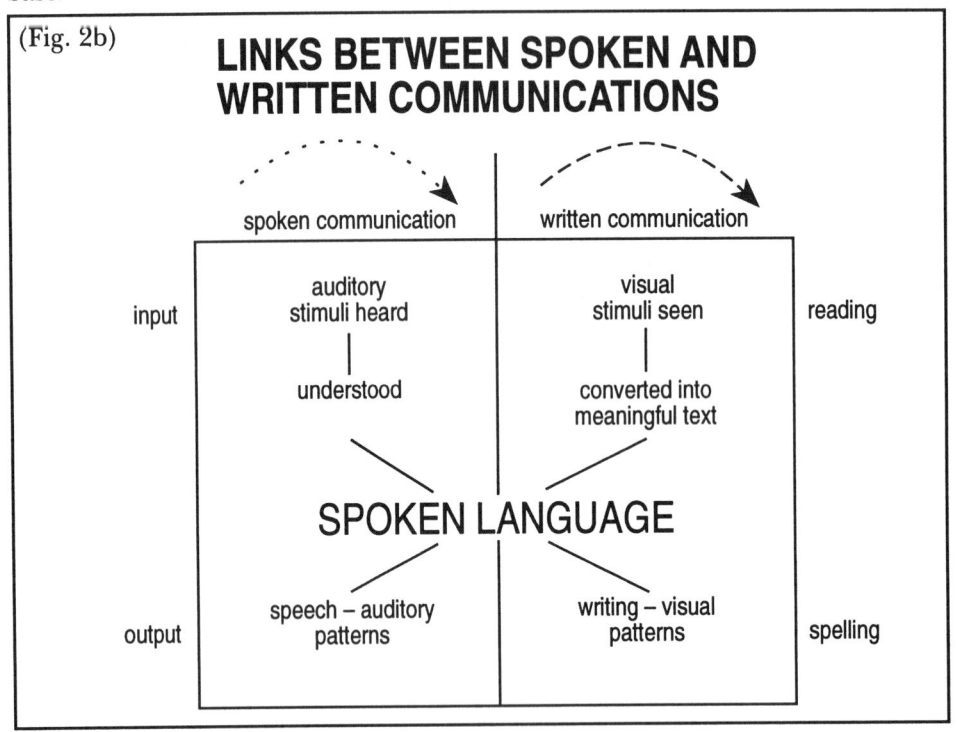

(Fig. 2b)

LINKS BETWEEN SPOKEN AND WRITTEN COMMUNICATIONS

```
                spoken communication      written communication

                    auditory                  visual
   input          stimuli heard           stimuli seen              reading
                        |                       |
                   understood              converted into
                                          meaningful text

                             SPOKEN LANGUAGE

                  speech – auditory       writing – visual
   output            patterns                patterns              spelling
```

Semrud (1989) suggests that dyslexia may be related to some underlying defect of a neurological nature in the brain upsetting the normal asymmetry necessary for establishing language skill. Hornsby (1984) states such a subtle disturbance in the arrangement of brain cells could result in two language areas referring messages across for analysis, leading to jamming and confusion. This anomaly of brain development, interacting with environmental and hereditary factors, would result in a developmental difficulty with language.

Normal development of the nervous system, and presumably of the brain too, may well occur only in response to the developing organism's life experience. If vital experiences do not occur at the critical times there may be permanent structural and functional defects.

Mann (1984) states that an unusual arrangements of brain cells may make them less efficient in language processing, resulting in greater problems when recognising shapes, giving them sounds, stringing them together, transferring sounds to shapes and writing them down. Sequences of sounds and shapes may not be easily remembered or expressed in a logical order. Mann reminds us that any attempt to explain the causes and manifestations of these problems can only be speculative due to our limited knowledge of cerebral processes. However, dyslexia is perhaps best thought of as a symptom, not a disease, a symptom of a large number of language disorders, or even a symptom-complex in itself.

Having discussed the links between spoken and written communication, shared brain mechanisms, and parallel language processing, it will now be useful to consider the importance of speech as a necessary foundation for reading and spelling. If the ability to read and write is related to competence in spoken language it may be expected that factors which make for competence in speech will improve literacy.

Children learn to read and write after they have learnt to say almost anything they need or want to say. Literacy is then a secondary skill learnt once a child has learnt to talk, to understand what is said, to recognise words as separate units of meaning, to hear sounds correctly and to blend them in his or her own speech. A child needs to be able to retrieve names of items rapidly – to have a vocabulary – and to have some syntactic knowledge of how words can be combined, and also the ability to code information phonetically according to its sounds. In addition literacy requires a more conscious level of awareness of phonology, semantics and syntax. (Snowling 1985).

EARLY LANGUAGE DEVELOPMENT

A closer examination of the linguistic skill which a child has normally developed by school age will help us to identify and understand the deviations that can occur, both before the development of literacy and associated with dyslexia during the school years. Figs 3 and 4 describe the levels of language.

Phonology refers to the sounds of a Language. Spoken language is made up of collections of sounds strung together in a sequence of contrasts to form words. Sounds are what we hear as opposed to letters which are the alphabetic name we give to some sounds. These sound contrasts distinguish between words of different meaning and make up the phonology of a language. By school entry children normally have an almost complete phonological system with fully intelligible speech, having acquired the system following a developmental pattern.

Chapter 26

Articulation refers to the physical ability to produce the sounds accurately with the tongue, lips and oral musculature moving appropriately. This is not a language skill. Children at school entry often have residual minor difficulties pronouncing the more complicated sounds such as 'th' and 'r' and will substitute with more easily articulated sounds. The term 'phonetic' refers to the way sounds of speech can be transcribed using phonetic symbols as opposed to letters, to cover sounds not directly correlated with our alphabet. Speech Therapists are familiar with the International Phonetic Alphabet which enables all speech to be transcribed and identified in an accurate and true form. Each phonetic symbol has an associated three term label which describes its voicing, place and manner of production. (fig. 3)

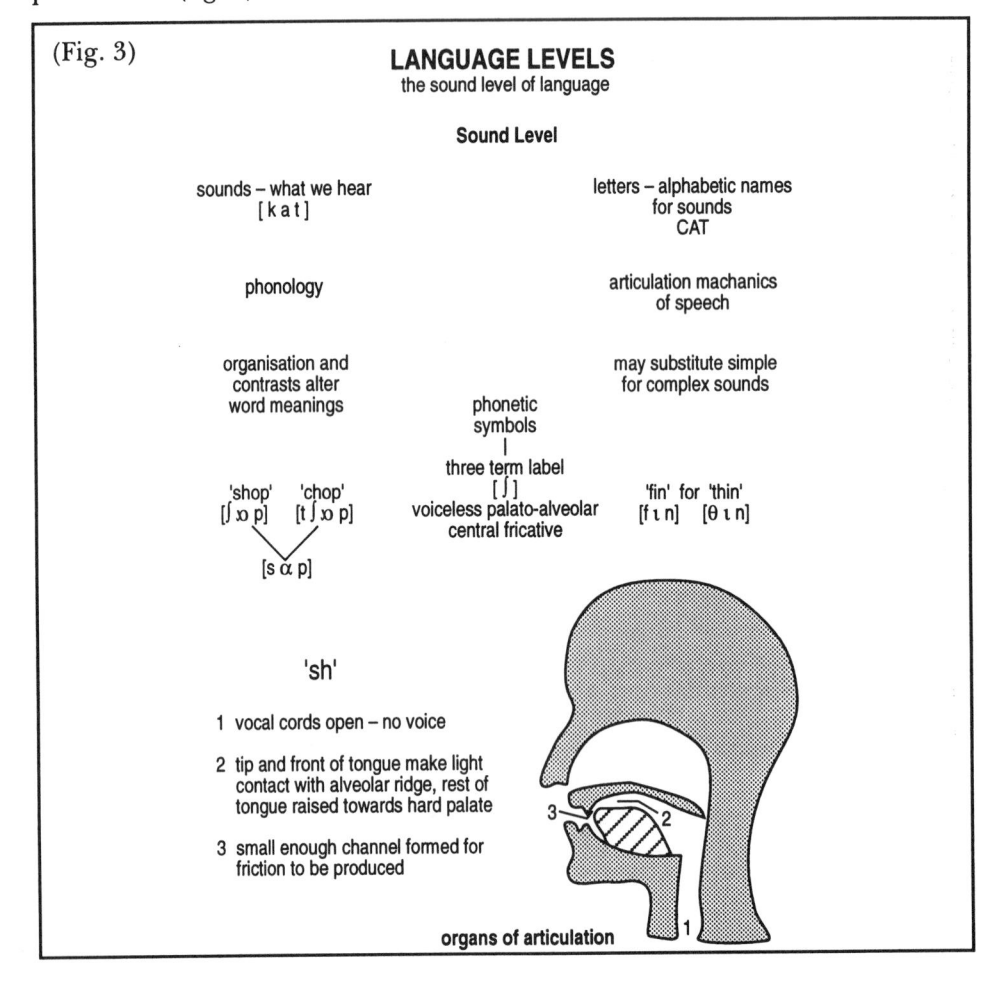

(Fig. 3) LANGUAGE LEVELS
the sound level of language

Sound Level

sounds – what we hear
[k a t]

letters – alphabetic names for sounds
CAT

phonology

articulation machanics of speech

organisation and contrasts alter word meanings

may substitute simple for complex sounds

phonetic symbols
|
three term label
[ʃ]
voiceless palato-alveolar central fricative

'shop'   'chop'
[ʃɒp]   [tʃɒp]

'fin' for 'thin'
[fɪn]   [θɪn]

[sɑp]

'sh'

1 vocal cords open – no voice

2 tip and front of tongue make light contact with alveolar ridge, rest of tongue raised towards hard palate

3 small enough channel formed for friction to be produced

organs of articulation

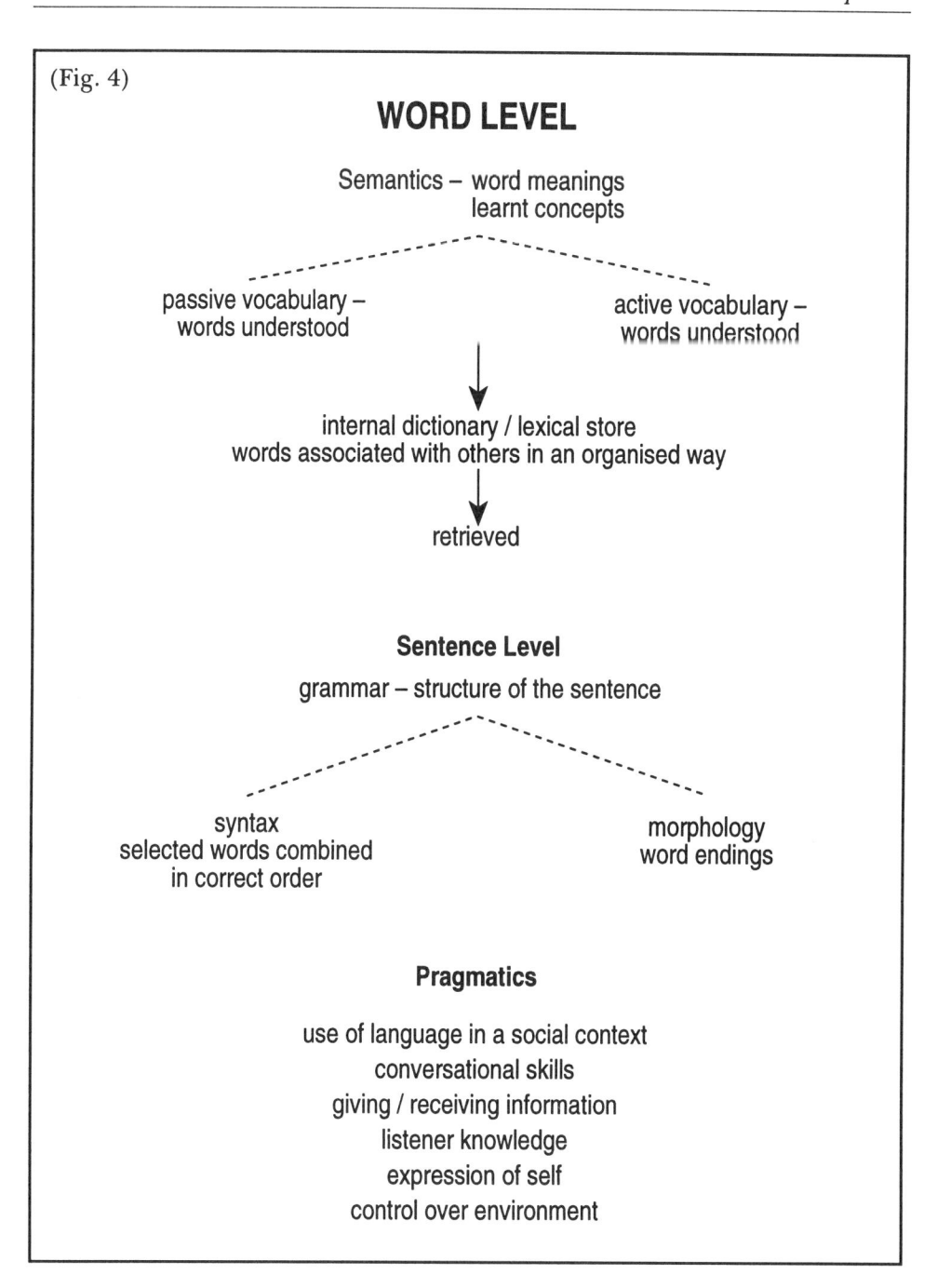

(Fig. 4)

WORD LEVEL

Semantics – word meanings
learnt concepts

passive vocabulary –
words understood

active vocabulary –
words understood

internal dictionary / lexical store
words associated with others in an organised way

retrieved

Sentence Level

grammar – structure of the sentence

syntax
selected words combined
in correct order

morphology
word endings

Pragmatics

use of language in a social context
conversational skills
giving / receiving information
listener knowledge
expression of self
control over environment

Semantics (fig. 4) refers to the meaning of words, the concepts behind the labels which we attach to the entities around us. These labels or words make up our vocabulary. We have a passive vocabulary (words we understand the meaning of) as well as an active vocabulary (words we use). We learn new vocabulary by learning how new words are associated with words we already know; for example with similar or opposite meanings, or as members of the same category. This makes up our 'internal dictionary' or lexical store. By school entry a child may have a vocabulary of many thousands of words but this number will double before the child enters secondary school.

At the sentence level words are combined according to syntactic rules governing word selection, word ending and word order. At school entry children are still increasing their understanding of complex sentences as well as learning the use of irregular syntactic rules in their own speech.

Pragmatics refers to the use of language in a social context, and refers to our skill at conversation, our ability to give and receive information, our awareness of listener knowledge and the way we use language to express ourselves and control our environment. By school entry a child is still learning the more subtle ways of using language; how, for instance to recognise such features as sarcasm, persuasion, implied requests and inference. It is the pragmatic aspect of language that is of particular relevance for the older age group. Many of these skills do not normally develop before the age of eight to twelve. This means that difficulties at the pragmatic level may not be obvious until later.

It is therefore vital to realise how much language development continues beyond the age of five years if we are to distinguish between normal and deviant features in a child's speech and language beyond this age.

Prior to five some children will struggle to acquire many of these skills. Some will progress through the expected order of acquisition but at a much slower rate, exhibiting a delay in language development at any or all levels. Others show different patterns of development with atypical features suggesting a disorder. Not all of these children will go on to have difficulties with reading and spelling but there is increasing evidence that particular kinds of verbal language difficulty are better predictors than others of later literacy failure.

PREDICTING LEARNING DIFFICULTIES

Bishop and Edmondson's (1987) study of prognostic indicators established that the likelihood of reading impairment in language disordered children depends upon the type and severity of the disorder. Those with isolated phonological disorder at the age of four are less at risk than those with semantic and syntactic as well as phonological impairment. Provided a child's language problem has resolved by the age of five and a half there should be little risk of a later literacy problem. However, persisting specific language impairment at this age will be likely to show itself in reading and spelling difficulty. Phonological difficulty becomes a more reliable predictor if still present at a later age.

Further studies looking at predictive behaviour have been carried out. Wiig, Semel and Crouse (1973) found that syntactic difficulties were significant precursors of reading failure. Stark (1984) states that children who have apparently recovered from early language impairment frequently go on to become late readers. Hornsby (1984) suggests that 60% of dyslexics were late or poor talkers. Mann (1984) found that tests of letter-naming, short-term memory, word repetition and phonological processing skill are better predictors of reading failure than IQ tests.

Snowling (1987) suggests that the ability to deal with speech at the level of the phoneme (i.e. at the sound level) is a good predictor of later reading development. Bradley (1980) suggests that phonological processing problems contribute significantly to reading failure.

Exactly what skills are of particular concern? The child needs to be able to segment the sound stream he hears into the component sound elements (phonemes) i.e. to divide words heard into their constituent sounds. This constitutes phonological processing. It renders the child capable of detecting initial, medial and final sounds in words, as well as identifying common or shared sounds in different words and so to have a sensitivity to rhyme and alliteration. This skill allows analysis of words into their component sounds and the blending of sequences of sounds into words, an important skill to be acquired before letter knowledge.

Snowling (1985) suggests that such phonological skills are vital as prerequisites for literacy, although other authorities such as Morais (1991) Integrating Theory and Practice consider that such skills develop as a consequence of exposure to the alphabet. Certainly, learning to read enhances phonological skills. Goswami and Bryant (1990) suggest that children are not interested in analysing words into smaller units until at least six years of age. However, they consider that the child's obvious and early natural interest in rhyme is based on the ability to hear the opening and closing of words – which constitutes a type of phonological skill of importance to reading success.

Bradley (1980) devised a training programme during which six to seven year olds were taught to be aware of the sounds in words and how these were linked to rhyme. By eight to nine years these children were eight to ten months further ahead in reading and seventeen months further ahead in spelling than controls who were taught to concentrate on the meaning. By twelve to thirteen years the children were reading at their appropriate age and twere wo years ahead of controls in spelling. Training in sound categorisation was more effective when it involved an explicit connection with the alphabet.

Speech sounds occur in a continuous, rapid flow of coordinated movements affected by neighbouring sounds rather than one sound fully articulated after another. Similarly, words have unnoticed boundaries in connected speech. A child's auditory processing skill allows her or him to understand the nature and boundaries of words, syllables and sounds. It is vital that this should occur before the learning of letter rules for reading and spelling.

Fig. 5 shows three stages of phonology: input, segmentation and output. Breakdown at each of these stages leads to particular difficulties for the child. (Snowling 1985).

Input refers to the awareness of salient features of sounds and the ability to discriminate between words which sound similar. The child who is unable to do this will confuse words by not being aware of subtle but important differences.

Segmentation is the intervening stage during which the child analyses words into sounds before translating these into letters and recognising shared sounds in different words. To analyse in this way the words must be held in the memory in a phonological form or code. Problems at this stage prevent children from segmenting and building words from sounds.

Output refers to the production of words; the pronunciation of words based on the retrieval of instructions that direct the necessary mouth movements. Problems at this stage render the child unable to pronounce some words accurately and consistently or to repeat words heard.

Symptoms of poor phonological processing will include a poor internal representation of sounds, inaccurate pronunciation of words, a slow increase in vocabulary with poor retrieval of words and poor acquisition of grammatical structure. In addition there will be difficulty in transferring to the alphabetic stage of literacy development and with the indirect route to literacy.

Having ascertained that phonological processing problems are likely to interfere with the child's progress in learning how to read and spell, and that

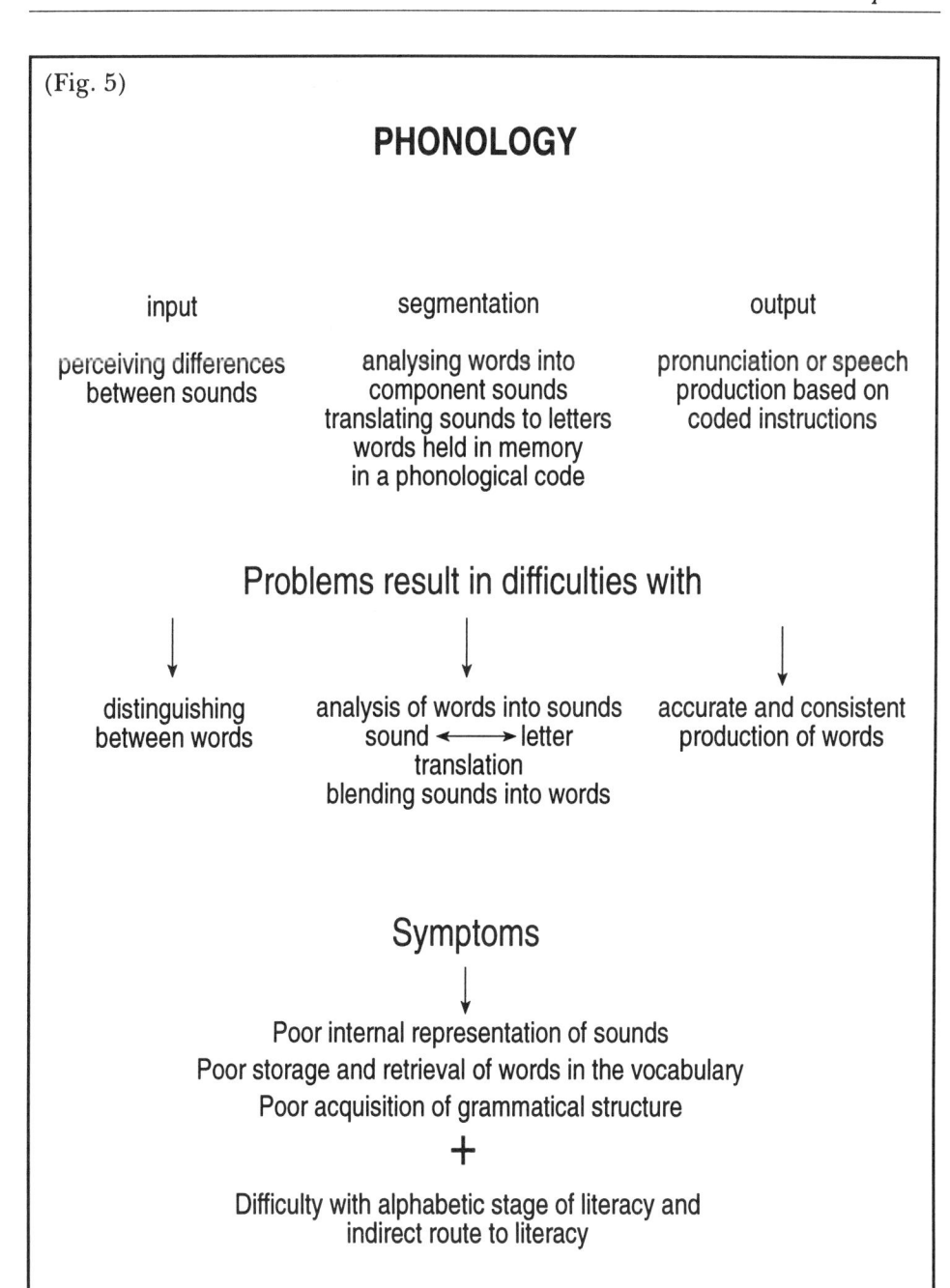

(Fig. 5)

PHONOLOGY

input	segmentation	output
perceiving differences between sounds	analysing words into component sounds translating sounds to letters words held in memory in a phonological code	pronunciation or speech production based on coded instructions

Problems result in difficulties with

↓	↓	↓
distinguishing between words	analysis of words into sounds sound ⟷ letter translation blending sounds into words	accurate and consistent production of words

Symptoms
↓
Poor internal representation of sounds
Poor storage and retrieval of words in the vocabulary
Poor acquisition of grammatical structure
+
Difficulty with alphabetic stage of literacy and indirect route to literacy

children requiring speech therapy at the preschool stage are more likely to be poor at these skills when at school, it is now important to consider dyslexia at school age.

DYSLEXIC PUPILS OF SCHOOL AGE

Is there any evidence that dyslexic children experience spoken language difficulty ? If there is this would provide further evidence that dyslexia may be a symptom of generalised deficit in verbal language. Obviously, not all children with dyslexia will have a problem with spoken language but those who do may have high level problems which are only identifiable by more complex language tasks and which are easily missed.

Snowling (1987) suggests these children are slower at retrieving words, use circumlocutions and have difficulty with category labels.

Renaldi (1991) suggests that word-finding difficulties may be evidenced in continuous speech by hesitations, revisions, discontinued utterances and even interruptions as the child struggles to use the utterance before it is forgotten. The older child will fail to organise his expressive language efficiently and will avoid social situations where there is a need to initiate conversation. These children will fail to understand ambiguous statements such as 'pull your socks up' and they will fail to appreciate the linguistic aspects of humour.

Thompson's (1984) evidence shows that children with dyslexia are liable to use less descriptive words and to use simple grammatical forms, with irregular verb tense errors.

Pavlidis and Miles (1981) suggest that children with dyslexia fail to understand more complex linguistic structures and need information put in a readily usable form to integrate with their own general knowledge.

German (1985) states that the child's failures are due to difficulty in attaching labels to incoming visual information – a verbal labelling difficulty. The child struggles to remember the articulatory-motor patterns of sounds in words affecting word-retrieval.

Renaldi (1991) suggests that gaps in the child's vocabulary reflect a difficulty in the understanding of certain concepts. Language serves as a 'learning bridge' to bring abstract concepts such as time within the child's reach. If language is made simple and used to represent familiar events, the child will eventually be able to understand the concept itself. Renaldi adds that these linguistic problems are frequently linked to emotional and cognitive factors, and that these difficulties are more specific and more severe than would be expected in a child with general developmental delay.

So it appears that children with dyslexia may have very subtle problems. These may show as deficiencies in their semantics, syntax and pragmatics. Phonology may also be impaired, resulting in inadequate processing of auditory signals. All these may have an adverse effect upon their development of vocabulary and on the ability to label words.

READING AND SPELLING ACQUISITION

How do these difficulties with words influence the development of literacy?

To explore this we must first understand how a child learns to read and spell from his or her first experiences with written language (see fig. 6). Reading is the process by means of which we attend to a written text, recognise letters and convert these to sounds, rehearse the sounds in a sequence either to ourselves or aloud and extract the sense of the text. To do this we need to develop a sight vocabulary – a store of words in memory that we rapidly recognise. We also need to develop a knowledge of our spelling system and our alphabet in order to decode or analyse words.

We can define two routes to this process, a direct visual route whereby we recognise the visual pattern of words and can rapidly attach a spoken label to it; and an indirect auditory route involving a process of deciphering the strings of letters in words and translating these to sounds. We can see how these two routes operate by looking at Frith's three phases to the acquisition of reading skill. These three phases are the logographic phase (matching the visual appearance of a written word to its spoken counterpart), the alphabetic phase (in which words are broken down into smaller units and letters are translated into sounds) and the orthographic phase (in which chunks of words are automatically recognised, only unfamiliar words having to be decoded letter by letter).

Frith also defines a pre-reading phase during which the child begins to learn about print and speech sounds, gradually recognising that letters represent specific sounds, and so building up a sight vocabulary. The fluent reader then becomes quicker at decoding and learns to recognise common spelling patterns. Reading to learn is the final stage when more efficient comprehension increases the reader's general knowledge from what has been read.

Chapter 26

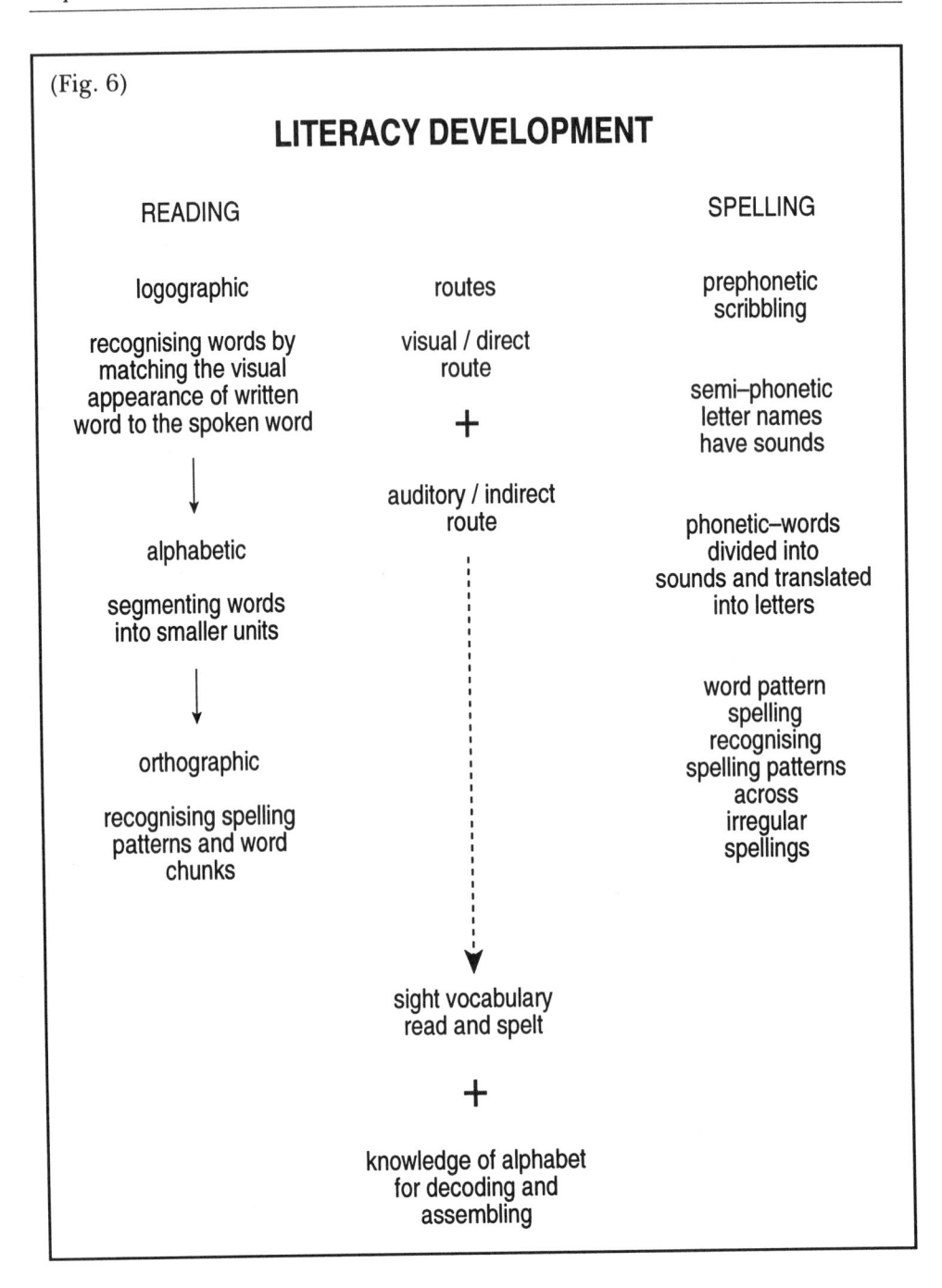

(Fig. 6)

LITERACY DEVELOPMENT

READING		SPELLING
logographic	routes	prephonetic scribbling
recognising words by matching the visual appearance of written word to the spoken word	visual / direct route	semi–phonetic letter names have sounds
↓	+	
alphabetic	auditory / indirect route	phonetic–words divided into sounds and translated into letters
segmenting words into smaller units		
↓		word pattern spelling recognising spelling patterns across irregular spellings
orthographic		
recognising spelling patterns and word chunks		
	▼	
	sight vocabulary read and spelt	
	+	
	knowledge of alphabet for decoding and assembling	

Specific Learning Difficulties (Dyslexia)

Spelling is the process by which we select exact letter representations of what we say to put on paper. Two routes are again used; a direct visual route where learned spellings of words are retrieved or addressed from the memory store; and an indirect phonic route when words are assembled letter by letter and spelt as they sound. Ehri (1991) describes a pre-phonetic stage of scribbling attempts at letters and numbers, a semi-phonetic stage when the child is aware that the names of letters have a sound to them, a phonetic stage when the child segments words into sounds and translating sounds into letters, and finally a word-pattern spelling when the child is able to distinguish common patterns of spelling common to many words, as well as learning irregularly spelt words.

We can therefore see that both reading and spelling require a decoding or phonic skill when words have to be segmented into sounds, sounds have to be recognised and discriminated, translated to and from letters, blended and pronounced. We know already that these are phonological skills which may well be impaired in children with dyslexia. In addition we know that reading and spelling depend on primary oral skills of vocabulary development, grammatical knowledge and comprehension skills that may also be lacking in the child with dyslexia.

Reading and spelling are complicated processes: phonological, visual, orthographic and contextual skills are all needed, at different times. Bryant and Bradley (1986) suggest that some children use the wrong skill at the wrong time. Perhaps the dyslexic reader copes with whole word 'visual' methods in developing a sight vocabulary but due to phonological difficulty fails to translate letters to sounds, or to remember letter-sound associations. The child fails to reflect upon the sound level of language and struggles to retain the phonological form of words in memory. Other readers with poor language skills may fail to use semantic, syntactic or contextual cues and although able to work out words from sounds may confuse meanings of word and fail to understand what has been read.

So we can see that the poor reader will present with a variety of reading and spelling problems. These will reflect different deficiencies in processing language and also different strategies in trying to compensate for those deficiencies.

ASSESSMENT

Is it possible to discover exactly what is going wrong by looking carefully at the presenting characteristics of the child's reading and spelling? It seems that we need to study more than the reading process and to check the spoken language skills as well.

An assessment will help us to make a diagnosis, to identify learning problems leading to the disability and to assist in the planning of remedial treatment.

An assessment must be able to distinguish between normal development and deviations from it. This requires a knowledge of normal language development particularly in its later stages. We need to analyse the presenting symptoms and to investigate their underlying nature. There is no "classic dyslexic". The nature of the dyslexic's difficulties change with time and with the child's development. We must adopt a descriptive approach to these children, rather than attempt to attach labels which mean different things to different people.

It is important, as with all language impairment, to understand the child with dyslexia in relation to his or her whole personal development. Emotional difficulties may either be the cause of a communication problem or may result from it. Subtle disorders may be missed or misconstrued. Failure to reason or understand may lead to a behaviour reaction which may be dismissed as disobedience. We must try to assess to what extent the child is distressed, lacks confidence, or is depressed and withdrawn.

Before commencing assessment a full case history will be taken from the parents. This will provide useful information regarding other indicators of dyslexia such as undetermined or crossed laterality, clumsiness, lack of concentration or poor pencil control in addition to signs of speech and language difficulty. Once at school the teacher can provide information on the child's written and spoken language skills to give the therapist a wider view of how the child copes in a variety of speaking situations. If a psychological assessment has been carried out such information will also be of great importance, as will pertinent information regarding any medical conditions such as hearing loss.

ASSESSING SPOKEN LANGUAGE

When assessing language skills both formal standardised assessments and informal assessment procedures are useful. Formal assessments give objective measures of ability comparing the child's performance with an age related standard. Speech therapists have a variety of standardised methods for assessing vocabulary, comprehension and the use of grammatical rules; although regrettably few that cover the adolescent years.

These are best combined with tasks given to check the child's conversational skills, descriptive and explanatory ability, and word association. The latter includes word selection tasks which reveal the child's storage and retrieval skills.

In addition phonological or auditory processing skills can be assessed using a variety of standardised tests of auditory memory, discrimination and organisation, as well as a variety of tasks to check segmentation, blending, rhyme and sound-letter conversion.

A speech therapist could conduct an oral examination if necessary and general intelligibility of speech will be checked. It is important to detect such conditions as dyspraxia, a motor programming problem with a characteristic picture of speech and written language impairment. Stackhouse (1991) reminds us that when children with speech and language problems do have reading and spelling problems as well this may be for a variety of reasons: speech problems arising out of poor health, physical problems such as cleft lip or palate or cerebral palsy, or fluctuating hearing and attention problems. Such children however are no more at risk than the normal population for 'specific' reading and spelling problems and so need to be diagnosed as such.

ASSESSING WRITTEN LANGUAGE

The child's written language performance also needs assessment. There are standardised tests giving age norms for reading and spelling. Error analysis may also be helpful in deciding whether there is a defect in the auditory or the visual pathways – where there is no detectable hearing or visual loss but the child appears unable to process heard or seen experiences. Thompson (1984) gives the following guide to an error analysis. An auditory channel deficit will have some of the following consequences for reading: substitution of sounds, poor sound blending, knowledge of letter names but not of their sounds, mispronunciations, wild guesses at words, poor 'sounding out' or phonic attack, substitution of words with similar meaning and poor sound-letter conversion. A visual channel deficit will result in reversals and inversions of words and letters, loss of place in text, omission and addition of words, ignored punctuation, substitution of visually similar words, confused order of letters, poor knowledge of spelling patterns and words spelt as they sound.

In the case of spelling, an auditory channel deficit will have the following symptoms: ends of words omitted, synonyms substituted, second letter of blends omitted, substitution with voiced/voiceless counterpart, confusion between high frequency sounds and those perceptually similar, confusion or omission of vowels, poor identification of middle part of word and wild guesses at spelling with at times no relation between sounds of words and letters chosen. With a visual channel deficit the speller will spell phonetically, mixing upper and lower case letters, reversing and inverting letters and producing words with incorrect letter sequences.

Children may perform adequately on testing but fail to transfer their ability to the classroom. They may be making poor use of their capabilities and instead of needing to learn new skills they should receive help with those which they already possess.

Can a speech therapist assess the performance of pre-school children at a pre-literacy stage in order to identify the child who is at risk? If so those with problems can be brought to the attention of the teacher at school entry by the speech therapist. Of course, not all children starting school with impoverished language skills will have been referred to a speech therapist. Similarly, not all children who have received speech therapy will be later candidates for learning support. Many parents will understandably wish their child to start school with no labels attached or special treatment awaiting them. The speech therapist will discuss the matter with parents if it is suspected that there may be reading difficulties. If phonological awareness and pre-reading skills appear to be lacking the therapist can suggest suitable advice regarding pre-literacy activities.

During therapy note can be made of the child's awareness of sounds, letters and rhyme as well as skills of listening and concentration. Speech therapy should of itself promote listening skills by concentrating attention on the sound of the words and by increasing the knowledge of how they are produced. Part of the therapy programme will be to show the parents how to stimulate the child's interest in the sound of letters, rhyme and rhythm. Certain play activities may help to alleviate some of the difficulties in the early school years.

PLANNING REMEDIATION

This leads to the third function of assessment: its role in planning remedial treatment. Having described the dyslexic child's individual reasons for failing, his or her strengths, weaknesses and compensatory strategies, it becomes possible to plan a remedial programme.

We can see with which modalities the child functions best: auditory, visual, vocal or motor, and we can use these senses to improve weaker areas. Snowling (1985) reminds us that the child may have been amenable to training in a way that has masked their underlying true reasons for failure. We are faced with the choice: either we apply treatment directly to the area of weakness or we promote an alternative strategy in an attempt to compensate. It is vital that we relate educational strategies to the individual's needs.

Can the child's needs be met with extra tuition alongside other poor readers, or does he require special teaching methods on his own ? Thompson (1984) suggests a different approach according to the type of dyslexia. Helping an auditory channel deficit by working through the visual modality with some training of auditory skills, and helping a child with visual deficit by working through the auditory modality with some training of visual skills. The dyslexic child with a mixed picture requires a multi sensory approach strengthening all senses: visual, auditory, tactile, and kinesthetic.

The speech therapist's training in phonetics as well as in linguistics has been shown to be beneficial to the successful management of the dyslexic child. Understanding what the sounds of speech are all about, by getting to know how we make them, can help with the difficult task of making sense of seemingly abstract sequences of noise heard at speed in a continuous flow of speech, especially if there are no clear breaks to distinguish where one sound ends and the next begins. Phonological problems need to be tackled individually, using the different senses to help the child find some way of representing and remembering speech at the sound level. One way of helping the child to link a spoken sound to its letter symbol and to remember this association for recall, is to link the sound with its oral movement, that is the auditory-articulatory relationship. Kinesthetic and tactile feedback can be a useful part of a multi sensory strategy. The child can be shown whether or not his vocal cords are moving, what part of the mouth the sound is made in and with what movement, and whether there is contact made or not, or a narrow gap allowing friction to occur. This phonetic knowledge will sharpen the child's pronunciation of words and help the sounds become controllable units. Where similar sounds are confused, as in the case of vowels, high frequency sounds, and blends, learning the 'feel' of the sounds will help to distinguish between them, for example what mouth shape is assumed for which vowel. Watching the oral movements on another speaker's face may help a child to remember the 'visual appearance' of sounds when they are spoken. Children can be shown how to help themselves, by being aware of their own speech and giving them clues about the required sounds and the word boundaries.

Experimenting with articulation and encouraging the child to talk things through, trying out words aloud while writing them, working rules through by saying them aloud in their own words, all these will help engage kinesthetic, visual and memory pathways.

Rehearsal of pronunciation of polysyllabic words by splitting them into syllabic units, each syllable beginning with a consonant sound if possible, will enable the child to see a long, difficult word as a series of short, easy units and enable the planning and sequencing aspects to become instinctive. New vocabulary can be introduced in this way too. When working on phonic skill with a child with a phonological problem affecting spoken word production, the therapist can advise the teacher on the order of acquisition of the sound system, so that the introduction of sounds and their correlated letter forms can be in an appropriate order of complexity.

There are various ways of helping a child to become aware of sound patterns and so to memorise them. For instance, he or she can be shown how vowel sounds determine rhyme (and the letters which are involved.) Showing how different words share common sounds whether initially, medially or finally will help the child to be aware of sound patterning in words and to retain these patterns by linking into memory.

Such sound categorisation practice will help with auditory discrimination and perception, (or input phonology), with the intervening stage of sound segmentation and blending, and with pronunciation (or output phonology). This in turn will help with the holding of the phonological form of words in memory and with the decoding processes of literacy.

The speech therapist's role in helping to plan support for the dyslexic with more subtle high level language problems begins with the careful identification of these. It should perhaps include increasing the ability of teachers to detect such problems. Once any problems have been identified, specific advice should be given regarding the linguistic experiences the child faces in the classroom. This might include encouraging the teacher to use readily understandable language and controlling sentences for length and complexity.

A child should be encouraged to let others know when she or he has not understood. Less obvious language such as metaphors should be explained and the child encouraged to read 'between the lines'.

New vocabulary should be carefully explained by relating to previously known words. All these measures help to produce an organised 'internal dictionary'. Teaching cueing-in methods to help with a word retrieval problem and encouraging the child to self-cue or substitute may also be helpful. A tape recorder can be very useful in developing listening, speaking and self-monitoring skills. The child's ability to judge his or her own speech performance is always worth encouraging.

Chapter 26

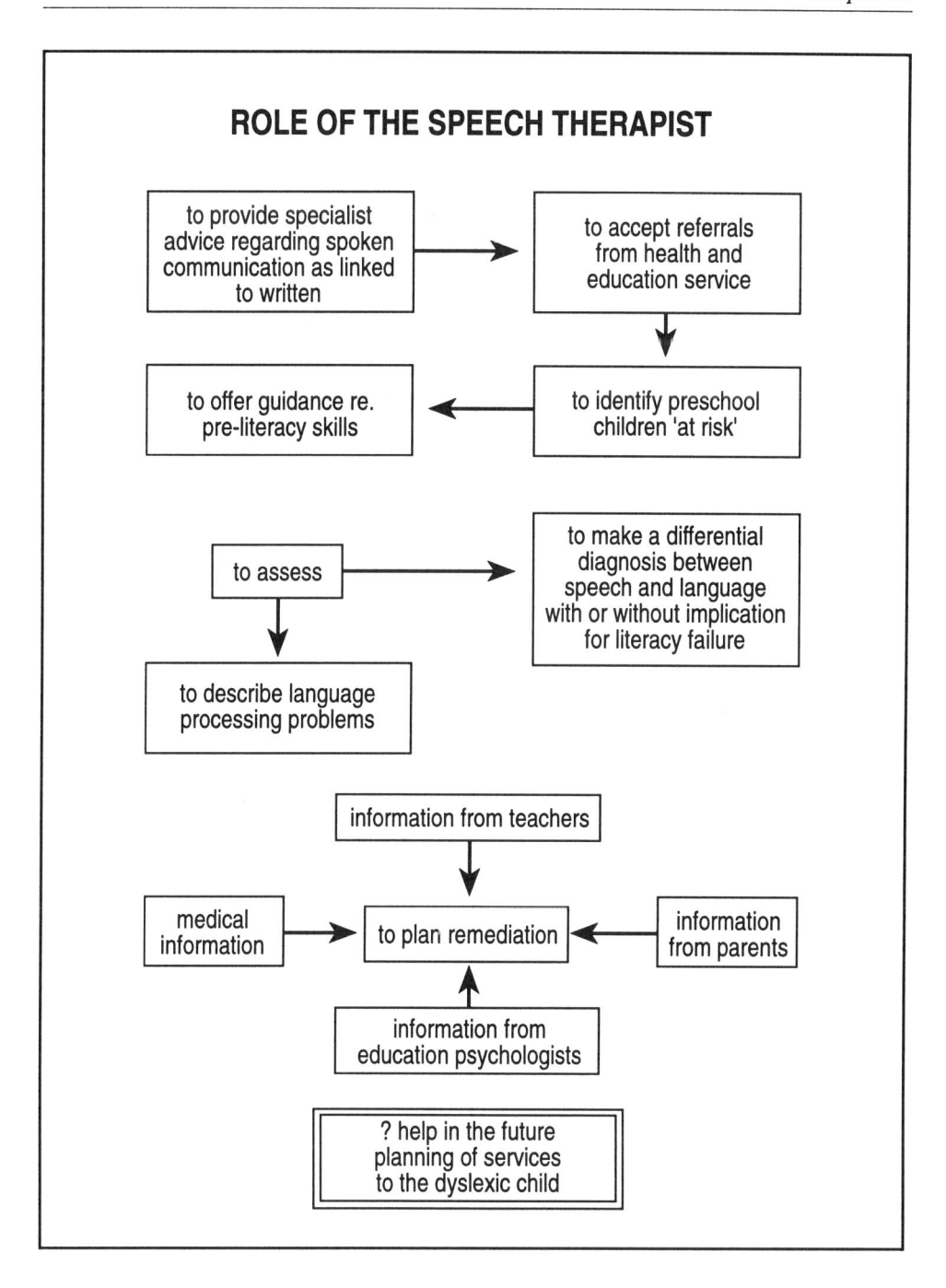

ROLE OF THE SPEECH THERAPIST

- to provide specialist advice regarding spoken communication as linked to written
- to accept referrals from health and education service
- to identify preschool children 'at risk'
- to offer guidance re. pre-literacy skills
- to assess
- to make a differential diagnosis between speech and language with or without implication for literacy failure
- to describe language processing problems

to plan remediation:
- information from teachers
- medical information
- information from parents
- information from education psychologists

? help in the future planning of services to the dyslexic child

Perspectives on Practice 375

Chapter 26

CONCLUSION

Since there appears to be links between spoken and written language it would follow that a specialist in speech should have a place in the management of a written language problem where a spoken component may exist.

Children with dyslexia do appear to suffer from a language disorder which sometimes affects spoken as well as written communication.

Evidence suggests that the child with dyslexia may have difficulties with spoken communication that are only noticed at a later stage by a skilled observer.

Dyslexia is not a condition that erupts at the reading and writing age in absence of early symptoms. Instead children at risk can be identified before they go to school if already presenting with speech and language delay. If dyslexia has precursors in the faulty language development of pre-school children, there may be useful preventative measures which can be undertaken at that age, which will have consequences for parents and for doctors and health visitors who are responsible for routine developmental care of children.

Once identified there follows the responsibility of early management to prevent the frustration and anxiety that may otherwise come. Assessment and guidance for parents and nursery teachers is a role the speech therapist already has. It should perhaps be extended to include specific advice regarding pre-literacy skills where necessary. Therapists should make and maintain contact with the relevant school for as long as required.

Therapists have a range of tests and skills at their disposal for accurate assessment of a child's performance. This allows a distinction to be made between a child showing normal features of later language development and one showing delayed or disordered development. Also between a child showing speech impairment which has no implication for literacy failure and one with underlying or more hidden language problems of significant relevance to literacy failure.

A description rather than a label should be provided for the benefit of the learning support team. This will detail results of standardised tests and task performances, based on the speech therapist's expertise in phonetic and linguistic analysis.

A reading and spelling error analysis will illustrate the effect of these problems and show at what stage their development has been arrested.

If dyslexia is a learning problem which is due to the absence of good reading and spelling models, and if suitable experiences given at an appropriate age can help, then it follows that a speech therapist's experience in the identification and correction of these difficulties may be very valuable in the learning support team.

If dyslexia reflects a difference in learning then it requires a difference in teaching. The question of who carries out remediation is a debatable one. In my own experience the speech therapist's role has been an advisory one with the learning support teacher implementing suggestions. This has been inevitable due to the limitations on my time and I have attempted to monitor developments after the initial-referral. The question of how to provide a useful service to the secondary school is a difficulty one, reflecting, I presume, the lack of attention given to children with language problems in this age group. Literacy development is often presumed to be complete by secondary school entry, at a time when many demands are placed upon it. Some language problems are only revealed at this stage in the child's education, and may surface as academic, social or behavioural problems.

Programmes of remediation are best based on the pooled knowledge of phonetics, linguistics, psychology and education. By sharing information derived from the various disciplines a greater understanding of the child's unfolding difficulties will be achieved. Speech therapists have experience of methods which are likely to be a considerable help to some of these children. Such methods should be used to supplement a teacher's own skills in the identification and care of language-disordered children in the classroom.

The speech therapist is in a very favourable position, being a professional accepted equally as part of the health and education services and so able to receive referrals from many sources.

Speech therapists do have special skills based on theoretical knowledge and clinical experience that can contribute to the management of children with dyslexia, although the extent to which they can fulfil the role I have described will perhaps depend on a degree of specialist knowledge not normally covered in basic training.

There is much to be learnt regarding the best age to concentrate intervention and the best ways of providing remedial treatment given the time constraints and the implications for the use of professional resources. Ultimately these constraints are often financial ones.

In the future it may be advantageous for the speech therapist to be included in planning the service to this client group. This would require changes in the way speech therapy services are currently resourced and organised.

REFERENCES

BISHOP D. V. M. and EDMONDSON A. (May 1987) 'Language impaired 4 year olds: distinguishing transient from persistent impairment. *Journal of speech and hearing disorder.* vol. 52.

BRADLEY L. (1980) *Assessing reading difficulties.: a diagnosis and remedial approach.* Macmillan.

BRYANT P. and BRADLEY L. (1986) *Children's reading problems.* Blackwell.

COLLEGE OF SPEECH AND LANGUAGE THERAPISTS (1991) *Communicating quality professional standards for speech and language therapists.*

CRYSTAL D. (1986) From 'The nature of specific language disorders in children and its assessment: The linguistic angle.' *Advances in working with language disordered children.* I.C.A.N.

ELLIS A. W. (1991) *Reading, writing and dyslexia.* Open University Press.

GERMAN D. (1985) 'Semantic word category in disnomia,' *British Journal for Disorders of Communication,* vol. 20, no. 2.

GOSWAMI V. and BRYANT P. (1990) *Phonological skills and learning to read.* Erlbaum Assoc.

HALES G. (ed) (1989. *Meeting points in dyslexia.* Proceedings of first International Conference on Dyslexia.

HEATON P. and WINTERSON P. (1986) *Dealing with dyslexia,* Better Books.

HORNSBY B. (1984) *Overcoming dyslexia.* Pub. M. Dunitz Ltd.

MANN V. (1984) 'Longitudinal prediction and prevention of early reading difficulty: Annals of Dyslexia.

MOGFORD K. and SADLER J. (1989) 'Child Language Disability,' *Multilingual Matters.*

NEWTON M. J., THOMPSON M. E. and RICHARDS I. R. (1978) *Readings in dyslexia.* L. D. A.

PAVLIDIS G. Th. and MILES T. R. (eds) (1981) *Dyslexia research and its applications to education.* Wiley.

QUIN V. and MACAUSLAN A. (1986) *Dyslexia: what parents ought to know,* Pelican Health Books.

RENALDI W. (Aug. 1991) *The Meaning of moderate learning difficulties at secondary school age.* College of Speech and Language Therapists Bulletin.

SEMRUD, HYND G. and SEMRUD-CLIKEMAN M. (1989) 'Dyslexia and brain morphology.' *Psychology Bulletin.* Vol. 106.

SNOWLING M. and THOMSON M. (eds) (1991) *Dyslexia – integrating theory and practice*. 'Neurological issues in dyslexia,' D. Duane; Metaphonological abilities and literacy,' J. Morais; 'The development of reading and spelling in children: an overview,' L. Ehri; 'Dyslexia: The obvious and hidden speech and lang disorder,' Stackhouse J. and Wells B. Proceedings of the second International Conference on Dyslexia. Whurr.

SNOWLING M. (1985) *Children's written language difficulties,* extract – quoting Wigg, Semel and Crouse (1973); and Frith. Stackhouse – Segmentation speech and spelling difficulties. Windsor. NFER Nelson.

SNOWLING M. (1987) *Dyslexia: A Cognitive Developmental Perspective.* Blackwell.

SNOWLING M. *et al* (1986) 'Segmentation and speech perception in relation to reading skill: a developmental analysis.' *Journal of Experimental Child Psychology.* vol. 41.

SNOWLING M., STACKHOUSE J. and RACK J. (1986) 'Phonological dyslexia and dysgraphia – a developmental analysis,' *Cognitive Neuropsychology,* no. 3.

SNOWLING M., VAN WAGTENDONB., STAFFORD C. (1988. 'Object naming deficits in developmental dyslexia,' *Journal of Research in Reading,* vol. 11, no. 2.

STACKHOUSE J. (May 1982) 'Investigation of speech and reading performance in speech disordered children.' *British Journal of Disorders of Communication.* vol. 52.

STACKHOUSE J. (1988) 'Relationship between spoken and written language disorders' in Mogford and Sadler's *Child's Lang Disability,* Vol. 1, Implications in an educational setting. Multilingual Matters.

THOMSON M. (1984) *Development Dyslexia, Its Natures assessment and remediation.* Arnold.

YOUNG P. and TYRE C. *(1990) Dyslexia or illiteracy.* Open University Press.

Chapter 27

LANGUAGE IN CONTEXT

EILEEN FRANCIS

INTRODUCTION

In the early 1970s little attention was paid to language in education issues and even less to the issue of communication in the classroom. The publication of texts by the Open University in the mid seventies (1972) and the Bullock Report 'A Language for Life' (1975) increased interest in language across the curriculum. The development of understanding provided by the disciplines of applied linguistics and social psychology, in relation to verbal and non-verbal communication, meant that the 1970s was the decade when communication became an issue for Scottish education. Teacher educators and subsequently teachers were able to claim that communication had intrinsic value as well as instrumental value for education. The subject of teacher talk and student talk became legitimate areas of study.

During the 1980s communication was subsumed into the wider concern for personal and social development programmes in the curriculum. In the 1990s, communication is back on the agenda in the context of discussion about values in education – 'communication' and 'respect for others' are key words in the values statements being produced by schools.

This contribution to 'Perspectives on Practice' asks you to consider the concept of language in context from the perspective of your own experience. How near or far from your own assumptions and expectations are the statements contained in this chapter?

THE SCHOOL IS A SPEECH COMMUNITY

Lakoff and Johnson (1980) have described the conceptual system, in terms of which we both think and act, as being fundamentally metaphorical in nature. They explain that we are not normally aware of our conceptual system and that we think and act automatically along certain lines for reasons which are not obvious. 'Concepts structure what we perceive, how we get around in the world and how we relate to other people. Our conceptual system thus plays a central role in defining our everyday realities'. Understanding our own conceptual system is the primary task of education and language is an important source of evidence.

Communication is based on the same conceptual system that we use in thinking and acting. Education, being a human enterprise taking place in relationships, needs to take the dialogue metaphor as a paradigm.

In the past the transmission metaphor in education has been dominant in Scotland. Progress was made with a dialogical approach to education in the 1980s, but recently the transmission metaphor has begun to compete for attention again as teachers discuss more efficient ways of increasing information flow to the student. The vocabulary of packing, sending, targeting and receiving tends to mask interpersonal aspects in education.

Tiberius (1986) has described the nature of the tension which exists between dominant and competing metaphors in education: 'Proponents of different metaphors tend not to confront each other; they talk to each other. However, they are like people talking different languages. They see different things when they look from the same point in the same direction. There is a tendency for misunderstanding as similar terms, concepts and experiments are used to convey new meanings in new contexts and in new relationships with each other'.

Those who promote the study of educational discourse tend to use specific terminology to inform other educationalists about their priorities in education. Such phrases as 'School is a place where the learner is empowered;' 'a community of learners;' 'and induction into a life-long learning process', give the impression that the school aspires to be an ideal speech community.

Saville-Troike (1982) describes speech communities as holding knowledge and behaviours in common. The speech community is characterised by patterns of language use, interpretation, rules of speaking and attitudes concerning language which are identifiably specific. What is of interest in the speech community is the range of interactional functions and domains present and the processes which separate, unify or stratify them. Effective communication requires individuals to orientate themselves by applying a set of rules in any given situation. Teachers need to identify the verbal and non-verbal forms appropriate to the community and to understand how they define and constrain interpersonal interaction in communication situations.

THE CLASS IS A GROUP.

The school is a communication system within which groups are constantly forming and reforming for the purpose of carrying out a variety of learning tasks. The teacher has two main functions: to maintain the group and to help the group to work. Learning tasks will not be achieved if the teacher gives greater attention to maintaining the group. It is helpful if the teacher has a sense of the group as a dynamic process and has developed process thinking skills (Bramley 1979) so that the double task of managing the group and managing the task is in balance.

Teachers and students are inextricably linked in the group process. It is for the teacher to decide which sessions during the day will highlight the process objectives of an activity and which will focus on content objectives. A class group in which both teachers and students have developed process thinking skills will be able to work effectively.

Process thinking enables us to understand that there are significant elements of the communication process which can be under the teacher's conscious control: the physical arrangement of the context in which learning is to take place; the organisation of the group within that context; the leadership style which will be adopted to accomplish the task. The imagery of the physical setting conveys the communication rules.

The student entering the classroom receives messages about the learning context. Tables and chairs are spaced for individualised learning, grouped for content-orientated work, placed in table-free circles for process-orientated work. Learning tasks need to be considered in relation to the most appropriate communication style to meet performance criteria: individualised work; paired work; groups of different sizes and compositions. In any one day the students will move through a series of different communication contexts. It is the teacher's task to observe how each is handled. Students will show different strengths and weaknesses in communication and individual preferences for specific learning contexts.

The leadership style of the teacher will be adapted accordingly, providing directive leadership when information-giving is required and a variety of styles which facilitate different types of groupwork (Francis 1985). The significant factor is for teachers to be aware that at one and the same time they are members of their groups as well as leaders. It is as if a semi-permeable membrane separates the leadership and membership regions of the group which allows initiating roles in communication to emerge from either region. When students initiate, teachers mediate the communication, maintaining responsibility for helping the students to manage themselves and the learning task.

While these three 'process shapers': physical setting, group composition and leadership style are under conscious control, groups have a dynamic of their own and function accordingly. Teachers need awareness and insight to analyse the dynamics of the group, understanding that the personal histories of the students and their expectations and assumptions about the learning process will affect the way in which the group works. These issues are addressed in the literature on psycho-dynamics, a body of knowledge concerning human functioning which gives priority to the role of emotional development and its effects on physical, social and intellectual growth.

COMMUNICATION STYLES ARE DIFFERENT

Individuals bring a variety of communication styles to the group. They need the capacity to analyse aspects of communication style which influence the group dynamic. How does a group member influence the group process: Is the group 'pushed' towards completion of a task or 'pulled' towards a resolution? Skilled communicators will use a combination of both styles.

Affiliative behaviour in a group helps it to work. Trower, Bryant and Argyle (1978) described affiliative behaviour as a combination of controlling and rewarding behaviours which communicate assertiveness and rapport. When the balance is inappropriate some participants appear aggressive, autocratic, or inappropriately dominant, while others, conversely, may appear indecisive, lacking in conviction or submissive.

Facial expression, eye contact and voice quality are more significant than verbal behaviour in communicating affiliative behaviour. One experiment (Mehrabian, 1977) provided the statistic 38% voice, 55% face and 7% verbal expression, to describe the relationship between verbal and non-verbal features in interpersonal communication. This statistic can be reassuring to students who are low contributors in groups. The way in which we listen to others can assert competence in learning as effectively as the amount of talk produced.

Research on discussion in Scottish classrooms (Francis, 1990) indicated that low contributors in the class group gain much from working together. They become more effective contributors as a result. High contributors, when placed with similar students have to address their own communication style and realise that listening is as significant as talking when completing a discussion task.

Swift, Gooding and Swift in Dillon (1988) describe the important of 'wait-time' between student-student and teacher-student interventions to encourage thoughtful responses. They observed that an increase in wait-time between contributions in a discussion had the effect of raising the cognitive level of a discussion.

Recently Tannen (1992) has described communication style in terms of a combination of features. She describes the way in which we communicate considerateness as 'rapport talk' and high involvement as 'report talk'. In practice teacher education appears to be more concerned with developing a communication style characterised by high involvement and report talk than with considerateness and rapport talk. Teachers are role models for students and they may project ambivalence in the learning context about communication styles characterised by sensitivity, perceptiveness and the capacity for reflection.

The value placed by teachers and students on different communication styles in the classroom will convey attitudes to aggressive behaviour. For example, in communication between boys and girls, between those from different ethnic backgrounds, and in a lack of tolerance of those who are observed as silent members of the group.

DEVELOP COMMUNICATION IN CONTEXT

If change is to occur in learning relationships, teachers will need genuine commitment and the inner belief that classroom discourse can be improved. In some schools the constraints are physical – group size and physical space communicate that student talk is of lesser significance than the role of the curriculum or of the teacher in classroom interaction. In these settings discussion activity may be marginalised and the emphasis placed on individualised or resource-based learning.

Parents and students still expect teachers to be the centre of classroom practice. Teachers are expected to be in control. Research on discussion shows that many students undervalue talk in education because they feel it is not as open to scrutiny as the written word. They distrust the transient nature of oral communication.

The discipline which helps educationalists understand language in context is applied linguistics. Literature produced by English language teachers for foreign language learners and by speech therapists working in clinical settings provides frameworks which are helpful in school-based learning environments. The pedagogical descriptions of applied linguistics, however, have been resisted by many educationalists who adopt a content-orientated rather than a process orientated approach to education.

Recently it has been encouraging to observe that there are attempts to reassess the contribution of applied linguistics in education. The establishment of the project on specific learning difficulties sponsored by the Scottish Dyslexia Trust at Moray House Institute and research initiated by the SOED on the role of the speech therapist in education indicates that this resistance is under review.

LANGUAGE IS CENTRAL TO THE LEARNING PROCESS

Nisbet, speaking at the National Forum for Educational Research in Scotland in 1991 stated:

'Learning results from a personal construction of knowledge: learning is not something that happens to students: it is something that happens by students. We need to give more attention to the motivation to learn, to the affective and social elements in learning .. building confidence is a crucial step in learning: student's perceptions of the task and of themselves, their self image, influence their learning profoundly. Our current focus on the cognitive aspects of learning needs to be balanced by the recognition of the learner as an active, feeling participant in the learning process'.

Educationalists who agree with this analysis have applied a range of alternative approaches to learning based on pedagogical descriptions which are different from those contained in familiar curriculum guidelines. Three approaches are provided here as an illustration.

(i) **Making thinking explicit: the metacognitive approach:**

This approach influenced by the work of Feuerstein, De Bono and Lipman states that where motivation and achievement are below the national norm we should look carefully at pupils' attitudes to their education. We need to encourage pupils' feelings of ownership and control of their education and this can be done by helping them to develop awareness and control of their own thinking processes. Students can develop thinking frameworks which can be applied across the curriculum as a strategy to tackle difficulties and to increase their ability for philosophical enquiry.

Students are encouraged to think explicitly using a self questioning procedure. When defining the task they can ask themselves 'What am

I supposed to be doing?' Next they might consider the transfer of learning experience: 'Have I done something like this before?' 'What will help me this time?' At the planning stage the questions to be addressed are 'What will I need?' 'How will I go about it?' Later when evaluating their performance they ask 'Did I do what I was supposed to do?' 'How could I do better next time?' 'What do I need to work on?'

Cross curricular programmes based on this approach are now being implemented in a number of schools in Lothian region and will become a feature of the new 5-14 curriculum.

(ii) **Learning to discuss**

The Standard Grade curriculum development programme provided the context for an experiment which aimed to make the discussion process explicit in the learning environment. It was suggested that the development of explicit understanding of the constituent elements of discussion skill should be on the agenda of all schools. A discussion profile of each student was produced on the basis of behavioural evidence (What did the students do in discussions?); cognitive evidence (How were the students thinking in discussion?); affective evidence (how did the students feel in discussion?) and interpersonal evidence (How were relationships managed in the discussion group?). The skills which were monitored for behavioural evidence included organising self for discussion; attending to others in discussion; listening to the content of the discussion; contributing to the discussion; responding to the contributions of others; observing and showing awareness of the roles others take; adopting different roles in discussion appropriate to context, and enabling the group to complete a discussion task.

The discussion development programme demonstrated how each of these skills could be further refined. For example the components of 'contributing skill' could be developed in the direction of proposing an idea; building an argument; supporting an argument; seeking information from others; giving information to others; disagreeing appropriately in argument. A range of activities and self assessment measures to help students with their own personal development of discussion skills were piloted in schools and made generally available to teachers in publications produced during the 1980s.

A teacher reporting on the effectiveness of the discussion programme commented on a particular task to improve contribution rate:

'It is quite clear that the pupils are learning about and improving their discussion skills. The task demonstrated that the quieter pupils are very capable of discussing ably but are clearly often submerged by the louder, more aggressive members. The success of the experiment was highlighted by the obvious enjoyment of the low contributors' group. The group with the highest contribution rate particularly enjoyed the challenge of the new group. They found it much harder work and made a real effort to observe discussion skill rules. When asked about the re-constituted groups everyone was pleased or just as happy as they had been previously – there were no negative comments.'

As the use of 'learning to discuss' programmes increases, more attention can be placed on the cognitive dimension of discussion. Learning objectives can focus on monitoring the quality of discussion performance. For example, the quality of reflectiveness – how thoughtful, reflective and searching do the students show themselves to be? Or the quality of consistency – how do the students demonstrate coherence, consistency and consecutiveness in though and argument?

(iii) **Differentiating Language in Context**

The metacognitive approach and the learning to discuss programme are finding a place within the framework of 5-14 developments for students of every ability. It is to be hoped that attention to these approaches will generate greater awareness and sensitivity to the needs of individual students, particularly those with specific language difficulties. The study of language in context challenges our assumptions on the traditional view of ability. Some potentially able learners show significant differences in their ability to process language. There is a need to re-consider our approach to language work with able and less able learners alike.

There are some students – labelled as having problems in terms of motivation and ability – who conceal a learning difficulty. Language difficulties are subtle, they do not always announce their presence.

They may not be documented in the school records. They may, however, affect potentially able students and interfere with their educational development.

Differentiating the language curriculum is dependent on developing accurate observation skills. Assumptions about the abilities of children should not be based on impressionistic observations. All observation is subjective and tends to encourage the use of value judgments: 'He lacks confidence.' 'She is talkative.' What do these descriptions mean and on what evidence are they based? When a teacher observes 'lack of confidence' are they referring to a child who contributes little in class? Whose face lacks expression? Who sits on the edge of the group? Who stares at the worksheet before beginning to work? Who fails to complete the work sheet in the time allowed?

Language investigations are ineffective if interpretations are based on psychological and social assumptions derived from observation of non-verbal and interaction behaviour. Difficulties with verbal behaviour which affect the capacity for learning may be masked by inappropriate attention to the psychological overlay of social interaction.

Studies carried out in schools in connection with the Moray House Special Educational needs course (Francis 1979,1985) showed that specific language assessment activities carried out during a 40 minute session could provide the teacher with useful information about the language processing abilities of a class group. Some students were revealed as highly able in their understanding of vocabulary and others less able. Some students had little difficulty in understanding a series of instructions while others showed problems in understanding and failed to complete tasks. Findings for receptive language abilities e.g. listening and understanding in context, were not necessarily matched by those for expressive language. The logic of cause and effect used in a story sequence might be observed in some students, but not in others. The amount and quality of the language produced in story telling was variable. Findings on auditory memory tended to be most variable. For example, some students were able to remember ten digits with ease, others had difficulty in remembering six.

Observations of students during a discussion activity provided a different perspective. Some of those who failed to sequence logically or to use complex and varied language constructions spoke a great deal in discussion.

The learning support service in schools should be able to demonstrate a range of specialised strategies which provide the evidence required for diagnostic assessment. However teachers should also consider developing a series of activities based on the vocabulary of the existing curriculum, the instructions required by the curriculum and a sample of specific tasks to assess the language differences within a class group.

Evidence from observations of student language should have an effect on the teacher's own use of language. The language of explanation can be considered more critically when there is an awareness that some students are less able to understand verbal complexity. Efforts can be made to ensure that instructions are succinct and carefully phrased. Instructions should be repeated if there is evidence of genuine misunderstanding rather than as a matter of course.

Research has shown that increased use of statements by teachers stimulates student interaction. Questions should be used to obtain information. Questioning as part of a ritual classroom game should be avoided. Communication is being used purposefully when there is an increase in the listening ability of the teacher and a greater understanding of the different learning styles in the class group. Deep structure learning needs to be valued more highly than surface structure learning based on memory.

APPLICATION TO A SPECIFIC CURRICULUM CONTEXT

The Geography curriculum at Standard Grade provides a specific context in which to test the application of the statements contained in this chapter. The 'Lurcher's Gully Enquiry' is a case study which is used for the investigation of conservation and economic issues to encourage understanding of the nature and purpose of environmental education. The investigation is based on groupwork, resource based-learning and discussion.

Understanding of the discussion process ensures that the groups are organised around low and high contributors: those who need more time to process language work together, while those who process language more quickly also work together.

During the simulation of the Lurcher's Gully enquiry, those who are linguistically able handle complex documents on conservation and economic issues on behalf of their peers. Those who are less able recreate the arguments of the conservationist, the developer or the ski-lift owner at an anecdotal level. The teacher mediates the experience so that each student constructs the argument at a particular reporting level – verbatim, process or conceptualised reporting. Students meet in pairs differentiating the arguments or matching similar arguments. Each level is valued as a different kind of contribution which needs to be considered for a thorough investigation of the topic. The different language levels of the debate can be highlighted and the need to integrate the various points of view emphasised.

In writing, the differentiation of the class group's work is developed in a similar way. As in any organisational system, those who are able to be responsible for the routine completion of questionnaires and worksheets are regarded as performing as valuable a function as those who create journalistic reports or speeches to Ministers of State or leaders of concerned bodies.

The language of 'core' and 'extension' which is often applied to the development of the curriculum for use in differentiated learning contexts has no relevance in this example – the work of every student is regarded as 'core' work.

Self assessment strategies which are included as a part of this learning system are vital so that students document the differences between one argument as compared to another and learn to understand the difference between anecdotal, verbatim and conceptualised reporting.

SUMMARY

This chapter emphasises that appropriate language in context is the key to the effective differentiation of learning. There is a need to understand the content of the student's language – their ideas, their formulation, their management in thinking. To understand the capabilities of the student in terms of the form of spoken language – the process of articulation, the amount and quality of vocabulary and syntax. To understand the use of language – in one to one, small group and large group interaction, and to understand the communicative context, not only of the learner, but also of the teacher and of the curriculum.

REFERENCES

BRAMLEY W. (1979) *Group tutoring: Concepts and case studies.* Kogan Page.

BULLOCK SIR A. (1975) *A Language for Life.* HMSO.

CASHDAN A.. et al (1972) *Language in Education.* Open University.

FRANCIS E. (1979) *Social Skills Training in Education.* Education in the North. Aberdeen.

FRANCIS E. (1985. *Learning to Discuss.* SCCC.

FRANCIS E., GILLON M., McKAY C. (1985) 'Communication for Special Educational Needs: A Multi-disciplinary Approach.' *British Journal of In-service Education.* Vol. 12.

FRANCIS E. (1988). 'Group Processes' in Dillon, J.T. (ed). *Questioning and Discussion: a Multi-disciplinary study.* Ablex Publishing Corporation. New Jersey USA.

FRANCIS E. (1990) 'Working Together on Discussion' in BRUBACHER M., PAYNE, R. and RICKETT K. (eds) *Perspectives on Small Group Learning: Theory and Practice.* Rubicon, Ontario, Canada..

LAKOFF G. and JOHNSON M. (1980) *Metaphors We Live By.* Chicago University Press.

MEHRABIAN A.. (1972) *Non-Verbal Communication.* Aldine-Atherton. Chicago.

SAVILLE-TROIKE M. (1982) *The Ethnography of Communication.* Basil Blackwell.

SWIFT, GOODING and SWIFT, (1988) 'Questions and Wait-time' In DILLON J.T. *Questioning and Discussion: A Multi-disciplinary Study.* Ablex Publishing Corporation, New Jersey, USA.

TANNEN D. (1990) *That's Not What I Meant.* Virago. London.

TIBERIUS R. (1986) 'Metaphors underlying the improvement of teaching and learning.' *British Journal of Educational Technology.* Vol. 17. No. 2.

TROWER P., BRYANT B. and ARGYLE M. (1978) *Social Skills and Mental Health.* Methuen.

SECTION 7

EMOTIONAL CONSIDERATIONS

Chapter 28

THE EMOTIONAL WORLD OF SPECIFIC LEARNING DIFFICULTIES

STEWART BIGGAR and JENNIFER BARR

It is the Wimbledon final. The players have won a set each. The newcomer is leading 4:1 in the final set. She loses the match.

Sports commentators can talk of an athlete having (or lacking) the self-belief and confidence that helps them to reach peak performance at the crucial moment. From another tack, people with a disability are often described as overcoming obstacles, showing great courage and determination. Are these mere colloquialisms? Or do self-belief and confidence, courage and determination, have psychological validity in the context of the everyday achievements of children? How are these achieved? By what processes? What can help and what may hinder?

In this chapter we argue that emotional factors lie at the heart of the experience of Specific Learning Difficulties, and we offer a tentative model of some of the processes involved. We hope to show that each child's view of him or herself – the unique, individual self-concept – is crucial to the way in which the child responds to and deals with their learning difficulty, and we describe some of the ways in which other children and adults can affect this self-view. It will be helpful first to highlight some key ideas.

SKILLS AND STRATEGIES

The work of Piaget (1971) and of Vygotsky (1962) has had a powerful influence on the way that psychologists see children's development. Piaget maintained that learning of all kinds involves the gradual altering of a mental model of the world, so that it fits with new information as it is gathered. The mental construction must accommodate to new knowledge as it is assimilated, and this adapted model then guides the search for additional data. Piaget talked of the process as being driven by the child's desire to achieve active mastery.

One of Vygotsky's contributions was to show how important other people are for a child's learning. Learning is a social and interactive process. In day-to-day life as in formal schooling, adults pick out for children those things which are important, they confer meaning on events and define what is to be learned; that is, they transmit cultural knowledge and values.

Wood (1989) offers an excellent discussion of these ideas and describes recent thinking. It is useful, he suggests, to think of learning as the development and refinement of skills and strategies. We do, quite literally, learn how to learn. This applies equally to playing football, having a conversation or reading a book. We refine our skills through using them, whether they be physical, social, or academic, and we develop higher order strategies as we practice them in different contexts. Fisher (1990) provides a useful account of the translation of such ideas into practice.

Bryant and Bradley (1985) and Goswami and Bryant (1990) argue that an important source of reading difficulties lies in the way a child approaches the task of reading. The job for the practitioner is to enable the child to understand the purposes and processes of literacy and thus to develop new and more effective strategies. It is not that a child who is failing to read does not use strategies, but that the strategies used are ineffective in enabling the learning to extract meaning from print: not learning to read or write conventionally is **also** a product of learning.

There seem to be many routes both to success and failure at reading. Bryant and Impey (1986) proposed the notion that children with dyslexic problems develop and rely on their own individual strategies just as normal children do. Seymour (1987), comparing case studies of normal and dyslexic readers, concluded there is little homogeneity in either group. Szeszulski and Manis (1987) compared the word recognition strategies used by dyslexic children and normal children matched for reading age. They found the strategies to be essentially similar, with the more advanced dyslexics indistinguishable from normals. The difficulties for the younger reading age dyslexics lay in the area of grapheme-phoneme correspondence rules.

Learning correspondence rules is important in the early stages of reading, but they can be fully used only by a child who already knows a good deal about literacy. Garton and Pratt (1990) describe important skills of pre-literacy. One of these, the child's level of phonological awareness, has been claimed to be the best single predictor of later reading success that we have (Bradley and Bryant, 1983; Goswami and Bryant, 1990). Skilled reading is a complex task depending on perceptual, cognitive and linguistic processes. Hall (1989) argues that readers do not proceed in strict sequence from basic perceptual units to overall interpretation of a text:

Rather, the skilled reader derives information from many levels simultaneously, integrating graphophonemic, morphemic, semantic, pragmatic, schematic and interpretive information simultaneously . . . The skilled reader is purposive and a continuous monitor of his or her own comprehension. (1989; 160)

SELF-CONCEPT

Johnston (1985) describes the extensive verbal reports of three adult disabled readers and concludes:

> . . . we need to consider more seriously explanations which stress combinations of anxiety, attributions, maladaptive strategies, inaccurate or non-existent concepts about aspects of reading, and a huge variety of motivational factors. (1985: 174)

Increasingly it is being recognised that even subtle influences on self-esteem can matter in children's learning. The interactive effects of self-esteem and skill development are, of course, unavoidable. There must of necessity be an interaction of some kind. Children who are confident and who acquire important skills easily can enjoy the benefit of a positive interplay between self-esteem and attainment. Other children, who may not have developed some crucial pre-literacy or social skills, and for whom the start of school becomes daunting and even frightening, may experience failure early on in their school careers.

What are the emotional consequences for a child who has been unable to develop effective skills and strategies in certain key areas of the curriculum and who is exhibiting specific learning difficulties? Searching for a model of the emotional processes involved in coping with specific difficulties, we considered the stages by which people often come to terms with other information – any information – that has a profound impact on their sense of self (there are useful parallels in thinking of a gay person 'coming out', or of a person assimilating the knowledge that they have contracted a serious illness). There can be an initial period of fear and confusion, where what the person expects of themselves is not what in practice it seems possible to achieve. Then there can be a stage of accurate identification and 'naming' of the difficulty, accompanied by a sense of relief that there is a reason, there is an explanation and it is not a question of fault or blame. As self confidence is slowly restored, the sympathetic understanding of at least one other person may be crucial. At a certain point the person may feel strong enough, or sure enough that 'this is who and how I am', that they are able to go public with the information. How well the reactions of others are handled at this stage depends both on the quality of available support, and on the emotional strength and confidence of the individual.

A study was undertaken in Dumfries and Galloway by one of the authors (Biggar, 1993). In the research a sample was constructed of twenty children of primary or secondary school age from across the Region, who had been identified as having specific learning difficulties (dyslexia). Information about the history and circumstances of the children was gathered from four sources:

- from the case psychologist or from case notes;
- from interviews with parents, who described their experiences in trying to make sense of the problem and in seeking help;
- from interviews with teachers, covering areas such as teaching methods, specialist training and resource allocation; and
- from interviews with the children, exploring their feelings. These interviews included assessments of self-concept using Battle's Self-Esteem Inventory (1981).

These sources offer quite different perspectives on the experience of specific learning difficulties, and a fuller account is available from the author. Here, we shall concentrate on the children's own experiences, and examples drawn from the case studies are presented under the headings of finding out, moving on, and going public. The final sections look at factors which appear to hinder and factors which foster good emotional progress.

FINDING OUT

The children in the study whose specific difficulties were in the area of reading often seemed to be the ones most affected by their own realization of failure. Children who were old enough and willing to reflect on their early years at school, claimed to have realized their difficulty before it became an issue for the adults. No doubt based on perceptions of their own performance up to that time, and their experience of developing mastery, the children assumed that they would continue to progress comparably with their peers. This expectation was made explicit by some children who had transferred to school with friends from playgroup or nursery. They reported becoming aware that they were not learning things which their peers seemed to find easy, and their first response was almost always to conceal or deny it.

It was this feeling of confusion and lack of understanding which the children reported they found most distressing. Certainly they tried to conceal their difficulty from friends, because friends – who also do not understand the problem – can 'section you out as being stupid', 'tease and humiliate you'. But there were also elements in many cases of concealment from self, of avoiding opportunities where failure might be experienced and of diversionary behaviour. There is no doubt that it was very painful for some children to admit their difficulty to themselves, and this could involve considerable self-blame. A young man whom we may call **A** could remember problems before P3, but in P3 he found that he 'could not read (his) own writing'. During that year A had four different teachers in succession. He reported thinking that they had each left because of him – this was his fault. During the following year it became clear to **A** that he was falling behind at nearly everything. He did not understand and he did not know what to do; he became quite anxious.

Literacy is highly valued in our culture and, as the medium for a great deal of the school curriculum, it has a prominent role. The rate at which children learn to read sometimes appears to be used as a measure of their overall ability to learn. While true for certain youngsters this can be a damaging assumption for those whose specific learning difficulties mean that though poor at reading, they are otherwise able. They may be driven to different forms of avoidance or concealment, and can be subject to a variety of definitions by teachers. In the sample two of the twenty children were first referred to the Psychological Service because of behaviour problems, though later these came to be regarded as stemming from specific learning difficulties. Moreover, in several cases where poor attainments were the stated reason for referral, these came with reports of associated behavioural patterns, including inattention, distractibility, laziness, immaturity and/or defiance.

Children themselves do not use these terms. Children talk of 'having a mental block', of 'stopping and starting', of 'facing a page of letters that make no sense' and of 'freezing'. They report feelings of embarrassment, humiliation, shame, anxiety and guilt. They can feel stupid, useless, frustrated and angry. They lose confidence in themselves as learners, and often they lose their friends.

Feelings of this kind were evinced by all but two of the sample. The longer such feelings were carried the more serious an issue their difficulties became. It looks as if becoming trapped in this desperate, private and lonely emotional state can delay the possibility of more useful learning. One pupil **R** held himself in very low esteem. He had little confidence socially, as measured by Battle's Inventory, and he thought poorly of his academic ability. He did not believe his parents understood in the least how he felt. **R's** measured reading and writing attainments on leaving school at sixteen were lower than they had been at age nine, despite several years of learning support. **R** emanated an air of great sadness, and yet he was reflective and articulate. He is now fully employed in a skilled trade.

MOVING ON

Starting to make sense of the difficulty for oneself seems to be an important step forward. The crucial role of peer relations is suggested by the case of **J**, a twelve year old girl. She had managed until P5 to conceal the extent if not the fact of her problem with maths. Her friends seem to have accepted that **J** would ask them questions and copy their answer, and to this extent they colluded with her. **J's** social confidence was reflected in other areas of her self-concept: she reported being teased 'a little bit' but it had not disturbed her: she described some of the techniques she had used to avoid doing sums in public, and she was clearly skilled at changing the subject and deflecting attention from herself on to others. Her difficulty was eventually discovered by her mother when she was unable to count the change after a shopping trip.

Other children testified to the relief they felt at having even one or two friends who understood that they found some things difficult, and whom they could openly ask for help. Having someone who did not tease them helped them to bother less about those who did. This remained important whether or not the children felt supported and understood by adults.

An element central to the children's construction of their difficulties is the way they think that they – and their difficulties are perceived by others. **S** described the friendship that developed with his learning centre teacher at primary school. Attending the centre brought taunts from his peers, he recalled, but being there was relaxing, purposeful and relieved his stress. His teacher did not define him as lazy or stupid, and she did not pressurize him to complete work. **S** understood that what she demanded of him was that he try his best. He emphasized the importance of support by someone you feel comfortable with. (We may note in passing that the importance of a close relationship with a trusted adult is highlighted by Marie Clay in the Reading Recovery Programme (1985). **S** described how his teacher's sympathetic approach had helped him see his difficulty more clearly, and so had reduced his fear and anxiety.

D the youngest child in the sample, had benefited from the identification of his motor learning difficulty pre-school, and felt supported by his parents and teachers. When he was also slow to begin reading, his difficulty was recognized early and appropriate learning support began. **D** is presently only seven but he was able to say:

'Teachers say it'll never go away, but I'll be able to work round it. I don't seem to be able to work round it now. I think I've got round something then it comes back and stands in my way.'

D was strong enough to be able to say of those who called him handicapped, 'I think they're just horrible people', but clearly he will need on-going sympathetic support to maintain his present positive approach to his difficulties.

GOING PUBLIC

The differences across the sample on measures of self esteem were very large. In fact these children's scores covered the full range from very high to very low on all three subscales of Battle's Inventory, that is on measures of social confidence, feelings about school and perceived parental support.

In general, those with difficulties in less restricting areas such as spelling saw themselves quite positively, especially if they believed that their difficulties had been recognised and were being tackled. Nevertheless, there were two children in the sample whose reading attainments exceeded their chronological age, yet who still regarded themselves as academically poor due to their spelling difficulties. There were other children whose academic attainments were actually poorer but who achieved greater confidence.

There is a stage beyond this, where children not only manage to make sense of their problem and to hold a positive approach to it, but become successful in overcoming feelings of public embarrassment. **S**, described earlier, was placed in a segregated, low-ability class on transfer to secondary school. He knew that he did not belong there but reported 'it took time to prove I wasn't different in other ways'. He did rejoin mainstream, and by third year 'everyone had forgotten'. His difficulty, which persists to the present day, was no longer an issue to him socially; having once felt different from others, **S** now felt normal. 'It is hard work and it wears you down'. The main benefit to **S**, however, was that the problem was now in the open, and it was in perspective.

By contrast, **T** felt he had done all the coping by himself. He did not acknowledge any particularly significant others. In spite of a learning difficulty severe enough to merit the preparation of material on audiotape in class and SEB examination concessions. **T** now attends a degree course at college. His parents had sought an independent assessment of his difficulties when he was thirteen. He recalled being told he was dyslexic and that he could either 'lie down and accept it' or else work very hard. Prior to this **T** had been exhibiting school phobia and complaints of illness which had no identifiable physical cause. In **T's** case the use of the dyslexic label had provided a useful explanation which reduced both his and his parents' confusion and distress. His parents no longer accepted (though previously they had) the school's assertion that T was a daydreamer who did not try. He himself no doubt benefited from his parents' reappraisal, and from the specialist support he started to receive, but what he regarded as more important personally was his own courage in declaring his difficulty and his determination to overcome it.

We have tried to draw common themes from the testimony of the children interviewed, even though each of their experiences was unique. Those who have succeeded in forming a view of their difficulties which, on the one hand, does not distort their sense of worth and, on the other, enables them to make progress, have done so by different routes and with different kinds of help. Those who have not been able to move on seem to have been hampered by similarly diverse factors. An interplay between self-image and academic progress is clearly evident from this study and even more crucial the importance of alleviating a child's feelings of guilt and self-blame as a pre-condition for progress. Children require help to reach a personal reconciliation with the fact of their difficulties and their chance of positive academic outcomes are improved when this help is prompt, sympathetic and on-going.

FACTORS WHICH HINDER EMOTIONAL PROGRESS

It is possible to identify several factors in the cases of these twenty children which seem to be associated with continued or exacerbated difficulties. The largely qualitative nature of the research does not permit any claims about causal relationships, though some may be suggested. (Robson, 1993). These are discussed under three general headings.

1   Inappropriate attributions

It has been noted that in many cases the poor attainments of children were attributed to behavioural patterns of inattention, distractibility, laziness, immaturity and/or defiance. Parents have generally regarded teachers as the experts and to an extent have believed and acted upon such definitions. In eight of the twenty cases, parents described the scenes of anger and distress which followed their attempts to apply pressure on their children to complete homework or extra assignments. The parents themselves became impatient and angry and the children became upset. For children who already feel confused and guilty, this increased pressure is not helpful. It may serve to damage the sense of alliance and support they have a right to expect from their parents, and it can hinder the process of reaching a true understanding of their difficulty. Even academically it doesn't work.

For some children the further failure they experienced was sufficient signal to their parents that explanations in terms of laziness were not adequate. Others, like **T**, began to exhibit behaviour of a neurotic kind before the perceptions of parents and teachers changed significantly. A few have carried these unfortunate labels throughout their school careers. If the only explanation offered to children who are failing is that the responsibility is theirs – that they are stupid or lazy or both – then in time they may come to believe it. What action can they take in self-defence?

2   Disagreement between adults

Avoiding, if we can, any questions of which view is 'correct', it was clear that in over half of the twenty cases the explanations of specific learning difficulty held by parents and teachers were at odds. This is consistent with the findings of the team from Stirling University (Riddell et al., 1993). If we take the children's self-esteem measures as an outcome and relate them to parent reports of disagreements with school, some interesting patterns emerge.

In cases where the disagreement has been particularly strong there is a tendency for children to feel that neither home nor school is on their side. Perhaps the problem turns into a focus on the dispute between home and school, such that neither is able to offer the confident reassurance which children so need. One exception was a fourteen year old girl, **K**, who scored very high on the measure of perceived parental support. However, she had been removed from school on the grounds that she was making no progress and was being bullied. Her scores on the academic and social confidence subscales were both very low. **K's** parents seem to have supported her general self-esteem but she was more emotionally dependent on them than a girl of this age might normally expect to be. She has not so far found ways to develop her own sense of worth or independent confidence. In purely academic terms, her difficulties were not severe, perhaps equivalent to those of **J** referred to earlier.

The outcomes for **J** have been quite different. Not only did her mother state specifically that she had tried to avoid any suggestion of blame or pressure towards her daughter, she also said she had withheld her doubts over the school's explanation for **J's** lack of progress. When **J** was diagnosed independently as being dyslexic, her mother resisted this label also, on the grounds that it might cause dissent with the school. Her mother strove for solutions for **J's** difficulty; she did not allow her own opinion or anxieties to confuse her primary aim of reaching a consensus in the approach of home and school. That she largely succeeded is suggested by **J's** high (at times very high) scores on different aspects of her self-concept, taken at the end of P7. She was rather more defensive than most children her age, but not so as to cast doubt on her clear statement that she expected to do well in secondary school. Her attainments have improved markedly.

J's success reinforces the suggestion that conflicts between home and school may be one cause of poor outcomes. In this example the flexibility of **J's** mother helped to create a positive ethos, but it might equally be the case that in different circumstances it is the professionals who may need to conciliate. Prompted by their understanding of the emotional world of learning, there may be occasions (e.g. where parents already hold strong views) that the professionals could make genuine and unpatronising attempts to seek common ground and workable compromise, even if this means moderating their own judgements for a time.

3   Verbal abuse

The effect of teasing by peers on a child with specific learning difficulties probably depends on that child's emotional resilience. All the children who were interviewed reported having been teased on account of their difficulties, but the importance of this was by no means the same for them all. Some of the children discussed earlier had been able to come to terms with their difficulty personally and socially, and for them teasing had either stopped or become unimportant. Others reported that it was serious and on-going. They remained defensive and secretive at school to avoid opportunities for ridicule. One of these was **M**, a girl of fourteen. She described her frustration at not feeling able to admit the extent of her difficulty in class, and therefore not getting help as she required it. **M's** self-esteem was uniformly low, even though she had skills that were well-developed in art, music and drama, and these were important to her.

M volunteered that her social and vocational skills course at secondary school had included a series of talks on various handicapping conditions. Why, she suggested, could this syllabus not be extended to include specific learning difficulties? Verbal abuse, or the fear of it, is at best unpleasant and, for emotionally vulnerable or exposed children, potentially quite damaging. An element of guided class discussion may indeed be useful.

FACTORS WHICH FOSTER EMOTIONAL PROGRESS

The preceding discussion suggests that a child's chances of emotional progress are best when certain conditions can be met:

- where there is an accurate description of the child's abilities and difficulties, uncluttered by anxiety or prejudice;
- where those adults who are significant for the child agree about the nature of the problem and how to tackle it;
- where they offer a construction or rationalisation which makes sense to the child, and which both preserves a sense of value, and anticipates progress; and
- where the child feels understood by a trusted adult.

Piaget writes of a child's desire to achieve active mastery, of wanting to understand and to be able to do things. Faced with failure, children's attempts to understand often result in doubts about their competence, and so damage their confidence. If the situation continues, the effects are compounded. For example, poor readers need both courage and encouragement to abandon strategies for learning which are ineffective. At the outset they have no first-hand evidence that better strategies can be found and so they may resist the attempts of others to teach them new skills.

There is an importance placed on literacy in our society, and difficulties with skills in this area can arouse strong feelings in parents. Children who are looking for some explanation or understanding of their lack of ability are sensitive to the heightened emotions of others. They may even in their own minds assume responsibility for having caused the upset themselves.

Without exception, the single most frightening event which poor readers reported was being asked to read aloud in class. It served no useful purpose in their eyes. Such children need to be helped to build their confidence. They are entitled not to be made anxious, not to be humiliated and not to be forced by another to disclose their difficulty in public.

There does not seem to be any single formula by which the needs of all children who have specific learning difficulties can be met, but this study does stress the importance of what Vygotsky called the 'better informed adult'. The children whose measured outcomes were better all round enjoyed a relationship of trust with someone who they were confident understood. Sometimes this was a parent, sometimes a teacher. Peers have also been an important source of support. If treated and respected as individuals, children do seem to be better at putting their difficulties into a wider perspective, and thus coming to terms with them. The requirements on a supportive adult seem to be:

- to be honest and open
- to remove guilt or blame
- to hold feeling for the child
- to preserve the dignity of the child
- to help the child to feel safe
- to maintain positive regard
- to value the child
- to act as the child's advocate

The circumstances of every child are different and the pattern of events which leads to the identification of a learning difficulty will always be unique. A child's emotional world is also a highly individual and personal place. In order to offer effective help, an adult needs some appreciation of how it feels for this child to have this difficulty. What we are arguing for in this chapter is a differentiation of the interpersonal to match the differentiation of the curriculum.

REFERENCES

BATTLE J. (1981). *Culture-free SEI: self-esteem inventories for children and adults.* Seattle: Special Child Publications.

BIGGAR S. (1993). *Specific Learning difficulties: A qualitative case study approach.* Unpublished project, University of Strathclyde.

BRADLEY L. and BRYANT P. E. (1983). Categorizing sounds and learning to read – a causal connection. *Nature,* 301, 419-421.

BRYANT P. E. and BRADLEY L. (1985). *Children's reading problems.* Oxford: Blackwell.

BRYANT P. E. and IMPEY L. (1986). The similarities between normal readers and developmental and acquired dyslexics. *Cognition,* 24, 1212-137.

CLAY M. M. (1985). *The early detection of reading difficulties.* 3rd edn. Auckland, NZ: Heinemann Education.

FISHER R. (1990). *Teaching children to think.* Oxford: Basil Blackwell.

GARTON A. and PRATT C. (1989). *Learning to be literate.* Oxford: Basil Blackwell.

GOSWAMI U. and BRYANT P. E. (1990). *Phonological skills and learning to read.* Hove, Sussex: Erlbaum.

HALL W. S. (1989). Reading comprehension. *American Psychologist,* 44, (2), 157-161.

JOHNSTON P. H. (1985) Understanding reading disability: a case study approach. *Harvard Educational Review,* 55, (2), 153-176.

MARSHALL C. and ROSSMAN G. B. (1989). *Designing qualitative research.* London: Sage.

MILLAR R., CRUTE V. and HARGIE O. (1992). *Professional interviewing.* London: Routledge.

PIAGET J. (1971). *Biology and knowledge.* Edinburgh: University of Edinburgh Press.

RIDDELL S., DUFFIELD J., BROWN S. and OGILVY C. (1993) *Specific learning difficulties: policy, practice and provision.* Department of Education, Stirling University.

ROBSON C. (1993). *Real world research: a resource for social scientists and practitioner-researchers.* Oxford: Blackwell.

SEYMOUR P. H. K. (1987). Individual cognitive analysis of competent and impaired reading. *British Journal of Psychology,* 78, 483-506.

SZESZULSKI P. A. and MANIS F. R. (1987). A comparison of word recognition processes in dyslexic and normal readers at two reading-age levels. Journal of *Experimental Child Psychology,* 44, 364-376.

THOMSON M. E. and WATKINS E. J. (1990). *Dyslexia: a teaching handbook.* London: Whurr.
VYGOTSKY L. S. (1962). *Thought and language.* Cambridge, Mass.: The MIT Press.
WOOD. (1989). *How children think and learn.* Oxford: Blackwell.

SECTION 8

PRACTICE, PROVISION AND RESOURCES

Chapter 29

SPECIFIC LEARNING DIFFICULTIES, LEARNING SUPPORT TEACHERS AND THE IMPACT OF CHANGING POLICY

SHEILA RIDDELL, SALLY BROWN and JILL DUFFIELD

INTRODUCTION

Between 1990 and 1992, a research team based at the Department of Education, University of Stirling, undertook a research project commissioned by the Scottish Office Education Department to investigate policy, practice and provision for children with specific learning difficulties. From the start, it was clear that we were investigating an area in which feelings run high. Even the term 'special learning difficulties' was disliked by some of those with whom we would be working; for them 'dyslexia' was the problem to be addressed and other labels were educationalists' jargon. This is not a matter of mere semantics; it goes to the core of how people conceptualise these kinds of difficulties, what they see as rational policy and how they believe the needs of these children should be met.

The views of learning support teachers, parents, voluntary organisations and education authority personnel on the nature of specific learning difficulties, ways of identifying children with these difficulties and appropriate forms of provision, were sought. This paper explores learning support teachers' ways of construing specific learning difficulties and the type of assistance they considered necessary. It then contrasts these views with those of education authority personnel and parents, reported in detail elsewhere (Riddell, Duffield, Brown and Ogilvy, 1992), and highlights the shifting conceptualisation of learning difficulties over the past twenty years from a child-deficit to a curriculum- and school-deficit model.

Within this context of changing ideas, learning support teachers have been encouraged to redefine their role, focusing on consultancy and co-operative teaching rather than individual tuition. This new role, however, has tended not to be welcomed by parents of children with specific learning difficulties, who have emphasised the needs of their individual child and argued that these cannot be met within normal classroom provision. Since government policy has continued to emphasise not only the new role for learning support staff, but also the rights of parents as consumers of educational services, there is potential for conflict between education professionals and parents of children with specific learning difficulties, as they struggle over competing definitions of the nature of the problem and its treatment.

Before turning to a discussion of the research findings which map out these tensions, we set the scene by looking at the relevant ideas embedded in two reports which have had a major influence on policy and thinking over the last decade and a half.

THE POLICY CONTEXT

The Warnock Report, the Progress Report of Scottish HMI and the SCOSDE guidelines

A central theme of the Warnock Report (DES, 1978) was the need to replace statutory categories of handicap with the notion of a continuum of special educational needs. Warnock maintained that there was no sharp dividing line between children with learning difficulties and others and that it was important to recognise the interaction between an individual and his or her environment as the source of learning difficulties. Modifying a child's learning environment, therefore, was likely to be an effective means of tackling their difficulties. Although envisaging a continuing role for special schools, Warnock indicated that most children with special needs should receive their education in mainstream schools.

The rejection of a child-deficit model was also evident in the report by Scottish HMI, published in 1978 and entitled **The Education of Pupils with Learning Difficulties in Primary and Secondary Schools in Scotland.** Inappropriate curricula and teaching methods were identified as the root cause of many pupils' learning difficulties:

> Many learning problems arise because the demands being made by schools are still too great for the linguistic competence of some of their pupils. (SED, 1978, para 4.9, p. 124).

HMI pointed to some of the dangers of withdrawing pupils for individual tuition, the traditional means of providing teaching support. It was argued that difficulties were likely to arise when pupils were re-integrated into their mainstream class, since they might have lost touch with the general work of the group. De-contextualised drilling in particular skills was seen as unlikely to be of long term assistance since pupils might well be unable to apply what they had learnt. Practice in specific skills was preferred and these skills should be context-specific and undertaken in mainstream classes. The report emphasised that the ultimate responsibility for dealing with children's learning difficulties lay with subject or class teachers.

> Pupils with learning difficulties should be taught, as far as possible, by class and subject teachers. If they are unable to give the proper kind of help, then the pupils involved should be given the additional support of a remedial teacher. That fact, however, does not reduce the class or subject teacher's responsibility for the pupils, or absolve him (sic) from continuing his (sic) own endeavours. (SED, 1978, para 4.11, p. 25).

This emphasis on the paramount responsibility of the class or subject teacher had implications for the continued existence of an autonomous remedial department. HMI commented:

> There has been a steady trend towards the establishment of separate 'remedial departments' in which they (remedial teachers) offer separate courses. Such a trend appears to be at odds with the indicators of our survey which suggest that remedial education is a whole-school responsibility and an inherent element of the work of subject departments. (SED, 1978, para 4.17, p. 27).

More than a decade later the Scottish Committee for Staff Development in Education (SCOSDE, 1990) published a document entitled **Guidelines for Diplomas in Special Educational Needs** which clarified and modified the recommendations of the HMI Report. Summarising the roles of learning support teachers, it suggested that they should be concerned:

(a) through consultation and collaboration, in helping class and subject teachers to plan and develop responses to the range of learning difficulties

(b) through consultation and collaboration, in the development of a differentiated curriculum at whole school and department levels to meet the range of learning difficulties found in mainstream classes;

Chapter 29

(c)   in supporting individual learners, either through direct teaching or through co-ordinating support from visiting teachers, parents or specialist services;

(d)   in working with management on the formulation and implementation of whole school or college policy;

(e)   in initiating and contributing to staff development related to their other roles.

Of particular interest to the research reported here, was the brief emphasis put by the Guidelines on learning support teachers being able to offer specialised individual help to children 'with specific learning difficulties, including those of a dyslexic kind' (para 4.1, p. 22) No elaboration of this point was provided however.

Our research was carried out, therefore, in a policy context where the Warnock Report, the 1978 Progress Report of Scottish HMI and the SCOSDE guidelines had instigated a shift in emphasis in provision for children with learning difficulties. Rather than seeing these children as the prime responsibility of the remedial teacher, the class teacher was seen as fulfilling the most important role in meeting their needs. The newly-styled learning support teacher was cast in a consultancy role, with individual tuition seen as less important than curriculum modification. Both Warnock and the SCOSDE guidelines recognised that children with specific learning difficulties might require individual tuition, but the implications of this not being in line with the general changes in policy were not pursued.

THE IMPACT OF POLICY DEVELOPMENTS ON THE PRACTICE OF LEARNING SUPPORT

What has been the impact of this change in policy, especially those parts which relate to the underlying causes of learning difficulties and the role of learning support teachers? The study conducted by Allan, Brown and Munn (1991) is one of the few pieces of research which has considered the implementation of the HMI's recommendations. Their work in one Scottish region identified problems that had arisen as a result of tensions within the views expressed by HMI on the role of the learning support teacher. On the one hand, it was argued that the new responsibilities, particularly consultancy and co-operative teaching, were considerably more exacting than the traditional work of small group and individual tuition. On the other hand, the HMI report implied that remedial teachers (now learning support teachers) no longer had prime responsibility for children with learning difficulties and did not require a departmental base from which to operate. It was unclear, therefore, whether the status of learning support teachers was being enhanced or downgraded and this had led to confusion in practice, as learning support and mainstream teachers attempted to delineate their respective functions and areas of responsibility. In secondary classrooms, there was a danger that the mainstream teacher either handed over all responsibility for children with learning difficulties to the learning support teacher, or attempted to retain complete control, interpreting any autonomous action on the part of the learning support teacher as a challenge to their own professional autonomy. The message of this research was that effective co-operative teaching and consultancy were not easily achieved.

A number of commentators south of the border have also noted weaknesses in the these kinds of approaches to learning difficulties. In her research on the work of learning support teachers, Bines (1988) found that teachers simply did not have enough time or resources to provide individual help and implement a more detailed and specialised approach to learning. She suggested that the goal of meeting the individual needs of all children was unrealistic and possibly misplaced. Rather, she suggested, teachers should tackle at an institutional level factors which led some children to be regarded as educational failures and accorded lower status:

> This could involve attempting to change conceptions of 'achievement', stressing the common rather than the different nature of teaching and learning processes for all pupils and also developing the social as well as the academic goals of the school. (p. 157).

Dyson (1990) has also expressed reservations, not least because the existence of learning support staff has led mainstream teachers to label some pupils as 'special' and hence someone else's responsibility. He has suggested that the learning support teacher should redefine his or her role as an effective learning consultant. Initial steps to achieving this would be the renunciation of the learning support department, the abandonment of the special needs label and the abdication of the specialist teaching role. The weakness in Dyson's argument, is its neglect of the fact that merely renaming learning support teachers is unlikely to change mainstream teachers' view of their function. What is clear is that both Bines and Dyson are advocating a shift even further away from the notion of the learning support teacher meeting the needs of children with difficulties on an individual basis.

Not all commentators, however, have agreed that learning support teachers should regard consultancy as their most important role. Moses, Hegarty and Jowett (1987), reporting on external support services to mainstream schools, found a marked evolution in the work for children with special educational needs. While the service's earlier role had concentrated on individual reading support, by 1984 they were dealing with a wider range of difficulties, in both primary and secondary schools and, significantly, were offering an advisory service to teachers as well as working directly with children. The authors of the report expressed reservations, however, about the new emphasis on consultancy rather than direct work with individual pupils.

Moses, Hegarty and Jowett were also interested in the question of **where** individual tuition should take place. They were aware that the practice of withdrawal from class had been the subject of considerable criticism, though not always for sound reasons. A new orthodoxy seemed, they suggested, to have been established in some quarters in which help inside the mainstream class-room is seen as the **only** solution and withdrawal was regarded as undesirable (p. 113) Despite its unpopularity among official policy makers, however, withdrawal has remained popular with junior school teachers. Gipps, Gross and Goldstein (1987) found that teachers regarded withdrawal as the most useful type of help that could be provided for children with learning difficulties and felt it should be extended to more pupils. Moses, Hegarty and Jowett (1987) concluded:

> Advisory and support services who wish to move away from this model of support may face a distinct lack of enthusiasm, if not actual opposition from schools and they need to be very clear about their reasons for rejecting this popular practice (p. 113).

Payne (1991) also defended withdrawing children from the mainstream class for individual tuition on an occasional basis. He claimed that teachers who practised this form of support had been led over recent years to feel like 'accomplices to some form of educational apartheid'. On the basis of interviews with pupils who had experienced both support in the mainstream class and temporary withdrawal for individual tuition, he found that they generally favoured the latter. He also stressed the need for a clear distinction to be drawn between temporary withdrawal and permanent segregation in a remedial or special class and listed the advantages of withdrawal identified by Gipps, Gross and Goldstein (1987).

The findings of Payne's research suggested that children withdrawn from the mainstream class for learning support worked harder on more appropriate work and developed a better relationship with the teacher. Other advantages arose from the support teachers' expertise and the privacy of the activity; these helped to avoid:

the distressing spectacle of a child forced to read aloud in a stumbling parody of fluency to a teacher who is intent on maintaining in the rest of the room, that very silence which is increasing the child's discomfort at his own obvious inability (p. 62).

The debates on the nature of learning difficulties and the role of the learning support teacher have had major implications for children with specific learning difficulties. Although Warnock and the 1978 HMI Report acknowledged that individual tuition may still be helpful for some children, the central thrust of policy was to blur distinctions between categories of difficulty, focus on within-school rather than within-child factors as the source of difficulties and concentrate intervention at the classroom and the school level rather than withdrawing the individual child. Some commentators have argued for an even tighter focus on systemic intervention rather than endeavouring to remediate individual children's difficulties (Dessent, 1987). A contrasting view, however, could argue that the reasons for rejecting the notion of difficulties residing within the child and abandoning individual tuition have been rooted in orthodoxy rather than sound educational judgement. Certainly this is the view of many parents of children with specific learning difficulties (see Riddell, Brown and Duffield in press) who continue to demand that the particular difficulties of their children are recognised and remedied by expert tuition delivered on a one-to-one basis.

But how do learning support teachers construe the nature of specific learning difficulties and appropriate focus of provision? It is to the views of this critical group of providers that we now turn.

THE RESEARCH FINDINGS

The nature of the learning support teachers' sample

In this strand of our research 400 questionnaires were distributed to learning support teachers in eleven Scottish regional authorities and six divisions of one large authority. An overall response rate of 59 per cent provided 206 completed questionnaires and 30 blanks. All but one of the 17 Scottish regions and divisions were represented. The response rate in different areas appeared to relate to the dominant view of specific learning difficulties within the region. In two regions, an earlier interview study had revealed strong opposition to the use of categories of learning difficulties (including specific learning difficulties) and here the response rate was particularly low.

In general, those who replied were highly experienced teachers, with only 19 of the 206 having less than 10 years' total teaching experience. The Diploma in Special Educational Needs was held by 36 per cent and these were significantly more likely to be secondary than primary teachers.

Learning support teachers' conceptualisation of specific learning difficulties and dyslexia.

An open-ended question asked learning support teachers to provide a definition of specific learning difficulties. More than a third (37 per cent) attached no particular meaning to the term and suggested that almost any learning difficulty might be described in this way:

Any specific factor preventing full access to the curriculum.

Problems due to medical, cognitive, developmental or acquired difficulties.

Some learning problem that can be identified and worked on.

However, 40 per cent indicated that specific learning difficulties were characterised by literacy difficulties and a discrepancy between attainment in this area and general ability. Although about a quarter agreed with the statement that children with specific learning difficulties were likely to have higher than average achievements in some areas, more than half suggested that children throughout the ability range might experience specific difficulties.

When asked whether they would ever use the term 'dyslexia' to describe a learning difficulty, 70 per cent indicated that they would, and those with ten or more years of teaching experience were more likely to use that term than their less experienced colleagues. Of those who used the term, the majority defined it as difficulty in decoding symbols, a much tighter definition than they had given to specific learning difficulties. A substantial number expressed reservations about use of the term dyslexia, however, suggesting that they would only use it with certain groups of people such as colleagues or the educational psychologist. Teachers who said they did not use the term explained that it was 'too generalised', that it referred to 'many difficulties, not one' and that it was 'too convenient a label'. A number of these answers conveyed irritation with parents 'latching on to the word' and 'wanting to call every learning difficulty dyslexia'.

On the matter of group distinctiveness of children with specific learning difficulties, we found an interesting difference between learning support teachers and other educationalists. Our interviews with education authority personnel had indicated a split between those who regarded children with specific learning difficulties as a discrete group (25 per cent of respondents) and those who felt their difficulties, although distinctive, should be seen as part of a general continuum (50 per cent). The remaining 25 per cent had also subscribed to the notion of a continuum of learning difficulties but had been opposed to the recognition of particular categories of difficulties within it. When the learning support teachers were asked whether children with specific learning difficulties formed a discrete group who were distinct from others with learning difficulties, however, two thirds agreed with this statement and a third disagreed.

In response to a question on the degree of priority attached to meeting the needs of children with specific learning difficulties, our respondents were almost equally split, with almost half saying they attached high priority to meeting their needs and the others claiming that it was impossible to say – they determined priorities on an individual rather than a group basis. A very small minority suggested that low priority was attached to meeting the needs of such children. However, comments written in the final open section of the questionnaire conveyed learning support teachers' anxiety as they attempted to establish priorities between the needs of children with global learning difficulties and specific learning difficulties. Such dilemmas were particularly acute in areas with high levels of social deprivation. One teacher commented:

> The problems are also found in a much larger group of children [than those diagnosed specific learning difficulties] who do not have 'higher than average achievements in other areas'. These pupils often benefit greatly from a structured individual approach but rarely get it . . . They have not the necessary pre-reading skills before they are required to begin learning to read and write . . . These children often come from language-deprived homes and live in socially deprived areas. Children who are diagnosed as having specific learning difficulties are almost always in my experience from socially advantaged backgrounds with parents who can effectively ask for help. Children from disadvantaged backgrounds with similar difficulties are unlikely to get specific help; the difficulties are blamed on their home background and lack of parental skills; schools and education authorities seem to think there is little they can do.

In attempting to summarise the views of this sample of learning support teachers, two findings are especially striking. First, a much higher proportion appeared to be conversant with (and ready to use) the term 'dyslexia' than with 'specific learning difficulties'. Secondly, they were much more likely than policy makers and managers to see specific learning difficulties (or dyslexia) as qualitatively different from global learning difficulties and to attach a high priority to meeting the needs of the former. In some ways, therefore, their stance might be seen as midway between that of local authority personnel and parents – almost all the parents in the research sample believed their children should be described as dyslexic and quite distinct from those with more global learning difficulties.

We have to be cautious, however, about claiming this as a generalisation across learning support teachers in Scotland. As we indicated in our comment on the response rate to the questionnaire, we suspect that those teachers who are opposed to any categorization of learning difficulties (and so to specific learning difficulties as a category) are under-represented in the sample. Given this caveat, we might also infer from these findings a certain lack of confidence about how to deal with children with these kinds of difficulties. On the one hand, those who come from privileged backgrounds may have parents who interfere in ways that are seen by the teachers as unhelpful. On the other hand, those from disadvantaged backgrounds may either not have their specific difficulties picked up (the assumption is made that social deprivation signals **global** learning difficulties) or receive inadequate support in the home.

If learning support teachers appear not to be confident at this general level of thinking about specific learning difficulties, can we expect things to improve as they get down to the more specific practical tasks of identification and assessment of those difficulties?

Learning support teachers' accounts of appropriate forms of identification and assessment.

Less than half of learning support teachers (42 per cent) expressed substantial confidence in their ability to identify children with specific learning difficulties, but a further 50 per cent reported some confidence. Teachers who used the term dyslexia and had more than ten years experience in learning support work were more likely to express confidence than others. Because dyslexia was defined more tightly than specific learning difficulties, it was not surprising that these teachers were more confident in their ability to recognise the phenomenon.

About 70 per cent of primary and 50 per cent of secondary learning support teachers claimed their school had systematic procedures for the identification of children with specific learning difficulties. In both primary and secondary schools, a team approach was used in identifying children with specific learning difficulties; however, class teachers in primary were more likely to be involved in this process than subject teachers in secondary. This suggested that the view advocated by HMI that children with learning difficulties are the prime responsibility of the mainstream teacher was less established in secondary than primary. Three quarters of the respondents said that formal diagnostic testing was used in their schools, either administered by themselves or the educational psychologist; about a third also used informal testing and observation to diagnose problems. This diagnosis was carried out mostly at primary school: 40 per cent of children were identified in P1-P3 and 40 per cent in P4-P7.

Overall, the learning support teachers conveyed feelings of confidence in their ability to identify children with specific learning difficulties and diagnose their problems. This was in marked contrast, however, with the perceptions of the sample of parents who singled out assessment as one of their major areas of dissatisfaction, complaining that the methods used by the learning support teachers were imprecise and inaccurate and schools were often reluctant to arrange an assessment by an educational psychologist. Furthermore, they felt that formal assessment was often conducted too late in a child's career for effective remedial action to be taken.

Location of provision
Moving on from the identification of specific learning difficulties to the meeting of needs, learning support teachers were asked where such children generally received their education. The most frequent response indicated this was in the mainstream class with some withdrawal. Education in the mainstream class without withdrawal was also common, particularly in the secondary school. Just under 10 per cent of the teachers reported that children would spend some time in a reading centre and 3 per cent identified withdrawal to a special class within the mainstream school.

Teaching methods and the role of the learning support teacher
In the context of the changing official conception of the role of the learning support teacher to one of greater consultancy and co-operation, together with parental anxiety about the lack of individual tuition for their children, how did the learning support teachers conceptualise their role? The teachers were asked to rank order the following aspects of their role: acting as a consultant to other members of staff; working co-operatively with class/subject teachers; direct teaching for individual pupils outwith the normal class; contributing to a range of special services within and outwith the school for pupils with learning difficulties; and providing and arranging staff development in relation to learning difficulties. **Figure 1** shows the numbers of learning support teachers who regarded particular aspects of their role as being of prime importance. Co-operative teaching was regarded as most important by 42 per cent followed by consultancy, (23 per cent); only 20 per cent saw individual tuition as the most important aspect of their role. **Table 1** compares primary and secondary learning support teachers' views of the

importance of individual tuition and shows that primary teachers saw it as much more salient for their work than did secondary teachers.

When given the opportunity to comment, teachers indicated that they had responded in different ways to requests to rank the different aspects of their role. For some, it appeared that priorities were clear-cut. One teacher for example, expressed a direct antipathy towards the role of individual tutor, commenting 'I have no time or inclination to tutor'. Another, however, who ranked individual tuition as the least important part of his work, was far more ambivalent. He wrote of 'a constant anxiety' as to whether withdrawing pupils for direct support should be promoted to greater importance.

Overall, it appeared that most of these learning support teachers had accepted Scottish HMI's re-definition of their role as consultants and co-operative teachers rather than individual remedial tutors. However, given the view of the majority of the teachers in our sample that children with specific learning difficulties have very distinctive needs, it is not surprising that some teachers experience conflict between different aspects of their role. One teacher expressed this conflict vividly:

> I am sole learning support teacher in a school of just over 600 pupils. Eleven children with Records of Needs, nine for specific learning difficulties. Various other pupils with less severe specific difficulties not recorded. Two pupils with severe specific learning difficulties have Reading Centre help two periods a week; the rest are the school's and my total problem. We also have traditional slow learners, a boy with muscular dystrophy and a boy with moderate learning difficulties. We rely on whole staff awareness and push to support these pupils. I am also involved in staff development and curriculum development. A tutu and fairy wand definitely required.

The combination of learning support teachers endeavouring to follow official policy on their new role, and the enormous practical pressures on them in schools, is generally bad news for parents of children with specific learning difficulties who are looking for individual tuition.

Guidelines and teaching materials for children with specific learning difficulties

By this time it will be clear that the learning support teachers were not at their most self-assured when thinking about specific learning difficulties. What, therefore, did they have to hand in the way of advice or material resources for this aspect of their work? Our respondents were asked whether they had any guidelines on appropriate teaching methods for children with specific learning difficulties. About 60 per cent said that they did and secondary teachers were more likely than primary to report that they had received guidelines from voluntary organisations. Those working in primary, however, were more likely to report an awareness of regional guidelines.

About 70 per cent of respondents said that they had teaching materials designed for tackling specific learning difficulties, but only 27 per cent regarded these as significantly different from those recommended for other learning and literacy problems. The minority who claimed that they used distinctively different materials said that these focused on structured approaches, repetition, breaking down outcomes into manageable sections, use of phonics, visual or auditory targeting, emphasis on hand-eye co-ordination and multi-sensory methods. An important feature was that the interest level was aimed at an older age group than the reading content. The majority who did not use special materials for children with specific learning difficulties said that all children benefited from carefully structured techniques and that there was no need to allocate scarce resources for distinctive items:

> The cost of supplying special material would be prohibitive. It is the teacher's approach that makes the difference.

Again, there was a marked contrast between the views of parents and teachers. Whereas a majority of the learning support teachers defended their use of a common approach for all children with learning difficulties, parents argued strongly for a distinctive approach for those with specific learning difficulties.

Learning support teachers' assessment of their effectiveness
In general, learning support teachers expressed a moderate degree of confidence in their ability to assist children with specific learning difficulties in overcoming their problems and in advising colleagues about the most effective courses of action. The number of years' experience as a learning support teacher seemed to be a crucial element in the overall level of confidence with those who had worked in this area for ten years or more expressing a significantly greater degree of confidence. Parents, however, took a much more critical view of the effectiveness of school provision. Although the progress report of HMI had established a new direction for learning support provision, the controversy remained particularly with regard to the scepticism among parents about the effectiveness of co-operative teaching and consultancy in comparison with individual tuition. Specific learning difficulties is an area where such controversies are likely to be in evidence since parents, supported by voluntary organisations, have been

clear in their demand for an individualised programme delivered by expert learning support teachers outwith the mainstream class. Such demands have cut across the view not only of HMI, but also of regional authority policies, which emphasise the whole school approach based on the delivery of a differentiated curriculum within the mainstream class.

DISCUSSION OF THE FINDINGS

In this paper we have drawn attention to two major strands of policy and thinking about learning difficulties which would be expected to have had a major impact on practice: new ways of conceptualising learning difficulties and new roles for learning support teachers. The report of the research has concentrated, therefore, on learning support teachers' perspectives on these two strands together with some comparisons with the views of policy makers/managers and parents. The distinctiveness of the research is its setting in the context of specific learning difficulties rather than special educational needs more generally.

Turning first to how learning support teachers think about the nature of specific learning difficulties, there was little evidence of consensus among the group. A significant minority seemed unfamiliar with the particular meaning of the term (and used it to refer to any learning difficulty), less than half were in line with the most widely accepted description (a difficulty, often in literacy, which is not reflected in achievement in other areas) and two thirds were at least as comfortable with the term 'dyslexia' as with 'specific learning difficulties'.

Despite the apparent uncertainty about the concept, two thirds of the sample of teachers saw children with specific learning difficulties as forming a discrete group with problems that are qualitatively different from those of children with more global learning difficulties. A rather smaller proportion of the teachers (about half) felt that this group should be given priority treatment; most of the others were committed to deciding priorities on the basis of the needs of individual children rather than the nature of their difficulties.

How do these perceptions match official policy? The findings from another part of our research suggested that the dominant view in regional authorities reflected that of Warnock and Scottish HMI reports in conceptualising a continuum of special educational needs. Specific learning difficulties were seen as lying along this continuum, according to their severity, and as being catered for within existing provision. Ideas of a discrete group of children and terms like dyslexia tended to be eschewed by regional personnel.

In contrast, the sample of parents of children with specific learning difficulties argued strongly that their difficulties were qualitatively different from those experienced by children of generally low ability. Furthermore, in the light of what they saw as their children's distinctive problems, they insisted that individual teaching delivered by expert tutors with specially designed materials was essential. They were unimpressed by notions of co-operative teaching in mainstream settings. (See Riddell *et al*, in press, for a further discussion of parents and local policy makers' perspectives.)

Learning support teachers, therefore, seemed poised between local authority personnel and parents. They were more likely than the former to recognise children with specific learning difficulties as a discrete group, but divided as to whether they should be accorded the high priority status requested by parents and unwilling to designate teaching materials as suitable only for children with specific learning difficulties – all those children with manifestation of difficulties in basic literacy could, many of them argued, benefit from such resources.

Turning to the second strand of policy and thinking, a new role for the learning support teacher, we found interesting differences between the primary and secondary teachers' ways of construing this area of special needs. In comparison with the secondary teachers, the learning support teachers in the primary sector expressed greater self-confidence in the systematic identification of children with specific learning difficulties, a more collaborative approach to the assessment of needs, a higher regard for withdrawal for individual tuition of pupils (and more frequent use of it) and a sharper awareness of regional guidelines on teaching methods in this area.

It seems likely that the primary teachers' confidence, in identifying these difficulties and undertaking withdrawal for individual tuition in the face of at least some official disapproval, stems from two factors. First, **all** primary school teachers see themselves as having responsibility (and appropriate training) for the development of basic literacy and numeracy and for becoming familiar with ways of picking up and then dealing with these problems. Secondly, collaborative approaches in general, and those reported by these teachers for the identification of children with specific learning difficulties in particular, characterise the ethos of many primary schools. The opportunities to discuss the problems, methods of identification and ways of meeting needs, and to hear from others about documents (such as regional guidelines) or materials that are available, are much greater within the collegial atmosphere of the (usually) small staff of the primary school. An environment of this kind is likely to foster close links between mainstream class teachers and learning support staff.

Chapter 29

The circumstances in which the secondary learning support staff found themselves were rather different. Confidence in the identification of specific learning difficulties and in the value of withdrawal for individual tuition were less apparent. There was a sense that identification and assessment of needs was seen as most appropriately carried out in the early years before secondary school, and that any learning difficulties persisting into the later years would be less amenable to remediation. Mainstream subject teachers characteristically see their main responsibility as teaching their subject. In relation to our research this seems to have had two effects. First, they tended to leave the learning support teachers to deal with any problems that arose; to a large extent, they seemed not to have moved on from the notion of the learning support teacher as the 'remedial expert'. Within this framework, learning support teachers could establish their own priorities but were likely to experience a degree of professional isolation. Secondly, the subject teachers were less favourably inclined towards withdrawal than were the primary teachers; children who are withdrawn are in danger of losing touch with the mainstream subject curriculum, and that curriculum is the subject teacher's first priority.

One of the implicit contrasts in this comparison of the primary and secondary sectors is between the way the mainstream primary class teachers and the mainstream secondary subject teachers view the role of learning support staff. The primary teachers may well be more ready to accept the recasting of the old remedial specialist into the learning support teacher who is expected to engage primarily in activities to enhance the work of the class teacher rather than to provide alternative programmes. The mainstream class teachers are prepared for this 'working-alongside' mode since they see the development of children's literacy as part of **their** role (just as it is for learning support teachers) and, as other research (Allan, Brown and Munn, 1991) has shown, primary teachers tend to be optimistic about the likelihood of remediation of young children's problems. Secondary subject teachers, however, seem to see things differently. They may (though some do not) accept the official conceptualisation of learning difficulties which rejects the idea that the child's inherent problems are the prime cause of failure and instead focuses attention on the possibility of inappropriate curricula or teaching methods.

They may also accept that old style remedial classes may exacerbate rather than alleviate children's learning difficulties, and that learning support teachers should operate largely in mainstream classrooms. What some at least find difficult is to abandon the notion that it is they who are in overall charge of the class, on account of their subject knowledge, and that the learning support teacher should be making use of his or her special expertise by supporting the lowest achievers (individual tuition within the mainstream classroom). The notion of equal partnership with the learning support teacher, or facilitation of that teacher's consultancy role, are often hard to sustain. Prognoses of the resolution of learning difficulties once a young person has reached secondary school tend to be much more pessimistic than in the primary; this pessimism nourishes the idea that the subject teacher should get on with stimulating the other children and leave the learning support teacher to deal with those who are having real problems.

The disparity between the primary and secondary sector, in the way mainstream teachers view the role of learning support teachers, reflects a general tension and lack of consensus which characterises this area. As our review of the literature showed, the value of the shift in role continues to be debated. On one side, there are calls for greater change so that learning support teachers become learning consultants. On the other, there is concern that the value of individual tuition has been too readily dismissed and that the research findings on the so-called failure of remedial education have been inconclusive.

This debate has particular relevance for specific learning difficulties. Whereas the parents of such children press for more individual tuition, policy makers at local authority level defend the importance of co-operative teaching and consultancy. The conflict seems likely to continue with learning support teachers occupying the uncomfortable middle ground with a sense of role uncertainty and insecurity. Few of our sample were aware of regional guidelines on provision which could be straightforwardly implemented as a way of avoiding the conflict; where such guidelines were available, they were sometimes regarded as unhelpful. There was some awareness, especially among secondary teachers, of guidelines from voluntary organizations. Since these tended to emphasise expert individual support, in line with parents' views, but the actual provision was overwhelmingly in mainstream classrooms with co-operative teaching and only some withdrawal, the resulting tensions were likely to have increased learning support teachers' unease about this aspect of their work.

Our survey has indicated that these learning support teachers feel themselves to be the victims of excessive expectation from both the education establishment and parents of children with specific learning difficulties. What can be said about the future of this piggy-in-the-middle state of affairs? In speculating about this, we turn to a recent document **Support for Learning: Special Needs within the 5-14 Curriculum** put out by the Scottish Consultative Council on the Curriculum (1993) as the outcome of an initiative, in collaboration with the Scottish Office Education Department, on staff development. In particular, we ask what it has to say about the conceptualisation of special educational needs and the role of the learning support teacher – the two issues upon which this final section of our paper has focused.

It is clear that the idea of a 'continuum of special educational needs which requires to be met through a range of provision' (part 1, p 5) is still a central idea. Quite what this is a continuum **of** is still not entirely clear. Since 'Pupils have special education (**sic**) needs when they face difficulties in, or barriers to, learning' (part 1, p 5) maybe it is a continuum of difficulties (more/less severe?) or barriers (harder/easier to overcome, or just one after another?). What the continuum does not tell us about is the diversity in the **nature** of the needs (or difficulties or barriers) that have to be faced. Perhaps this is because 'The special educational needs of the majority of pupils relate to problems in a particular aspect of the curriculum' (part 1, p 5) and so the continuum looks rather like the continuum of attainment targets in the 5-14 curriculum itself.

Beyond this, it is acknowledged that some pupils have special educational needs because of 'specific problems', but we are reminded that the 'system of labelling pupils has been replaced with a description of their learning needs' (part 1, p 5) What are parents of children with specific learning difficulties to make of this? Well quite a lot, as it happens, since a diagram showing 'learning difficulties considered from the standpoint of individual problems' (part 1, p 6) includes 'specific learning difficulties' as one distinct element. What its significance is difficult to say since the 'code' of the diagram is almost indecipherable, but it has a prominent position which it did not have before.

Turning to the role of the learning support teacher, we are given five main elements (in this order): consultancy, teaching and tuition, co-operative teaching, specialist services and staff development. In comparison with the SCOSDE guidelines cited earlier three things might be said: consultancy still retains its central role, specialist services are included for the first time and teaching and tuition seemed to have gained prominence (by putting this second in the list the alphabetical order is broken). Both the 'specialist services' and the 'tuition' open the door on one-to-one work rather wider. Furthermore, teaching and tuition includes 'providing special programmes in reading and writing for pupils with dyslexia'. Not only is central government recognising a special case here, it is conceding a change in nomenclature from 'specific learning difficulties' (back) to 'dyslexia'.

How parents and voluntary organisations will react to this remains to be seen. They may be content to rest their case or they may reject it as inadequate and simply a fudge to placate them. The document itself in several places reminds them of the power that parents now have, not just to be kept informed but also to be much more active in the decision making. Teachers are reminded that 'In partnership with parents they can decide what is to be taught and how it is to be taught'. Schools are advised to consider the following in planning pathways.

> Parents of pupils with special educational needs should be fully involved in the planning process. Their views will be of particular importance in specifying programme aims and in analysing decisions about the selection of curriculum content (part 1, p 16)

The luckless learning support teacher may still be caught between the other two powerful forces and schools will have to consider ways of reducing this pressure. That might be done by putting more emphasis than there seems to be at present on their consultancy role, ensuring they play a major part in the decisions about provision for children with special needs (including specific learning difficulties) and providing support for them in interactions with parents so they are not left unaided to shoulder the public responsibility for unpopular decisions. However, the reality is that the more time learning support staff devote to consultancy, management and decision making, the less time there will be for individual tuition and that is unlikely to help relationships with parents of pupils with specific learning difficulties.

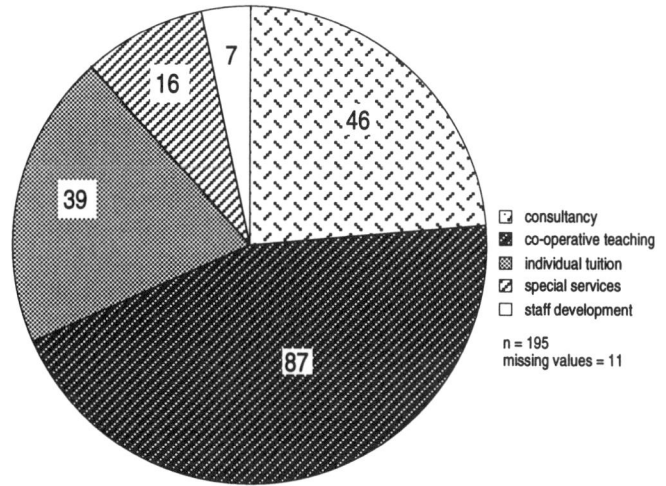

Figure 1

Learning support teachers' view of the most important aspect of their role (numbers).

- consultancy: 46
- co-operative teaching: 87
- individual tuition: 39
- special services: 16
- staff development: 7

n = 195
missing values = 11

Chapter 29

Table 1: Learning support teachers' views of the importance of individual tuition outwith the class by sector. (Rank 1 is most important, Rank 5 least important). (Result of chi-square test).

	Rank 1	Rank 2	Rank 3	Rank 4	Rank 5	Total
Primary	29 (27.6)	28 (26.7)	21 (20.0)	22 (21.0)	5 (4.8)	105 (57.4)
Secondary	8 (10.3)	14 (17.9)	20 (25.6)	16 (20.5)	20 (25.6)	78 (42.6)
Total	37 (20.2)	42 (23.0)	41 (22.4)	38 (20.8)	25 (13.7)	183 (100,00)

p<.001   Missing values + 23

Table 2: Confidence in assisting pupils with SLD reported by more and less experienced learning support teachers.   (Result of chi-square test).

	Confident	Sometimes	Not confident	Total
1 - 9 years experience	26 (25.0)	70 (67.3)	8 (7.7)	104 (54.7)
10 or more years experience	44 (51.2)	36 (41.9)	6 (7.0)	86 (45.3)
Total	70 (36.8)	106 (55.8)	14 (7.4)	190 (100.0)

p <.001   Missing values = 16

Table 3: Confidence in advising teachers about SLD reported by more or less experienced learning support teachers.   (Result of chi-square test).

	Confident	Sometimes	Not Confident	Total
1 - 9 years experience	22 (21.4)	71 (68.9)	10 (9.7)	103 (53.9)
10 or more years experience	39 (44.3)	43 (48.9)	6 (6.8)	88 (46.1)
Total	61 (31.9)	114 (59.7)	16 (8.4)	191 (100.0)

p <.001   Missing values = 15

REFERENCES

ALLAN J., BROWN S. and MUNN P. (1991) *Off the Record: Mainstream Provision for Pupils with Non-Regarded Learning Difficulties in Primary and Secondary School*, Edinburgh, Scottish Council for Research in Education.

BINES H. (1988) 'Equality, community and individualism: The development and implementation of the "Whole School Approach" to Special Educational Needs' In Barton L .(ed). *The Politics of Special Educational Needs*, London: The Falmer Press.

DEPARTMENT OF EDUCATION AND SCIENCE (1978) *Special Educational Needs* (The Warnock Report), London: HMSO.

DESSENT T. (1987) *Making the Ordinary School Special*, Lewes, Falmer Press.

DYSON A. (1990) 'Effective learning consultancy: a future role for special needs co-ordinators?' *Support for Learning* 5, 3, 116-127.

GIPPS C., GROSS H. and GOLDSTEIN H. (1987) *Warnock's 18%: Children with Special Needs in Primary School*, Lewes, Falmer Press.

MOSES D., HEGARTY S. and JOWETT S. (1987) *Meeting special educational needs: support for the ordinary school* Educational Research 29, 2, 108-115.

PAYNE T. (1991) 'It's cold in the other room', *Support for Learning* 6, 2, 61-65.

RIDDELL S., DUFFIELD J., BROWN S. and OGILVY C. (1992) *Specific Learning Difficulties: Policy, Practice and Provision*. Department of Education, University of Stirling.

RIDDELL S., BROWN S. and DUFFIELD J. (forthcoming) 'Parents' and professionals' conceptualisations of specific learning difficulties: A case of a paradigm clash' in Riddell S. and Brown S. (eds) *Children with Special Educational Needs: Policy and Practice in the '90s*, London: Routledge.

SCOTTISH EDUCATION DEPARTMENT (1978) *The Education of pupils with Learning Difficulties in Primary and Secondary Schools in Scotland. A progress Report by HM Inspectors of Schools*, Edinburgh: HMSO.

SCOTTISH COMMITTEE FOR STAFF DEVELOPMENT IN EDUCATION (1990) *Award Bearing Courses within the Three Tier Structure: Guidelines for Diplomas in Special Educational Needs*, Edinburgh: SCOSDE.

SCOTTISH CONSULTATIVE COMMITTEE ON THE CURRICULUM (1993). *Support for learning: Special Needs within the 5-14 Curriculum*. Dundee: SCCC.

Chapter 30

A FRAMEWORK FOR PRACTICE

LINDA CUMMING

INTRODUCTION

In order to meet satisfactorily pupil needs within the area of specific learning difficulties, it is important to focus attention upon aspects other than the most obvious one of the individual child or young person and his immediate learning and teaching requirements. The delivery of a service to such pupils involves not only a system of provision but also good inter-agency liaison, staff development organisation, material resources availability and a willingness to communicate with, and involve, parents at every stage. Somehow all of these aspects have to amalgamate into a recognisable structure which will profit the pupil, satisfy his parents and which is realistic and manageable for schools and the Authority.

Most practices have evolved over time and in response to a variety of stimuli. Most recently, perhaps, the 5-14 Development Programme has emphasised to all working in the field the importance of pupil access to the normal curriculum and, equally, the requirement in many cases to amend and adapt programmes to suit individual needs. Computer technology, for example, has had a huge impact especially in the area of word processing, and as hardware and software packages become even more sophisticated so teaching approaches and staff training needs continue to change and develop.

STAFF DEVELOPMENT

While formal methods of staff development and information dissemination certainly have a place in the scheme of things, much valuable work is done through ongoing contact between learning support, class and subject teachers and staff of Advisory and Psychological Services. Teachers who have experience of pupils with specific learning difficulties will have learned much from case discussions with staff of these services. School staff obtain advice, for example, on appropriate teaching strategies, as well as on materials and professional books which are available either through School Library Services or the Psychological Service if the pupil in question has been referred to that Service. Some Library Services are fortunate in having special needs departments and specialist librarians.

Formal staff development opportunities are usually available to specialist and learning support staff through college-based Diploma courses or local in-service. Increasingly though, there is a need to train class and subject teachers in a more structured way, and at a level beyond what might be assimilated if they happen to be working closely with Learning Support or specialist colleagues. Although planned activity time has decreased of late, some schools will have taken the opportunity to invite local Psychological Service or Advisory staff to give presentations. Equally, if special educational needs in its most general sense is a priority within Authorities, then opportunities may present themselves for specific learning difficulties of a dyslexic nature to be on the agenda. Such staff development exercises can only be at the awareness-raising level but if they are backed up by straightforward written information, including definitions and indicators, suggestions for further reading and local authority contacts, then the exercise will have been worthwhile.

There is a need, therefore, for concrete information on identification, further assessment, teaching strategies and resource suggestions to be developed centrally and to be disseminated to class and subject teachers through learning support staff. If there are good links, for example, between staff of the Psychological Service and the Advisory Service, then there are distinct possibilities for collaborative work in this respect. Small working groups, for example of senior learning support teachers, are another source of expertise to be tapped to the benefit of colleagues.

Staff who have used the many computer programs and packages on the market, will be aware of their value as motivators and as alternative methods of recording. In addition to Regional in-service opportunities, every school appears to have at least one in-house computer buff who is usually only too eager to help a colleague in (technological) distress!

INTERVENTION PROCEDURE

Pupils may not only encounter difficulties in different areas of the curriculum, they may also show different levels of difficulty. Intervention procedures therefore have to attempt to cater for these factors by trying to ensure that school and specialist personnel are involved at the most appropriate stages.

In order to meet the needs of pupils with learning difficulties it may be necessary to formalise intervention procedures by trying to ensure that staff at each stage of the identification, assessment and teaching process are aware of their responsibilities and of Authority expectations. These are that class and subject teachers, perhaps in consultation with learning support staff, should be capable of identifying a pupil with specific learning difficulties and that they will, thereafter, become jointly responsible, at a level appropriate to the degree of difficulty encountered, for some form of direct intervention. Further assessment will undoubtedly take place and the learning support teacher will contribute to planning and delivering a programme which takes account of the demands of the 5-14 guidelines.

Experienced learning support staff should feel confident in their assessment of pupil needs, and it may not be necessary to involve either Advisory or Psychological Service or other agencies. If there are serious concerns, schools may have access to Advisory Teachers who may be able to offer suggestions for further work or who may suggest a referral to the Psychological Service. It is very probable, in any case, that the school psychologist will be aware of the pupil through regular consultation with school staff.

Staff should be encouraged also to involve parents in their plans for the pupil and to deal sympathetically with parent concerns.

It can be a source of some concern to professionals that parents are often quite determined in requesting Psychological Service intervention at a stage long before which school and Advisory staff would deem it desirable or even necessary, and during which pupils are, in fact, making good progress. For that reason and, in any case in this more accountable age, authorities may be considering formalising school-based assessment and intervention procedures so that parents know what can be made available within school and what may be necessary in the future by way of specialist provision. Staff too can then be aware of their obligations in the process.

SPECIALIST PROVISION

Beyond the in-school procedure which will certainly have involved class and learning support teachers and may have included parent help, it may be thought necessary to formally involve the Psychological Service.

More specialised provision will vary tremendously among authorities but is possible that if pupils are referred to the Psychological Service, specialist teachers, dealing principally with pupils with specific learning difficulties, will work with individual pupils either directly, or in a staff and resource support role on a long-term basis.

Authorities are now prepared to consider the opening of a Record of Needs for pupils with specific learning difficulties. Additional resources can be made available for pupils with severe difficulties and these often take the form of dictaphones, word processors and other forms of computer technology. In a very few instances, Supervisory Assistants may have been appointed to help support in their local school, pupils with severe difficulties who require help with organising their workload and with reading texts. They may also tape materials and scribe for the pupil.

CASE STUDIES

Difficulties can and do occur at various stages of the intervention process as this brief case study illustrates. It particularly highlights how slow progress can be when a widely discrepant profile emerges, and how difficult and time consuming it can be for staff to support an anxious parent.

Case Study 1 – Louise

Louise was first assessed by a clinical psychologist when she was seven years old. Her parents had referred her to their GP because of concerns regarding Louise's very slow progress at school and behaviour problems at home, although the school, a very sympathetic one, had already identified difficulties and support was being provided.

She was referred on to the Psychological Service some months later. She had presented as a fairly lively and chatty girl whose pre-school development had been normal. A fine hand tremor was noted but neurological investigation yielded nothing of note. Her performance on BAS sub-tests was very variable – average and above average in some verbal tests and in digit span, but extremely poor in non-verbal sequencing tasks and in construction/jigsaw type activities. A WISC-R gave a similar profile. Overall, Louise's attainments and ability profile were characteristic of a younger child but with some strengths which suggested a specific learning difficulty. Handwriting and drawings were very immature. On the Neale Analysis of Reading Ability her reading skills seemed only mildly delayed but she had little by way of blending skills for spelling.

The school psychologist and specialist teacher made arrangements to meet with the class teacher and learning support teacher to plan a programme. General advice on specific learning difficulties was given to the class teacher. The programme for Louise aimed to improve her reading skills by accessing taped stories and through paired reading, to develop her blending skills through use of a well known structured scheme and tapes, and to increase her self confidence and reduce anxiety by minimising the level of written work required and by carefully grading her programme of work. Louise's mother agreed to undertake the paired reading at home.

Louise made slow progress and her mother became even more anxious. At age 8 the parents requested that a Record of Needs be opened. Further assessment at this stage yielded a similar pattern to that obtained previously, although her learning and other behaviours were more mature and she displayed less anxiety in the school situation. She was reading at around the seven year level and spelling skills were around the six year level.

In the event a Record was not opened, as it was judged that support could be adequately provided in the existing setting. Louise received input from the school learning support teacher and the specialist teacher regularly visited on a consultative basis.

Louise is now in P6, a happier and more confident girl who in language work is functioning as a member of a class group, albeit at a level below that of most of her classmates. Although there are difficulties still in following instructions and in comprehension, she is altogether a more organised and more motivated child, though still seeming immature for her years. Reading fluency has improved and she is able to identify and correct her spelling errors.

The learning support teacher, in consultation with the class teacher, organises most of Louise's language work. Her aim is to make Louise and her group more independent by, for example, ensuring that they have been taught simple reference skills. The work programme, though, is still very well organised and structured so that success at each stage is assured. The involvement of the specialist teacher is now minimal.

As important as the progress Louise has made is the fact that her mother recognises that progress, and has come to terms now with the fact that this is and will continue to be, slow. All the staff concerned have worked hard, not just in terms of planning and teaching and evaluating Louise's progress but also in supporting an occasionally very demanding parent.

Chapter 30

Case Study 2 – Ewen

This case study illustrates a fairly common pattern among pupils with specific learning difficulties and is an example of a successful in-school intervention programme.

Ewen's difficulties, particularly in written work, had been for some time the subject of discussion between his mother and staff of his small, rural school. The school found Ewen to be a likeable, lively and enthusiastic pupil whose performance in maths was satisfactory, whose oral reading had taken some time to develop and was still not considered to be fluent, and whose spelling and written work were felt to be 'careless' and 'slapdash'. His oral reading was still hesitant but he was able to gain meaning from what he read. The school felt that the parents' hectic lifestyle was somewhat responsible for Ewen's poor reading performance in that there had not been sufficient practice at home and promises to help with homework tasks were often not fulfilled.

The school had a small amount of learning support input per week but this had always been targeted at two pupils with poor overall attainments.

The Headteacher contacted the Advisory Service with a view to helping to assess Ewen's difficulties. The learning support teacher had already carried out standardised tests as follows:

Chronological Age: 7 years 9 months

Neale Analysis of Reading Ability (old version)   Accuracy   7 years 8 months
                                                  Comprehension   8 years 4 months

Schonell Graded Word Spelling   7 years 0 months

An informal assessment of Ewen's written work showed that he wrote the minimum possible when required to do functional or creative writing tasks even on topics which he enjoyed, and that he displayed a tendency to spell unknown words phonetically. He was right-handed and most letters were correctly formed although his handwriting was not neat. A check of phonic skills showed Ewen to be competent at blending simple three and four letter words but having great difficulty with vowel diagraphs and common irregular words.

A meeting with his mother confirmed that there had been no concerns regarding early development and that Ewen enjoyed good health. His mother was

Perspectives on Practice

concerned that Ewen might be dyslexic because of a family history of learning difficulties.

The learning support teacher, having had an opportunity to observe and work with Ewen, was now well aware of the discrepancies between his performance in reading and writing tasks and his apparently well-developed verbal skills and competence in maths. It was agreed that she would work with Ewen for two short spells during the morning she was at the school, one to work on re-drafting a piece of the previous week's writing and to prepare the spelling tasks for the week ahead, and the other to work on reading.

A structured spelling programme was used and, in addition, personal words required for writing were written on small cards to be studied using the look, cover, write and check approach. These were to be kept in an envelope while being learned and transferred to another once mastered. It was hoped that this approach would boost Ewen's confidence in spelling and, moreover, could be checked by a class-mate if necessary. He was encouraged to increase his writing output gradually, and his teacher encouraged not to correct every mis-spelling, but to select only a few words per week for further study. Computer games were used to reinforce spelling tasks and Ewen was able to use the word processing facility on occasion to type up particularly good pieces of writing.

Some in-service work on spelling difficulties was done with staff since it was felt that other pupils might benefit from a more structured approach in this area.

Ewen remained on the same reading scheme, but decoding skills were practised using games. Oral and written activities designed to improve his use of context cues were also used.

Ewen was brought to the notice of the school psychologist and it was decided that a referral was not necessary at this point. His parents agreed to assist with spelling work at home. This input was somewhat erratic but nonetheless, even in a few months Ewen was showing improvements. He was responding to the attention of the learning support teacher and to a carefully structured programme continued by his class teacher. It should be possible, given parental support for the programme in hand, for Ewen to continue to make gains.

CONCLUSION

Although Louise and Ewen presented as two very different children in terms of their assessment profiles and learning styles, they were both considered to have specific learning difficulties. Both benefited from very structured programmes which focused on those difficulties while taking account of curricular and personal strengths. The strategies and resources used differed according to need and much thought was given to those which would boost their confidence in tackling particular areas of the curriculum.

Consideration was given to planning within the framework of the 5-14 Development Programme, making justifiable amendments and adaptations as required.

Both general and specific advice was given to staff and parents, and the help of the latter was solicited in both cases.

Specific Learning Difficulties continue to enjoy much media attention. While this is the case school and local authority staff will sometimes have difficulties convincing parents of the worth of their recommendations. Only continuing support and staff development will ensure that all staff have the confidence to assure parents that their children's needs are in fact being met. Good local authority links with a local branch of the Dyslexia Association can be helpful in this respect, as the Association can give information to parents and, most importantly, can encourage parent/school discussion of the difficulties.

* The views in this chapter are the author's and do not necessarily represent those of Central Region Education Authority.

Chapter 31

THE USE OF RESOURCES TO ACCESS LEARNING SKILLS

ANNE F. PHILIP

INTRODUCTION

Irrespective of the debate highlighted in the research regarding the aetiology and the teaching of dyslexic children, the classroom environment would be extremely lack-lustre without a range of teaching resources. This chapter will focus on the variety of resource material which can be used and adapted by the teacher to develop a range of skills among dyslexic children and additionally to facilitate and enhance a positive self-concept.

WHAT IS A RESOURCE?

A resource can be defined as 'any supply which will meet a need'. Such a supply can include books, equipment, teacher adapted materials, the teacher and the learning environment. Resources, however, should be placed within a context. That context includes both the needs of the learner, teaching methods and the classroom setting. Often the dyslexic learner is a very bruised and damaged individual and this needs to be appreciated in developing and using resources. Additionally, the school policy, the environment for learning, the method of study, the demands of the syllabus, including the 5-14 programme in Scotland and the National Curriculum in England, and the primary difficulties experienced by the child also need to be borne in mind when identifying and developing suitable resources for dyslexic children.

THE TEACHER

The teacher is clearly a major resource. In an ideal world the teacher should be interested, informed, enthusiastic, possess a sense of humour, display considerable patience, have a 'herculean constitution' and an ever welcoming smile.

Chapter 31

DEVELOPING RESOURCES

A Teaching Framework for Dyslexic Children.

Such a framework should include a number of different aspects all of which are important and need to be considered in the development of resources (Fig. 2).

Check List (Fig. 2)

- Alphabet
- Name & Address
- Units of Time - Money
- Mathematical Symbols
- Compass Points
- Use of: dictionary
  - atlas
  - encyclopaedia
  - library
- Reversals (correction)
- Cursive Writing
- Auditory Perception
- Visual Perception
- Spelling Rules
- Syllabification
- Basic Sight Vocabulary
- Social Sight Vocabulary
- Outlaws
- Reading with some competence
- Writing with some competence
- Sequencing
- Orientation

Chapter 31

The Alphabet

The sounding of the letters of the alphabet is of great importance. These letters are the tools of reading. There are many different representations of letters currently available, such as plastic letters and wooden letters (Galt). Letters can also be put on to cards and can be used in a variety of ways in the teaching process. The cards can be hung on a 'washing line' across the room so that not only can they be readily seen by the children, but they also can be moved together to form various kinds of digraphs and blends (see Fig. 3).

(Fig. 3)

Alphabetic order is also very important for the use of dictionaries, telephone books and other reference texts. If possible the use of the actual resource, dictionary or telephone book is preferable. Dictionaries can be divided easily into four parts, for example A-D: E-L: M-R: and S-Z.

The child can be helped to remember this division through the use of a simple mnemonic such as:

'Alphabetic Entry Makes Sense'.

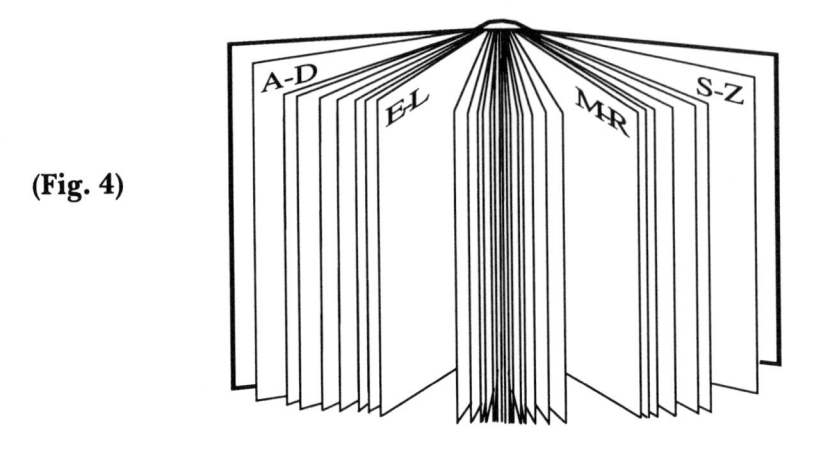

(Fig. 4)

The use of the alphabet can be reinforced through the use of games. Such games can include arranging the children in alphabetic order according to their surname or Christian name.

Name and address

It is important that the child can spell his or her own name and address. This can sometimes prove difficult for dyslexic children and a card, like a credit card, can be made to help reinforce the correct spelling of the child's name and address.

Units of Time and Money

It is sometimes necessary to reinforce units of time and money. There are many ways in which this reinforcement can be achieved. These can include:

- **an egg timer** instead of a clock. This provides the sense of time and highlights particular units of time, e.g. three minutes on an activity.
- **a festival folder** in which the months of the year are highlighted including the special events of each month.
- **use of real money**. This can reduce any loss of learning which can occur when learning needs to be transferred to other contexts. The use of real money replicates real situations more readily than using 'toy money' or counters.

Mathematical Symbols

It is important to ensure that the child has a real understanding and appreciation of mathematical symbols. Graphics can help to make the meaning of symbols clearer to children. (For examples of this see Mathematics and Dyslexia – Ann Henderson).

Syllabification

This process can make spelling easier because the word is broken up into syllables. It is important to highlight syllabification for dyslexic children, since this process can be quite difficult for them to acknowledge (Bradley, 1988).

It is useful therefore to ensure that the child is aware of the natural syllabic breaks in words. This can be done by actually marking them on the word or by breaking larger words into small ones e.g. 'fire/place'. The Stott Reading Programme provides many useful examples of strategies for syllabification.

Chapter 31

Basic sight vocabulary

This is necessary, not just to provide the child with a working vocabulary which can help in the comprehension of reading passages, but also to give the child a degree of confidence from being able to read at least some words. This basic sight vocabulary should include words which can be described as a 'social sight vocabulary – some everyday commonly used words' (Fig. 5 and 6).

(Fig. 5)

a	for	make	she
about	from	me	so
an	get	more	some
and	go	must	that
are	goes	much	the
as	had	my	their
at	has	new	them
back	have	no	then
be	he	not	there
been	her	now	they
before	here	of	this
big	him	off	to
but	his	old	too
by	I	on	two
call	if	one	up
came	in	only	want
can	into	or	was
come	is	other	we
could	it	our	well
did	just	out	went
do	like	over	were
does	little	right	will
down	look	said	with
first	made	see	you

442   *Specific Learning Difficulties (Dyslexia)*

Outlaws (Fig. 5a)

In addition to Basic Sight Vocabulary is the list of Outlaws – words for reading and spelling which make life tough.

ache	else	please
across	enough	push
again	even	put
against	ever	queue
all	every	quite
almost	eye	ready
alone	few	school
also	friend	shone
always	find	such
among	four	sugar
amongst	fourth	their
answer	full	these
any	give	those
anyone	gone	though
away	half	through
because	height	use
beauty	how	useful
beautiful	instead	usual
become	island	very
behind	kind	walk
biscuit	learn	what
both	many	when
busy	money	where
business	most	which
buy	mother	why
caught	next	
child	none	
children	nothing	
deny	often	
door	once	
either	people	

Perspectives on Practice

Chapter 31

Social Sight Vocabulary (Fig. 6)

```
DOCTOR              NURSE              CHEMIST            EMERGENCY
POISON              PRESCRIPTION       FIRST AID          SURGERY
Take three tablets twice per day       DENTAL SURGERY

TOILETS             LADIES             GENTLEMEN          GENTS
VACANT              ENGAGED            PUBLIC

PUSH                PULL               ENTRANCE           EXIT
WAY IN              WAY OUT

WAIT                CROSS NOW          GIVE WAY           ONE WAY
STOP                GO                 NO LEFT TURN

OPEN                CLOSED             PAY HERE
PAY AS YOU ENTER

POLICE              STATION            RAILWAY            BUS
SCHOOL

TELEPHONE           POST OFFICE

PRIVATE             PARKING

RESTAURANT

Make up real life situations
Where possible find true to life signs
```

Writing

Some writing competence should be encouraged. An excellent framework for the development of such skills can be found in the 5-14 development programme (English Language). The use of a word processor can also be included in the resources for the development of written language.

Listening

It is unwise to assume that the pupil is listening. Brief exercises to strengthen listening skills can therefore be useful. Such exercises can include:

- the use of music at the beginning of a lesson to help children 'switch on' their 'listening ears'
- reading stories, particularly those constructed by the child
- dictation

- listening bingo
- asking the children to go outside to hear six different sounds
- listening to, and acting on, verbal instructions.

Talking

Talking and discussion can be a great strength and thus a source of success for the dyslexic child. It is important therefore that this should be fully utilised. This may be done by:

- encouraging children to tell stories in small groups and tape them,
- reading sentences in rotation with a partner,
- providing a 'help sheet' which outlines a framework for a talk, thus encouraging the child to give a structured talk (see Fig. 7).

Title Help Sheet (Fig. 7)

> Title of Talk..
>
> Jot down ideas at random - any how!
> Select the best
> Make up talk
> Reduce to note form
> Rehearse - aim to interest the audience -
>   not to fill the Albert Hall
> Tape yourself - how you sound
>   - think of your audience
> Enjoy yourself!

Reading

Reading has a variety of strands including information, enjoyment, silent reading and reading aloud. It is inecessary for the teacher to become aware of the child's reading preferences – this may not be reading aloud – and to acknowledge this in order that some enjoyment may be possible from reading.

It is advisable to explain to the child different types of reading and their functions. These include:

- s**kimming** – a telephone book for numbers,
- **scanning** – selecting parts of a book for interest,
- **understanding** – scrutiny, reading carefully in order to, for example, follow instructions.

The pleasure in reading can come from activities such as:

- **News corner**

This might include a daily paper, some school information, extracts from the school diary, reading out events involving the child or even their daily diary.

- **Personal Anthologies**

A collection, made by the child, of those poems, passages from books, words and even jokes which have had some impact on them.

- **Vocabulary of reading**

Helping the child to understand the vocabulary of reading, including:

- reading aloud,
- silent reading,
- top of page,
- foot of page,
- letter,
- word,
- sentence,
- paragraph,
- roman numeral,
- index,
- contents,
- cover.

It is also important to ensure that the child's eye movements in reading are correct. It is possible the child may require some specific eye tracking exercises. There are a number of useful resources for this including the Word Tracking Series (Ann Arbor Publishers) which includes high frequency words and proverbs. Some of the activities to enhance scanning and eye tracking include writing particular words in lines of text.

Chapter 31

Frameworks for Reading (Fig. 8)

Book Review

Title ....
Author ....
Publisher ....
Outline of Story:
N.B. who, where, what, why, when, how.
List most important characters

Describe - looks: personality.

Enjoyment level ....

Reading for Information / Comprehension

1. Look at passage
   N.B. Title: extract: author: illustration:
   layout: type: shape: length of paragraph.

2. Skim:
   What is it about?
   What is the purpose of writing?

3. Read all questions

4. Read again   (Big 6)

5. Answer questions - follow the directions and instructions.

   who   = person   how = in what way
   where = place   why = for what reason
   when = time   what = (many answers)

Character Sketch

Character Sketch

Book..
Author...
Name of Character..............................
Age..
Appearance.......................................

Would you like to meet him?
Where in the book do you meet him?
What was he doing / saying?

Perspectives on Practice

Chapter 31

Writing

Important aspects of writing include the following:

- functional,
- imaginative,
- personal,
- language,
- spelling,
- punctuation and structure,
- handwriting and presentation.

All should be given some focus. The child may need particular help with creative writing. Such help may include encouraging five paragraph essays; providing a list of possible opening sentences to each of the paragraphs; writing postcards; writing letters. Other useful writing activities include form filling and completing applications. Note taking is also a useful skill to develop (see Fig. 9).

LAYOUT OF NOTES: Pointers (Fig. 9)

1   Notes may be laid out in graphic or linear style

⬅——— 2   Leave good margins. ———➡

(THESE BLANK AREAS CAN BE USED FOR AMENDMENTS OR ADDITIONS)

3   Use plenty of space.

Small undivided work is difficult to read

4   To emphasise important points or equations or formulae:-

     (a)   CAPITALS   (d)   highlighter pen

     (b)   <u>Underline</u>   (e)   coloured pens

     (c)   ⬜ BOX ⬜

5   Legibility

6   <u>Abbreviations</u> may help

=	equals	&	and
∝	proportional to	N.B.	take note of
>	greater than	i.e.	that is
∴	therefore	≠	is not equal to
e.g.	for example	⊄	not proportional to
cf	compare	<	less than
		∵	because

When taking notes omit small words- (a: the.........etc.) shorten words.

Spelling

Spelling needs to be taught, where possible in context, or at least some reason needs to be given to explain why there is a need for functionally correct spelling. There are a number of aids available to assist with spelling such as the Franklin Spellmaster, dictionaries, and specific computer programmes such as PAL (Predictive Adaptive Lexicon) which can help with spelling, punctuation and structure. Spelling should be taught in some context which helps to emphasise the point that we write to communicate not spell. It can be noted that often awareness of being a poor speller can lead to reluctance to write.

Handwriting and Presentation

It is important that the child develops a good, correct handwriting grip. Rubber grips and non-slip pencils can be useful to help with this. Some strategies which can help with handwriting include:

Chapter 31

- Sellotaping along the margin which helps to provide the child with a starting point,
- the use of 'braille paper' which allows the lines to be felt,
- a green spot on the page to indicate the starting position, and a red spot to show where one should stop.

Study Skills

For the dyslexic child study skills are an essential part of the teaching programme. A number of very useful publications exist on study skills, but the teacher can also employ some strategies which can also help. These include:

- displaying information on graphic posters,
- use of mind maps,
- classroom pin board,
- the logging of information to help with recall,
- help with planning a daily routine, the dyslexic learner is ofern 'lost in time and space' so this time plamming is essential
- help the child to find the learning style most suited to him/her.
  For example background noise, or no background noise, music, silence, bright light, dim light (Dunn & Dunn, 1992).

Resources are indeed a crucial component of any teaching programme for dyslexic children. There are many excellent commercially available resources, but additionally the teacher can adapt materials to facilitate the learning and teaching process for the dyslexic child. Any resource, however, must consider not only the content of a lesson or a skill, but the holistic needs of the child and therefore should aim to enhance and develop a positive self-concept – which in itself will facilitate learning.

SOURCES AND RESOURCES

This list of books, publications and equipment can be useful to the teacher. The list is by no means definitive but I would hope that it would be helpful to those involved in teaching dyslexic learners. These resources are never complete in themselves but are more to be used, often in part, when they are relevant, when a different approach is needed or when all else fails. They are wonderful teaching tools and should be used accordingly.

General

Plastic letters: Galt clinging letters. James Galt & Co.
Letterland L. Wendon: Letterland Ltd.
Learning through Play: Jan Marzolla & Janice Lloyd. Unwin Paperbacks.
Entertaining and Educating Young Children: Robyn Gee. Usborne Publishing.
Early Childhood Resource Book: Merle B. Karnes. Winslow Press.
Building Auditory and Visual Perception Skills: LDA.
A Manual for the Training of Sequential Memory and Attention. Pruna S. Klein and Allen A.Schwartz. Academic Therapy Publications.
Gill Cotterell Check List. LDA.

Dictionaries and Reference

A Sentence Dictionary: Eric Neal. Hulton Educational Publications.
Collins First Dictionary: Collins (both give definitions by using the word in a sentence).
ACE Spelling Dictionary: David Mosely and Catherine Nicol, LDA. (can be difficult for some children to use because of the reference method).
Spell it Yourself. G. T. Hawker. Oxford University Press (very clear layout as a spelling check).
Oxford Children's Picture Dictionary. Oxford University Press (words presented as groups under themes e.g. fruit and vegetables).
Pergammon Dictionary of Perfect Spelling: Christine Maxwell. Wheaton.
Collins Concise School Dictionary: Collins. (clear layout).
Pocket Dictionary: John Grisewood. Kingfisher Books (clear and well illustrated).
Atlas: Folens Ordnance Survey World Atlas. Folens. (very clear and concise – now with photo-copiable material).
Letter Tracking: Ann Arbor.
Globes of the World either as free standing or as transparent 'balloon' reproductions which can be suspended in a classroom.
Library and friendly librarian – an invaluable resource.
CD-ROM (Reading Only Material which gives access to information in encyclopaedias on computer, very often with illustration, animation and even voice over).

Listening

Oral comprehension: LDA.
Fast Forward: Joyce Dring: LDA.
Reading and Thinking tapes: LDA.

Remedial Spelling: Violet Brand: Egon Publishers. (part of the Spelling Made Easy series and an excellent source of dictation work).
Alpha to Omega: Beve Hornsby and Frula Shear: Special Educational Needs (Marketing) (for dictation exercises).
Books on tape which can be found in may good booksellers and record shops.

Talking

Springboards for Writing: Brenda McNeal: Academic Therapy Publications (lists of sentences and paragraphs which can be used for oral work as well as part of a very good writing scheme).
Novels and stories to encourage talk: e.g. The Iron Man: Ted Hughes.
Any by Roald Dahl.
Help Yourself Stories: Nelson.

Reading for Information

(some of these will obviously cover various strands of any programme but I have divided reading into 2 main categories – for information and enjoyment).
Reading Alive and Library Alive: Gwen Gawith: A & C Black.
Headwork books 1-8: Chris Culshaw & Deborah Waters: Oxford University Press (books 1-4 are particularly good containing cloze, matching, deduction, sequencing, classification).
English Headwork books 1-4: Chris Culshaw and Deborah Waters. OUP.
Way Ahead English books 1-4: Gareth Price: LDA. (includes – following directions, writing skills, collecting information, the media).
New Treasury of English books 1-4: Eithne Roycroft: Folens. (grammar, comprehension, nature study all presented so clearly and with good illustrations).
Language Patterns books 1-6: ed. Donald Moyle. Cassell (includes stories for enjoyment as well as workbooks and teacher resource books – a well laid out scheme for the smaller group).
Word Power books 1-4: Helen McLullich. Oliver & Boyd. (with Wordpower Assessment Tasksheets which are photo-copiable, this is excellent material).
Wide Range Reading Skills Workbooks: Oliver & Boyd. (a little old fashioned but useful).
Cloze procedure:
- Words for Living,
- Which Word,
- Words in their Places: Lynn Hutchison: Hodder & Stoughton.

False Teeth and Vampires: Astronauts and the Black Death: Christopher Jarman: LDA.

Chapter 31

Prediction

Start Thinking.
Keep Thinking.
Stories for Thinking: Lynn Hutchison: Hodder & Stoughton.
Directions: John Cooper: (all books in this series cover essential reading skills – skimming, scanning, speed reading, prediction, reference skills, study skills, also photo-copiable material) Oliver & Boyd.
What's that You're Reading: Sandra Gilfeather: Edward Arnold. (comprehension exercises using pictorial material).
Tests in English Comprehension: Betty Kerr: Macmillan.
Reading for Meaning books 1-4 George A Carr: Hodder & Stoughton (old fashioned but good short passages).
Primary Language Programme books 1-7: Masson, Monoghan, Thomson: Heinemann.
I See What You Mean books 1 & 2: Kilpatrick, McCall, Palmer: Oliver & Boyd.
What's the Idea: Graham R. White: Oliver & Boyd: (for summary and report writing).

Reading for Enjoyment

Books of pupil's own choice.
Anthologies and collections are an excellent way of getting the flavour of a book and perhaps encouraging the child to read more.
I Like This Story: Puffin.
Meet my Friends: chosen by Kaye Webb: Guild Publishing (characters and their adventures).
Openings: ed. Roy Blatchford: Antony Rowe Ltd. (good collection of stories with follow on activities included at the end of the book).
Reading 2000. 1-5. Oliver & Boyd. (good novels and back-up activities).
Headwork Stories 1 & 2: Chris Culshaw: OUP. (good stories and questions).
Twists: Gordon Hogg: Hodder & Stoughton: (stories with a twist in the tail – there is associated work but good for the stories alone).
Usborne Puzzle Adventures (various) Usborne Books.
The Black Knight, The Longship Invaders etc: Michael Thomson: LDA.
Learning with Letts: Letts. (to quote – English activities with additional maths and science based on an exciting adventure story: different, well presented and fun).
Sea Hawk Main Readers: S. K. McCullagh: E. J. Arnold.

Poetry

Lizard Over Ice: Gervasse Phinn: Nelson.
Any collection by Brian Patten: Roger McGough.
Choral verse where the effect of group reading can support weaker readers – chosen from A. A. Milne: T. S. Eliot's 'Old Possum's Book of Practical Cats'.

Writing

Really Useful Picture Series: Learning Materials Ltd.: (several books with pictorial material for encouraging writing).
My Book About Myself: Learning Materials Ltd. (excellent framework for personal writing).
Finish the Story. Books 1-4: Kate Fitzsimmons: Learning Materials Ltd.
Tell Tale: Gordon Hogg and Graham Turnbull: Edward Arnold.
Brain Waves photo-copiable material.
Using the Newspaper to Teach Social Studies: Marilyn Olson: Dale Seymour Publications. (useful different approach to writing and reading making use of newspapers).

Spelling

Spelling and Tables: Folens: (concise lists with dictation).
Exercise Your Spelling books 1-3: Elizabeth Wood: Hodder & Stoughton. (also excellent photo-copiable material).
Spelling Made Easy. Books 1-3: Violet Brand: Egon Publishers Ltd.
Super Spelling Book books 1-6: Charles Cuff: Longman.
Alpha to Omega: Beve Hornsby and Frula Shear + Activity Packs: Beve Hornsby and Julie Pool: Heinemann.
Space to Spell: More Space to Spell: Frula Shear: Special Educational Needs (Marketing).
Attack: Jean Richards: Reeves Hall Hepworth Norfolk. (very good associated material).
Catchwords books 1-6: Charles Cripps: Harcourt Brace Jovanovich.
Hand for Spelling: Charles Cripps: LDA.
Sounds O.K. books 1-3: Tony Walsh: Folens: (very clear presentation).
Step-by Books: Constance Milburn: Arnold Wheaton. (a source of fun activities).
500 Word Book: Learning Materials Ltd.

Spellbound: Elsie T. Rak: Educators Publishing Service (structured phonic programme).
Put it Right: Violet Brand: (Egon Publishers Ltd. (proof reading).
Franklin Spellmasters: small computer aids to spelling: FLS Services, Fareham.

Structure and Punctuation

Teaching Written Expression: Diana Phelps-Terasaki: Academic Therapy Publications. (different and effective way of looking at sentence structure).
First Aid in English: Angus Maciver: Robert Gibson.
Mind Your Language books 1-4: U. E. Palmer and Peter Brinton: Oliver & Boyd (well illustrated and fun grammar).
Master Your English: Punctuation: Davies, Dillon, Egerton-Chesney: Basis Blackwell (very handy little book).
Punctuation in its Place: Don Shiach: Hodder & Stoughton.
Language and Languages: Derek Strange: Oxford University Press (good activities).
Introduction to Language: Aphir, Crawshaw, Roselman, Williams. Hodder & Stoughton. (should the dyslexic learner study a modern language – this provides good and interesting background).

Handwriting

Handwriting Activities books 1 and 2: Thomas Barnard: Wardlock Educational.
Building Handwriting Skills in Dyslexic Children: Ed. John I. Arena: Academic Therapy Publications.
Handwriting: a second chance: LDA.
Pencil grips: LDA and Early Learning Centre.
Hand Huggers: Berol (John Menzies).
Penmaster: Phillips: Phillips High Street Oxford: (handwriting guide).

Study Skills

Basic Study Skills: Charles Milward: Macmillan.
Research Skills book 1-3: James McCafferty: Edward Arnold.
Improve Your Study Skills: Doug Humphries: CRAC.
Super Student: Carel.

Thinking Skills

Critical Thinking Activities: Dale Seymour Publications.
Reading and Thinking: Arthur Evans and Looking and Thinking: Arthur Evans. Learning Materials Ltd.
Basic Workbooks for Everyday books 1-4. Arnold Wheaton (good variety of material).
Brain Busters: Peter D Thoms: Arnold.
Electronic games such as Simon.

Exercise

Sensorimotor Activities: Academic Therapy Publications.
Motor Education and Perceptual Training: A. E. Tansley: Arnold Wheaton.
Switching on: Dr Paul E. Dennison.
Graded Activities for Children with Motor Difficulties: James Russell: Cambridge University Press.
Sensory Integration and the Child: Jean Ayres: Western Psychological Services.
Tracking Books: Ann Arbor.
Take Time: Mary Nash-Wortham and Jean Hunt: Robinswood Press: (fascinating variety of activity).

Mathematics

Ginn Mathematics Scheme: Ginn. (clearly laid out).
Mathswise books 1-3: Ray Allan, Martin Williams: Oxford University Press (good book for practice exercises).
See the Maths books 1 & 2: Sandra Gilfeather: Edward Arnold.
Dyslexia: basic Numeracy: Vicki Burge: Helen Arkell Dyslexia Centre.
On the Track to Problem Solving: Margaret McDougall, Rae Cook: Nelson: Blackie.
Number Practice books 1-4: A. J. Stables: Schofield & Sims.
Visual Maths: Educational Insights: (for number bonding up to 10).
Maths and Dyslexics: Anne Henderson: St David's College, Llandudno: (this book contains very good graphics on mathematical symbols (page 29).
Tables Teacher: Early Learning Centre: (Marvellous pencil case which revolves to provide answers to the tables).

Self-Esteem

Every Letter Counts: Susan Hampshire: Bantam Press: (collection of letters from those with dyslexic problems who have survived.
Unicorns are Real: Barbara Meister Vitale: Jalmar Press.
Free Flight: Barbara Meister Vitale: Ann Arbor: (both contain a fresh approach and numerous sayings which help boost the confidence).
Breakthrough Learning: Barbara Given: George Mason University, USA.
No Easy Answers: the Learning Disabled Child: Sally S. Smith, US Dept. of Health Education and Welfare.
Self-Assessment Forms: writing, reading, listening, Folens: (all photo-copiable).
Language User's Handbook: Tony Ramsay: E. J. Arnold. (for older pupils at the end of their tether – good for dipping into).
Computers, computer aids e.g. PAL, word processors.

Boxes of Ideas

Unique Reading Games.
The Reading Box.
Aston Portfolio.
Building Receptive and Expressive Language Skills.
Getting the Main Idea et alia (good 'no book approach').
Mathsteps: LDA.

Microtechnology
(See chapter 13)

For Older Pupils

Writing Workshop: Richard McRoberts: Macmillan. (an excellent guide to the craft of writing).
English Plus: T. McSweeney and M. Elam: Longman. (a practical scheme of work for the examination years – essays, punctuation, spelling, spoken English, comprehension).
The Oxford English Programme National Curriculum Stage 3: J. Selly, F. Green, D. Kitchen. Oxford University Press.
Subject Spellchecks. Spelling for Exams: E. G. Stirling.
Help for the Dyslexic Adolescent: E. G. Stirling: Better Books.
Highlight English books 1 and 2: Susan Duberly + Teacher's Resource Pack: Heinemann.
Enjoying English books 1-3: (extracts from novels, plays, poems well presented in themes).
Enjoying Poetry: More Enjoying Poetry: Appreciating Poetry: (an excellent selection of poetry and a superb teaching book). All by Sadler, Haylar, Powell. Macmillan.
Look it up: Peter Forrestal: Nelson: (a good handbook for help in the conventions of writing).
Take any Book: Richard Bain and Ali Cooper: GCSE. (very good for book reviews).
Spelling it Out: R. Pratley: BBC Publications.
Word Mastery: J. Conlan and M. Henley: Oxford University Press.
Spelling Matters: Bernard R. Sadler: Edward Arnold.
Mathematics Foundation Skills 11-14 yrs: Michael Ashcroft: Letts.
Problem Solving Pack: Edward Arnold.

And Not Forgetting

Learning Difficulties in Reading and Writing: A Teacher's Manual: Reason & Boote: NFER Nelson.
Specific Learning Difficulties: Dyslexia: Margaret Crombie: Jordanhill College of Education.
Fantastic Ideas for Frenzied Teachers: Christine Syme: Collins Educational.
Special Needs Information press: a monthly publication with very pertinent articles. 23 Saxholm Way, Southampton.
This Book Doesn't make sens çens sns scens sense. Jean Augur: Antony Rowe Ltd.
Reading Problems: Identification and Treatment: Peter Edwards: Heinemann.
Monaco Hang UP a/V Storage: Don Cresswell (for displaying the pupils' 'Best Work').

REFERENCES

BRADLEY L. (1988) 'Rhyme Recognition and Reading and Spelling in Young Children' in Masland R. L. and Masland M. R. *Pre-School Prevention of Reading Failure*. Parkton, Maryland. York Press.
DUNN R. and DUNN K. (1992) *Teaching Elementary Students Through Their Individual Learning Styles*. Allyn & Bacon, Massachusetts. (1992).

NOTES ON CONTRIBUTORS

NOTES ON CONTRIBUTORS

Jenni Barr

Jenni Barr qualified in Scotland as an educational psychologist before embarking on four years of research with Margaret Clark in Birmingham, looking at aspects of policy and provision for pupils with learning difficulties. She published 'Understanding Spelling' (SCRE, 1983) based on her doctoral thesis and for the last ten years has been employed in a variety of educational psychologist posts in Central and Fife Regions, and as a senior lecturer at Strathclyde University concerned with psychologist training. She remains committed to the generic work of an educational psychologist and to the importance of educational research in local authority settings.

Stewart Biggar

Dr Biggar is an educational psychologist with Tayside Region Psychological Service having recently completed post graduate training in educational psychology at Strathclyde University. He has accumulated a range of experiences in areas of research, university-tutoring, training and adult basic education.

Gordon Booth

Gordon Booth is currently Acting Regional Educational Psychologist for Grampian Region. Having had a long-standing interest in the problems faced by dyslexic children and their families, he regards it as a particular achievement to have been instrumental in setting up in 1978 the first of several special Learning Units for pupils with specific learning difficulties in Grampian and in having been associated with the specialist training of teachers in this field.

Morven Brown

Morven Brown is Learning Resources Co-ordinator at Daniel Stewarts and Melville College and the Mary Erskine School. A psychology graduate she trained as a primary teacher and then worked for the Child Guidance Service in Lothian Region as an educational psychologist until 1980, since this time she became interested in dyslexia and specific learning difficulties. She has been involved with the Edinburgh Dyslexia Association since the early 1980s. Her present post involves the development of support for learning throughout the school-age range.

Pat Brown

Pat Brown is at present in charge of a Reading Unit in Lothian Region which specialises in teaching pupils with Specific Learning Difficulties. Her interest in metacognition developed during the time she worked as a primary learning support teacher whilst studying for a Masters degree at Edinburgh University. She regularly presents seminars and workshops on aspects of metacognition at both local and national levels.

Sally Brown

Sally Brown in Professor of Education at the University of Stirling and was formerly director of the Scottish Council for Research in Education. Her current research interests are primarily in the field of special educational needs and teachers' thinking about teaching and learning. Once upon a time she was a physics teacher.

Helen Calcluth

Helen Calcluth has 20 years experience in teaching at Primary and Nursery levels. In 1987 she completed the British Dyslexia Diploma course. Over the last six years she has developed the PASS Programme to tackle the problem of specific learning difficulties in the mainstream classroom situation. The Programme is a multi-sensory, structured phonics programme which can be effectively used as an intervention programme in the whole-class situation or a remediation programme in the individual or group situation.

Catriona Collins

Dr Catriona Collins is Principal Teacher at George Watson's College, where she is in charge of the Learning Support Department (including a Dyslexic Unit for Secondary pupils). For the past six years she has been the Course Tutor for the RSA Diploma Course for teachers of pupils with specific learning difficulties. She obtained a Ph.D. in Psychology.

Margaret Crombie

Margaret Crombie is a part-time Lecturer in Specific Learning Difficulties at Moray House Institute, and a teacher of children with specific learning difficulties in the Renfrew Division of Strathclyde. She is the author of Specific Learning Difficulties (Dyslexia) A Teacher's Guide and is currently engaged in research into second language learning for pupils/students with specific learning difficulties.

Linda Cumming

Linda Cumming has worked in primary learning support and as a specialist teacher with Central Regional Psychological Service. She is now Advisory Teacher (Primary Learning Support) and is concerned mainly with policy, curriculum and staff development issues as they relate to pupils experiencing a wide range of learning difficulties.

Sheila Dobie

Sheila Dobie is Head of Department Movement Studies at Moray House Institute, Heriot Watt University. She initially trained in physical education followed by studies at the Laban Centre. A specialist interest led to an Advanced Diploma in Severe and Profound Learning Difficulties at Cambridge University and an MEd (SEN) at Stirling University. She is an Associate of the Institute of Neuro-Physiological Psychology and was awarded an OBE in the New Year's Honours 1991.

David Dodds

David Dodds is currently principal learning support special needs teacher at Boroughmuir High School. He has worked in secondary learning support since 1980, before which he was a primary teacher. He developed an in-service package on supporting pupils with specific learning difficulties/dyslexia in the secondary school while on part-time secondment from 1990/92.

Fernando Almeida Diniz

Fernando Almeida Diniz is Head of Department at Moray House Institute of Education, Heriot-Watt University and Chairperson of the Advisory Committee for the Specific Learning Difficulties Project. After teaching in special and mainstream schools, he lectured at the University of Greenwich, London, where he was Head of Division and Reader in Special Needs in Education. He has extensive international experience and has held visiting professorships at universities in Germany and Spain.

Morag L. Donaldson

Dr Morag Donaldson is a lecturer in the Department of Psychology, University of Edinburgh. Her teaching and research interests lie mainly in the area of language development in pre-school and primary school children. She is author of *Children's Explanations: a Psycholinguistic Study*. (Cambridge University Press, 1986).

Jill Duffield

Jill Duffield is a Resarch Fellow at the Department of Education, University of Stirling, and a former modern studies teacher. As well as the specific learning difficulties research she has taken part in the evaluation of pilot primary foreign language projects in Scotland, She is currently investigating how schools support the progress of lower achieving pupils, with Sally Brown and Sheila Riddell.

Marie Dougan

Marie Dougan is Senior Teacher – Learning Support (Information Technology) – Lothian Region. She graduated from Glasgow University with a degree in Biological Sciences, and taught Biology and General Science in secondary schools before moving into the Special Education sector in 1978. She has held her present post with responsibility for micro-technology and special education for 7 years and is currently undertaking a series of modules in Specific Learning Difficulties at Moray House.

Eileen Francis

Eileen Francis initiated the Specific Learning Difficulties Project at Moray House Institute. Until 1991 she was a Senior Lecturer at the Institute and contributed to courses provided by the Department of Curriculum and Support Studies. She is a member of the College of Speech and Language Therapists and of the Scottish Institute of Human Relations. Currently she is working independently on research and training projects.

Janet Hunter

Janet Hunter is a learning support teacher at Riccarton Primary School. She has considerable experience in the area of dyslexia and is engaged in promoting whole school aspects of assessment and teaching of children with learning difficulties. She is currently undertaking the modular courses in specific learning difficulties at Moray House.

Ros Hunter

Ros Hunter is assistant adviser in Borders Region with responsibility for Learning Support and Special Educational Needs. She is currently seconded to the Scottish Consultative Committee on the Curriculum to work on a national project promoting differentiation.

Vicky Hunter

Vicky Hunter is Principal Teacher, Learning Support at James Gillespie's High School, Edinburgh. Formerly Principal Teacher, Learning Support at Blackburn Academy, West Lothian. Prior to that Teacher in Charge, Support Unit, Dunfermline High School. She is interested in teaching children's thinking skills and understanding of their own learning styles, and is currently co-developer in James Gillespie's of 'Skills for Learning', which is a thinking skills course for all first year pupils.

Rhona Johnston

Dr Rhona Johnston gained her B.A. and Ph.D. in Psychology at the University of Hull. She then trained as a primary school teacher at Dundee College of Education, and worked for two years as a secondary school remedial teacher in Fife schools. Since 1979 she has been a lecturer in Psychology at University of St Andrews.

Mary Kiely

Mary Kiely taught initially in a rural primary school. After a break to bring up a family, she taught in a psychiatric unit and a unit for severely maladjusted pupils before her present post as a senior teacher in the learning support department of Dumfries Academy.

Sionah Lannen

Dr Sionah Lannen is an educational psychologist currently employed with Lancashire Education Authority. Following teacher training at Dundee she taught in Fife Region as a primary teacher, and learning support teacher. She then embarked on post-graduate training in educational psychology at Glasgow University before taking up posts in Canada, at Ottawa University and Western Quebec School Board. She has had a long-standing interest in specific learning difficulties in relation to teaching, assessment and teacher training.

Jean Miller

Jean Miller has been Headteacher of Portree Primary School in the Isle of Skye since January 1991. Prior to that she was Headteacher of a large primary school with a special class for pupils with moderate learning difficulties and a Special Education Unit for pupils with severe and profound learning difficulties. She was very active in promoting the integration of SEN pupils into mainstream and was a member of a Highland Region Working Party on Integration.

Rosemary McGhee

Rosemary McGhee is a Learning Support Teacher at Elgin High School. Initially trained as a Home Economics teacher she has completed RSA Diploma for Teachers of Children with Specific Learning Difficulties.

Marysia Nash

Marysia Nash is a speech and language therapist specialising in specific developmental language disorders and dyslexia. She works at the Royal Hospital for Sick Children in Edinburgh and the Burgh Language Unit in Musselburgh.

Anne O'Hare

Dr Anne O'Hare is Consultant Paediatrician, Community Child Health. Senior Lecturer, Department of Child Life and health, University of Edinburgh and honorary Consultant to Neurology Department, Royal Hospital for Sick Children.

Anne F. Philip

Anne Philip is specialist teacher responsible for students with specific learning difficulties at the High School of Dundee. Since joining the staff at the High School of Dundee in 1980 she has established a Learning Skills Centre which serves both as a resource base and a support classroom for students with specific learning difficulties. Anne has made a number of conference and seminar presentations on dyslexia and the use of resources.

Gavin Reid

Gavin Reid is Coordinator of the Specific Learning Difficulties Project at Moray House Institute/Heriot-Watt University, with responsibility for the development of teacher training in Specific Learning Difficulties. Following a lengthy period as a teacher in Grampian Region, he completed Post-Graduate training at Glasgow University in educational psychology before taking up employment as an educational psychologist in Grampian and Fife Regions. During that time he developed his interest in specific learning difficulties through involvement in research and staff development. He has presented conference papers on specific learning difficulties nationally and internationally.

Jennifer Reid

Jennifer Reid is a speech and language therapist who has specialised in the treatment of pre-school and primary school children with specific language impairment. She is currently working as a research fellow in the Department of Psychology, University of Edinburgh.

Sheila Riddell

Dr Sheila Riddell is a lecturer in the Department of Education, University of Stirling. Having graduated from Sussex University in 1976, she worked as an English teacher for seven years before enrolling for a PhD at Bristol University in 1984. The topic of her research was gender and option choice in rural comprehensive schools. She moved to Scotland in 1988 and took up the post of Research Fellow in the Department of Education, University of Edinburgh, working on a project in the area of special educational needs. Since moving to Stirling University in 1989, she has continue to research and write in the areas of special educational needs, gender and education and school effectiveness and improvement.

Nicola Robinson

Nicola Robinson is a speech and language therapist, currently employed in the community in Midlothian. She trained at Queen Margaret College in Edinburgh and has worked with a range of speech and language disorders with adults and children. She has developed an interest in the provision of services for children with written and spoken language disorders. Her chapter on the role of the speech therapist is based on a presentation which she made at the Annual Conference of the Edinburgh and South East Dyslexic Association in September 1991.

Sylvia Russell

Sylvia Russell is the Coordinator of Learning Support Services for Lanarkshire. She ran a Psychological Service Reading Centre for many years before changing to a peripatetic school based service. She is author of the Phonic Codecracker Programme (Jordanhill Publications 1992) and has completed a series of the Moray House modules in specific learning difficulties.

Keith Topping

Dr Keith Topping develops and researches methods for non-professionals (such as parents or peers) to tutor others in fundamental skills (eg reading, spelling, writing) and higher order learning (science, maths, etc), for use across a wide age range in many different contexts. He is the Director of the Centre for Paired Learning at the Department of Psychology, University of Dundee, where he also directs the postgraduate professional training course in educational psychology and the Higher Education Effective Learning Project.

George Turner

George Turner is Curriculum Development Officer – Microcomputers and Special Education, Fife Region. He graduated from Edinburgh University in Electrical Engineering and worked in the computer industry before returning to Edinburgh University and Moray House College and entering the teaching profession as a secondary maths teacher. He then taught in Special Education before taking up his current post responsible for all aspects of micro-computing in Special Education in Fife Region.

Charles Weedon

Dr Charles Weedon is Principal Teacher Learning Support at Perth Grammar School. After leaving the Royal Navy, he took an Edinburgh B.Ed., then worked as an English and Maths teacher, and taught in Shetland, Fife and Tayside. His M.Ed and Ph.D research focused on writing and reading skills.

SUBJECT INDEX

Symbols

5-14   10, 387, 388, 430, 432, 437, 438, 444

A

absence   184
absent   309
achievement   70, 71, 81, 89, 105, 145, 148, 156, 233, 386
achievements   191, 340
achieving   315
acid   52
analytic   48, 60
anxieties   105, 107, 139, 248, 403
anxiety   11, 42, 52, 53, 72, 141, 145, 156, 232, 233, 248, 249, 255, 277, 320, 376, 396, 398, 399, 404, 434
anxious   237, 247, 250, 303, 304, 398, 404, 433, 434
aphasia   318, 321, 335
arithmetic   30, 36, 38, 44, 274, 280, 281, 282, 283, 286, 287, 288, 289
arrow   204, 222, 223
assess   3, 270
assessed   339, 341, 350
assessing   66, 190
assessment   2, 4, 5, 6, 9, 10, 14, 16, 17, 18, 19, 21, 22, 24, 26, 27, 28, 30, 31, 32, 33, 34, 35, 36, 37, 38, 39, 42, 43, 44, 45, 46, 47, 49, 50, 51, 52, 53, 55, 57, 58, 60, 61, 63, 66, 72, 73, 76, 81, 82, 83, 88, 93, 32, 133, 134, 146, 147, 150, 152, 153, 180, 185, 190, 191, 252, 253, 323, 325, 326, 333, 336, 341, 349, 350, 351, 352, 354, 355, 369, 370, 371, 372, 376, 379, 380, 387, 389, 390, 391, 431, 432, 434, 435, 436
assignments   56, 116, 124, 125, 189, 196, 267, 401
attainment   28, 35, 54
attainments   8, 72, 74, 76, 94, 132, 339, 341
attention   14, 18, 21, 46, 49, 50, 51, 55, 56, 58, 68, 71, 74, 76, 145, 149, 177, 232, 246, 249, 250, 251, 252, 253, 255, 347, 371, 372, 377
attitude   6, 42, 88, 89, 107, 174, 175, 177, 179, 188, 197, 270
attitudes   28, 382, 385, 386
auditory   14, 15, 29, 37, 38, 39, 41, 56, 59, 60, 67, 69, 72, 75, 85, 94, 128, 129, 130, 136, 137, 146, 148, 157, 158, 162, 163, 176, 184, 186, 203, 204, 216, 217, 226, 228, 252, 253, 279, 280, 321, 322, 324, 333, 344, 347, 350, 355, 364, 367, 371, 372, 373, 374, 389
automatic   83, 129, 259, 264, 268

automaticity   203, 205, 206, 219, 221, 247, 249, 250, 255
automatisation   16
automisation   149

B

'b' and 'd'   262
b/d   39, 80
BAS   433
behaviour   10, 47, 50, 56, 57, 62, 106, 107, 108, 111, 176, 192, 291, 294, 295, 296, 304, 357, 358, 363, 370, 384, 389, 398, 402, 433, 434
behavioural   71, 81, 144, 148, 152, 184, 241, 318, 327, 328, 329, 330, 331, 334, 336, 345, 377, 387, 398, 401
behaviours   147, 235, 320, 328, 331, 382, 384
birth   71, 76, 77, 143, 144, 150, 152
brain   47, 67, 68, 69, 71, 72, 76, 77, 188, 279, 280, 354, 357, 358, 359, 379
British ability scales   52

C

central nervous system   148
clumsiness   144, 148, 1152, 92, 370
clumsy   67, 145, 151, 152, 153
co-ordination   67, 73, 150, 152
cognitive   5, 6, 9, 11, 45, 46, 47, 48, 49, 50, 51, 52, 53, 55, 57, 61, 62, 63, 64, 69, 72, 76, 143, 146, 147, 152, 200, 201, 202, 204, 205, 212, 213, 214, 216, 220, 222, 232, 275, 277, 278, 279, 280, 286, 287, 288, 292, 293, 294, 297, 300, 302, 303, 304, 305, 306, 318, 322, 331, 333, 334, 339, 345, 385, 386, 387, 388, 395, 406
communication   9, 11, 20, 174, 179, 180, 318, 319, 326, 330, 331, 332, 335, 336, 381, 382, 383, 384, 385, 390, 392
communicative   318, 319, 320, 323, 326, 328, 330, 331, 332, 334
community child health   65, 66, 77
comprehend   194
comprehension   7, 9, 14, 18, 19, 20, 29, 36, 37, 38, 47, 49, 50, 52, 53, 54, 55, 56, 59, 63, 70, 71, 77, 95, 106, 109, 123, 124, 125, 200, 209, 211, 212, 213, 214, 215, 218, 219, 220, 222, 223, 234, 239, 240, 241, 247, 251, 253, 275, 292, 293, 296, 297, 298, 299, 300, 301, 302, 305, 306, 308, 309, 319, 320, 324, 326, 332, 333, 339, 341, 344, 345, 346, 347, 348, 349, 352, 367, 369, 370, 396, 406, 434, 435, 442, 451, 452, 453, 457
computer   40, 41, 87, 96, 98, 101, 102, 103, 107, 108, 109, 110, 111, 113, 154, 157, 158, 159, 160, 161, 162, 163, 164, 165, 166, 171, 172, 312, 313, 430, 431, 433, 436, 449, 451, 454, 456

computers   173, 176, 178, 190
concentration   18, 49, 50, 51, 71, 370, 372
confidence   11, 19, 29, 39, 41, 51, 59, 85, 88, 89, 101, 104, 106, 107, 111, 114, 138, 232, 233, 239, 240, 258, 268, 270, 370, 386, 389, 394, 396, 397, 398, 399, 400, 402, 404, 434, 436, 437
confident   54, 55, 396, 402, 404
congenital   275, 279, 280
consult   65, 66
consultancy   5, 7, 11, 32, 37, 42, 45, 46, 52, 53, 61, 65, 66, 429
consultation   4, 32, 33, 88, 111, 431, 432, 434
consultations   108
consultative   434
consulting   111
counselling   105, 112, 183, 232, 244
curricula   54
curricular   176
curriculum   4, 5, 6, 8, 9, 10, 11, 14, 21, 22, 43, 45, 46, 52, 53, 55, 61, 80, 86, 90, 93, 94, 95, 108, 111, 112, 114, 115, 117, 124, 125, 135, 173, 174, 180, 183, 186, 187, 194, 195, 196, 197, 235, 243, 267, 268, 272, 274, 284, 285, 292, 300, 301, 381, 385, 386, 387, 389, 390, 391, 396, 398, 405, 430, 431, 437, 438, 457

D

decode   130, 201, 211, 214, 230
decoding   14, 15, 19, 50, 98, 106, 107, 201, 203, 207, 208, 210, 211, 212, 213, 214, 215, 218, 219, 221, 227, 246, 247, 250, 252, 294, 295, 296, 299, 303, 307, 308, 347, 348, 436
deficiencies   144, 147
deficits   146, 151
developmental   143, 144, 145, 146, 148, 149, 150, 151, 152, 153
diagnose   26, 93, 97, 104, 131
diagnosis   5, 32, 34, 35, 36, 37, 81, 147, 151, 354, 370, 379
diagnostic   16, 21, 30, 31
dictaphone   312, 313
dictaphones   180, 191, 433
differentiate   48
differentiated   93, 94, 96, 108, 173
differentiating   111, 215, 388, 389, 391
differentiation   4, 6, 9, 93, 94, 112, 114, 116, 117, 124, 183, 186, 391, 405
discrepancies   5, 14, 19, 20, 22, 436
discrepancy   19, 20, 25, 35, 39, 94, 212, 346, 349

discrepant   433
discussion   6, 9, 85, 89, 91, 93, 97, 115, 117, 120, 121, 122, 123, 124, 125, 156, 213, 216, 261, 269, 270, 278, 299, 302, 309, 310, 314, 381, 384, 385, 387, 388, 389, 390, 392, 395, 403, 445
distractability   52, 53, 58
dyscalculia   273, 274, 279, 280, 281, 286, 287, 288
Dyslexia Association   67, 437
dyspraxia   323, 324, 343, 344, 345, 347, 353, 371

E

educational psychologist   6, 45, 46, 47, 48, 51, 53, 55, 61, 63, 1105, 06, 173, 183, 185, 193, 341, 349, 350
educational psychologists   3, 83, 200, 202
embarrassment   85, 86, 398, 400
emotional   10, 20, 29, 34, 81, 183, 184, 186, 191, 197, 232, 241, 318, 384, 394, 396, 397, 398, 401, 403, 405
emotionally   402, 403
emotions   404
environment   15, 20, 48, 55, 56, 65, 66, 71, 143, 146, 154, 175, 194, 196, 249, 254, 320, 438
environmental   318, 320, 358
exam   84, 85, 86, 87, 88
examination   189, 190, 197, 400
examinations   10, 165, 172
extracted   258
extraction   185, 193
eyesight   34, 35

F

factors   47, 53, 58, 61, 67, 69
failure   5, 6, 15, 16, 23, 35, 40, 41, 68, 89, 97, 100, 104, 144, 145, 148, 232, 277, 278, 315, 395, 396, 397, 398, 402, 404
family history   67, 74, 81, 436
fluency   53, 55
frustration   104, 304

G

game   96, 97, 98, 112, 113, 390
games   41, 54, 136, 137, 210, 330, 331, 332, 436, 441, 455, 457

genetics   5, 69, 77
gestalt   188, 214, 215, 220
global   60
grammatical   318, 320, 321, 323, 324, 326, 332335,
group   45, 48, 54, 55, 58, 59, 60, 81, 82, 83, 85, 93, 94, 96, 97, 100, 108, 118, 120, 121, 122, 123, 124, 125, 128, 129, 130, 131, 132, 133, 134, 176, 299, 301, 308, 309, 382, 383, 384, 385, 387, 388, 391, 392
groups   34, 233, 239, 382, 383, 388, 390, 431
guidelines   5, 174, 177, 386, 429, 432

H

hand   184, 190, 193, 195
handedness   67, 76, 77
handwriting   8, 30, 40, 97, 99, 100, 102, 106, 110, 111, 137, 138, 139, 146, 154, 175, 257, 258, 259, 260, 261, 264, 265, 266, 267, 268, 269, 270, 271, 311, 312, 313, 433, 435, 448, 449, 455
handwritten   156
hardware   163, 166, 167, 430
hearing   34, 35, 38, 70, 318, 335, 336, 337, 370, 371, 379
hereditary   358
history   34, 35
hyperactivity   144

I

identification   5, 7, 10, 15, 116, 9, 20, 21, 23, 24, 47, 54, 55, 56, 66, 93, 114, 184, 185, 186, 192, 193, 195, 396, 399, 405, 431
identify   3, 5, 9
immature   201, 433, 434
immaturity   67, 106, 184, 192, 319, 398, 401
impulsive   278
impulsivity   144
in-service   431, 436
inattention   299, 300, 398, 401
indicators   36, 81, 362, 370
individual   5, 9, 10, 28, 30, 32, 34, 35, 38, 41, 42, 45, 47, 48, 52, 54, 55, 58, 60, 62, 94, 96, 100, 108, 110, 112, 128, 130, 132, 134, 147, 148, 149, 187, 189, 190, 195, 198, 201, 203, 204, 207, 211, 213, 218, 219, 220, 221, 223, 258, 297, 300, 321, 323, 325, 326, 327, 328, 331, 334, 428, 429, 430, 432
individualised   73, 106, 174, 193, 259, 383, 385

Perspectives on Practice

individually   116, 121, 122, 124
inherited   69, 76
intellectual   46, 51
intelligence   51, 64, 68, 74, 77, 144, 184, 195, 273, 276, 333
intelligent   63, 94
interaction   8, 30, 32, 54, 55, 58, 61, 204, 212, 214, 216, 248, 253, 291, 295, 382, 385, 389, 390, 391
interactive   31, 201, 202, 212, 214, 216, 219, 223, 247, 248, 294, 299
intervention   6, 10, 15, 16, 17, 18, 26, 35, 66, 68, 81, 82, 111, 130, 131, 134, 144, 145, 146, 147, 148, 149, 151, 211, 220, 232, 234, 242, 303, 325, 326, 327, 328, 329, 330, 331, 332, 333, 334, 335, 336, 337, 342, 347, 350, 431, 432, 433, 435
interventional   145, 146
interventions   292
IQ   50, 51, 54, 56, 63, 69, 70, 73, 74, 75, 275, 280, 339, 349

J

no entries

K

kinaesthetic   20, 39, 40, 146, 147, 148, 156, 203, 218
kinesthetic   60, 94, 99, 373

L

language   6, 8, 9, 34, 38, 54, 56, 58, 62, 66, 67, 68, 69, 70, 71, 72, 75, 77, 96, 97, 101, 102, 103, 110, 114, 115, 116, 117, 118, 121, 131, 145, 146, 149, 157, 158, 184, 187, 189, 190, 192, 193, 200, 201, 203, 206, 210, 211, 215, 216, 219, 220, 222, 223, 273, 274, 277, 278, 279, 280, 281, 283, 287, 318, 319, 320, 321, 322, 323, 324, 325, 326, 327, 328, 329, 330, 331, 332, 333, 334, 335, 336, 337, 338, 339, 340, 341, 342, 343, 344, 345, 346, 347, 348, 349, 350, 351, 352, 353, 354, 355, 357, 358, 359, 360, 362, 363, 366, 367, 369, 370, 371, 372, 374, 376, 377, 379, 380, 381, 382, 385, 386, 388, 389, 390, 391, 392
laterality   37, 53, 80, 81, 370
laziness   26, 398, 401, 402
lazy   104, 399, 402
learning   291, 292, 294, 295, 296, 297, 299, 300, 301, 302, 303, 304, 305, 306
learning style   14, 20, 21, 22, 23, 24, 45, 48, 52, 55, 56, 57, 60, 61, 62, 63, 313
learning styles   5, 6, 8, 94, 112, 187, 211, 217, 218, 220, 221, 278, 390
learning support   10, 34, 42, 51, 54, 82, 111, 114, 130, 173, 178, 180, 183, 184, 185, 191, 196, 309, 355, 372, 376, 377, 390, 399, 428, 430, 431, 432, 433, 434, 435, 436

liaise   95, 106
liaison   54, 86, 95, 108, 111, 183, 186, 193, 196, 341, 430
linguistic   70, 318, 319, 321, 322, 323, 326, 327, 328, 329, 330, 331, 332, 333, 334, 335, 336, 395
linguistics   323, 336, 352, 381, 385, 386
listening   19, 37, 38, 39, 116, 117, 247, 248, 253, 372, 374, 384, 387, 389, 390, 444, 445, 451, 456
literacy   5, 7, 9, 10, 16, 35, 39, 44, 47, 49, 50, 67, 89, 92, 95, 96, 103, 141, 191, 192, 194, 200, 203, 205, 210, 220, 222, 223, 232, 233, 239, 240, 242, 244, 245, 248, 256, 303, 305, 306, 329, 338, 339, 341, 342, 343, 345, 346, 347, 348, 354, 355, 357, 359, 362, 363, 364, 367, 372, 374, 376, 377, 380, 395, 396, 398, 404
literate   166
LS   173, 174, 175, 178, 179, 180

M

material   47, 48, 49, 51, 52, 54, 55, 56, 60, 82, 83, 87, 103, 114, 116, 121, 125, 154, 161, 162, 174, 178, 180, 233, 238, 239, 240, 309, 400
materials   2, 6, 40, 138, 297, 430, 433, 438, 450, 454, 455
mathematics   7, 8, 72, 103, 185, 193, 273, 274, 275, 276, 277, 278, 279, 280, 281, 282, 283, 284, 286, 287, 288, 289, 441, 456, 457
maths   112, 115, 145, 174, 243, 314, 399, 435, 436
medical   35, 66, 68, 70, 72, 76, 106, 354, 355, 370
medicine   65, 76, 77, 78
memorise   96, 103, 106

memory   15, 16, 18, 19, 39, 40, 49, 50, 51, 52, 53, 62, 63, 64, 69, 70, 72, 80, 81, 94, 95, 99, 105, 110, 138, 144, 147, 148, 154, 155, 163, 164, 165, 167, 176, 186, 189, 195, 202, 203, 204, 205, 206, 207, 208, 211, 216, 230, 231, 249, 255, 280, 281, 283, 293, 296, 319, 322, 336, 349, 363, 364, 367, 369, 371, 373, 374, 389, 390
metacognition   9, 105, 188, 212, 213, 219, 291, 292, 293, 294, 297, 301, 302, 305
metacognitive   21, 45, 55, 107, 193, 292, 293, 294, 295, 296, 297, 299, 302, 303, 304, 305, 306, 386, 388
micro-technology   7
microcomputer   16
microcomputers   154
microtechnology   16, 173, 178
model   234
modelling   188, 219, 248, 251, 253, 300, 301, 303, 327, 331
motivated   162, 166, 235, 434

motivation   7, 8, 29, 57, 59, 88, 89, 104, 105, 178, 187, 189, 191, 192, 196, 249, 253, 254, 255, 256, 258, 259, 261, 265, 270, 292, 311, 314, 320, 331, 333, 386, 388
motivational   304, 396
motivator   98, 102
motivators   431
motor   16, 17, 25, 38, 67, 71, 73, 77, 78, 106, 137, 139, 143, 144, 145, 146, 147, 148, 149, 150, 151, 152, 153, 156, 192, 193, 247, 250, 252, 255, 274, 280, 288, 323, 343, 366, 371, 372, 399
movement   143, 144, 145, 146, 147, 149, 150, 151, 152, 153
multi-sensory   40, 41, 60, 73, 82, 83, 94, 95, 96, 99, 100, 103, 110, 128, 129, 130, 134, 136, 137, 139, 1189, 92, 203, 204, 219, 220, 222, 223, 373

N

names   15, 359, 369, 371
naming   81, 227, 229, 253, 349, 350, 351, 353
nervous system   355, 358
neurological   5, 11, 67, 71, 76, 149, 150, 184, 273, 274, 275, 277, 279, 280, 288, 354, 358, 380
neurology   65, 76, 77, 78, 355
number   27, 29, 30, 81, 82, 83, 184, 185, 187, 192, 274, 275, 276, 280, 281, 283, 284, 285, 287, 288, 311, 313, 314
numbers   53, 103
nursery   7, 15, 192, 397

O

observation   32, 39, 42, 47, 50, 51, 57, 60, 61, 185, 188, 389, 390
observational   47, 57, 58, 60, 63
observations   29
observe   259, 261, 307, 308
organisation   2, 3, 8, 49, 51, 52, 53, 58, 95, 104, 155, 205, 216, 275, 276, 371
organisational   51, 58, 176, 177, 274, 285
organise   51, 53
organised   434
organising   6, 47, 104, 105, 109, 187, 188, 387
orientation   53, 81
over-learning   203, 206
overlearning   247

476   *Specific Learning Difficulties (Dyslexia)*

P

paediatric   65, 66, 70, 72, 73, 75, 76, 77, 146
paediatrician   5
paediatricians   47
paired reading   8, 88, 98, 101, 111, 98, 233, 234, 236, 237, 239, 240, 242, 243, 245, 247, 248, 256
parent   185, 236, 237, 239, 241, 242, 243
parental   6, 320
parents   2, 3, 4, 8, 10, 12, 32, 33, 35, 38, 42, 46, 66, 72, 88, 91, 98, 102, 104, 111, 112, 174, 176, 179, 232, 237, 239, 241, 242, 243, 244, 247, 248, 249, 250, 251, 253, 254, 320, 326, 328, 331, 370, 372, 376, 379, 397, 398, 399, 400, 401, 402, 403, 404, 429, 430, 432, 433, 434, 435, 436, 437
peer   85, 115, 125, 203, 210, 216, 314, 340, 258, 399
peers   96, 97, 103, 104, 107, 165, 232, 233, 237, 243, 249, 307, 312, 322, 328, 329, 397, 403, 404
perception   145, 147
perceptual   143, 144, 145, 146, 148, 149, 151, 152
phonic   36, 41, 54, 56, 82, 83, 128, 130, 131, 134, 202, 204, 206, 209, 211, 217, 218, 234, 369, 371, 373, 435
phonics   95, 96, 98, 108, 135, 136, 230, 339, 344, 346
phonologic   321, 323, 324, 326, 327, 331, 333, 336, 343, 344, 348
phonological   7, 8, 14, 15, 16, 17, 19, 23, 24, 37, 47, 49, 50, 62, 69, 70, 106, 192, 201, 202, 203, 207, 208, 209, 210, 211, 215, 218, 219, 220, 222, 223, 225, 226, 227, 228, 229, 230, 231, 246, 253, 303, 342, 343, 344, 345, 347, 349, 351, 352, 353, 359, 363, 364, 369, 371, 372, 373, 374, 379, 380, 395, 406
phonology   41, 252, 318, 324, 336, 359, 364, 367, 374
physical   143, 144, 146, 149, 150, 151, 152, 153
policies   3, 4
policy   3, 4, 10, 12, 85, 86, 189, 429, 438
pragmatic   323, 324, 326, 327, 330, 335, 336, 396
pragmatics   323, 326, 335, 362, 367
praise   89, 105, 194, 235, 236, 242, 250, 314
praising   327
pre-school   66, 70, 71, 145, 150, 151, 152, 226, 231, 291, 340, 342, 354, 372, 376, 433
primaries   34
primary   7, 12, 20, 38, 39, 50, 51, 82, 84, 93, 95, 97, 99, 100, 101, 102, 105, 108, 112, 130, 131, 173, 174, 176, 185, 189, 192, 193, 194, 195, 196, 257, 272, 397, 399, 403, 428, 429
primary school   295

processing   47, 48, 49, 50, 52, 53, 56, 62
profile   5, 35, 37, 38, 42, 45, 49, 51, 52, 201, 283, 284, 387, 433, 436
profiles   144, 145, 151
programme   2, 4, 5, 6, 8, 10, 26, 30, 31, 35, 36, 39, 40, 41, 42, 72, 73, 76, 77, 93, 95, 96, 97, 98, 101, 102, 105, 106, 107, 108, 110, 113, 128, 129, 130, 131, 132, 134, 146, 147, 148, 151, 162, 188, 190, 193, 202, 203, 204, 210, 211, 215, 217, 218, 258, 259, 297, 303, 306, 330, 381, 387, 388, 430, 432, 433, 434, 435, 436, 437, 438, 441, 444, 450, 452, 453, 457
programmes   6, 7, 11, 14, 21, 51, 52, 54, 55, 82, 83, 86, 92, 45, 147, 152, 226, 327, 328, 331, 334, 449
programs   156, 157, 161, 162, 163, 164, 166, 167
psychological   20, 23, 24, 45, 47, 62, 63, 64, 88, 89, 145, 150, 151, 153, 191, 198, 370, 389, 394, 398
psychological services   430
psychologist   132, 133, 394, 397, 406, 432, 433, 436
psychologists   2, 3, 291
psychology   377, 379

Q

no entries

R

read   47, 49, 50, 51, 53, 54, 55, 56, 57, 58, 59, 62, 63, 64, 66, 67, 68, 69, 70, 71, 72, 73, 74, 77, 78, 176, 395, 398, 404, 406
readers   83
reading   7, 8, 9, 14, 15, 16, 17, 18, 19, 20, 23, 24, 25, 29, 30, 31, 35, 36, 37, 38, 39, 41, 42, 44, 80, 81, 83, 85, 86, 87, 88, 89, 91, 92, 93, 94, 95, 96, 97, 98, 100, 101, 102, 103, 104, 106, 107, 109, 110, 111, 112, 113, 123, 128, 131, 132, 138, 141, 142, 145, 148, 149, 160, 161, 163, 172, 173, 174, 175, 176, 178, 180, 185, 191, 192, 194, 195, 196, 200, 201, 202, 203, 204, 205, 206, 207, 208, 209, 210, 211, 212, 213, 215, 216, 217, 218, 219, 200, 220, 221, 222, 223, 224, 225, 226, 227, 228, 229, 230, 231, 232, 233, 234, 235, 236, 237, 238, 239, 240, 241, 242, 243, 244, 245, 246, 247, 248, 249, 250, 251, 252, 253, 254, 255, 256, 274, 278, 281, 282, 287, 288, 291, 292, 293, 294, 295, 296, 297, 299, 300, 301, 302, 303, 304, 305, 306, 307, 308, 309, 319, 329, 335, 337, 338, 339, 340, 341, 342, 343, 344, 345, 346, 347, 348, 350, 351, 352, 353, 354, 355, 357, 358, 359, 362, 363, 364, 367, 369, 371, 372, 376, 377, 379, 380, 395, 397, 398, 400, 406, 431, 433, 434, 435, 436, 440, 441, 442, 443, 444, 445, 446, 447, 451, 452, 453, 454, 455, 456, 457, 458
reading recovery   81, 399

reciprocal teaching   299, 300, 301, 303, 304, 305, 306
record   26, 28, 31, 32
record of needs   88, 173, 433, 434
recording   204, 222
records   34, 42, 105
referral   29, 34, 35, 69, 192, 348, 349, 398, 432, 436
referrals   258, 377
reflexes   147, 148, 152
remedial   34, 36, 39, 72, 73, 146, 147, 150, 152, 185
remediation   81, 117, 149, 162, 232, 323, 326, 351, 372, 377, 380
report-writing   31
reports   185, 186
resource   6, 7, 183, 184, 198, 385, 390, 397, 406, 430, 431, 432, 433, 437, 438, 451, 452, 457
resources   3, 7, 10, 45, 46, 53, 57, 60, 61, 86, 116, 233, 243, 248, 438, 439, 444, 446, 450
reversal   106
reversals   18, 34, 35, 37, 53

S

scotopic sensitivity   18, 23, 24, 252
Scottish Dyslexia Trust   2
scribe   86, 89, 196, 312, 313, 433
scribes   19, 20, 180
scribing   312, 313
secondary   7, 12, 34, 39, 42, 86, 87, 110, 111, 114, 125, 127, 137, 173, 175, 189, 195, 196, 257, 258, 262, 265, 270, 307, 309, 311, 312, 313, 397, 400, 403, 428, 429
self esteem   253, 257, 258, 270, 278
self image   191, 192, 197, 249, 386
self worth   292
self-concept   59, 89, 438, 450
self-confidence   233
self-esteem   8, 10, 19, 39, 75, 85, 104, 105, 107, 315, 396, 397, 402, 403, 406
self-image   102, 111, 232, 313
semantic   363, 396, 379
semantics   359, 362, 367
sensory   5, 50, 60, 144, 146, 147, 148, 150, 151, 152, 184, 188, 189, 192, 274
sequence   41, 81, 115, 116, 121, 124, 125, 389
sequences   154, 343, 349, 352, 359, 363, 371, 373, 376

Perspectives on Practice

sequencing   15, 36, 39, 52, 58, 59, 67, 80, 81, 95, 101, 104, 128, 129, 138, 157, 163, 280, 322, 452
social   28, 32, 34, 54, 55, 66, 75, 86, 145, 232, 239, 248, 275, 278, 283, 291, 300, 302, 309, 319, 330, 332, 333, 357, 362, 366, 377, 381, 384, 386, 389, 392, 394, 395, 396, 398, 399, 400, 402, 403, 406
software   154, 159, 160, 163, 164, 165, 166, 167, 169, 170, 171, 172, 191430
spatial   274, 276, 279, 281, 287, 288
specialised   185
specialist   5, 10, 81, 83, 86, 87, 132, 183, 202, 221, 232, 245, 376, 377, 397, 401, 430, 431, 432, 433, 434
speech   9, 34, 47, 58, 66, 67, 70, 72, 73, 77, 149, 163, 164, 192, 193, 247, 250, 318, 320, 321, 323, 324, 326, 328, 330, 331, 335, 336, 337, 338, 340, 341, 342, 343, 344, 345, 348, 349, 350, 351, 352, 353, 354, 355, 357, 358, 359, 360, 362, 363, 364, 366, 367, 370, 371, 372, 373, 374, 376, 378, 379, 380, 381, 382, 385, 386, 391
speech therapist   354, 355, 360, 370, 371, 372, 373, 374, 376, 377, 378
spell   47, 54, 55, 62
spelling   6, 9, 30, 35, 36, 37, 38, 39, 40, 41, 44, 69, 70, 81, 82, 83, 84, 86, 87, 91, 93, 97, 98, 99, 100, 101, 102, 104, 106, 107, 108, 109, 110, 111, 112, 113, 128, 130, 131, 132, 133, 134, 135, 136, 137, 138, 139, 141, 142, 145, 148, 154, 158, 159, 160, 162, 163, 174, 175, 176, 178, 185, 187, 190, 191, 192, 195, 202, 204, 215, 220, 221, 222, 224, 229, 242, 243, 258, 270, 293, 303, 311, 313, 314, 315, 316, 338, 340, 341, 342, 343, 344, 345, 347, 350, 351, 352, 353, 357, 358, 359, 362, 363, 364, 367, 369, 371, 376, 377, 380, 400, 433, 434, 435, 436, 441, 443, 448, 449, 451, 452, 454, 457, 458
strategies   5, 6, 7, 9, 15, 21, 22, 26, 29, 33, 35, 36, 39, 42, 46, 47, 48, 50, 57, 83, 86, 94, 100, 101, 103, 107, 114, 135, 136, 138, 139, 141, 144, 146, 147, 151, 154, 156, 174, 175, 177, 188, 191, 194, 196, 200, 201, 202, 203, 206, 207, 209, 211, 213, 216, 218, 220, 222, 292, 293, 294, 295, 296, 297, 298, 299, 300, 301, 302, 303, 305, 306, 307, 308, 309, 311, 313, 314, 323, 325, 344, 347, 369, 372, 390, 391, 394, 395, 396, 404, 430, 431, 437, 441, 449, 450
strategy   4, 9, 14, 105, 138, 149, 161, 248, 292, 293, 294, 295, 297, 298, 299, 300, 301, 302, 303, 304, 305, 306, 343, 386
stress   97, 104, 109, 246, 247, 249, 396, 397, 399, 401, 404
stressed   156, 166
structure   95, 100, 101, 105
structured   41, 51, 54, 55, 56, 82, 83, 86, 94, 95, 96, 97, 98, 106, 114, 128, 131, 134, 137, 138, 175, 176, 192, 202, 211, 217, 233, 240, 243, 303, 326, 331, 332, 431, 434, 436, 437
structuring   109

study skills   189, 450, 453, 455
support   2, 4, 7, 10, 12, 34, 42, 46, 47, 50, 51, 54, 57, 82, 85, 86, 88, 89, 91, 93, 98, 100, 104, 108, 111, 154, 155, 156, 157, 158, 160, 161, 164, 165, 171, 173, 174, 175, 176, 177, 178, 179, 180, 183, 184, 185, 186, 187, 188, 191, 192, 194, 196, 197, 198, 202, 210, 211, 213, 215, 217, 223, 247, 248, 249, 251, 397, 399, 400, 401, 402, 404, 428, 429
supporting   7, 101, 106
supportive   97, 304, 306

T

tactile   60, 94, 146, 148, 203, 218, 322
tactual   20
tape   86, 87, 92, 97, 98, 101, 103, 108, 116, 125, 176, 180, 181, 191, 195, 248, 309, 312, 374, 433, 434, 445, 451, 452
tape-recording   31
taped   42, 54, 56, 180
tapes   20, 178, 309
taping   313
technique   156, 162, 164, 233, 234, 235, 236, 237, 242, 243, 244, 399
techniques   54, 56, 68, 70, 73, 75, 115, 141, 146, 187, 188, 197, 203, 204, 206, 222, 275, 325, 327, 331, 333, 334
technology   7, 16, 72, 154, 155, 161, 162, 164, 167, 172, 187, 190, 191, 197, 430, 433
test   14, 16, 17, 18, 19, 26, 27, 28, 29, 30, 31, 32, 33, 35, 36, 37, 38, 39, 42, 44, 47, 51, 52, 53, 57, 61, 62, 63, 117, 123, 131, 132, 133, 148, 153, 237, 239, 240, 241, 242, 294, 300, 303, 307, 313, 314, 315, 316
testing   35, 38, 84, 131, 136, 185, 253
tests   177, 185, 211, 218, 326, 339, 346, 349, 350
therapist   9, 318, 320, 323, 326, 327, 328, 330, 331, 338, 341, 342, 348, 349, 350, 351
therapists   66, 385
therapy   34, 73, 74, 75, 76, 77, 146, 150, 151, 152, 192, 328, 331, 332, 333, 342, 348, 349, 351, 352
thinking   26, 30, 145, 151, 188, 191, 197, 213, 215, 216, 217, 220, 247, 252, 275, 276, 286, 302, 303, 304, 382, 383, 386, 387, 391
tracking   18, 53, 54, 55, 109, 252, 253, 446, 451, 456
training   3, 5, 7, 11, 82, 84, 85, 86, 88, 89, 114, 145, 146, 147, 152, 184, 188, 191
tuition   185, 186, 258, 259, 372, 428
tutor   248, 253
tutorial   121

Perspectives on Practice

tutoring   17, 98, 115, 233, 234, 237, 239, 240, 242, 244, 294
tutors   111, 232, 234, 235, 236, 237, 239, 240, 241, 242, 243, 244

U

under-achievement   71
underachieving   144
understanding   27, 29, 47, 57, 83, 84, 88, 97, 98, 104, 105, 115, 117, 121, 122, 123, 124, 125, 276, 277, 278, 281, 282, 283, 284, 286, 294, 295, 296, 297, 301, 305, 308, 314, 315, 316, 346, 348, 349, 381, 382, 384, 387, 389, 390, 396, 397, 402, 403, 404, 406, 441, 446

V

verbal   35, 36, 39, 48, 49, 52, 53, 56, 62, 67, 69, 71, 72, 73, 105, 276, 277, 279, 281, 286, 288, 338, 339, 341, 342, 343, 344, 346, 347, 349, 350, 353, 381, 382, 384, 389, 390, 392, 433, 436
visual   5, 7, 8, 14, 16, 17, 18, 23, 25, 29, 37, 39, 40, 41, 52, 53, 54, 56, 59, 60, 67, 68, 69, 70, 71, 73, 74, 77, 78, 80, 94, 95, 99, 100, 101, 109, 110, 115, 121, 129, 130, 135, 136, 137, 139, 141, 144, 146, 148, 154, 155, 163, 167, 176, 184, 186, 202, 204, 215, 221, 225, 228, 229, 230, 251, 252, 253, 276, 279, 280, 322, 328, 343, 344, 346, 347, 355, 358, 366, 367, 369, 371, 372, 373, 451, 456
visually   247
vocabulary   35, 36, 38, 39, 40, 44, 47, 53, 55, 56, 87, 96, 97, 103, 116, 137, 157, 158, 241, 320, 330, 332, 346, 348, 349, 351, 357, 359, 361, 362, 364, 366, 367, 369, 370, 373, 374, 382, 389, 390, 391, 442, 443, 444, 446
vocational   191

W

WISC   51, 52, 62, 63
WISC-R   433
withdraw   85, 86
withdrawal   85, 95, 204
withdrawn   86
word blindness   68
word processing   173, 174, 175, 178, 430, 436
word processor   312, 444, 456
word processors   178, 180, 190, 195, 197, 433
worksheet   123, 125, 389
worksheets   95, 97, 108, 111, 162, 164, 391
write   176, 180, 181, 359, 395, 404

writing   7, 8, 9, 31, 32, 35, 37, 39, 40, 41, 42, 54, 55, 62, 73, 77, 82, 84, 86, 88, 91, 92, 97, 99, 100, 101, 105, 106, 107, 109, 110, 111, 112, 113, 117, 124, 131, 137, 138, 139, 145, 146, 148, 149, 154, 155, 156, 163, 173, 174, 175, 176, 177, 180, 181, 192, 193, 242, 243, 258, 259, 260, 264, 265, 266, 267, 268, 269, 270, 271, 274, 311, 313, 339, 340, 354, 359, 373, 376, 379, 391, 398, 435, 436, 444, 446, 448, 452, 453, 454, 456, 457, 458

written   26, 30, 32, 52, 53, 54, 55, 58, 59, 116, 124, 125, 174, 180, 187, 189, 190, 192, 193, 194, 195, 196, 310, 312, 313, 340, 342, 343, 344, 347, 352, 353, 354, 355, 357, 358, 359, 367, 370, 371, 376, 380

X

no entries

Y

no entries

Z

no entries

AUTHOR INDEX

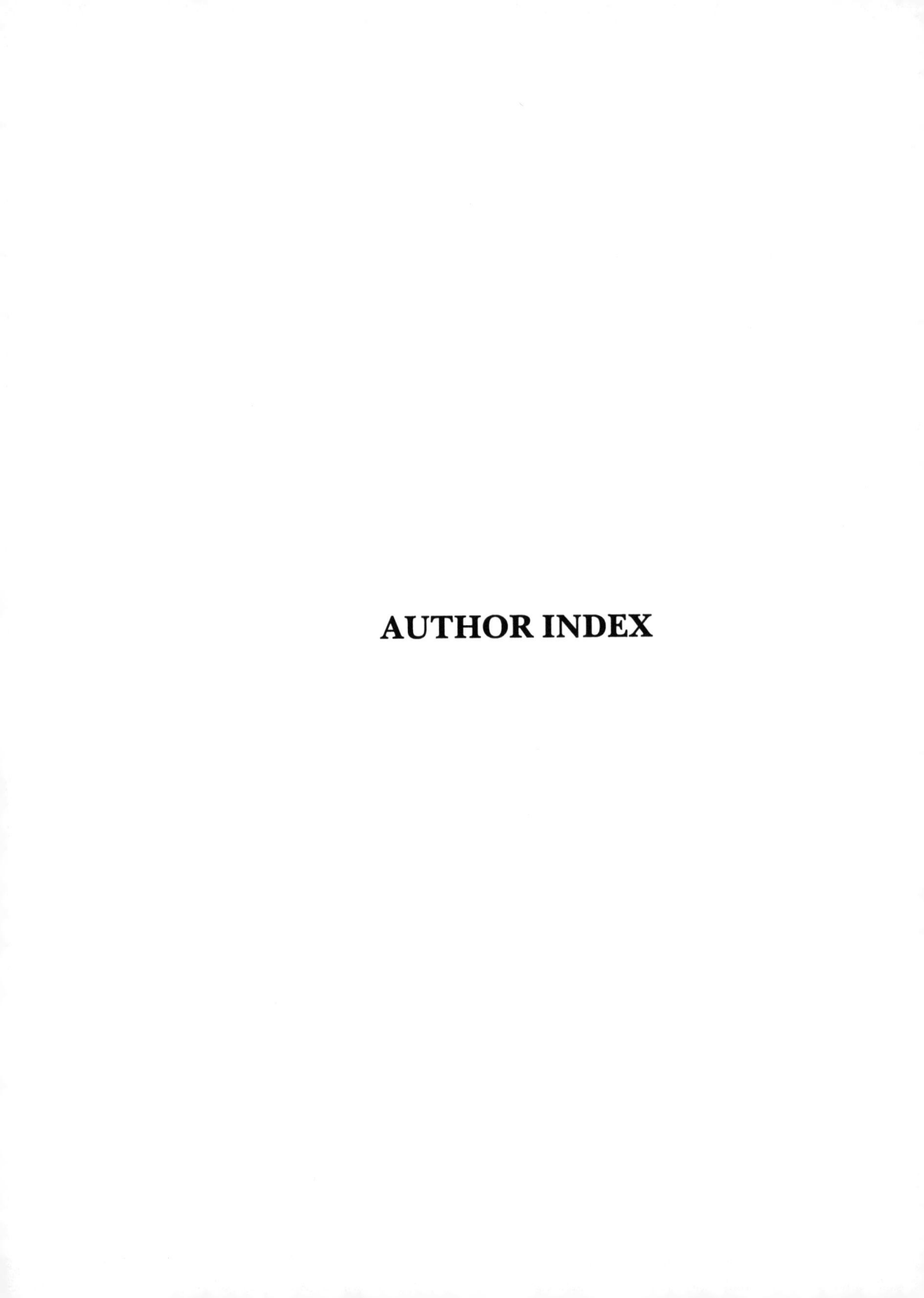

AARON P. G. 19, 50, 212.
ABEL SMITH A. E. 143.
ACKLAW J. 88.
ADAMS C. 338, 345.
ALESSI S. 296.
ALLAN J. 116, 412, 424, 456.
ALLARDYCE B. 277, 280, 281.
ALLEN D. A. 324, 343, 345, 346, 347.
ALSTON J. 272.
ANASTASI A. 51.
ANDERSON R. C. 246.
ANDERSON T. 296.
ARENA J. I. 455.
ARGYLE M. 384.
ARKELL H. 81.
ARMBRUSTER B. 292.
ARNOLD H. 209, 210.
ASHCROFT M. 457.
ASTBURY J. 144.
AU K. H. 213.
AUGUR J. 202, 458.
AUSUBEL D. 276.
AUXTER D. 147.
AYRES A. J. 146, 147, 456.
BADDELEY A. D. 49, 50, 318.
BAIN R. 457.
BAKER L. 213, 292.
BAKKER D. J. 247.
BALD J. 83.
BANAS N. 52.
BARNARD T. 455.
BATTLE J. 397, 400.
BAX M. 66, 67.
BECK I. 213.
BELL N. 214.
BELMONT J. 298.
BIGELOW E. R. 17.
BIGGAR S. 397.
BINES H. 413.
BISHOP D. V. M. 17, 67, 69, 317, 318, 320, 323, 339, 342, 343, 345, 362,
BLACKMORE C. 253.
BLAGG N. 216.
BLATCHFORD R. 453.
BLEY N. S. 279.
BLIGHT J. 81.
BLYTHE P. 147, 148.
BOCHNER S. 329.
BOOTE R. 84, 458.
BORGER H. 145.
BORKOWSKI J. 292.
BRADLEY L. 15, 16, 49, 83, 100, 106, 110, 208, 209, 226, 228, 246, 252, 303, 318, 363, 369, 395, 441.
BRADY S. 15.
BRAMLEY W. 383.
BRAND V. 137, 452, 454.
BRIGGS S. 202.
BRINTON P. 455.
BROWN A. L. 213, 214, 216, 292.
BROWN J. K. 72.

BROWN S. 409, 412, 413, 424.
BRUCK M. 207.
BRUNER J. S. 248, 330.
BRYANT B. 384.
BRYANT P. E. 16, 49, 83, 106, 205, 207, 208, 209, 226, 228, 246, 252, 303, 318, 342, 363, 369,395,
BUDOFF M. 330.
BULL S. 211.
BULLOCK SIR A. 381.
BURGE V. 456.
BUTKOWSKY I. S. 249.
BUZAN T. 51.
CAPUTE A. 145, 147.
CARBO M. 20, 94, 211, 217, 218, 249.
CARR G. A. 453.
CASHDAN A. 210, 217, 303, 380.
CERMAK S. 145.
CHALL J. S. 206.
CHALMERS 70.
CHASTY H. 49, 204, 205, 216, 217.
CHEEM A. I. 48.
CHINN S. J. 278, 279.
CHOMSKY N. 330.
CLARK D. B. 204, 215.
CLAY M. M. 81, 252, 399.
CLAYDON J. 316.
COCKROFT W. H. 279.
COLTHEART M. 225.
CONANT S. 330, 331.
CONLAN J. 457.
CONNELL P. J. 332.
CONTI-RAMSDEN G. 320, 322, 346.
CONWAY J. 72.
COOK R. 456.
COOPER A. 453, 457.
COTTERELL G. 451.
COWDEN J. E. 144.
CRAIG F. 251.
CRAIK F. I. N. 50.
CRATTY B. J. 144.
CRESSWELL D. 458.
CRIPPS C. 40, 100, 454.
CROMBIE M. 81, 95, 458.
CROSS D. 301.
CRYSTAL D. 322, 325, 357.
CUFF C. 454.
CULSHAW C. 452, 453.
CURTIS M. E. 50.
CURTISS S. 321.
CUTFORTH N. 146.
DAHL R. 452.
DARKE S. 249.
DE BONO E. 386.
DE QUIROS J. 147, 149
DEAN E. C. 331.
DELOCHE G. 279, 280.
DENIS V. 316.
DENNISON P. 456.
DESSENT T. 415.

DETTERMAN D. K. 51.
DEWART H. 326.
DICKSON L. 277, 279.
DILLON J. T. 384.
DOBIE S. 250.
DOCKRELL J. 47,49, 50.
DOLLAGHAN C. 347.
DONALDSON M. L. 325.
DONALDSON M. 329.
DOUGLAS G. 47,48.
DRING J. 451.
DUANE D. 358.
DUBERLY S. 457.
DUFFIELD J. 409, 415.
DUFFY F. H. 60.
DUNLOP P. 17.
DUNN K. 20, 48, 94, 211, 217, 450.
DYSON A. 413.
ECHWALL E. E. 212.
EDMUNDSON A. 339, 362.
EDWARDS D. 214.
EDWARDS P. 458.
EHRI J. C. 207, 208, 209, 369.
EICHSTAEDT C. 147.
EISENSON J. 320.
ELAM M. 457.
ELBERT J. C. 70.
ELIOT T. S. 454.
ELLIOT C. D. 82
ELLIS N. C. 208.
ENTWHISTLE N. 291, 307.
ESSON J. 72.
EVANS A. 16, 241, 455.
EYSENCK M. W. 249.
FARNHAM-DIGGORY S. 279.
FAWCETT A. J. 15,16, 205, 250.
FEUERSTEIN R. 386.
FEY M. E. 327.
FIELD J. 147.
FISHER J. G. 148.
FISHER R. 395.
FITZSIMMONS K. 454.
FLAVELL J. H. 295.
FLETCHER P. 322.
FLOYD A. 275, 276, 278.
FORRESTAL P. 457.
FOSTER S. H. 327.
FOWLER A. E. 15.
FOWLER S. 17, 74.
FOX B. 208.
FRANCE L. 88.
FRANCIS E. 383, 384, 389.
FRITH C. C. 139.
FRITH U. 138, 202, 367.
FROSTIG M. 146.
FURTH H. 145.
GALABURDA A. M. 68.
GALE A. 46.

Chapter

GALLAGHER T. M. 322.
GALLAGHUE D. 146.
GARMAN M.
GARNER R. 293.
GARNHAM A. 50, 297.
GARTON A. 395.
GARWOOD S. G. 143.
GATHERCOLE S. E. 318.
GAWITH G. 452.
GEE R. 451.
GERMAN D. 366.
GESCHWIND N. 68.
GILES G. 275, 276, 277.
GILFEATHER S. 453, 456.
GILLBERG I. C. 67.
GINSBURG H. 277, 280, 281.
GINSBURGH P. 277.
GIPPS C. 414.
GIVEN B. 456.
GODFREY B. 146.
GOETZ E. 296.
GOLDSTEIN H. 414.
GONZALEZ E. G. 279.
GOODMAN K. S. 201, 254.
GOSWAMI U. 49, 202, 207, 208, 363, 395.
GRISEWOOD J. 451.
GROSS H. 414.
GRUNDY K. 322.
GRUNWELL P. 322.
GUNN M. 346.
GUPTA Y. 88.
HALL W. S. 395.
HAMPSHIRE S. 456.
HARRIS J. 327.
HARRIS K. 18.
HARVEY R. 278.
HASLAM R. H. A. 75.
HAWKER G. T. 451.
HECHT B. 330.
HECHTMANN L. 75.
HEGARTY S. 413, 414.
HEGDE M. 328.
HENDERSON A. 145, 441, 456.
HENLEY M. 457.
HEWISON J. 88.
HICKEY M. 202.
HIEBERT J. 276.
HIRSH-PASEK K. 227.
HITCH G. 282.
HODGES 249.
HOGG G. 453, 454.
HOLLIGAN C. 227.
HOLMES B. J. 52.
HORNSBY B. 81, 82, 83, 358, 363, 452, 457.
HOWELL J. 331.
HOWLIN P. 331, 338, 339.
HUGHES T. 452.
HULME C. 204, 226.

HUMPHRIES D. 455.
HUMPHRIES T. 146.
HUNT J. V. 71, 143, 456.
HUNTER-CARSCH M. 107, 215.
HUTCHISON L. 452, 453.
IMICH A. J. 45.
IMPEY L. 395.
INGRAM D. 322.
INHELDER B. 321.
IRLEN H. 18.
JAMES W. H. 69.
JARMAN C. 452.
JOFFE L. 276, 279, 281.
JOHNSON D. 281.
JOHNSON M. 381, 389.
JOHNSTON J. R. 321.
JOHNSTON P. H. 396.
JOHNSTON R. S. 211, 227.
JORM A F. 49 209.
JOWETT S. 413, 414.
KALAKIAN L. 147.
KARNES M. B. 451.
KASTON N. 347.
KAUFMAN A. S. 52.
KEPHART N. 146.
KERFOOT S. R. 45.
KERR B. 453.
KINSBOURNE M. 69.
KIPHARD E. 146.
KITHCEN D. 457.
KLEIN H. 349.
KLEIN N. K. 143, 144.
KLEIN P. S. 451.
KLENK L. 292.
KNIGHT-JONES E. B. 143.
KNOWLES W. 326.
KOLERS P. A. 279.
KOSC L. 274, 280, 281.
KRUTETSKII V. A. 279, 280.
KYD L. 18.
LA BERGE D. 201.
LABAN R. 146.
LAKOFF G. 381.
LANE C. H. 204.
LANNEN S. 16, 46.
LANSDOWN R. 275.
LARCOMBE T. 277.
LARGO 71.
LASZLOW J. 146, 147.
LAW J. 72.
LAWRENCE D. 105, 106, 232.
LEES J. 327.
LEINONEN E. 322.
LEONARD L. B. 319, 320, 327, 328, 330.
LERNER J. 143.
LESGOLD A. M. 50.
LEVINE M. D. 72, 73.
LEWIS C. 274, 282.

Chapter

LIBERMAN I. Y. 208.
LIEBECK P. 277.
LINDSAY G. 239, 241.
LIPSON M. 301.
LOCKHART R. S. 50.
LOSSE A. 145.
LOVELESS E. J. 274, 279.
LUNDBERG I. 16, 226.
MacIVER A. 455.
MAELAND A. F. 143, 145.
MAGNUSSON E. 339, 340.
MANIS F. B. 49, 395.
MANN V. 15, 342, 359, 363.
MARIA K. 212, 213.
MARLOW N. 71.
MARSHALL J. C. 227.
MARZOLLA J. 451.
MASIDLOVER M. 326.
MATARAZZO J. D. 52.
MATTSON P. D. 145, 146.
MAXWELL C. 84, 451.
McCAFFERTY J. 455.
McCLELLAND R. J. 253.
McCLENAGHAN B. 146.
McCONNEL C. 338.
McCULLAGH S. K. 453.
McDOUGALL M. 456.
McGETTRICK P. 18.
McGLOWN D. 147.
McGOUGH R. 454.
McKENZIE B. E. 17.
McKEOWN M. 213.
McLULLICH H. 452.
McNEAL B. 452.
McROBERTS R. 457
McSHANE J. 47,49,50.
McSWEENEY T. 457.
McTEAR M. M. 322.
MEEK M. 246.
MEHRABIAN A. 384.
MELLETS D. 321.
MERCER N. 214.
MESSICK C. 321.
METZGER R. L. 73.
MILBURN C. 454.
MILES T. R. 80, 81, 82, 349, 366.
MILLER A. 248.
MILLER J. F. 317, 320.
MILNE A. A. 454.
MILWARD C. 455.
MONTAGUE M. 292.
MOORE P. 300.
MORAIS J. 226.
MORRIS H. 72.
MORRISON D. C. 147, 148.
MORSE R. 330.
MOSELY D. 451.
MOSES, D. 413, 414.

MOYLE D. 452.
MUNN P. 412, 424.
MURRAY E. 148.
MYERS M. 296.
MYKLEBUST H. R. 281.
NASH-WORTHAM M. 456.
NAUCLER K. 339, 340.
NEAL E. 451.
NELSON C. 148.
NICOL C. 451.
NICOLSON R. I. 15,16, 205.
NIKLASSON M. 215.
NISBET J. 105, 107.
NOLL M. 328.
NYE C. 326,331.
O'HAGEN F. G. 45.
O'HARE A. E. 72.
OAKHILL J. U. 50, 297.
OBRIST C. 250.
OKA E. 299.
OLIVER C. E. 73.
OLSEN R. 209, 218.
OLSON M. 454.
ORTON J. 203, 277, 279, 280.
OSTLER C. 104.
OXLEY. 100.
PALINCSAR A. 214, 216, 292.
PALMER U. E. 455.
PALSIO N. 145.
PARIS S. 296.
PASK G. 278, 302.
PATTEN B. 454.
PAVLIDIS G. T. 18, 366.
PAYNE T. 85, 414.
PECORA R. 328.
PENNINGTON B. F. 69, 208.
PERFETTI C. A. 50.
PETERS M. 110, 313.
PETERSON P. 302.
PHELPS-TERASAKI D. 455.
PHINN G. 454.
PIAGET J. 321, 394, 404.
PINKERTON F. 253.
PLUNKETT S. 275, 277.
POLLOCK J. 101.
POLYA G. 275, 276.
POOL J. 454.
POSTLETHWAITE K. 272.
PRATLEY R. 457.
PRATT C. 395.
PRELOCK P. 321.
PRICE G. E. 48, 452.
PRUTTING C. A. 322.
PUMFREY P. D. 18,21, 52, 80, 82,89, 248, 249, 250, 251, 253. 272.
PYFER J. 145, 147, 148.
RABAN B. 272.
RACK J. P. 209, 218, 227.
RAK E. 454.

RAMSEY T. 456.
RAPIN I. 324, 343, 345, 346, 347.
RAVEN S. C. 35,36.
REASON R. 18,21, 52, 80, 82, 84, 89, 200, 202, 211, 248, 250, 253, 272, 458.
REID G. 16, 45, 205.
RENALDI W. 366.
REVELL K. 88.
RICHARDS J. 454.
RIDDELL S. 402, 409, 415, 423.
RIDER B. 147, 148.
RIDING R. 47, 48.
ROBBINS C. 207.
ROBERTS G. R. 252.
ROBSON C. 401.
ROGERS M. 66.
ROOT B. 98.
ROSEBERGER P. B. 68.
ROSENBLOOM L. 343, 344, 345.
ROTHERY A. 278.
ROURKE B. P. 281.
ROUTH D. K. 208.
ROWE M. 204.
ROYCROFT E. 452.
RUMELHART D. R. 213.
RUMSY 69.
RUSSELL J. 456.
RUSSELL S. 98, 99, 107.
RUTTER M. 80, 338, 339.
SADLER B. R. 457.
SAMUELS S. J. 201.
SASSOON R. 272.
SAVILLE-TROIKE M. 382.
SCHWARTZ A. A. 451.
SCOBLE J.100, 240.
SCWARTZ R. 321.
SEALE T. W. 70.
SEAMAN D. 327.
SELLY J. 457.
SEMRUD H. G. 358.
SERON X. 279, 280.
SEYMOUR P. H. K. 47, 395.
SHANKER J. L. 212.
SHANKWEILER D. 70, 208.
SHARE D. L. 209, 274, 282.
SHARMA M. C. 274, 279, 280.
SHAVWITZ S. E. 68.
SHEAR F. 83, 452, 457.
SHEEHAN R. 143.
SHERBOURNE V. 146.
SHERRILL C. 145, 146.
SHIACH D. 455.
SHUARD H. 278.
SHUCKSMITH J. 105, 107.
SIEGEL L. S. 51, 94,107.
SILVA P. A. 71, 329.
SIMPSON M. 291.
SINGLETON C. H. 15, 16, 47, 80, 88, 109.
SKEMP R. R. 275.

SKUSE D. 319.
SLINGERLAND B. H. 203.
SMILEY S. 295.
SMITH B. R. 322.
SMITH F. 201.
SMITH S S. 456.
SMITH 70.
SNOW C E. 319.
SNOWLING M. J. 47, 80, 138, 209, 218, 227, 344, 349, 350, 359, 363, 364, 366, 372.
SOLITY J.211.
SOVIK N. 145.
SPENCE L. 346.
SPIERS P. A. 277, 280.
STABLES A. J. 456.
STACKHOUSE J. 338, 342, 344, 347, 348, 350, 371.
STANOVICH K. E. 15, 49, 50, 51, 201,205,212.
START K. R. 321.
STEIN J. F. 17, 74.
STERNBERG R. G. 51.
STEWART-BROWN S. 74.
STIRLING E. G. 87, 349, 457.
STOWE J. 18.
STRANGE D. 455.
STUART A. 250.
SUMMERS S. 326.
SUTHERLAND G. 18.
SVEISTRUP H. 147.
SWANSON M. 144.
SWANSON W. I. 45.
SWING S. 302.
SYME C. 458.
SZESZULSKI P A. 49, 395
TALLAL P. 321.
TANNEN D. 385.
TANSLEY A. E. 456.
TATE M. 343.
TAYLOR J. 272.
TEMPLE C. M. 227.
TENNANT M. 47.
TERRELL B. 321.
THOMS P. D. 455.
THOMSON G. B. 211.
THOMSON M. E . 52, 80, 81, 206, 207, 210, 253, 366, 371, 372, 453.
THORNTON C. A. 279.
TIBERIUS R. 382.
TIZARD J. 88.
TOPPING K. J. 49, 88, 100, 235, 237, 239, 240, 241, 242, 243.
TREIMAN R. 207, 227.
TROWER P. 384.
TURNBULL G. 454.
TYRE C. 88, 242, 248.
URWIN S. 327.
VYGOTSKY L. S. 300, 394, 404.
WALKER P. 282.
WALSH T. 454.
WATERLAND L. 203, 210, 246.
WATERS D. 452.
WATKINS E. J. 80, 81, 253.

WATSON D. R. 253.
WEBSTER A. 338.
WEEDON C. 274, 282.
WEINER B. 246.
WELLS B. 344, 350.
WENDON L. 83, 96, 451.
WERNER D. B. 73.
WESSEL J. A. 146.
WHEATLY G. H. 279.
WHITE G R. 453.
WHITELEY M. 237, 240.
WHITMORE K. 66,67.
WIGGLESWORTH C. 240.
WILCE L. S. 209.
WILKINS A. 18.
WILKINS A. 74.
WILLIAMS J. P. 214.
WILLIAMS M. 456.
WILLOWS D. M. 249.
WILLS I. H. 52.
WISE B. W. 208.
WOLFENDALE S. W. 235, 237, 242.
WOOD E. 454.
WRIGHT A. 18.
WRIGHT J. 210, 217. 303.
YOUNG P. 88, 242, 248.
ZANGWILL O. L. 253.

ZUBRICK 71.